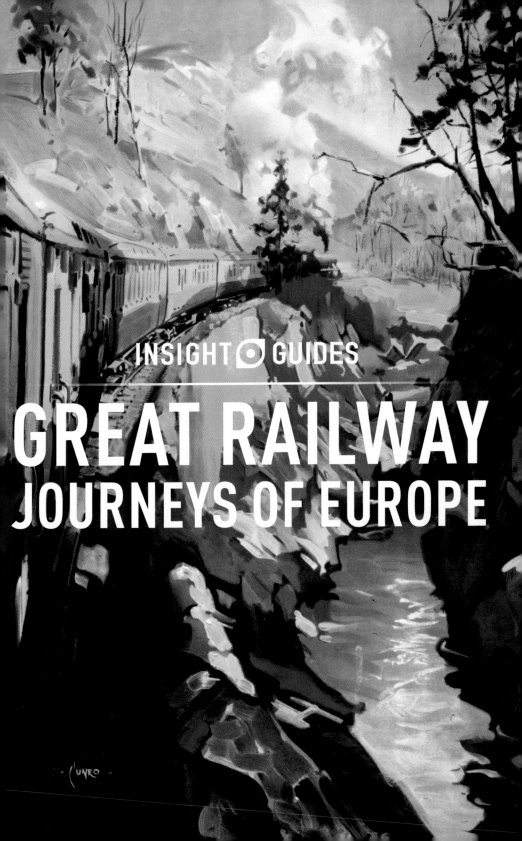

INSIGHT ● GUIDES

GREAT RAILWAY
JOURNEYS OF EUROPE

◉ Walking Eye App

YOUR FREE DESTINATION CONTENT AND EBOOK AVAILABLE THROUGH THE WALKING EYE APP

Your guide now includes a free eBook and destination content for your chosen destination, all for the same great price as before. Simply download the Walking Eye App from the App Store or Google Play to access your free eBook and destination content.

HOW THE WALKING EYE APP WORKS

Through the Walking Eye App, you can purchase a range of eBooks and destination content. However, when you buy this book, you can download the corresponding eBook and destination content for free. Just see below in the grey panels where to find your free content and then scan the QR code at the bottom of this page.

Destinations: Download your corresponding essential destination content from here, featuring recommended sights and attractions, restaurants, hotels and an A–Z of practical information, all for free. Other destinations are available for purchase.

Ships: Interested in ship reviews? Find independent reviews of river and ocean ships in this section, all available for purchase.

eBooks: You can download your free accompanying digital version of this guide here. You will also find a whole range of other eBooks, all available for purchase.

Free access to travel-related blog articles about different destinations, updated on a daily basis.

HOW THE DESTINATION CONTENT WORKS

Each destination includes a short introduction, an A–Z of practical information and recommended points of interest, split into 4 different categories:

- Highlights
- Accommodation
- Eating out
- What to do

You can view the location of every point of interest and save it by adding it to your Favourites. In the 'Around Me' section you can view all the points of interest within 5km.

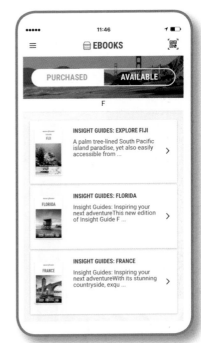

HOW THE EBOOKS WORK

The eBooks are provided in EPUB file format. Please note that you will need an eBook reader installed on your device to open the file. Many devices come with this as standard, but you may still need to install one manually from Google Play.

The eBook content is identical to the content in the printed guide.

HOW TO DOWNLOAD THE WALKING EYE APP

1. Download the Walking Eye App from the App Store or Google Play.
2. Open the app and select the scanning function from the main menu.
3. Scan the QR code on this page – you will then be asked a security question to verify ownership of the book.
4. Once this has been verified, you will see your eBook and destination content in the purchased ebook and destination sections, where you will be able to download them.

Other destination apps and eBooks are available for purchase separately or are free with the purchase of the Insight Guide book.

CONTENTS

Travel tips

EUROPEAN RAIL TRAVEL

COUNTRY BY COUNTRY A–Z

FURTHER READING 364

Maps

Inside front cover European Railways:
  Regional Maps
Inside back cover European Railways:
  Featured Route Maps
LEGEND
$\mathcal{P}$ Insight on

THE BEST OF:
EUROPE'S RAILWAY JOURNEYS

The Royal Scotsman passes Loch Dubh.

CLASSIC JOURNEYS

Settle–Carlisle. Britain's most spectacular main line, through wild, hilly countryside with great walks from stations. See page 113.

Seville–Madrid. The dash across the southern *meseta*, Spain's central plateau, lined with olive groves, ends in the splendid station of Atocha with its tropical garden. See page 172.

Geneva–Milan. The train is by far the best way to enjoy the picturesque northern shore and vineyards along Lake Geneva, which just happens to be special enough to be a Unesco World Heritage Site. See page 187.

Train passing Lake Geneva.

LUXURY TRAINS

The Royal Scotsman. There's no more stylish way to see Scotland than a journey aboard this sumptuous train. See page 106.

The Venice Simplon-Orient-Express. Its history, immaculate period carriages, outstanding food and perfectly delivered service make this the most romantic of trains. See page 80.

El Transcantábrico. Luxury on the narrow-gauge railway along the Bay of Biscay on Spain's northern coast. See page 165.

Grand suite on the Venice Simplon-Orient-Express.

SCENIC BYWAYS

Garabit Viaduct, France.

Wales. See page 116.
Clermont Ferrand–Nîmes. This meander through the Cévennes Mountains and the valleys of the Massif Central called for impressive engineering works. See page 136.
Trier–Koblenz–Giessen. Both parts of this journey astride the Rhine follow rivers but the landscapes are very different. See page 258.
Sweden's Inlandsbanan. Few railways in Europe traverse such remote country as this seasonal line up the spine of the country. See page 280.

Shrewsbury–Swansea. Linking a succession of spa towns, this line traverses some of the finest landscapes in

Glacier Express on the Oberalp Pass.

MOUNTAIN RAILWAYS

Le Train Jaune. Yellow narrow-gauge trains clatter across the hills of the Cerdagne with the mountains of the Pyrenees seldom out of sight. See page 153.
The Glacier Express. Europe's finest mountain railway journey, between Zermatt and St Moritz, is extremely popular, so booking is vital. See page 192.
The Harz Mountains. The narrow-gauge network, made up of three lines, that threads the historic landscapes of the Harz is one of the most characterful in Europe. See page 262.

ISLAND RAILWAYS

Corsica. An efficient metre-gauge railway runs through spectacular mountains and valleys, and is the best way to see the island. See page 154.
Mallorca. The island has a developing and efficient railway system, but the most scenic journey remains the link between the capital and Sóller. See page 177.
Sardinia. The astonishingly circuitous 4.5-hour journey between Arbatax and Cagliari takes you through the tangled *macchia* and ancient woods of the Seulo Mountains. See page 224.

The Brocken Railway runs through the Harz Mountains.

The Soller Tramway, Mallorca.

The Thames-Clyde Express, hauled by The Duchess of Sutherland locomotive, crosses the Ribblehead Viaduct in the Yorkshire Dales National Park.

Cogwheel railway with Mount Schynige Platte in the background, Bernese Oberland, Switzerland.

The AVE high-speed line passes La Pena de los Enamorados (Lover's Rock), in Andalucía, southern Spain.

The Falkenstein Bridge passes over the Niederfalkenstein Castle, Austria.

EUROPEAN RAIL TRAVEL

The magic of train travel lies in its ability to provide an endlessly changing procession of landscapes and cultures

Train track runs along the coast in Calabria, Italy.

'Dear Victoria, gateway to the world beyond England. How I love your continental platform, and how I love trains anyway. Snuffing up the sulphurous smell ecstatically, so different from the feint, aloof, distantly oily smell of a boat. But a train, a big snorting hurrying, companionable train with its big puffing engine, sending up clouds of steam and seeming to say impatiently, "I've got to be off, I've got to be off, I've got to be off", is a friend.'

This book is for those who can identify with these words, written by Agatha Christie, or who think they might be able to, given the chance. Of the various modes of travel, only sailing ships and the grand liners have rivalled the train in the affections of their users and the wider public. For a century and a quarter, their appeal was bound up with the atmosphere and character of the steam railway, which artists, composers and novelists sought to capture. Yet even today, with the romance of steam confined to heritage railways and the occasional forays of museum locomotives, railways continue to exercise an immense appeal.

ICE train in Diersfordt, Germany.

Even at its most basic, the train remains one of the most civilised forms of overland transport. The freedom train travel gives to work, read or stare out of the window with one's thoughts is, for millions each day, unrivalled. As the playwright Stephen Poliakoff said, one of the joys of train travel is the way the landscape rolls past the window like a film at the cinema.

For travellers intent on exploring and experiencing a country, train travel has its rewards. Robert Louis Stevenson said that the best way to see a country was from the window of a train. After all, what can you learn from the window of a plane? For Paul Theroux 'A train isn't a vehicle. A train is part of a country. It's a place.' Although European trains are not the mobile souks of a country such as India, they still offer the opportunity to meet people; only the most reclusive of rail travellers are without their stories about people met and conversations enjoyed.

This book highlights some of the great European railway journeys and gives advice on how to use the railway networks, including a range of passes that make train travel both simpler and cheaper. Most of the journeys have been selected for the scenery that passengers enjoy, though some are included as important links between other journeys or as epic transcontinental migrations that call for a couple of nights' rest and recuperation at their end. Though air travel has whittled away the number of overnight trains, there are still enough left to create that unrivalled sense

of anticipation that accompanies the late evening departure of a long train of sleeping cars from beneath a dark vault of ironwork. By dawn it may have crossed several borders, and passengers awake to quite different landscapes and architecture, best appreciated from a seat in the restaurant car for breakfast. Part of the magic of European rail travel is the variety of landscapes and cultures encountered in such a compact area. In just a few hours the train can have migrated from western affluence to eastern influences and from northern chill to southern warmth.

By travelling by train rather than plane or car, you are making a major contribution to minimising the environmen-

Crossing the Laxgraben Viaduct, Switzerland.

tal impact of travel. With tourism one of the fastest-growing global industries, it is more crucial than ever that more environmentally friendly forms of transport are chosen by individuals and encouraged by governments.

HOW WE CHOSE THE JOURNEYS

The routes in the book have been chosen either for their scenic merit or because they are notable in other ways. For instance, the Paris–Marseille and Seville–Madrid high-speed lines are included because of the remarkable speed and smoothness of the journey. Others, such as Paris–Moscow, have to be considered 'great' journeys for their romance and history. It is worth nothing at this point, that this is a subjective exercise.

With such a huge number of routes to choose from, and with limited space, we have focused on regular, scheduled services that appear in national rail timetables (and the European Rail Timetable). In a few instances, other, privately operated, routes have been included; these vary from the five-star luxury of such famous 'cruise trains' as the Venice Simplon-Orient-Express and El Transcantábrico, to small mountain railways such as La Rhune in the French Pyrenees. Her-

Wood panel detail on the Orient Express.

itage railways, however, have not generally been described: selected listings of these, together with railway museums of note, can be found at the end of each 'journeys' chapter, with their locations marked on the relevant maps.

The decision was made to concentrate on the journeys themselves rather than the start and end points of the route. A brief list of essential sights has been included for the major cities where the routes begin or end or through which they pass.

Electrified track in Altenbeken, Germany.

1952 British Rail poster titled 'On Early Shift', depicting a train approaching Greenwood Signal Box, New Barnet.

DECISIVE DATES

The Rocket in 1876.

1758
First railway authorised by the British Parliament, from Middleton Colliery to Leeds.

1778
First railway built in France, at the mouth of the Loire.

1794
First use of flanged (wooden) rails, at Otaviga mines in Hungary.

1804
First locomotive successfully hauls load at Merthyr Tydfil, South Wales.

1812
Matthew Murray's engine begins work at Middleton Colliery in England.

1825
Stockton and Darlington Railway opened.

1827
First public railway in France opened, running from StÉtienne to Andrézieux.

1829
Stephenson's *Rocket* achieves 46km/h (29mph) at the Rainhill trials in England.

1830
Canterbury and Whitstable Railway and Liverpool and Manchester Railway opened.

1834
First railway opened in Ireland, from Dublin to Kingstown (Dun Laoghaire).

1835
First railway in Belgium opened between Brussels and Malines. First railway in Germany opened, Nuremberg to Fürth.

1836
First London railway (Spa Road to Deptford). First railway in Russia opened, running from St Petersburg through Tsarskoe Selo to Pavlovsk. World's first narrow-gauge railway opened, Ffestiniog Railway, North Wales.

1838
Electric telegraph first used, on the Great Western Railway from London.

1839
First railway in Italy opened, from Naples to Portici.

1841
First Thomas Cook-organised excursion train.

1842
Queen Victoria's first railway journey. First major rail crash, when 48 died on the Versailles–Paris express.

1844
First railway in Switzerland opened, from Basel to St Louis. J.M.W. Turner paints *Rain, Steam and Speed, the Great Western Railway.*

1848
First railway opened in Spain, from Barcelona along the Costa Brava to Mataró.

1849
First railway opened in the Netherlands, running from Amsterdam to Haarlem.

1851
Moscow–St Petersburg line opened.

1854
First railway opened in Norway, between Christiana (Oslo) and Eidsvoll.

1855
The world's first special postal train travels between London and Bristol. Thomas Cook runs the first continental rail tour and initiates a foreign exchange service.

1856
First Portuguese railway opened, Lisbon to Carregado. First railways opened in Sweden, Gothenburg to Joosered and Malmö to Lund.

1862
William Frith paints *The Railway Station at London Paddington*.

1863
First underground railway opened, from Bishop's Road to Farringdon Street, London. Gas lighting introduced in carriages on North London Railway.

1869
First railway opened in Greece, between Athens and its port, Piræus.

1871
Europe's first rack railway opens in Switzerland, climbing to Rigi from Vitznau.

1874
First use of Pullman cars in Britain, on the Midland Railway. First Pullman car sleeping service in England, St Pancras to Bradford.

1878
First Tay Bridge opened.

1879
First run of dining car with kitchen in Britain, London King's Cross to Leeds. Collapse of first Tay Bridge. First practical electric railway, Berlin Trades Exhibition.

1882
Gotthard Tunnel opens, becoming the first railway link through the Alps.

1883
Britain's first public, electric railway opened, at Brighton. Orient Express introduced.

1886
Severn Tunnel opened in Britain.

1887
Second Tay Bridge opened in Scotland.

1890
Forth Bridge opened in Scotland. World's first underground electric railway opened, the City and South London.

1893
First elevated railway opened, in Liverpool.

1895
First film of a moving train, shot by Louis Lumière at La Ciotat.

1898
Switzerland opens the world's first electric rack railway, between Zermatt and Gornergrat.

William Frith's 'The Railway Station', depicting London Paddington, 1862.

1900
First section of Paris Metro opened.

1904
City of Truro reaches 164km/h (100.2mph) (disputed).

1906
Simplon Tunnel opened.

1915
Britain's worst rail disaster, at Quintinshill, with 227 killed.

1921
German railways nationalised as Deutsche Reichsbahn.

1922
Grouping of Britain's railways into "Big Four".

1924
Arthur Honegger wrote symphonic movement, *Pacific 231*.

Aftermath of the Quintinshill rail disaster, 22 May 1915.

1926
Golden Arrow (La Flèche d'Or) introduced, London–Paris. Nationalised Société Nationale des Chemins de Fer Belges (SNCB) created.

1928
World's longest non-stop run inaugurated, London–Edinburgh 629km (393 miles).

1932
Flying Hamburger, first high-speed diesel train, enters service, Berlin–Hamburg.

1934
Agatha Christie's *Murder on the Orient Express* published.

1938
World speed record for steam, 202km/h (126mph) by *Mallard*, England. Nationalised Société Nationale des Chemins de Fer Français (SNCF) created.

1939
World record set for diesel-electric traction in Germany, 213km/h (133mph).

1945
German railways split into Deutsche Reichsbahn (DR) in East Germany and Deutsche Bundesbahn (DB) West Germany.

1948
British Railways created, following nationalisation by the Labour government.

1951
World's first preserved railway reopened, Talyllyn Railway in Wales.

1955
World electric speed record set in France, 331km/h (205.7mph).

1967
Le Capitole trains between Paris and Toulouse become the world's first rail service to be timetabled to run at 200km/h (124mph).

1968
British Rail withdraws standard-gauge steam.

1972
The first InterRail passes were introduced for travellers aged 21 or under, giving one month's unlimited train travel in 21 countries for £27.50.

1976
Introduction of High Speed Trains (HSTs) capable of 200km/h (125mph), between London and Bristol/South Wales.

1981
First Ligne à Grande Vitesse (LGV), Paris–Lyon. New world speed record set in Germany, 406.9km/h (252mph).

1989
Inauguration of LGV Atlantique, Paris–Le Mans/Tours. New world speed record set in France, TGV-Atlantique, 482.4km/h (301.5mph). Introduction of InterCity Express (ICE) trains.

1990
Introduction of X2000 trains in Sweden. New world speed record set in France, TGV-Atlantique, 513.3km/h (319.5mph).

1991
Introduction of ICE Hamburg–Munich trains.

1993
Start of TGV Nord services, Paris-Nord–Pas de Calais.

1994
Formal merger of Deutsche Bundesbahn and Deutsche Reichsbahn, reuniting German Railways as Deutsche Bahn. Channel Tunnel opened, 6 May.

1996
Introduction of Thalys, Paris–Brussels.

1998
Switzerland's Semmeringbahn becomes the first railway to gain Unesco World Heritage Site status.

2000
Øresund Bridge opened linking Denmark and Sweden, 1 July. Opening of the LGV Méditerranée, Valence–Avignon–Marseille.

First electric test drive at the North Portal of the Gotthard Base Tunnel.

2003
Opening of first stage of Channel Tunnel rail link in England.

2004
Madrid–Lleida high-speed line opens.

2006
Berlin Hauptbahnhof opens, Europe's largest multi-level railway station.

2007
World speed record set by TGV, at 574.8km/h (359mph), 3 April. LGV Est opens for Paris–Strasbourg/Basel TGV services, 10 June. Lötschberg Base Tunnel in Switzerland opens, 15 June. Full opening of Channel Tunnel Rail Link/HS1 into London St Pancras, 14 November.

2008
Madrid–Barcelona high-speed line inaugurated on 20 February.

2014
Completion of the new high-speed hub, Rotterdam Centraal station in the Netherlands, with its innovative boomerang-shaped canopy.

2016
Gotthard Base Tunnel – the world's longest traffic tunnel – opens, running through the Swiss Alps.

2019
Crossrail project is due to be completed in September, offering new rail travel options across London.

1950s British Rail poster promoting travel to Yorkshire.

JACK MERRIOTT.

KNARESBOROUGH

YORKSHIRE

THE GROWTH OF RAIL TRAVEL

The impact of the railways was enormous. They opened the world to commerce, widened social perspectives and facilitated military campaigns

It is not often that the likely impact that an invention will have on the fabric of society is immediately apparent. The steam locomotive was one exception. Few in Britain who witnessed the opening of the Stockton and Darlington or Liverpool and Manchester railways can have been in much doubt that they were witnessing a turning point in world events. The same cannot be said even of the motor car: the Caledonian Railway of Scotland commissioned a photograph in the early 1900s showing its largest express engine dwarfing a car, ridiculing the pretensions of this flimsy conveyance.

The sense of an historical watershed was encouraged by the rapid development of this new form of locomotion. Writing in the late 19th century, the American Charles Francis Adams pointed out that 'the great peculiarity of the locomotive engine, and its sequence, the railroad, was that it burst rather than stole or crept upon the world. Its advent was in the highest degree dramatic'.

IMMEDIATE BENEFITS

The hyperbolic rantings of some early sceptics, denouncing the very concept of railways as 'a dupe of quackery', were soon made to look absurd by such simple and irrefutable evidence as a reduction in the price of coal in Leicester from 18 to 11 shillings a ton following the opening of the Leicester & Swannington Railway in 1832–33.

What is more, most people found railway travel agreeable: a friend of Sir Walter Scott wrote in 1838 that the speed of 45kmh (28mph) was attained so smoothly that he had 'felt more dizzy when whirled along by four horses at the rate of ten or eleven miles in the hour'. When

Robert Stephenson and his locomotive, The Rocket.

Queen Victoria made her first railway journey, from Slough to London in June 1842, she described herself as 'quite charmed'.

Reactions to the steam locomotive itself varied. Except for those who had worked in textile mills or watched a steam engine pumping water out of mines, no one had seen a machine on this scale, and certainly not one that moved or was so physically expressive of its purpose. The British radical MP John Bright described his response to the first sight of a locomotive at Rochdale in 1839: 'It was a new thing and I think the power, speed and the grandeur of these great locomotive engines can never grow old, and that we can never regard them without wonder and without admiration.'

The children's author Beatrix Potter was enthralled by them: 'To my mind there is scarcely a more splendid beast in the world than a large Locomotive... I cannot imagine a finer sight than the Express, with two engines, rushing down this incline [from Kingswood Tunnel to Dunkeld on the Highland Railway line].'

In contrast, the parish clerk of a Wiltshire clergyman was quite overcome when he was taken to witness the passage of a train on the newly opened Great Western Railway: 'he fell leapt to their feet in fear that they were about to be crushed.

But it was not just the locomotive that inspired awe. Over a century before Bright saw his first steam engine, the largest single-span bridge in Britain had been constructed across a remote burn in County Durham to carry a waggon-way linking a coal mine with the River Tyne. Opened in 1727, the Causey Arch was hailed as a feat comparable with the Via Appia; people came from far and wide to see it, and it was commemorated in published prints.

King Louis-Philippe, Queen Victoria and Prince Albert aboard the Royal Carriage, 1846.

prostrate on the bank-side as if he had been smitten by a thunderbolt! When he had recovered his feet, his brain still reeled, his tongue clove to the roof of his mouth, and he stood aghast, unutterable amazement stamped upon his face. It must have been quite five minutes before he could speak, and when he did it was in the tone of a Jeremiah. "Well, Sir, that was a sight to have seen; but one I never care to see again! How much longer shall knowledge be allowed to go on increasing?"'

If that seems far-fetched, it should be remembered that when the first film of a moving train, shot by Louis Lumière at La Ciotat station in southern France, was shown to the public in 1895, some people in the front row

BUILDING THE NETWORKS

The speed with which European rail networks were built reflects how quickly most governments, businessmen and entrepreneurs realised that this was an invention that would have a major impact on economic, social and political life throughout the world. At a local level, towns that rejected the chance to be on a mainline railway soon stagnated or atrophied, and manufacturers without easy access to a railway were soon at a severe commercial disadvantage. Most countries had varying periods of feverish railway construction, as well as the inevitable financial crises and scandals.

The approach adopted by governments towards the railway routes themselves varied enormously. At one extreme was Britain, with a *laissez-faire* policy in which competition was encouraged; at the other was the autocratic decision of Tsar Nicholas I to link Moscow and St Petersburg by a straight line, ignoring the needs of the historic towns of Torzhok, Valday and Novgorod, through which the railway could easily have been routed.

Prudent governments learned from the mistakes of others and adopted a more cautious approach. Leopold I of Belgium sought the advice of George and Robert Stephenson in devising a rational network. After some years of cantonal bickering, the Swiss government asked Robert Stephenson to plan a system. The French government came up with a Paris-focused network and the novel idea of building the infrastructure, including stations, and leaving private companies to lay the track and undertake all operations. Slow progress by these companies due to financial problems compelled the government to guarantee a minimum rate of return.

Europe understandably looked to Britain, the pioneer, for practical help – not only with planning, surveying, financing and building railways, but also with the provision of locomotives and other equipment. It was a measure of the standing in which British engineers were held that the Piedmontese were unwilling to buy shares in

---

The great steam age was romanticised – and immortalised – by J.M.W. Turner's painting, 'Rain, Steam and Speed', in 1844.

---

their own Turin–Novara railway until they heard that the Cheshire-born contractor Thomas Brassey had taken a large number of shares as part payment for the work.

But British engineers and contractors were soon joined, and gradually displaced, by nationals of other European countries, most of which quickly developed the workshops and skills to build most of their own equipment.

GRAND OPENINGS

The scale of most official openings reflected the importance attached to railway transport during the second half of the 19th and the

early 20th century: they were an opportunity for a free ride, verbose speeches, sumptuous banquets and possibly the conferring of some awards if a monarch or prime minister was present.

If the drawings and lithographs of early French and Italian openings are to be believed, they eclipsed anything staged in Britain. For the celebrations in Nantes of the inauguration of the railway to Angers in 1852, pavilions fronted by classical columns were erected alongside the line and plinthed statues placed between

The opening of the Stockton & Darlington Railway, 1825.

the running lines along which four locomotives moved in parallel. There was more pomp at Strasbourg the same year: four locomotives were positioned before an immense dais with steps up to a canopied altar, so they could be blessed by the city's archbishop.

This trend reached its zenith with the 1862 opening of the first railway in the Papal States, between Rome and Velletri. Inclement weather kept the Pope away, but the train was blessed by his chaplain, the Archbishop Prince of Hohenlohe, surrounded by the prelates of the Apostolic Court, the musicians of the Sistine Chapel and regiments from Rome and France.

The distinguished guest list at these prestigious events was often international. When

William Huskisson, President of the Board of Trade, was hit by Stephenson's Rocket and killed while officiating at the opening of the Liverpool–Manchester line in 1830. He is thought to be the first person to die in a train accident.

Thomas Brassey's railway between Cherbourg and Caen was opened, not only were Louis Napoleon and Empress Eugénie pre-

The Flying Scotsman in 1948.

sent, but so was Queen Victoria. The tradition continues for the few railway openings of major consequence: on 6 May 1994, Queen Elizabeth II and French President François Mitterand formally opened the Channel Tunnel.

THE IMPACT OF THE RAILWAYS

The substantial reduction in transport costs brought about by railways had far-reaching consequences. Lower prices for all kinds of products combined with the opening up of new markets to increase the demand for manufactured goods. The commuter train removed the limits to urban growth, and rail links led to a major increase in trade between nations.

Railway construction also played a significant role in the 19th-century unification of disparate kingdoms and duchies into nation states – notably in Germany and Italy. Even in long-established countries, construction of the railway system engendered nationalist feelings. In Switzerland, for example, disapproval of the leading role of French and German financiers in Swiss railways led to strong public pressure for the system to be nationally controlled. The railways were nationalised in 1902 after a public referendum.

From the use the Prussians made of the railways in suppressing the uprisings of 1848 or the dispatch of 30,000 troops from Russia to Hungary the following year, it was evident that railways would play a major role in future conflicts. However, the Franco-Prussian War of 1870–71 emphasised the limitations: in speeding mobilisation, railways were only as efficient as the co-ordination between railway and military authorities, and this was often poor. Distribution from railheads was weak; and railways were susceptible to sabotage.

Inevitably, lines built for political rather than economic reasons were unprofitable, often barely able to cover their running costs. State guarantees to pay the interest on loans to fund construction were a common way of ensuring that marginal lines – intended to foster unity or encourage development of rural areas – were built. Many of the railways in the Balkans were planned for geo-political reasons.

⊘ THE FLYING SCOTSMAN

One of the world's most famous trains, the *Flying Scotsman* began the 629-km (393-mile) service between London King's Cross and Edinburgh in 1862. After dining cars were added in 1900 (previously the train had stopped for a 20-minute lunch break at York), the *Scotsman*'s journey became the longest non-stop run in the world when even the break for a locomotive and/or crew change was eliminated in 1928 by the provision of corridor tenders, allowing a crew change on the move. In 1934 the train made the world's first 160-kmh (100-mph) run. *The Flying Scotsman* locomotive still runs today, under the auspices of its owner, the National Railway Museum.

RUNNING ON ECONOMIC LINES

Perhaps the major instance of state construction of railways for economic and social benefits took place in France, where over 20,000km (12,500 miles) of minor lines were built as feeders to the principal routes under an act of 1880 embodying the Plan Freycinet. This incorporated a plan of desired secondary lines together with a poorly-devised financial framework under which they would be built and operated.

Many of the rural metre or narrow-gauge networks – like those of other European countries – were routes of great character. Penetrating quiet corners of the French countryside, such railways had an immense impact on areas that had remained more or less unchanged for centuries. Suddenly there was more than a local market for produce, thanks to cheaper and faster transport to nearby towns. To meet the extra demand, better farm equipment and fertilisers were brought in by train.

While this cheaper 'imported' equipment threatened the livelihood of local tool makers, new job opportunities were created by the ease with which villages and towns could be reached. This broadened social circles and offered the chance to look beyond the immediate community for employment. The range of goods in village shops increased, and daily newspapers broadened the focus of people's interest and concerns.

THE GROWTH OF TRAVEL AND TOURISM

The speed of train travel compared with that of a horse-drawn coach, coupled with the middle classes' ability to pay long-distance fares, opened up opportunities that would have been unthinkable to previous generations. As the Maine-born poet Edna St Vincent Millay put it:

My heart is warm with the friends I make,
And better friends I'll not be knowing,
Yet there isn't a train I wouldn't take
No matter where it's going.

Before the railways, most people scarcely travelled a day's walk from their birthplace, and the only ones who could visit other countries were the very rich on a Grand Tour, or men willing to risk the uncertainties of life as a sailor or soldier. The railway opened up unprecedented opportunities, although it was to be several

decades before the middle classes started venturing abroad in large numbers; first came the day excursion.

Thomas Cook claimed to have run the 'first public excursion train' (a special train at reduced fares) in England when he organised a temperance outing from Leicester to Loughborough in July 1841. In fact, such trains are almost as old as the railways, and the first instance is thought to have been an excursion on the Bodmin & Wenford Railway in June 1836. What is beyond question, however, is the impact of Cook's

Thomas Cook advertising poster.

excursion, for he went on to arrange more special trains to further the cause of temperance, in which he passionately believed, gaining unrivalled experience in their organisation. In the summer of 1845 he applied his knowledge to a commercial excursion, and produced for the journey the first in a long line of handbooks. These had a 'threefold advantage – they excite interest in anticipation; they are highly useful on the spot; and they help to refresh the memory in after days'.

Although Cook's first conducted tour to Scotland in the following year was something of a disaster, it 'transformed me from a cheap Excursion conductor to a Tourist Organiser and Manager'. After coming perilously close to bankruptcy, Cook recovered and went on to build up the business that remains a byword in tourism. It was a short-lived decision by Scottish railways in 1862 to stop issuing cheap tourist tickets that compelled Cook to expand his operations to the Continent, leading holidays to Paris and Switzerland the following year. By the end of the century, there were few places in Europe served by railways that Thomas Cook did not cover: in 1894 he added the 'almost undiscovered country' of Herzegovina, and in 1899 the first group arrived in St Petersburg for a journey

London, Brighton & South Coast Railway poster, 1901.

on the newly opened Trans-Siberian Railway to Vladivostok.

The event that made the railway excursion a part of British life was the Great Exhibition of 1851. People went to great lengths to save the money for a visit, and over 6 million admission tickets were sold. For many, it was their first long-distance train journey, and 165,000 of them travelled by Cook-organised excursions.

HOLIDAYS FOR ALL

Gradual reductions in working hours from the mid-19th century went hand-in-hand with the idea of the excursion train and a growing ability to pay the fares. In 1871 the British government created four bank holidays, and within a decade

a week's holiday at the seaside was the goal of many families. Blackpool doubled in size in each decade between 1870 and 1900.

The earliest recorded works excursion was in 1840, when the marine and steam engine builder R & W Hawthorn of Newcastle chartered a train for its workers and their families to have a day in Carlisle. But it was the restorative air of the seaside that attracted most day-trippers, and works outings enabled many to see the sea for the first time. Sporting fixtures also generated good business: 82 special trains were run for the 1887 St Ledger Day race in Doncaster, for example.

The demand for tickets often exceeded expectations, requiring additional carriages and locomotives: an excursion to Brighton in 1844 ended up with 60 carriages and six locomotives. Even scheduled holiday trains, like the Cornish Riviera Express, would sometimes run in several portions, so great was the demand for tickets.

By the final quarter of the 19th century, the middle classes were starting to venture abroad in considerable numbers, leading to unkind caricatures in satirical publications. As places were popularised by the middle class, aristocratic patrons moved to pastures new. By the beginning of the 20th century, tourism was becoming an international phenomenon – as indicated by the cosmopolitan guest list at popular resorts.

Most 19th-century monarchs had trains built specially for them. The first carriage designed for royalty was adapted for the Dowager Queen Adelaide by the London & Birmingham Railway in 1842.

A DIFFERENT CLASS OF TRAVEL

The provision of three classes of carriage by the Liverpool & Manchester Railway set a pattern for rail travel around the world. Some made do with two; the Prussians offered a choice of four, with a special class for military use; and the Montpellier–Sète Railway in France felt a need for five classes. As the surviving Bodmin & Wenford Railway carriages of 1834 in the National

Railway Museum in York testify, passengers in third (or lower) class at first had to make do with roofless, open wagons, some without so much as a bench to sit on. Holes were drilled in the floor to act as drains. Besides the coal smuts and smoke, wind and rain, passengers would have to endure the stench of rendered animal fat or vegetable oil that was used as a lubricant for axle bearings, before relief arrived in the form of mineral oil. Some French railways sold spectacles to protect the eyes of passengers travelling third class or in one of the curious,

comfortably upholstered seats with arm- and head-rests. Yet it took many decades for passengers to receive the facilities now taken for granted: for much of the 19th century the only heating came from metal foot-warmers hired from stations; the absence of toilets spawned a variety of contraptions allowing people to relieve themselves with some decorum; and not until 1879 was it possible to eat in a restaurant car on a British train.

Railways were unwilling to add amenities that would increase the weight of trains,

Liverpool and Manchester Railway in 1831. At the top are 1st-class carriages, with 2nd and 3rd-class carriages below.

double-decker suburban carriages with open upper seats. The witty cartoons of French caricaturist Honoré Daumier are a testament to the tribulations of such travel.

Even when third-class passengers were afforded a roof and upper sides to carriages, they were denied a view because the use of expensive glass was restricted to a few tiny windows to provide light at a high level. But even this was an improvement on slow and uncomfortable coach travel, whose services became redundant once a parallel railway line was opened for business.

For early first-class passengers, railway travel was far more agreeable. The skills of the stage-coach builders were developed to provide

in turn requiring more powerful locomotives that burned more coal. They often had to be coerced by governments into raising standards.

In Europe the carriage divided by internal walls was quickly adopted as the usual layout, following construction of the first compartment carriage in 1834; during the 20th century many European railways began to move away from compartment stock.

LUXURY CARRIAGES

George Mortimer Pullman, born in New York State in 1831, had a huge effect on the improvement of railway carriages. His train journeys, selling furniture made by his cabinet-maker brother, gave him the idea for carriages that would make travel by train a pleasure rather than an endurance. Although Pullman's carriages made his name synonymous with luxurious style and service, many contemporary accounts suggest that the reality was very different. Nonetheless, Pullman's ideas attracted the attention of a man who shared his objectives. James Allport, General Manager of the Midland Railway, met Pullman during a tour of America in 1872. Allport's interest was primarily in day saloons rather than the sleeping cars with which

Touring America, Nagelmackers was unimpressed by what the Pullman company offered, but was quick to see that the real value of their services was 'through running'. At that time, trains generally terminated at borders or at the end of a company's line, requiring frequent changes on long journeys. Nagelmackers believed that luxury-carriage services that crossed national and commercial boundaries would promote international travel. He would attach carriages to trains, railway companies would charge a normal fare in return

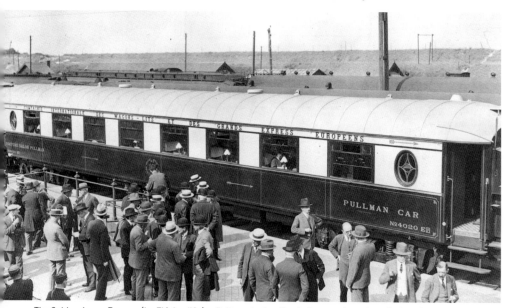

The Golden Arrow Express (La Fléche d'Or), a Pullman train, after its inaugural run from Paris to Calais, 1926.

Pullman was associated, so when the first Pullman-car train on a revenue-earning journey in Europe left Bradford for London St Pancras on 1 June 1874, it comprised four carriages with a mixture of open saloons and compartments and a single sleeping car.

In the same month, the Pullman Palace Car Co., as the European subsidiary was entitled, signed the first contracts with railways in Italy. Although the Pullman company later provided carriages for such British trains as the Southern Belle and Harrogate Pullman, most of the opportunities in Europe were lost to a company founded by the other great name behind the development of luxury carriages, the Belgian Georges Nagelmackers.

for free haulage, and Nagelmackers would make money from a surcharge for use of his carriages.

SETBACKS AND OPPORTUNITIES

Plans to launch a Paris–Berlin train were stymied by the outbreak of the Franco-Prussian War in 1870, but Nagelmackers quickly seized the initiative and used his five new carriages for an Ostend–Brindisi service for Britons catching Peninsular & Oriental Steamship vessels bound for Alexandria and Bombay through the newly opened Suez Canal. 'The P&O Express' was such a success that Nagelmackers ordered five more carriages and, together with P&O, built a luxury hotel in

Brindisi where passengers could await the boat in comfort.

As soon as the Franco-Prussian war ended, P&O abandoned Nagelmackers, after the French had refused to allow his coaches to use the much faster new route through the Mont Cenis Tunnel. Having built it, the French wanted to hold on to the revenue it generated.

Nagelmackers was in trouble. No one was willing to offer a route for the 10 carriages of his newly-registered Compagnie Internationale des Wagon-Lits et Grands Express Européens (CIWL). He was saved by the arrival in Britain from America of Colonel William Mann, with two boudoir cars, superior to Nagelmackers' carriages. The two men formed a partnership and gradually won business, helped by the fact that the Prince of Wales (later Edward VII) travelled in one of the cars to his brother's wedding in St Petersburg. In due course, Mann became homesick for America and sold out to Nagelmackers, leaving him to complete the rout of Pullman's European efforts and dominate luxury international train services.

> King Boris III of Bulgaria not only loved riding on the Orient Express but also used his regal prerogative to take over as driver and run it at full throttle while travelling through his realm.

THE ORIENT EXPRESS

The most famous train created by CIWL was undoubtedly the Orient Express, which first ran on 4 October 1883 from Gare de Strasbourg (now Gare de l'Est) in Paris to Constantinople (Istanbul). The thickly-carpeted, gas-lit carriages were panelled in teak, walnut and mahogany and decorated with Gobelins tapestries. Passengers sat on leather upholstery, slept in silk sheets, ate with silver cutlery and drank out of crystal glasses. On the first run, brass bands greeted the train at intermediate stations, and after Bucharest the King of Romania invited the passengers to break the journey at his new summer palace.

Other long-distance or international trains followed: by 1914 CIWL had 32 luxury trains in service. None, however, captured the public imagination like the Orient Express, helped by the many novels and, later, films which used it as a setting. For more on the history of the Orient Express, see page 228.

PORTMANTEAUS AND PARASOLS

Travelling light is a necessity imposed by air travel. Until habits began to change, or standards fall, depending on your point of view, it

Dining car on the Orient Express, c.1885.

would have been unthinkable for men to have appeared for dinner at a smart hotel in anything less than a suit. For women, a different dress and hat for each day was *de rigeur*. Cartoonists, and paintings such as Frith's *The Railway Station*, give some idea of the huge quantities of luggage with which people travelled.

The 1859 *Official Guide to the London & North Western Railway* advised that travellers should 'take as little luggage as possible; and ladies are earnestly entreated not to indulge in *more* than seven boxes and five small parcels for the longest journey'. The 3rd Duke of Sutherland had an entire train when he migrated between his Staffordshire and Highland homes.

Another reason for several luggage vans on international trains was that those who could afford to travel to other countries often did so for much longer than a fortnight's holiday, partly of course because it took them longer to get there. Families would often stay for months on end, like the characters in some of Thomas Mann's novels and short stories, bringing with them governesses or nannies to look after the children. Noël Coward was particularly fond of long trans-continental railway journeys, and when he set off for the Far East

Poster for the Golden Arrow (La Fléche d'Or), c.1927.

in 1929, he took 27 pieces of luggage and a gramophone.

THE GOLDEN AGE

For those with the wherewithal to pay for the best, the quality of carriages and service on the Trains de Luxe from the late 19th century to the outbreak of World War II has never been surpassed. Between the wars, the railway companies introduced many new amenities: telephones and secretarial services on some German trains; a hairdressing salon on the *Flying Scotsman*; chromium-finished cocktail bars; observation saloons with armchairs.

More routes were added beyond the borders of Europe, making possible comfortable

rail travel to the Middle East and Asia. The Simplon-Orient Express offered connections with the newly introduced Anatolia and Taurus expresses, so that from Paris one could reach Baghdad in 6 and a half days, Tehran in 8 and Karachi in 12. International sleeping and dining cars continued to be operated mostly by CIWL, although Germany had its own operating company, Mitropa.

Many of the most famous trains were introduced between the wars. The well-known La Flèche d'Or between Calais Maritime and Paris began operation in 1926; it was made up entirely of Wagon-Lits Pullmans and covered the 294km (184 miles) in 195 minutes. The English Pullman equivalent between Dover and London Victoria, also known as the *Golden Arrow*, began in 1929. Another train from Calais was the equally famous Train Bleu, a colloquial term for the all-blue stock of the train that served the Côte d'Azur. This had through coaches for Interlaken, Bucharest, Vienna and Constantinople, which were attached to other expresses at Paris, although in summer there were enough passengers to justify a direct train, avoiding Paris and stopping only for locomotive changes. In 1936 the Night Ferry, composed of specially-built Wagons-Lits coaches, made its first journey between London Victoria and Gare du Nord in Paris via the Dover–Dunkerque rail ferry.

The pioneering work by Swiss and Italian railway engineers on the use of electric traction before World War I was expanded into progressive electrification schemes in most European countries, and diesel traction, too, was developed. Germany's *Flying Hamburger* became one of the best-known examples of the latter, the two-car articulated unit averaging 124kmh (77mph) over the 285km (178 miles) between Berlin and Hamburg.

WAR AND DECLINE

The railways had suffered during World War I but the damage inflicted during World War II was even greater and more widespread. Some lines were so badly damaged that they never reopened. As happened after 1918, large numbers of army lorries were sold off, giving a boost to road haulage at the expense of the railways. The rapid growth of the car industry also helped to foster the idea that the age of the railways was over.

By the 1930s wealthy, long-distance travellers were starting to go by plane. For three decades the railways fought a losing battle. The road lobby had become much more influential and some politicians stood to benefit financially from the decline of the railways.

The mostly nationalised railways did what they could to modernise with the funds granted them, but motorway and road building received a higher priority. Gradually the classic names of rail expresses began to disappear. Throughout Europe, steam traction was being replaced by electrics and diesels. Few countries executed the process with greater haste or waste than Britain, where locomotives with only eight years' working life were sent for scrap (it was not unusual for steam locomotives on the Continent to become centenarians, although 40–50 years was more usual).

The demise of steam was heralded by British Railways' 1955 Modernisation Plan, outlining a major electrification programme supplemented by diesels. Dozens of untried diesel designs were ordered, some proving so disastrous that they survived for less than five years. In 1963, Dr Beeching produced his infamous plan, ordered by a government that clearly saw road transport as an evolutionary successor to railways. The plan envisaged widespread closures of rural and duplicated railways, including – with customary myopia – the only north–south main line built to accept continental-sized rolling stock. The electrification programme was scaled back to keep the diesel fleet occupied, and between January 1963 and December 1968, the steam locomotive fleet went from 8,767 to three, and British track mileage fell from 76,068km (47,543 miles) to 54,361km (33,976 miles).

The shock of the 1973 oil crisis, coupled with growing concern about the damage to health and to the planet from pollution, prompted a review of transport thinking. With new roads becoming badly congested almost as soon as they were built, it became obvious that greater mobility did not mean greater accessibility. It was time to rethink the role of the railways.

THE RENAISSANCE OF RAIL

Few inventions enjoy a second life, but the congestion and pollution produced by road vehicles have prompted a re-evaluation of the role of rail transport. Central to this change of thinking has been a realisation that it is impossible to build a way out of congestion. US cities such as Los Angeles have failed to reduce congestion however much land and money are thrown at road building, and the result has been air quality so bad that on some days children and the elderly are advised to stay indoors.

Poster encouraging people to travel by rail in the 1950s.

Consequently, forward-thinking cities have revived or built tram (or light rail) networks, and high-speed railways are helping to reduce long-distance car travel as well as relieving pressure on airports by eliminating the need for internal flights – very few have operated between Paris and Lyon since the opening of France's first Ligne à Grand Vitesse in 1981.

The high-speed trains that run on these routes are not as luxurious as the grand expresses of the inter-war years, but they are nonetheless smooth and comfortable. A higher proportion of transport investment by national governments and the European Commission is now being directed at railways, helping to raise standards of comfort and operational reliability.

Liverpool station and entrance to
the tunnels, Merseyside, 1831.

ENGINEERING FEATS

The building of the railways required extraordinary feats of engineering – viaducts, tunnels and bridges that allowed the tracks to surmount all obstacles

Railway engineering was the wonder of the 19th century. Canals had produced some outstanding aqueducts and tunnels, but because barges were used almost entirely for freight traffic, few people were aware of such achievements as Pontcysyllte Aqueduct in Wales or the 17th-century Canal du Midi in southern France, linking the Mediterranean to the Atlantic. Passenger trains enabled people to see for themselves the magnificent structures that were soon the subject of paintings, aqua-tints, lithographs and engravings, reproduced by such publications as the Illustrated London News as well as national and local newspapers.

IMPRESSING THE FAMOUS

It was as much the civil as the mechanical engineering that impressed the actress Fanny Burney when she accompanied George Stephenson on the footplate of the *Northumbrian* for a journey along the Liverpool & Manchester Railway: 'You can't imagine how strange it seemed to be journeying on thus, without any visible cause of progress other than the magical machine, with its flying white breath and rhythmical, unvarying pace, between these rocky walls, which are already clothed with moss and ferns and grasses; and when I reflected that these great masses of stone had been cut asunder to allow our passage thus far below the surface of the earth, I felt that no fairy tale was ever half so wonderful as what I saw. Bridges were thrown from side to side across the top of these cliffs, and the people looking down upon us from them seemed like pigmies standing in the sky'.

Admiration for the achievements of leading civil engineers gave the profession a new

Trisanna Viaduct, Austria.

standing. Portraits were commissioned and honours were bestowed on the most successful. This esteem was reflected in the willingness of royalty to open new railways or bridges. Queen Victoria was in Newcastle two years running for such occasions: to open Robert Stephenson's High Level Bridge in 1849, and the magnificent Central Station a year later.

The need for extensive civil engineering works was due to the limited ability of the adhesion steam locomotive to climb gradients. Anything steeper than 1 in 40–50 would require a banking or pilot engine, and a gradient of 1 in 100 – the stipulation for the Settle & Carlisle railway – was considered an ideal maximum. Standard-gauge railways cannot follow the contours of hills in the way canals do, and engineers realised that speeds would soon increase, making gentle curves even more important. Consequently, railways required earthworks on a scale far exceeding anything in the canal age.

BUILDING THE FORMATION

For most of the 19th century, mechanical aids to railway construction were limited. The majority of railways were built using picks, shovels and wheelbarrows wielded by vast armies of itinerant workers, nicknamed navvies after the canal-

George Stephenson instructing navvies in the 1820s.

building 'navigators' of the 18th century. Living in basic, temporary accommodation thrown up by contractors, often in shanty towns miles from the nearest settlement, navvies soon developed a reputation for hard drinking and violence. The fear they instilled in local residents was generally unjustified, but there were occasional riots that required military as well as police force to quell.

Apart from bridges and tunnels, the two basic elements of a railway were the cutting and the embankment. Wherever possible, the spoil from the former was moved via a rudimentary waggon-way to create the latter, but where no embankment was needed the spoil was removed by barrow runs. These were crude wooden inclines up the cutting sides to allow spoil to be spread on surrounding land. Haulage was usually by means of a horse-pulled rope mounted over a pulley at the top of the embankment; a man at the rear of the barrow steered it up the boards. It was dangerous work, as both horses and men sometimes slipped in muddy conditions; if the barrow fell on the same side as the navvy, he could easily be injured.

British navvies had a reputation for hard work, and they were sometimes employed on early continental railways, such as the Paris–Rouen line built by Thomas Brassey. The cuttings attracted many Frenchmen, one of whom was heard to exclaim: *'Mon Dieu! les Anglais, comme ils travaillent!'* (My god! Those English, they work hard!). The use of a foreign workforce was a continuing feature of railway construction: many of Switzerland's railways relied heavily on Italian labour.

VIADUCTS AND BRIDGES

The early railway engineers could draw on the experience of road bridges and canal aqueducts for the railways. What was remarkable was the proliferation of designs using the basic materials of stone, brick, iron and wood in varying combinations, usually determined by the location of the structure and the availability of materials. Provided good stone and mortar are used, such structures are probably the most durable, requiring little maintenance. Wooden structures were cheap and quick to build, and there are still a few major ones in use, such as the 759-metre/yd Barmouth Bridge across the Mawddach Estuary in Wales.

> *The expression 'It's like painting the Forth Bridge' has entered the English language as a way of describing any interminable task.*

The study of metallurgy was still in its infancy, and some limitations were discovered the hard way: the problems of cast iron were tragically highlighted in 1847 when Robert Stephenson's skew bridge across the River Dee at Chester collapsed as a train was crossing, with the loss of five lives. The use of cast iron in spans of over 30 metres/yds was blamed. Insufficient allowance for the effect of wind, coupled with shoddy workmanship, was held responsible for one of the most tragic railway disasters, when all 13 of the high girders of Scotland's Tay Bridge fell into the water during a storm in 1879, taking a train and 75 lives with it. Its designer, Thomas Booch, had failed to address the problem of vertical cracks in the wrought-iron piers. He merely bound them with hoops rather than curing the cause – the pressure exerted on the

examples include the lattice girder bridges over the River Kinsig at Offenburg, north of Freiburg in Germany, and the crossing of the Garonne at Bordeaux, both approached by turreted, crenellated gateways with neo-Gothic arches.

A bridge that relies entirely on its form is the graceful, cantilever and lattice-girder Forth Bridge across the Firth of Forth in Scotland. Opened in 1890, the bridge was one of the first major structures to use steel rather than wrought iron; over 50,000 tons of steel held together by 6.5 million rivets were used

Britannia Bridge over the Menai Straits in Wales, built by Robert Stephenson and opened on 18 March 1850.

cylinders by the Portland cement with which he had filled them.

AESTHETIC REQUIREMENTS

Most engineers intended their structures to make a positive contribution to the landscape through the use of sympathetic materials, elegant design or embellishment. Sometimes the last was forced on the company by conditions attached to the sale of land. The beautifully situated, 13-arch Knucklas Viaduct in Wales is a classic example of the way railway companies were happy to spend money on decoration. The crenellated parapet is supported by corbels and at each corner of the viaduct is a semi-circular castellated turret with arrow slits. Other

⊘ RACK RAILWAYS

The ability of trains to climb steep gradients varies according to the type of traction – electric traction can cope with steeper gradients than steam locomotives – the nature of the railway and the radius of curves. To allow trains to climb mountains, various engineers have developed an original idea of John Blenkinsop, superintendent of Middleton Colliery near Leeds, for a cog mounted on the engine to engage a toothed rail. Blenkinsop's toothed rail was positioned outside the two running rails, whereas all subsequent systems have had the rack rail placed centrally between them. Most rack systems have been the work of Swiss engineers.

on the 2,529-metre/yd long bridge. This was the world's largest cantilever bridge until 1917 when it was overtaken by the Quebec Bridge in Canada. For a century, until Railtrack altered the maintenance arrangements, the task of keeping the steelwork protected from the elements required a full-time team of 29 painters (see box).

SOME RECORD HOLDERS

One of the most famous steel viaducts in the world is the Garabit Viaduct designed by Gus-

One of the most complex bridge types is the swing bridge, which allows shipping to pass 'through' a bridge where there would otherwise be insufficient height. One of the largest in Europe is the Caronte Bridge across the Marseille–Rhône canal just to the west of Marseille.

The title for Europe's longest railway bridge (with road deck above) passed to the Øresund Bridge linking Denmark and Sweden on its opening on 1 July 2000. In addition to the 7,243 metres/yds of the bridge

Fades Viaduct, a railway viaduct, crossing the River Sioule in the Puy-de-Dôme département of France.

tave Eiffel over the River Truyère on the scenic line between Béziers and Neussargues (see page 139). Opened in 1884, it has the seventh-highest arch in the world at 112 metres/yds and is now painted in a surprising shade of pink. For 67 years France had the highest railway bridge in the world: Fades Viaduct, across the Sioule River in the Puy-de-Dôme on the railway between Clermont-Ferrand and Montluçon via Volvic, has four unequal spans on masonry piers at a maximum height of 132.5 metres/yds. It was built between 1901 and 1909. This record was held until 1976 when Serbia's five-span Mala Rijeka Viaduct opened, eclipsing the Fades Viaduct by almost 50 percent, at 198 metres/yds.

is a 4,055-metre/yd artificial island created from the spoil produced by boring a 3,510-metre/yd tunnel at the western (Danish) end.

THE ALPINE TUNNELS

The Alps were the greatest challenge to Europe's railway engineers. Tunnels were needed, but the sheer height of the mountains made it impossible to adopt the usual tunnelling methods, whereby the sinking of a number of shafts would enable headings (tunnelling faces) to be established at several points in addition to those at each end. Spoil could be taken up, and equipment and lining materials lowered down the shafts, which would finally be lined to act as ventilation shafts. This greatly increased the speed of boring, as well as making train operation in steam days less smoky.

The principal drawback of working without intermediate shafts was that it reduced the engineers' knowledge of the rock strata that were likely to be encountered. There was no knowing where poor rock might be met, leading to rock falls that could crush the tunnel workings, or where an explosive charge might release a torrent of underground water. Second, there was greater room for error in making sure the two workings met in the middle. Yet so skilled did the engineers become that the two centre lines of the 14.6-km (9.1-mile) Lötschberg Tunnel met with an error of just 25.7cm (10in) horizontally and 10.2cm (4in) vertically.

Although it was the Swiss who inevitably gained the most experience in tunnelling, with a greater percentage of its route kilometres in tunnel than any other country, it was a tunnel between France and Italy that first penetrated the Alps. Construction of the Mont Cenis Tunnel took 14 years (1857–71). The 13.6-km (8.8-mile) bore was built by Thomas Brassey, but much credit must go to his agent, Thomas Bartlett, who improved a pneumatic drill designed by Germain Sommeiller, driven by water-powered compressors that hammered the rock face at 300 strokes a minute. The compressed air helped ventilate the torrid workings.

The first link between Italy and central Europe was provided by the 14.99-km (9.5-mile) Gotthard Tunnel, which began immediately to the south of Göschenen station. For almost eight years, from June 1872, labourers drawn mostly from northern Italy toiled night and day with compressed-air rock drills and explosives to meet the punishing schedule agreed by the engineer, Louis Favre.

Accepting severe penalties in the event of failure, he committed himself to having the tunnel open in eight years; it took 10, but by

Railway between Passhohe and Meiringen, Brunig, 1890.

⊘ EUROPE'S HIGHEST AND WIDEST

Europe's highest railway bridge, at 198 metres/yds high, spans Serbia's Mala Rijeka gorge, which is located near Kolasin on the scenic line between Belgrade and the Adriatic coast at Bar, in Montenegro.

The greatest concrete span in Europe is on the Salzburg–Villach line in Austria. The Pfaffenberg–Zwenberg Bridge has a concrete arch span of 200 metres/yds and sits at 120 metres/yds high. It was constructed in 1971.

The world's longest brick viaduct, part of the London & Greenwich Railway, was opened in 1836. The 878 arches stretched for 6km (3.75 miles) and used around 60 million bricks.

The longest traffic tunnel in Europe is the twin-bore Gotthard Base Tunnel, which passes through the Swiss Alps, which opened in 2016. In total, the tunnel runs for 57km (35.5 miles), and links Erstfeld with Bodio, in the cantons of Uri and Ticino respectively.

The world's largest brick-built bridge is the Göltzsch Viaduct, rising in four series of arches across the valley of the Göltzsch River between Mylau and Netzschkau, in Germany. The bridge was originally completed in 1851, spanning 574 metres (1,883ft) and standing at 76 metres (256ft) high.

that time Louis Favre was resting in the grave-yard by Göshenen church, having died of a heart attack in the tunnel workings in 1879, aged 53.

With teams naturally working from both ends, the breakthrough came in February 1880, when a drill of the southern section suddenly shot through into empty space. The sounds of the other team's workings had been heard for two months, so they were prepared for this moment. The section engineer on the southern side handed through the tiny

Diggers meet in St Gotthard Tunnel, 1880.

opening a tin box containing a photograph of Favre – the '*Capo*' or boss, who was always meant to be the first to pass through the tunnel.

THE HUMAN COST

The human cost of tunnel boring was huge. On the Gotthard, deaths caused by accidents averaged about 25 a year, with casualties in the hundreds. Even if workers emerged externally unscathed, they might have contracted one of the illnesses that stem from breathing rock dust, explosive fumes and stale air.

The two single-bore Simplon tunnels were the second major Swiss Alpine tunnels to be

built, the first between 1898 and 1906, the second brought into use in 1921. Tunnellers worked in extreme discomfort: 8km (5 miles) from the north portal of the Simplon Tunnel, the temperature was 52.8°C (127°F). When additional fans proved ineffective in reducing the temperature, engineers resorted to spraying ice-cold water around the rock face. To allow flexible train working when repairs were required, the two tunnels were enlarged at the midway point into a large, single chamber with crossovers between tracks. Until around 1960, when remote control from Brig was set up, the signal box at this extraordinary location deep in the mountain was manned 24 hours a day.

THE LÖTSCHBERG TUNNEL

One of the most difficult tunnels to construct was the Lötschberg Tunnel, between Kandersteg and Goppenstein, on the line between Spiez and Brig in the Bernese Oberland. Boring began in 1906 using about 4,000, mostly Italian workers, housed in huge camps at each end. The southern work camp was buried by an avalanche one February night in 1908, killing 12 men, but worse was to come inside the tunnel workings. The engineers were confident that with at least 183 metres/yds between the tunnel and the floor of a valley under which they were tunnelling, they would meet nothing but rock. However, on 24 July 1908, a charge was detonated which released so much glacial debris and water into the workings that 1,554 metres/yds of the tunnel were filled, killing 25 workers.

After months of trial borings and discussion it was agreed that there was no alternative but to block off the affected section and all the inundated equipment with a wall 10 metres/yds thick, and divert the tunnel to the east. The two bores met in March 1911, and the tunnel was opened to traffic in 1913, creating one of Europe's last, and most spectacular, main arteries.

The Austrian Alps are penetrated by a shorter tunnel: the Arlberg Tunnel, which opened in 1884 and is 10.25km (6.3 miles) long, was built for traffic between France and Austria via Switzerland and lies on the impressive line between Bludenz and Innsbruck.

THE CHANNEL TUNNEL

The first recorded suggestion of a tunnel under the English Channel was made in 1802 by a French mining engineer, who envisaged tunnels linking the shores, with a central island where horses could be changed.

The first official agreement between the British and French governments over the idea was signed in 1875, and in 1881 the visionary railway manager Sir Edward Watkin initiated work through the Anglo-French Submarine Railway Company. Before British military authorities got the jitters the following year and persuaded parliament to cancel the project, a total of 4km (2.5 miles) had been excavated from Shakespeare Cliff and at Sangatte in the Pas de Calais. Work was not to resume for almost a century: in 1973, trial borings began, but two years later the newly elected Labour government again stopped work at the moment the first boring machine was ready.

The scheme was revived under Margaret Thatcher, and after a tendering process Eurotunnel emerged as the successful consortium. Construction work commenced soon after the Channel Tunnel Act was passed in July 1987. Boring began in February 1988 to create two parallel rail tunnels and between them a smaller service tunnel.

Underwater tunnels pose particular difficulties because of the steep gradients needed at each end to take the track well below the floor of the water, and because of the need for pumping equipment in case the tunnel is breached. With these and other obstacles to contend with, and in common with so many major civil engineering projects, costs for the Channel Tunnel soon escalated way beyond the estimates, leading to acrimonious disagreements between the contractors and Eurotunnel. The strain on Eurotunnel's financing was immense, and it was a great achievement of co-Chairman, Sir Alastair Morton, that the consortium of banks was held together, not only during construction but through the difficult first few years before operations made a profit.

The tunnel finally opened in May 1994, well behind schedule. Almost inevitably, things got off to a bad start when a train full of journalists got stuck mid-tunnel. There were various operational difficulties and a serious fire in 1996, though without loss of life. But soon the system was running smoothly. For the first time it was possible to travel from the UK into Europe quickly and comfortably without having to suffer the tedious travails of air travel or ferries. With further journey time reductions, the train has become the obvious choice, reducing the demand for air services between these cities. The 50.45-km (31.35-mile) tunnel is used by three different types of train: passenger-carrying Eurostars

Boring equipment in the Channel Tunnel.

between London St Pancras and Paris/Lille/Brussels/Amsterdam; Eurotunnel's shuttle trains carrying cars and lorries; and through rail freight services. Through passenger trains are also operated from London to Marseille and Disneyland Paris, and during the skiing season to Marne la Vallée and Bourg-St-Maurice.

The high-speed line linking Paris and the tunnel was ready for the 1994 opening; on the British side work had not even begun. Only in 2003 was the first stage of the Channel Tunnel rail link opened. Its full opening, in late 2007, allowed journey times between the capitals of 2 hours 20 minutes at speeds of 300kmh (186mph).

STATION ARCHITECTURE

So imposing were many Victorian stations that they were called "Cathedrals of Steam". Some have been preserved and adapted for innovative purposes

The advent of railways produced a whole new area of work for architects. In contrast to canals, where nothing more innovative was required than lock-keepers' cottages and warehouses, railways called for an entirely new range of buildings. Stations, goods sheds, locomotive depots, carriage sheds, signal-boxes and water towers were all unprecedented types of structure.

With so many hundreds of thousands of examples, it is hardly surprising that quality varies enormously, ranging from some of the finest buildings of any kind in the urban landscape to some that are little more than ersatz bus shelters. Most countries have a rich variety of well-designed station buildings that add enormously to the pleasure of rail travel.

The principal reason for this diversity is that, for the most part, railways were built and maintained by private companies, before amalgamation reduced their numbers or nationalisation brought state ownership. Inevitably, most effort and money went into station buildings, but even some of the more utilitarian structures were embellished with decorative details. Many buildings were standardised, none more so than minor station buildings in France, where a station in Normandy looks much the same as one in Corsica.

Paddington and its slender columns, London.

ADAPTING AND HARMONISING

As the new railway transport system required buildings with a whole set of new requirements, it was seldom feasible to adapt existing buildings. There are very few examples of railway stations occupying adapted structures, but a few stand out. Britain's impecunious Eastern Counties Railway adapted a Georgian mansion for its station at Enfield in 1849, and the Great Northern Railway devised the grandest residence for its stationmaster at Bourne, in Lincolnshire, by converting the early 17th-century Red House, also used as a ticket office. In Switzerland, a Graubünden chalet of 1720 became the station of Celerina Staz.

Some railway companies were conscious of their responsibilities to an historic town and tried to harmonise their station buildings with the prevailing style or materials. Others adopted standard designs and brought in bricks of a different hue from those made by the local works, or used brick where stone predominated. But most railways used an eclectic mix of styles for their stations that reflected both local circumstances and the preferences of the architect and, occasionally, the client. Ghent St-Pierre was built to reflect the medieval architecture of the Belgian town, while the neo-Gothic of Battle station in Sussex echoes nearby Battle Abbey. In important cities and towns, railway companies often went to great lengths to create a building that would engender civic pride, as well as reassure those wary of rail travel by the solidity, and in many cases a familiar and domestic style, of their buildings.

Helsinki Central station.

CREATING THE RIGHT IMPRESSION

The first company to lavish money on buildings to impress and inspire confidence was the London and Birmingham Railway. Its stations at each end of the line were 'to the modern city what the city gate was to the ancient city' to quote Carroll Meeks. At Euston, a massive Doric portico was erected as the entrance; when built in 1837 its columns were the tallest in London. Both this and the Ionic-columned equivalent at Curzon Street in Birmingham were designed by Philip Hardwick, who later worked with his son on the equally magnificent Great Hall and Shareholders' and Directors' rooms at Euston. The application of classical architectural precepts to station design set a pattern in which

earlier styles were used to mask the functionality of the station.

With his customary attention to detail, the engineer of the Great Western Railway, Isambard Kingdom Brunel (1806–59), designed many of the railway buildings between London, Bristol and the West Country. Tudor styling was applied to his masterpiece, the station and train shed at Bristol Temple Meads, which opened in 1841, with a magnificent hammer-beam roof reminiscent of Westminster Hall.

The second station at Paddington is another of Brunel's triumphs. The three spans of his roof (a fourth was added in 1916) look as impressive today as they did on their completion in 1854. They are helped by the unusual transepts that were created for long-discarded operating practices. The Moorish decorative scheme was devised by Matthew Digby Wyatt.

The outstanding London terminus, however, is newly restored St Pancras, on account of the immense Gothic-Revival hotel and station designed by Sir Gilbert Scott, and the great train shed roof by W.H. Barlow. The two exemplify the 19th-century contrast between the atavism of station façades and the cutting-edge technology employed to build the monumental coverings of platforms and trains. The immense cast-iron ribs of the train shed were made by the Butterley Iron Company in Derbyshire and extend far below the platforms. They meet to form a depressed Gothic arch 33.5 metres (36.5 yds) above the platforms.

Beneath the platforms, in the once dark undercroft, barrels of Burton beer were stored, and Barlow had to design it to accommodate the maximum number of barrels. Few stations have been designed using a barrel of beer as the unit of measurement.

Today St Pancras receives Eurostars after their sprint from the Channel Tunnel on the high-speed line, and the grand rooms and corridors of the Midland Grand Hotel have now been sympathetically restored to their former glory, reopened in 2011 as a luxury hotel, the St Pancras Renaissance Hotel, befitting for a building with Grade I listed status. It was out of use for more than a quarter of a century, and 76 years after it last served as a hotel.

PARISIAN GREATS

The Gare St-Lazare will always be associated with the series of 12 paintings commissioned from Claude Monet in 1877. The novelist Emile Zola praised them as 'terrific views of railway stations. You can hear the trains rumbling in, see the smoke billow up under the huge roofs'.

The Gare du Nord was reconstructed in 1889 to produce the station seen today, and most recently adapted to act as the terminal for Eurostar trains from London and Thalys trains from Brussels. It is the busiest station in Europe in the world. Designed on the monolithic scale favoured by totalitarian regimes, it has a façade 185 metres/yds long and platforms covered by five steel arches, the central one having a span of 72 metres/yds. The public spaces are decorated with 2,400 tons of marble.

An emphatically modern, Nordic style was employed by Eliel Saarinen for his design of Helsinki Central station in 1918, at a time when Finland was still under Russian dominance. On either side of the round-headed entrance stand four pink-granite giants holding globes that light up at night.

St Pancras station, London.

numbers of passengers.

The Gare de Lyon was transformed around 1900 with the tall, ornate clock tower added. Someone familiar with these stations a century ago would have no difficulty recognising them today, and it is this sense of continuity – alone among the various categories of railway buildings – that partly explains their ability to evoke the sense of romance many still associate with rail travel.

POLITICAL STATEMENTS

In some countries the station was a political or nationalist statement. The classic example of the former is Milan Central station. Opened in July 1931, it is one of the most grandiose in

The chandeliered stations of the Moscow Metro were designed to impress visitors as well as Muscovites with the achievements of the Soviet Union. Foreigners are often surprised by the generous space of the public areas as well as their palatial decoration, with marble walls, stucco work and murals.

STATIONS AND SOCIETY

Stations became imbued with all kinds of associations that developed because the railway station soon began to rival the market as the focal point of the community. People out for a stroll would wander down to the station to watch the arrival of a train or two. The Railway Children of Edith Nesbit's eponymous novel were doing nothing unusual by taking in their Yorkshire country station during walks.

Meetings and partings invested stations with emotional connotations: the trysts under the station clock; the anticipation of going on holiday; the sadness of setting off for war, wondering if the receding view of a waving handkerchief would be the last sight of a loved one; the different aura of a station at the beginning and end of school term. These themes were increasingly picked up by poets, novelists, painters, photographers and film-makers.

have been the fulcrum of the story, such as in *Brief Encounter* (filmed at Carnforth station in Lancashire), the poignant tale of doomed love that is forever associated with Rachmaninov's *2nd Piano Concerto*; or in Vittorio de Sica's *Indiscretion of an American Wife*, set almost entirely in Rome's Stazioni Termini. Harry Potter and his fellow wizards take the fictitious Hogwart's Express to Hogwarts School from platform 9¾ at Kings Cross, accessed by magic through a brick wall. A popular sign for the platform has been erected, much to the appreciation of the

Milan Central station.

The French novelist and poet Théophile Gautier (1811–72) wrote: 'These cathedrals of the new humanity are the meeting-points of nations, the centre where all converges, the nucleus of huge stars whose iron rays stretch out to the ends of the earth'. After the more or less conventional depiction of stations during the 19th and early 20th centuries came the work of painters such as Giorgio de Chirico and Paul Delvaux, for whom the station became a symbolic setting for the depiction of emotional states of mind or a metaphor in a dream-like composition.

STATIONS ON FILM

Countless films have used stations as important components in the plot or as a motif, and some

many hundreds of thousands of fans. Horsted Keynes station on the Bluebell Railway in Sussex was adapted into Downton station for the TV series *Downton Abbey*. A Czech country station was the scene for the film *Closely Observed Trains*, based on the wartime story by Bohumil Hrabal about an adolescent's longing for sexual initiation, obligingly provided by a member of the resistance movement as his reward for taking part in the destruction of an ammunition train.

DECLINE AND WRECKING BALL

The sense during the immediate post-World War II decades that the railways' loss of market share was an inexorable process did nothing to help those fighting to prevent the destruction of landmark railway buildings. Thousands of kilometres of line have been closed throughout Europe, stripping stations of their function. Some main lines have become secondary routes, making today's passengers wonder at the lavish scale of remaining buildings.

The greatest single loss in Britain was, perhaps, the Euston Arch. Its destruction in 1962 was made all the more regrettable by the dullness of the station that replaced the old one, as well as by the fact that the arch could easily have been incorporated in the new station plan. Its destruction did, however, alert many people to the value of Victorian buildings, and a wide cross-section of railway structures are among the many 19th-century buildings now given statutory protection.

A similar fate almost befell Zürich's Hauptbahnhof, designed by Jakob Friedrich Wanner and completed in 1871. A proposed office development above the concourse was scrapped in the face of a public outcry, and the station has now been sensitively restored.

Europe has lost nothing on the scale of New York's magnificent Pennsylvania Station, based on the Baths of Caracalla in Rome, which was torn down in 1963 to make way for a skyscraper, despite public protest. Nonetheless, Britain, in particular, has suffered some major losses, such as Nottingham Victoria, Birmingham Snow Hill, Glasgow St Enoch and Manchester Central (though the train shed has been converted to an exhibition hall). Countries ravaged by war have had many older structures destroyed. France lost 100 large and almost 1,000 smaller stations during World War II.

RENAISSANCE

Since the nadir of the 1960s, most railway administrations have taken progressively better care of their legacy of historic buildings, encouraged by the clear preference of passengers for a refurbished historic building with character rather than the bland, utilitarian replacement that seemed the usual alternative.

Besides providing improved facilities for passengers, restored stations often have surplus space that can be rented out, sometimes for a complementary activity such as a café or cycle hire agency. This provides an income for the railway and enhances the feeling of security if a station is unstaffed at any time.

In Britain, the work of the Railway Heritage Trust, set up in 1985 to award grants for conservation work, has helped to save hundreds of buildings. In Portugal the stations decorated with azulejos tiles in many parts of the country are being given the care they deserve. In Finland, agreement was reached between various organisations in 1998 that 872 different railway buildings at 85 locations should be preserved; they range from locomotive depots to railway staff housing as well as stations.

Oriente station, Lisbon.

INNOVATIVE NEW DESIGNS

As governments and the EU recognise the need to increase use of railways if the quality of life in towns and cities is to be improved, money for imaginative station designs is being found. Some of the most exciting work has been by Spanish-born architect Santiago Calatrava. In Portugal he designed Lisbon Oriente station, adjacent to the Expo '98 site, covered by a striking, delicate roof supported by 60 symmetrical steel and glass 25-metre (82ft) high 'trees'. Calatrava has also designed buildings for Zürich Stadelhofen and the TGV station at Lyon Satolas airport.

In Britain, the reconstruction of London's Liverpool Street station showed how an unwieldy and impractical edifice built piecemeal during the Victorian era could be adapted and enhanced without sacrificing its character. British Rail's own architects not only created a station that is a pleasure to use, but designed the scheme around the need to keep the busy commuter station open. Another triumph has been the transformation of London Bridge station. Bombed in wartime and unsatisfactorily patched up during the following decades, it was dramatically remodelled during 2011–18, into an efficient transport hub with a new concourse, shops and new platforms, allowing it to increase peak hour capacity by up to 30 per cent.

Manchester Liverpool Road, which has been incorporated into the Museum of Science & Industry; and Brunel's original train shed and station at Bristol houses a venue for business conventions and leisure events, the Engine Shed.

Smaller stations often make splendid homes: signal-boxes can become summer-houses; the goods shed a garage and store; the gap between a twin-platformed station can become a swimming pool or sunken garden. Modest-sized stations are easy to adapt to commercial uses such

Gare d'Orsay, Paris.

SAVED BY CONVERSION

A range of ingenious uses has been found for 19th-century stations, largely in order to save them from demolition. Some of the grander stations have made outstanding art galleries and museums. The best-known example is the Gare d'Orsay in Paris, which has been adapted brilliantly to become the city's principal gallery for 19th-century art, the Musée d'Orsay. Where better to hang Monet's paintings of Gare St-Lazare than a former cathedral of steam?

Other examples include Berlin's oldest station, the Hamburger Bahnhof, which became the city's Museum of Modern Art in 1996; the oldest terminal station in the world,

as restaurants, hotels, offices, banks, tourist information centres, bookshops and craft workshops. The station at Pocklington on Humberside became a school sports hall. Appropriately for a village with strong religious connections, Little Walsingham's station was converted into a Greek Orthodox church.

Even old locomotive depots have been adapted: in France, the roundhouses at La Rochelle, Metz Frescaty and Béthune have been converted into retail accommodation, while in Britain the London & Birmingham Railway roundhouse at Camden has been put to various uses, including a theatre. The imagination applied to their rescue is also a tribute to the original quality of construction.

RAILWAY HOTELS

In common with the railway itself, the railway hotel began in Britain. The first purpose-built hotel was at Euston station, occupying two facing buildings on either side of the former Doric Arch and linked by an underground passage. On one side the Victoria Hotel was a 'dormitory' for third-class passengers, while on the other, the Euston was suitably appointed for first-class passengers.

Other hotels soon followed at the railway junctions of Derby, Swindon and Normanton. The Midland Hotel at Derby was to establish a pattern for railway and other hotels in the way it emulated a country house by being set in its own grounds with an ornamental fountain in the forecourt. Opened in 1842, it has the distinction of being the oldest purpose-built station hotel in continuous use as a hotel.

It spawned a number of country-house establishments such as the West Country hotels of the Great Western Railway, at Tregenna Castle near St Ives and North Bovey Manor near Moretonhampstead. Golf provided the principal attraction at some country hotels, such as Gleneagles and Turnberry. The railways also used hotels to bolster passenger takings on trains serving resorts, such as the Zetland Hotel at Saltburn-on-Sea where the Stockton & Darlington Railway made sure there was an entrance door almost opposite the place where carriages halted.

Other hoteliers sometimes complained of the threat railway hotels represented to their businesses, as happened prior to the opening of the North Eastern Railway's first hotel in York in 1853.

In the days when some railway companies operated their own steamship services, hotels designed to serve passengers changing between train and ship were a natural extension of their business operations. The first was the Royal Pavilion Hotel at Folkestone, built by the South Eastern Railway (SER) and opened in 1843 for passengers using the steam packet service to Boulogne. Charles Dickens was a regular guest at the SER's Lord Warden Hotel in Dover.

Despite the success of the Euston hotels, it was another 15 years before another railway-owned hotel opened in London, although over a dozen followed before the end of the century. The French Renaissance edifice at Paddington exemplified the tendency of railway hotels to be at the forefront of architectural and technical developments, the Great Western Royal Hotel having fireproof staircases, electric clocks and an elaborate bell system. It was the first of many large hotels. The zenith of the railway hotel as far as opulence – and rates – were concerned was reached in the magnificent Midland Grand Hotel at St Pancras, which closed in 1935 but reopened in 2011.

Hotel Schreiber, perched on Mount Rigi, Switzerland.

Other railways in Europe followed the British example and set up their own hotels, but not on anything like the same scale. It was far more usual for hotels adjacent to stations to be built by independent hotel companies. Not even the Canadian Pacific Railway matched British railway companies in the scale and extent of its hotels, although Ireland had a good number, such as those of the Great Southern & Western Railway at Killarney, Dublin, Limerick Junction, Caragh Lake, Cork and several others.

In Switzerland, some hotels atop mountains or near stations were railway-owned, while others, like the outstanding Hotel Schreiber on Mount Rigi, were independently financed and operated.

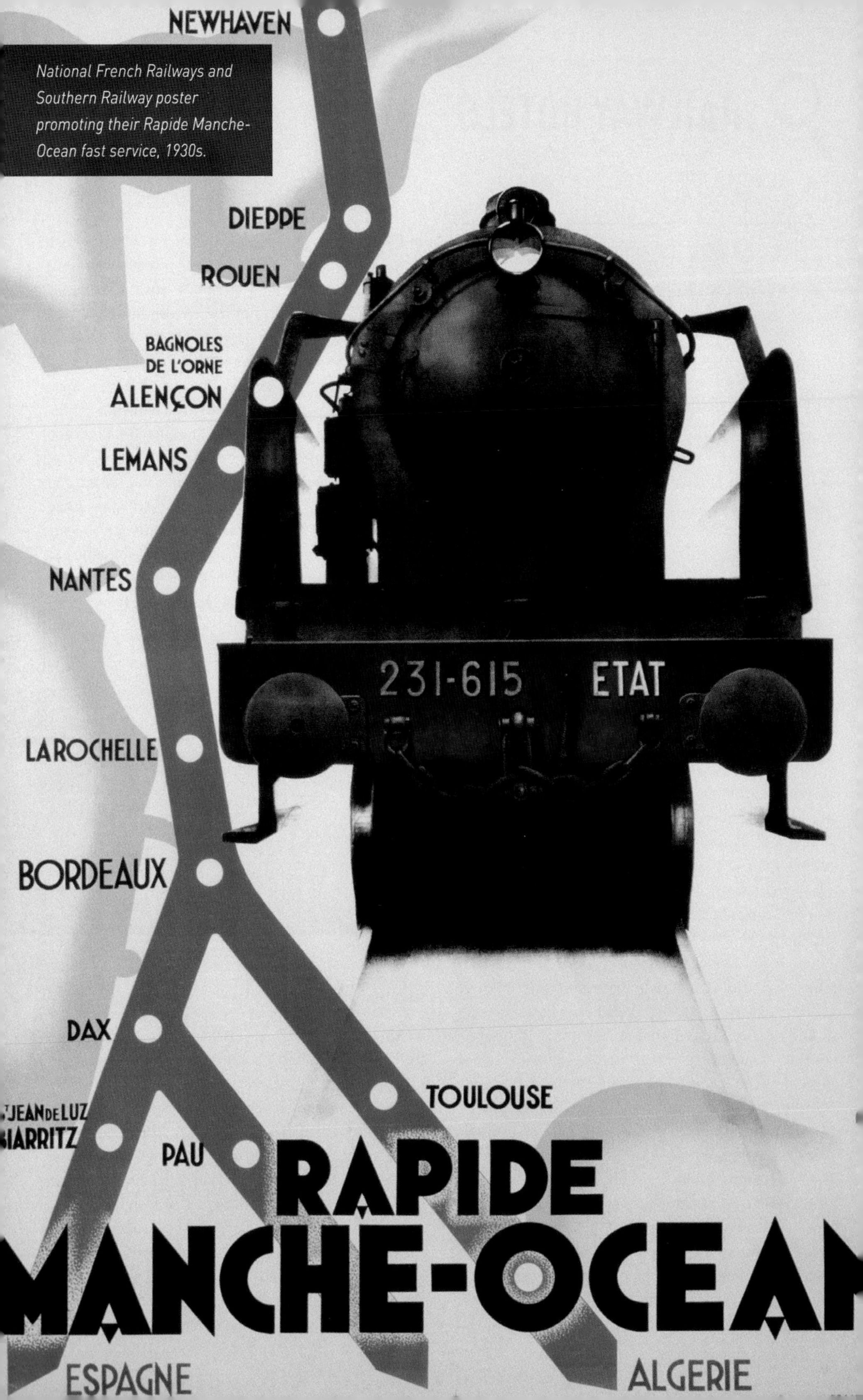

NEWHAVEN

DIEPPE

ROUEN

BAGNOLES DE L'ORNE

ALENÇON

LEMANS

NANTES

231-615   ETAT

LAROCHELLE

BORDEAUX

DAX

TOULOUSE

S^tJEAN DE LUZ
BIARRITZ   PAU   **RAPIDE**

MANCHE-OCEAN

ESPAGNE   ALGERIE

THE PURSUIT OF SPEED

Speed has always held a fascination. In today's world it is essential for commercial success but must always be balanced against safety concerns

Speed has been a major objective of railway engineers since the 1829 Rainhill Trials, the contest to decide on the motive power for the Liverpool and Manchester Railway. The ability of a locomotive to reach a speed of 16kmh (10mph) was regarded as essential. The trial was won by the Stephensons' entry, the *Rocket*, which amazed everyone but its builders by reaching the 'very high velocity' of just over 46.4kmh (29mph).

Within two decades, speeds of 96kmh (60mph) were being achieved in daily service on the Great Western Railway, confounding those who had predicted dire consequences for human health if the body was subjected to speeds much higher than the gallop of a horse.

THE BUSINESS OF SPEED

The average speed of trains has always had an intricate relationship with railway economics. Raising average speeds requires an investment in better track and faster locomotives which consume more fuel; journey times fall and more passengers or freight are attracted on to trains, and revenue rises. However, the correlation – and the trade-off with the higher costs – is imprecise and naturally varies with time and place. Today the competition is with air and road transport, and the dramatic impact on market share as a consequence of slashing rail journey times by high-speed lines and trains has been perhaps the dominant driving factor in railway investment since the 1980s.

But human nature being what it is, it is speed records that capture the public imagination, and railway managers have used this fascination to maximise publicity almost from the start.

A horse-rider races the Carlisle Express, 1938.

In Britain the principal battleground has been the Anglo-Scottish routes: in 1888 and 1895 the east and west coast lines (operated by the Great Northern, North Eastern and North British companies on the east coast, and the London & North Western and Caledonian on the west coast) indulged in racing bouts to reach the remote Scottish junction where the two routes converged for the final section to Aberdeen. Newspapers carried excited daily reports on the previous night's runs and lauded the victor.

RAILWAY RIVALRY

The rivalry resumed in the 1930s, with the two railways adopting streamlining for locomotives and carriages in an effort to capture the world speed record for rail transport. The London & North Eastern Railway (LNER) finally secured a lasting victory with the *Mallard*'s achievement of 201.6kmh (126mph) between Grantham and Peterborough in 1938. During this period of public rivalry, crowds gathered by the line-sides to see each new contender for the headline-grabbing timings; cinema newsreel film crews added to the coverage.

Although it was these exploits that attracted media attention, neither route was served by the train with the fastest average speed. That

Trans Europ Express poster, 1964.

distinction went to the Great Western Railway's *Cheltenham Flyer*, which in 1932 averaged an astonishing 114.2kmh (71.4mph) over the 123km (77 miles) between Swindon and London Paddington, making it the fastest train in the world. That record, however, did not remain with Britain for long.

In 1935 German Railways introduced an articulated, two-car diesel train with open seating and a tiny bar on the *Flying Hamburger* service between Berlin and Hamburg, averaging 123.8kmh (77.4mph) and taking 138 minutes for the journey. This was only four minutes less than the fastest InterCity Express (ICE) until December 2004 when trains were accelerated to cover the 285km (177 miles) in 90 minutes.

A few years before *Mallard* set the standard, efforts had been made to capture the steam record from the current holder in Britain, the LNER's Pacific *Silver Link* with a speed of 181kmh (112.5mph), by streamlining a Class 05 4-6-4. In 1936 this rather sinister-looking machine achieved 200.4kmh (124.5mph) at Neustadt an der Dosse, just west of Berlin. It held the world record until it was eclipsed by *Mallard* in 1938.

ELECTRICS AND DEDICATED LINES

Electric traction had held greater promise than steam since the extraordinary run in 1903 of a German AEG railcar which reached 210.2kmh (130.6mph) on a military railway between Marienfelde and Zossen, an astonishing speed for the time. This remained the world record for electric power for half a century until, in 1954, French

---

⊘ PUSHING TECHNOLOGY TO THE LIMIT

Whatever the stage of development or form of traction, pushing locomotives to their design limits and beyond entails risk. This has been brought home on a number of occasions during official or semi-official attempts to break records or cut journey times. In 1896 a northbound sleeping car train was derailed at Preston through running too fast. Timings were immediately eased and a ban put on any resumption of racing.

Competition between two railways to whisk disembarking transatlantic passengers from Plymouth to London resulted in disregard of a speed restriction and a serious accident at Salisbury in 1906, when 28 people were killed. In 1937 the press run of the London

Midland & Scottish Railway's new Coronation Scot came within a hair's breadth of disaster when it entered a series of 32kmh (20mph) cross-overs at almost 96kmh (60mph), causing the train to lurch so violently that people were thrown to the floor and crockery sent flying. Luckily the train just kept to the rails.

In 1955 French Railways' record-breaking run with electric BB9004 very nearly came to grief when the track was severely distorted by fierce hunting (oscillation) of the locomotive's bogies. A new world record of 331kmh (205.7mph) was set, but a photograph taken of the buckled track was suppressed and did not appear in print until 1981.

Railways began a series of remarkable runs that were to help the country become the first in Europe to enjoy dedicated high-speed lines and trains.

The move towards high-speed lines has been one of the principal post-World War II developments in railway operation, pioneered by Japanese National Railways with the opening of the Tokaido line between Tokyo and Osaka in 1964. Its immediate commercial success in doubling the number of passengers within a year convinced others that this was the way to achieve a renaissance of rail travel.

exports, as great interest surrounded the project, not least from the United States and Canada.

Unfortunately, it was not to be: a combination of Treasury parsimony, delays due to the sheer number of technical innovations designed into the train, industrial disputes and an exaggerated fear of tilt mechanism failure, causing the train to foul the loading gauge, were the prime factors that put paid to the APT in 1981. Development work was abruptly halted and the train put into store. By mid-1986 most of the APT vehicles were in a scrapyard.

The ill-fated Intercity APT, alongside a miniature steam train at Crewe Heritage Centre.

The Japanese had chosen to build new lines laid out for speed, with gentle curves and an absence of slower-moving, local passenger or freight trains. This avoided the compromises of track cant (angling to allow higher speed) and signal spacing that have to be made on a mixed-use railway.

TILTING TRAINS

The only alternative (and a cheaper one) is a tilting mechanism that allows trains to run through curves at a higher speed. During the 1970s it looked as though Britain would assume a commanding lead in tilt technology, as British Rail worked on the Advanced Passenger Train (APT), which was intended to take over inter-city routes. A successful outcome held the promise of healthy

Yet, as so often with British-invented technology, others were able to develop it commercially. A Talgo tilting train entered service between Madrid and Zaragoza in 1980, and was later extended to Barcelona, while in Italy Fiat developed a successful, active tilt system, allowing tilting Pendolino trains to enter commercial service in Italy in 1988.

These operate over conventional lines as well as sections of high-speed line, while striking, Pininfarina-designed, non-tilting, high-speed trains, the ETR 500 class, have, since 1993, been built for services over Italy's growing high-speed network, with routes operating east–west from Turin through Milan to Venice and north–south from Milan to Naples via Bologna, Florence and Rome.

THE TGV

France has eschewed tilting trains, developing the longest network (2,647km/1,645 miles, plus 670km/416 miles under construction at the time of writing) of dedicated high-speed lines (Ligne à Grande Vitesse), following the opening of LGV Méditerranée in 2001 and LGV Est in 2007. The Train à Grande Vitesse (TGV) has been able to set many new records since the first orange, grey and white sets entered service in 1981 with the opening of the first LGV between St-Florentin near Paris and Lyon. The LGV network from Paris also extends to Rennes and Bordeaux in the west and the Channel Tunnel in the north, Strasbourg in the east and Marseille in the south. Plans to extend the network and run high-speed trains across the borders into Italy and Spain are in motion.

ICE SERVICES

German Railways originally opted for non-tilting, high-speed trains for its new high-speed lines, known as Neubaustrecke, on which construction began in 1973. ICE services began in

ICE train in Germany.

⊘ A LACK OF INVESTMENT

For almost a century and a quarter, Britain's railways were at the forefront of global technical development, which was reflected in the country holding the world speed record for steam traction from 1938.

Although the launch of the InterCity 125 in the 1970s was a somewhat needed boost, in general the fragmented model for the privatisation process of the late-1990s weakened an industry already suffering from several decades of under-investment by central government.

A major blow to industry prestige was the abandonment of plans for the operation of tilting trains at 225kmh (140mph), following the 2002 collapse of Railtrack, a conglomerate that owned much of the railway infastructure throught the UK.

In 2015, the high-speed north–south line (HS2) was planned and costed at over £55 billion. By 2018, the project was still in its infancy, with the line from London scheduled to be extended to as far as Birmingham by 2025 and Manchester by 2032. Maglev trains – equipped with a special hoovering mechanism that gives them remarkable power to accelerate and decelerate quickly – were considered for the HS2 project, but ultimately their running costs over long distances rendered them unfeasible.

1991 between Hamburg and Munich via Hanover, Frankfurt, Mannheim and Stuttgart. Attractively-styled, new generation ICEs, including diesel tilting versions, have been brought into use, gradually taking over more main line services. A first generation ICE briefly captured the world record in 1988, reaching 406.8kmh (252.8mph) before commercial services began. In 1990, France won back the record. Now the Italian trains have edged ahead of Spain and Germany, closely followed by the Eurostar and TGV.

Yet despite the maxima being reached on new high-speed lines elsewhere, in 1991 British Rail had more trains running at averages over 160kmh (100mph) than any other European country. That position has been steadily eroded as ever more generous levels of investment in other western European countries have raised performance of their flagship services.

THE EUROPEAN HIGH-SPEED NETWORK

Today France boasts the fastest European average speeds. The LGV Méditerranée allowed an hour or more to be slashed from the schedules of many trains between Mediterranean coast stations and northern France. It is possible to leave Marseille at 3.25pm and be in London just after 10pm. In 2016 the TGV Est was extended to Strasbourg; the shortest journey takes 1hr 44 mins for 406km (252 miles) at 235kmh (176mph).

The success of the TGV has encouraged other European countries, which are now rapidly catching up with France. Spain is currently in second place, with the Alta Velocidad España (AVE) trains, based on the French TGV design. Over 46 AVE trains a day run at speeds up to 310kmh (193mph).

Germany's ICE trains offer the third-fastest timings, linking 32 major cities in the country, and serving others over the border. In 2017 a new line between Berlin and Munich shaved two hours off the journey time between the two cities, with the 623km (387-mile) trip now taking just 3 hours 55 minutes.

Norway takes the laurel for the fastest link between a capital city and its national airport, which is provided by the Gardermobanen line between Oslo Sentral and Gardermoen Airport.

The current fastest service covers the 52km (32 miles) in 19 minutes at an average speed of 164.2kmh (103mph).

EXTENSIONS AND PROSPECTS

Further extensions are under construction on the high-speed networks of France, Germany, Italy and Spain. However, the upgrade of the West Coast main line in Britain, intended to allow Virgin tilting trains to travel at a maximum of 225kmh (140mph), has been scaled back to 200kmh (125mph) and there is no prospect of a

An AVE high-speed train arrives in Valencia.

north–south high-speed line (HS2) until at least the late 2020s.

The prospects for speeds much higher than 350kmh (219mph) are limited by the steel wheel/steel rail interface, which has led Central Japan Railway (JR Central) to invest large sums in magnetic levitation (maglev) technology; a test track has been built in Yamanashi prefecture.

Although a world record has been established with a speed of 603kmh (374mph), a programme of intensive trials and research to reduce construction and operating costs cannot overcome the fundamental problem that integration with conventional trains is bound to be difficult and limited.

HERITAGE

Early railway engineers and entrepreneurs had little thought for posterity, but the preservation and appreciation of historic railways is now big business

Railway preservation in its various forms is now so well established in Europe that it is hard to imagine how slowly the idea took hold. Today, when collecting all manner of things has become the focus of many people's lives, we almost take it for granted that either an institution or an individual, somewhere, will save significant items of our cultural past for future generations. Yet for a century or more after the opening of the Stockton and Darlington Railway in 1825, few countries had any sort of policy to safeguard their railway heritage.

PRESERVATION BEGINS

Most of the early efforts to preserve railway artefacts came from either the museum world or from prescient figures in the railway industry. In Britain, it was the former, and began with the opening in 1857 of London's South Kensington Museum, the institution that would later become the Science Museum. It took charge of the remains of the Stephenson's *Rocket* in 1862. In most other European countries it was the railway staff themselves who took the initiative.

The catalyst for popularising the concept of preservation was the celebration of various anniversaries marking the founding of railway companies. In 1875, for example, the North Eastern Railway organised events to mark the jubilee of the Stockton & Darlington Railway, which it had taken over in 1863. Yet even then, no consideration was given to the future of any of the celebrated locomotives that took part. Only when its successor, the London & North Eastern Railway (LNER), organised the centenary would things be different.

Settle–Carlisle steam train tour.

AUSTRIA LEADS AND NORWAY FOLLOWS

In Austria, as early as 1885, Dr Baron von Röll, a senior officer of the newly created State Railways, suggested forming a collection of relics that would commemorate the achievements of the railway pioneers. The board approved and von Röll was given the job of setting up a museum. In 1893, an exhibition was opened to the public in the administration building opposite Vienna West station. The State Railway Museum contained some choice early items, such as an 1834 horse wagon and the narrow-gauge locomotive *Gmunden*, dating from 1854.

Donations from Austrian private railways and contracting firms flooded in, encouraging ideas of a new and larger building. In 1896 the museum was placed under the Presidential Office, but it was not until 1914 that space was found in the new Technical Museum for Trade & Industry for some of the full-size locomotives and rolling stock. The outbreak of war delayed the opening until 1918, but the collection survived World War II. Today most of the exhibits have been moved to the Eisenbahnmuseum at Strasshof (see page 274).

In Norway the idea for a railway museum came from the Norwegian Stationmasters'

Old express train at DB Museum in Nuremberg.

Association in 1895, and work started at once to collect suitable material. Initially housed in a room at Hamar station on the Oslo–Trondheim line, the collection later found a new home nearby where old railway buildings were re-erected and opened to visitors in 1930. In time this was outgrown, and the museum moved to its present site 3km (2 miles) north of Hamar, beside Lake Mjøsa, in 1955 (see page 297). The site has been laid out as a railway station with running lines for demonstration. Locomotives of three gauges are on display. Some of the rooms in the reconstructed buildings have been restored to their original condition, while others house themed exhibitions.

PRESERVATION IN ITALY AND GERMANY

The National Museum of Science & Technology in Milan (see page 229) is housed in a pavilion from the 1906 Expo and the displays range from 19th-century Italian locomotives to electric engines in use in the 1960s.

In Germany the legacy of the pre-unification states has led to a number of museums being devoted to railways and transport, or having sections on the subject. One of the oldest is the Deutsches Museum Verkehrzentrum in Munich (see page 274), which first opened in 1925 and displays artefacts that have been collected since 1903. In Berlin, the Deutsches Technikmuseum (see page 274) has adapted the workshops and roundhouse locomotive depot outside the old Anhalter station in an imaginative way. The collection contains 40 locomotives and carriages, including the first electric train, invented by Werner Siemens, as well as an exhibit on the fate of Berlin Jews deported by the Nazis between 1941 and 1945.

THE LATECOMERS

Despite its international importance, Britain was slow to recognise its early railway history. There were a few isolated instances of companies preserving a particularly historic item, such as the South Eastern Railway's saving of the Canterbury & Whitstable Railway's 1830 *Invicta*, but no national guidance. Not until after World War I was there much effort by the railway companies to take account of their past, and even then some railway officials behaved like philistines when it came to history.

Two eminent chief mechanical engineers scrapped historic locomotives that had been laid to one side by their predecessors. In 1906, G. J. Churchward cut up the magnificent, broad-gauge *North Star* and *Lord of the Isles*, and in 1932 Sir William Stanier ordered the same fate for a collection of engines that had been assembled at Derby on the London Midland & Scottish Railway.

It was not until the LNER organised a splendid cavalcade of locomotives, many hauling carriages or wagons, to mark the centenary of the Stockton & Darlington Railway (SDR) in 1925 that serious thought was given to establishing

Britain's first railway museum. This opened in a former locomotive works in York in 1927, and was broadened by locomotives that came from non-LNER constituent railways.

Nonetheless, for years it remained a small regional museum. Things began to change with the opening of the British Transport Museum at Clapham in London in 1963, which included artefacts from all parts of the country, although it was light on Great Western Railway (GWR) material because a museum devoted to the GWR had been opened at Swindon the year before.

Train maintenance, DB Museum Halle, Germany.

There was no room for expansion at Clapham so the museum was superseded by the National Railway Museum (NRM; see page 124), which opened in 1975 in a former locomotive round-house at York; this received the contents of the older York railway museum, which was then closed. The NRM has become an immensely successful enterprise, attracting half a million visitors a year. Within historic buildings associated with the beginnings of the Stockton and Darlington Railway in the town of Shildon, Locomotion opened in 2004 as another national collection of railway vehicles. More railway engines and carriages can be found in a former station at Darlington, now home to the Head of Steam Railway Museum.

Another country that had been rather slow in creating a national museum was France. Its National Railway Museum, the Cité du Train (see page 158), opened in 1976 in the Alsatian town of Mulhouse, close to the border with Switzerland. As the largest railway museum in Europe, it focuses primarily on standard-gauge engineering, with less devoted to the social and economic aspects of railways compared with the large collection of steam and electric locomotives and rolling stock.

THE AMATEURS TAKE OVER

People are often quite emotional about railways. Many who never set foot on a train all year would be among the first to be upset by the idea that their local train service might be axed. When the Lynton & Barnstaple Railway was threatened with closure in 1935, for example, almost everyone came to the protest meeting in Barnstaple by car. Whatever the reasons for the feelings that railways generate, this emotional attachment has induced hundreds of thousands of people all over the world to give up large amounts of their spare time and money to preserve something they value.

For most people, the steam locomotive has always been at the heart of railways' appeal, and it was to save some notable examples that the first voluntary efforts were made. It is a measure of the allure of steam that these unofficial preservation schemes would, in time, eclipse the work of the official sector and become the custodians of far more artefacts than the formal museum sector.

One of the earliest instances of a group of individuals preserving a locomotive occurred in 1927 when the Stephenson Locomotive Society took the decision to buy from the Southern Railway a condemned Stroudley 0-4-2 dating from 1882, No. 214 *Gladstone*. It was placed on loan at the LNER's museum in York, where it was joined in the early 1930s by one of the first locomotives thought to have reached 160kmh (100mph), *City of Truro*. This began to give the museum a national rather than a merely regional scope.

PRESERVING WORKING RAILWAYS

The idea of preserving a working railway appears to have had its origin in the United

States, where, in 1937, the Save the Bridgton Narrow Gauge Railroad Club suggested buying one of the delightful narrow-gauge railways in Maine. Regrettably, the owners preferred to see it scrapped rather than kept for posterity, but the scrap merchant had a greater sense of history than the railroad company and set aside the locomotives and carriages. These were later used on the now-closed Edaville Railroad in Massachusetts, which was created by a fruit farmer after the war.

Baie de Somme historic train.

The idea of preserving an entire working railway resurfaced after World War II, when the Welsh narrow-gauge Talyllyn Railway (see page 127) was under threat of closure. A meeting was called, resulting in the formation of the Talyllyn Railway Preservation Society in 1950, which took over and reopened the line the following year.

Standard-gauge railway preservation soon followed, with successful attempts in 1960 to save the historic Middleton Railway in Leeds and the picturesque country branch line in Sussex, now well-known and loved as the Bluebell Railway (see page 124).

Since then, 'amateur' railway preservation throughout Europe has taken different forms.

Besides those societies that have assumed ownership of a railway, others have taken advantage of light passenger traffic at weekends, or an absence of traffic on freight-only private lines, to operate passenger trains. This arrangement is common in Germany, Switzerland and France. Another accepted form has been the establishment of a railway museum in a former locomotive works or depot, with a short running line for demonstration purposes. Sometimes these have become bases for locomotives operating over the national railway network.

Some countries now have hundreds of heritage railways and museums, ranging from small, family concerns in converted stations or goods sheds, to major tourist enterprises employing dozens of people and playing a major role in the regional tourism industry.

A distinction should also be made between tourist railways – those lines that have been preserved solely because they pass through attractive scenery – and heritage railways that have been saved for overtly rail-related reasons. The latter often aim to give visitors an experience of travel in a different age, perhaps recreating stations to look as they did before World War I or in the 1930s and with their staff (often volunteers) dressed in appropriate uniforms. Some railways have enough stations to restore each one to reflect a different period.

The principal museums and preserved railways are listed at the end of each chapter, but some deserve a second mention.

AUSTRIA

Two of the country's outstanding railway attractions are not heritage railways in the more usual sense of being closed lines saved by third-party efforts, since neither of Austrian Railways' metre-gauge rack railways has ever been closed. Both the Puchberg–Hochschneeberg and the St Wolfgang–Schafberg lines continue to use steam power as well as diesel, with a mixture of century-old and recently built locomotives.

The small town of Jenbach on the main line to the east of Innsbruck has long been a draw for railway enthusiasts. To the north is the rack railway up to the Achensee (see page

238), worked by three steam engines dating from 1899; to the south is one of Europe's oldest independent railways, the Zillertalbahn (see page 239), which uses steam and diesel traction for its tourist trains over the 32km (20 miles) to Mayrhofen. Besides the traditional black tank engines, it has a former Yugoslavian 0-8-2, built in 1909.

An amateur interest in railways is almost as old as the railways themselves. The Railway Club, founded in 1899, spawned hundreds of imitations catering for myriad specialist interests.

BRITAIN

Britain has more heritage railways operating daily services over a longer season than any other European country. Many are now substantial businesses, offering lunch and dining trains, engine-driving courses, themed weekends and Christmas 'Santa Specials' to attract more visitors. Yet each has an individual character, influenced not only by its surroundings but also by the interests of those who created and run it. Some try to preserve the atmosphere of a Great Western branch line with Brunswick green locomotives and chocolate-and-cream coloured carriages, barrows of period suitcases or milk churns on the platforms, and posters of West Country resorts to admire while warming your hands before the fire blazing in the waiting-room grate.

Some of the best-known heritage railways are the 'Great Little Trains of Wales', narrow-gauge lines with immense appeal, thanks to the glorious scenery through which they pass and the perennial appeal of smaller gauges. The Ffestiniog Railway (see page 125) provides a valuable transport link between the National Rail terminus at Blaenau Ffestiniog and Porthmadog, situated on the scenic line between Shrewsbury and Pwllheli. The Ffestiniog line played such an important part in the development of narrow-gauge railways worldwide that in 1870 the Russian Tsar sent emissaries to witness one of its innovations – the trial runs of double-boilered, articulated steam locomotives.

Another railway, this time linking Porthmadog with the North Wales coast, is the Welsh Highland Railway (see page 127), a 40km (25-mile)-line to Caernarfon, the rolling stock of which includes Pullman coaches and other vintage carriages as well as three locomotives that are over 150 years old. The railway serves the start of several walks up the highest mountain in Wales, Snowdon, and also winds through the precipitous Aberglaslyn Pass.

Further south, the pretty journey up the Afon Fathew valley from Tywyn to Abergynolwyn, and

Snowdon's rack railway.

⊘ SNOWDON'S RACK RAILWAY

Great Britain is not over-endowed with high mountains, and the only historic rack railway it possesses provides an alternative means of reaching the summit of Mt Snowdon, in Wales. Using the technology that the Swiss made their own, after a pioneering effort by Americans, the Snowdon Mountain Railway (see page 127) has taken millions to the 1,086-metre (3,563-ft) peak since the operation began in 1897. Four steam and four diesel locomotives propel trains slowly up the 7.6km (4.7 miles) of track, the mountain falling away on both sides above Rocky Valley and providing views as far as the Isle of Man, and even Cumbria on a clear day.

on to Nant Gwernol at the foot of the old slate quarries, will always remind anyone associated with railway preservation that this is where it all began. It was the example of the Talyllyn Railway pioneers that inspired others to believe that such schemes could be made to work. Even when the railway's prime function was conveying slate, Britain's favoured roofing material, the tourist potential of the line was apparent, as people used it to reach the impressive Dolgoch waterfalls.

Guard on the Bluebell Railway.

A FEW FAVOURITES

It is almost invidious to select a few of the dozens of preserved standard-gauge railways in Britain, as each one has individual qualities to attract visitors. For the pleasure of riding in superbly restored period carriages between stations renovated to look as they did in 1900, in the 1930s and the 1950s, it is hard to better the Bluebell Railway in Sussex (see page 124). Its multi-platformed, intermediate station at Horsted Keynes still has the atmosphere of a deeply rural junction, where one might have half an hour to linger over a pint of draught beer by the refreshment-room fire while waiting for an onward connection. Its fleet of locomotives and carriages reflects the fact that it

had plenty of choice during its formative years in the 1960s.

Another early venture was the Keighley & Worth Valley Railway (see page 125), always seeming much longer than the 7.6km (4.7 miles) between the main line junction at Keighley and the village of Oxenhope. It, too, has plenty of carriages that would have been lit by oil or gas when new, as well as half a dozen engines that were in use when Victoria was on the throne. The line passes through Haworth, famous as the home of the Brontë sisters, who shared the vicarage with their father and brother.

For a dramatic setting and the authentic appearance of a North Eastern Railway branch line, the North Yorkshire Moors Railway (see page 126) is outstanding. Running south from a junction with the Esk Valley line at Grosmont, the railway climbs at a steep gradient up into the moors at Goathland and through lovely Newtondale to the market town of Pickering. The goods shed at Goathland has been imaginatively restored as a café, retaining a sense of its original function by using open wagons for seating areas and barrels as seats.

The distinctive character of the branch lines that served West Country holiday resorts is captured by several railways (see pages 126 and 127): the West Somerset, between Bishops Lydeard and the sea at Minehead; the Paignton & Dartmouth, running alongside the Dart estuary and through Devon woods to rejoin the sea at Torbay; the South Devon, along the Dart Valley from Totnes; and the Swanage Railway. The last performs a useful public transport function by relieving traffic congestion around popular Corfe Castle by operating trains from a park-and-ride station at Norden. Steam trains operate on the stretch from Swanage to Norden, while diesel services carry on north to Wareham via the National Rail station.

Almost every preserved railway is single track, not least because most of them are based on branch lines or secondary routes that never had need of more. A notable exception is the Great Central Railway (see page 125) in the east Midlands, running over what was a double track main line between Loughborough and Leicester.

Following reopening with a single line, a second track has been relaid for much of the 12.8km (8 miles), offering the rare sight of steam trains passing at speed.

EASTERN EUROPE AND GREECE

Most of the small number of tourist and heritage railways in eastern Europe have their origins in state activity rather than individual initiatives. Many of these are former forestry and mining railways which have been resurrected as heritage lines since the fall of the Iron Curtain. Examples are the Hronec Forest Railway in Slovakia (see page 311), the Szalajka Forest Railway in Hungary (see page 309), and the 600-mm (1 ft 11 5/8-in) gauge Znin Railway (see page 321) from Znin to Wenecja and Gasawa in Poland.

A remarkable enterprise is the Wolsztyn Experience in Poland (see page 312), offering the opportunity to drive and fire steam locomotives under the eye of the regular crew on service trains between Wolsztyn and Poznan.

In Serbia, the remarkable series of spirals and tunnels on the 760-mm (2 ft 5 7/8-in) gauge line from Mokra Gora to Sargan has been rebuilt, having lain derelict since closure in 1974. The Sargan Mountain Railway (see page 321) is the heart of a tourism development scheme that also includes a 600-mm (1 ft 11 5/8-in) gauge line into the forest.

One of the most notable revivals in the late 1990s was the enchanting Pelion Railway in Greece (see page 321), running through olive groves along the flank of Mt Pilion, with views over the Pagasitic Gulf. The trains, with open-balconied wooden coaches, were initially hauled by the original French-built tank engines dating from before World War I, but these have been replaced on most trains by diesel-powered, steam-outline affairs.

FRANCE

Many of France's private lines are tourist rather than heritage railways, focusing on provision of a train service over a particularly scenic stretch of railway rather than trying to recreate or preserve a period railway experience. Probably the best-known heritage railway in France is the Chemin de Fer (CF) du

Vivarais (see page 158), running through the hills of the Ardèche between the Rhône-side town of Tournon and Lamastre, noted for its gastronomy. The founder of the society which saved the Vivarais took his inspiration from a visit to the Talyllyn Railway.

Operated mostly by Swiss-built, articulated steam locomotives, the Vivarais also has some inter-war railcars whose remarkable ugliness exudes character. The railway follows the River Doux past the St-Josephe vineyards, which produce one of the best Côte du

Train à Vapeur des Cévennes.

Rhônes, and a medieval stone-arched bridge that was once the largest arch of its kind in the world.

Operating daily over a long season, the standard-gauge Train à Vapeur des Cévennes (see page 159) runs from Anduze to St-Jean du Gard. Trains climb nearly all the way from Anduze across some fine viaducts and past a park of oriental plants at La Bambouseraie.

HISTORIC AND MILITARY LINKS

Very different is Le Chemin de Fer de la Baie de Somme in Picardy (see page 158), which runs along both sides of the Somme estuary, past willow-lined streams and bird-filled marshes.

It perfectly conveys the character of the myriad networks of narrow-gauge railways that once meandered through much of rural France. The 27km (16.8-mile) line serves the historic seaside towns of Le Crotoy, Noyelles-sur-Mer, Cayeaux-sur-Mer and St-Valery-sur-Somme, from where William the Conqueror set sail for England in 1066.

The battlefields of World War I were supplied by networks of quickly laid, narrow-gauge railways that could bring men, munitions and supplies to the front. One of these forms the

Luzern's Verkehrshaus der Schweiz locomotive.

basis of the remote CF Froissy–Cappy Dompierre (see page 159) to the east of Amiens. After the war these networks became part of the local transport infrastructure, carrying agricultural produce as well as raw materials to, or products from, brickworks, quarries and sugar refineries. Some of the steam locomotives that work most trains have World War I connections, and there is a museum explaining the origins of the line and its historical significance. The most successful standard-gauge railway in France is the Train à Vapeur des Cévennes (see page 159), from Anduze to St-Jean du Gard, thanks to its daily service over a long season. Trains climb nearly all the way from Anduze across some fine

viaducts and past a park of oriental plants at La Bambouseraie.

GERMANY

The survival in East Germany of some steam-worked narrow-gauge railways until the reunification of Germany in 1990 has been a helpful legacy for tourism in those areas. Their retention and development makes them the principal destination for visitors in search of regular steam operations, supplemented by new heritage railways such as the Preßnitztalbahn between Jöhstadt and Steinbach. In western Germany there is a strong tradition of regionally-owned railways, often operated by surprisingly modern trains. Some accommodate local preservation societies and allow them to run special trains at weekends, although few operate more than one or two days a month. In the Harz Mountains near Wernigerode, the narrow-gauge railways of the Harzer Schmalspurbahnen take in some wonderfully timeless landscapes (see page 262).

The country's first museum line was an 8km (5-mile) metre-gauge operation between Bruchhausen-Vilsen and Asendorf (see page 275) to the south of Bremen, which has steam and diesel locomotives that have operated since 1899. One of the shortest but most delightful railways is the 2km (1.2-mile) Chiemseebahn in Bavaria (see page 275), between the Munich–Salzburg line at Prien and the pier at Stock, where boats leave for Ludwig II's palace at Herrenchiemsee. Its principal locomotive is a tram engine of 1887, and its appropriate rolling stock is four-wheeled.

One of Germany's finest working museum collections is the Eisenbahnmuseum Bochum-Dahlhausen (see page 274), near Essen. There is an elevated signal box and administration building containing various exhibitions. A shuttle railcar links the S-bahn station and museum on operating days, and trains also run between nearby Hattingen (terminus of S-bahn line 3), Wengern Ost and Hagen.

SWITZERLAND

One of the two remarkable Swiss developments of the 1990s was the construction of a batch of new rack steam locomotives in Winterthur for the lines up the Rothorn and to Rochers-de-Naye. Overlooking lakes Brienz and Geneva respectively, the two railways were the only Swiss rack lines using steam on a daily basis until the latter sold its locomotive to the former. The locomotives are capable of one-person operation, and even have a timing device to light themselves up in the morning. The Brienz Rothorn Bahn already used steam as well as diesel traction.

The other impressive initiative was the gradual reopening of the former metre-gauge line over the Furka Pass (see page 193), using locomotives repatriated from Vietnam. The line runs from a junction with the Brig–Chur line at

Steam train in Germany.

Realp and climbs over the summit in tunnel to drop down to Gletsch and Oberwald. The line runs along track formerly used by the Glacier Express, which now takes an all-season route through a tunnel.

The Blonay–Chamby line (see page 206) above Montreux and Vevey is Switzerland's principal heritage railway, with a large collection of well-maintained steam and electric traction, and a wonderfully scenic line on which to demonstrate them. Luzern's Verkehrshaus der Schweiz (see page 208) is Europe's largest transport museum, where the railway section provides a fascinating insight into the particular challenges faced by those building and operating railways in such a mountainous country.

EXCURSIONS ON NATIONAL RAILWAYS

Most railways have programmes of excursions organised by national or private operators, using sets of every-day carriages or privately-owned rakes (strings of carriages) of historic vehicles hauled by steam, diesel or electric traction. Probably the best-known private operator is the Venice Simplon-Orient-Express (see page 80), but there are many others, taking passengers to special events such as sporting fixtures, or running over scenic routes.

Many are aimed specifically at railway enthusiasts. In Britain the first example of a railway enthusiasts' special train using a preserved locomotive on the main line was in 1938, when the Railway Correspondence & Travel Society chartered the now restored Great Northern Railway 'Single' No. 1 and its historic train. Since then charter trains have become common in most countries, commemorating the passing of a particular class of locomotive, the closure of a line or the anniversary of a notable event in railway history.

The most elaborate events are German 'Plandampfs', which entail preserved locomotives taking over both passenger and freight service trains on one or more secondary lines, sometimes over several days. They attract people from all over Europe to ride behind and photograph steam engines on 'ordinary' trains rather than special workings.

The future of heritage railways seems rosy, given the perennial appeal of steam and railway travel, although they have to overcome occasional obstacles raised by officials in national governments or the EU – the latter even proposed that all hot surfaces on a steam locomotive should be painted a fluorescent colour. It was to counter such absurdities, and represent their collective interests, that the European Federation of Museum & Tourist Railways (fedecrail) was formed in 1994.

But heritage railways have become such big business in many parts of Europe that they now represent a powerful element of the tourism industry. In Britain alone, in 2014, they generated an estimated £250 million to the UK economy and attracted 8.4 million passengers, a nine percent increase on the previous year.

Fishing beside the Inlandsbanan, Dorotea, Sweden.

Train du Montenvers by Mer de Glace, Chamonix, France.

Train linking Alicante and Elche passes by ripening oranges in the Valencian countryside.

An Italo NTV high-speed train in Rome.

JOURNEYS

A detailed guide to Europe's best railway journeys, with
routes traced on the accompanying maps

Choosing fewer than 100 railway journeys from the tens of
thousands offered by the railways of Europe is obviously a subjective affair. The selection included in this book is based on the
professional judgements of its writers, who aim to describe the
best possible trips but also to offer the reader great variety.

Rail travel allows passengers to cover great distances by the
fastest trains, or slow the pace right down by changing trains
and breaking the journey at the most promising places. The
book combines both kinds of journey, but if there is a bias, it is

*The Rhaetian Railway,
Switzerland.*

probably towards routes through hills and mountains; the appeal of a railway
line is often related to the degree of difficulty of its construction, reflected in
the tunnels and viaducts as well as the impressive views that usually accompany the most heroic conquests of the railway builders.

The journeys are intended to emphasise not only direct connections
between departure and arrival points between, but also the many possible
diversions that can be made on the way. Most rail passes – often valid for
a given number of days within in a month – allow enough flexibility for the
indulgence of such whims.

One fact needs to be stressed before you set off: the railways set the pace,
not you. Rail travel of course entails reading many timetables, but this is generally much easier than is commonly supposed and our writers have tried to
take some of the hard work out of it by telling you exactly where to look for the
route you want to take. The best reference tool is the European Rail Timetable,
published quarterly in both print and digital forms, which is indispensable for
anyone who wants to get around the continent with ease.

While getting there is often as enjoyable as the journey, the train traveller
needs to know what there is to see and do at each stop along the way. The
book provides plenty of such information, briefly describing the landscapes,
towns and villages along the way. If you really love railways, you will also
appreciate the details of narrow-gauge lines – often maintained by teams of
railway enthusiasts, museums and heritage trains in each country.

Be aware that railways are dynamic things. Times can change; delays
occur; trains are cancelled or rerouted. Lines sometimes close because of
lack of funding. Great Railway Journeys of Europe aims to be an essential part
of your planning and preparation. As the doors close and the whistle blows,
you can be sure of a fascinating and memorable trip ahead of you.

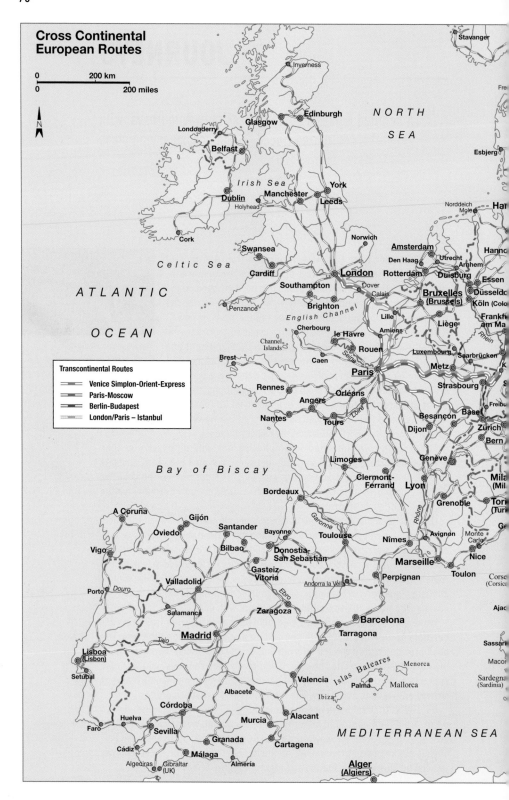

Cross Continental European Routes

0 — 200 km

0 — 200 miles

N

Transcontinental Routes
- Venice Simplon-Orient-Express
- Paris-Moscow
- Berlin-Budapest
- London/Paris – Istanbul

NORTH SEA

Stavanger

Inverness

Edinburgh

Glasgow

Londonderry

Belfast

Esbjerg

Irish Sea

York

Dublin
Holyhead
Manchester
Leeds

Cork

Norddeich Mole
Ham

Celtic Sea

Swansea

Norwich

Amsterdam
Hanno
Den Haag
Utrecht
Arnhem
Hann

Cardiff

London
Rotterdam
Duisburg
Essen

ATLANTIC

Southampton

Dover
Calais

Bruxelles
(Brussels)
Düsseldo
Köln (Colo

OCEAN

Penzance

Brighton

Lille

Frankf
am Ma

English Channel

Cherbourg

le Havre
Amiens

Liège

Channel
Islands
Caen
Rouen

Luxembourg
Saarbrücken

Brest

Seine

Metz

K

Paris

Rennes

Orléans

Strasbourg

Angers

Loire

Besançon

Basel

Freibu

Nantes

Tours

Dijon

Zürich

Bern

Limoges

Genève

Bay of Biscay

Clermont-
Ferrand
Lyon

Mila
(Mil

Bordeaux

Rhône

Grenoble

Tori
(Tur

A Coruña

Gijón

Santander
Bayonne

Toulouse

Avignon
Monte
Carlo

Ge

Oviedo

Bilbao

Donostia-
San Sebastián

Nîmes

Nice

Vigo

Garonne

Marseille

Toulon

Gasteiz-
Vitoria

Corse
(Corsica

Valladolid

Andorra la Vella

Perpignan

Porto

Douro

Ebro

Ajac

Salamanca

Zaragoza

Barcelona

Sassari

Madrid

Tarragona

Tajo

Maco

Lisboa
(Lisbon)

Valencia

Islas Baleares

Menorca

Sardegna
(Sardinia)

Setúbal

Palma
Mallorca

Albacete

Ibiza

Córdoba

Murcia

Alacant

MEDITERRANEAN SEA

Huelva

Faro

Sevilla

Granada

Cartagena

Cádiz

Málaga

Almería

Alger
(Algiers)

Algeciras
Gibraltar
(UK)

Moskva
(Moscow)

Riga

Daugavpils

Smolensk

Baltic Sea

Kaunas

Bryansk

Malmö

Vilnius

Kaliningrad

Minsk

Sassnitz

Gdańsk

Kursk

ostock

Szczecin

Białystok

Warszawa
(Warsaw)

Kyiv
(Kiev)

Berlin

Zhytomyr

Poltava

Poznań

Lublin

Vinnytsya

Zaporizhzhia

eipzig

Dresden

Wrocław

Kraków

L'viv

Praha
(Prague)

Katowice

Ostrava

Plzeň

Košice

Chernivtsi

erg

Brno

Iaşi

Chisinau

Odesa

ensburg

Donau

Bratislava

Debrecen

urg

Linz (Danube)

Wien
(Vienna)

Oradea

Cluj-
Napoca

ien

Salzburg

Budapest

Graz

Villach

Timişoara

Braşov

Ploieşti

Constanţa

BLACK

Zagreb

SEA

Trieste

Ljubljana

Craiova

Bucureşti
(Bucharest)

ento

Venezia

Rijeka

Beograd
(Belgrade)

Dunarea (Danube)

Ruse

Varna

Bologna

Sarajevo

Niš

zè

Ancona

Split

Sofiya
(Sofia)

Istanbul

Metkovic

Priština

Plovdiv

Pescara

Cetinje

Podgorica

Skopje

Adriatic Sea

Tiranë

Alexandhroupoli

Roma
Rome)

Foggia

Thessaloníki

Bari

Nápoli

Lecce

Larisa

Aegean

Lésvos
(Lesbos)

İzmir

Kerkyra
(Corfu)

Sea

rrhenian Sea

Ionian
Sea

Patra

Athina
(Athens)

Palermo

Messina

Rodhos
(Rhodes)

Reggio di Calabria

Sicilia
(Sicily)

Catania

Kriti
(Crete)

Siracusa

MEDITERRANEAN SEA

Iráklion

Venice Simplon-Orient-Express navigating the Brenner Pass, Austria.

CROSSING THE CONTINENT

Crossing Europe by long-distance express train remains the epitome of romantic travel; although the Golden Age may be long gone, today's express trains are mostly smooth, fast and comfortable

The idea of boarding a train and striking out across the Continent to reach a distant destination has appealed to romantics since the dawn of the railway age. As the European network evolved through the 19th century, the concept of international train travel took hold; the first international train travelled the relatively short journey between Strasbourg and Basel in 1841, but it wasn't long before fast express trains were covering much greater distances.

Thomas Cook was at the forefront of the new form of travel, and in part thanks to his pioneering vision, the concept of the Grand Tour on the railways gradually became fashionable. Soon the well-to-do were boarding the boat train from Victoria to link with Wagons Lits services on the Continent. Often the development of long-distance railways was linked with the shipping company routes to India and the Orient; the railways transported mail and passengers to meet the liners, firstly to Spain, and, after the opening of the Suez Canal in 1869, to Brindisi, Athens and Port Said.

MODERN LONG-DISTANCE RAIL TRAVEL

In modern Europe, the ultra-fast trains operating between such cities as London and Paris, Madrid and Seville will

get you to your destination as quickly, if not quicker, than a plane. Longer journeys, such as Paris to Madrid and Rome, are obviously quicker by air, but travelling overnight in the supreme comfort of the new class of 'Train Hotels', which feature single- and double-occupancy cabins with en suite showers, is an infinitely preferable option.

Europe's longest rail journey on one single train is the Paris to Moscow run, which departs twice weekly (three times in summer) and takes

Main attractions

Budapest: Vár (Castle), Matyás Church & Fishermen's Bastion, Gellért Baths and Gellért Hill, Hungarian National Museum, Parliament building, Fine Arts Museum Istanbul: Topkapi Palace, Blue Mosque, Hagia Sophia, Grand Bazaar, Chora Monastery, Hippodrome, Archaeological Museum, Sunken Palace.

Maps on pages 81, 87, 93

Interrailing.

⊙ Essentials

Distance: 1,073km (1,058 miles)

Duration of journey: 28 hrs 30 mins (2 days, 1 night)

Frequency of trains: 2 per week March to November (London–Venice departures on Thursday and Sunday; Venice–London on Wednesday and Saturday)

Boarding the Venice Simplon-Orient-Express in Victoria, London.

46 hours. Other epics include Berlin to Kiev, and the Budapest to Istanbul route (see page 87). The Yugoslav war of the 1990s severely disrupted the routes leading southeast from Western Europe to Greece and Turkey, and there are still no direct trains from Vienna to Athens. The Olympus service travels between Ljubljana and Thessaloniki, and on to Athens during June to October. The Trans-Balkan connects Budapest and Thessaloniki via Romania and Bulgaria. The line between Croatia and Sarajevo, severely damaged in the war, re-opened in 2001.

The perennially popular Interrail pass (Eurail for non-Europeans) makes many cross-continental routes popular with backpackers, especially during summer. The most popular routes radiate out from the tourist hubs of Paris, Prague, Rome, Florence and Barcelona. In the following chapter are two classic rail journeys that cross Europe; north to south on the Orient Express, and west to east on the Paris to Moscow route.

THE VENICE SIMPLON-ORIENT-EXPRESS

London's Victoria Station may seem an incongruous place to set off on a 1,703-km (1,058-mile), 28.5-hour journey in consummate luxury to the timeless city of Venice. The mêlée of tourists consulting the destinations boards; commuters rushing hither and thither; perplexed travellers listening to inaudible announcements; all are soon left behind at the specially-reserved check-in lounge at the eastern side of the station, just before the entrance to Platform One.

Baggage is tagged, your seat assignments on Belmond British Pullman are noted on your boarding card, and the number of the allocated Wagons-Lits on the continental portion of the train marked on your ticket. Almost unnoticed, the 10 chocolate and cream Pullman cars have arrived at Platform 2, and smartly uniformed personnel are standing beneath the individual carriage name signs to welcome their guests.

Your fellow passengers collect their belongings and make their way towards the train. The *frisson* is tangible. Perhaps their Pullman carriage will be that in which Grace Kelly travelled after she became Princess Grace of Monaco; or the one in which the *beau monde* once rode to the Casino at Monte Carlo; or the special car in which members of European nobility were carried to the Coronation of Queen Elizabeth II in 1953.

Audrey, *Cygnus*, *Ibis*, *Ione*, *Lucille*, *Minerva*, *Perseus*, *Phoenix*, *Vera* and *Zena*; the classical names of the carriages hark back to a more distinguished era and rekindle the golden age of railway travel. Each one is shining and polished like a new toy and has a style entirely its own. *Phoenix* and *Zena* (used in the 1976 film *Agatha*) are distinctly Art Deco; *Ione* and *Ibis* have an Edwardian feel to their marquetry, with a frieze of roses and

Greek dancing girls. They are even more opulent now than they were when they ran in such famous trains as the Brighton Belle, the Queen of Scots and the famous Cunarder boat trains.

BON VOYAGE

At 11.15am precisely, the electric locomotive takes the strain and this idiosyncratic train takes its leave from London's busy terminus. Within seconds you are crossing the Thames, past the imposing chimneys of Battersea Power Station on the left, before being plunged into the sprawling urbanisation of the metropolis, epitomised by Brixton with the bronze statues of commuters on the Y-shaped platform. Inside your coupé or table for two, the champagne corks have popped and the time has come to toast this journey in time, space and splendour.

Bromley South, Orpington, Chelsfield, the unremarkable leafy suburbs flash past your window. By now you're finishing the first of three courses of the lunch that is served en route to Folkestone. Heads turn to the left, and then across the carriage, attempting to glimpse the apple and cherry orchards of Kent – not for nothing is this county called the Garden of England. Another Limoges china plate is filled with poached salmon, accompanied by mint-flavoured new potatoes and a variety of salad leaves. The scene outside is now punctuated by whitecapped oast houses – testimony to the ancient art of brewing, although most have now been converted into private homes.

The chalk hills of the North Downs lie off to the left, as does the highspeed line for Eurostar trains bound for France, Belgium and Holland. You are now approaching the vast array of marshalling yards that lead to the Channel Tunnel, and before long the train slows as it reaches Folkestone West. Here, the train will stop and you will board a luxury coach that will take you to

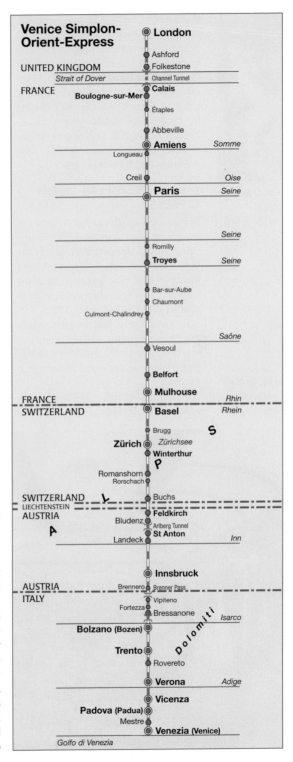

Venice Simplon-Orient-Express

London
Ashford
Folkestone
Channel Tunnel

UNITED KINGDOM
Strait of Dover
FRANCE
Calais
Boulogne-sur-Mer
Étaples
Abbeville
Amiens — Somme
Longueau
Creil — Oise
Paris — Seine
Seine
Romilly
Troyes — Seine
Bar-sur-Aube
Chaumont
Culmont-Chalindrey
Saône
Vesoul
Belfort
Mulhouse — Rhin
FRANCE
SWITZERLAND — Basel — Rhein
Brugg
Zürich — Zürichsee
Winterthur
Romanshorn
Rorschach
SWITZERLAND
LIECHTENSTEIN — Buchs
AUSTRIA — Feldkirch
Bludenz — Arlberg Tunnel
St Anton
Landeck — Inn
Innsbruck
AUSTRIA — Brennero — Brenner Pass
ITALY — Vipiteno
Fortezza — Bressanone — Isarco
Bolzano (Bozen) — Dolomiti
Trento
Rovereto
Verona — Adige
Vicenza
Padova (Padua)
Mestre
Venezia (Venice)
Golfo di Venezia

A Lalique glass panel in the Cote d'Azur Restaurant Car.

The Piano Bar on board the Venice Simplon-Orient-Express.

the nearby Channel Tunnel terminal. After a brief rest stop, your coach will board a vehicle-carrying carriage of Le Shuttle for the 35-minute journey through the Channel Tunnel. Light refreshments will be served on board. Once on French soil, the coach heads for Calais Ville station, where, awaiting you amongst a collection of railway vehicles like a cardinal among curates, is Europe's most elegant train.

THE VENICE SIMPLON-ORIENT-EXPRESS

Drawn up like Grenadier Guards in gleaming royal blue and gold livery, stand the 17 sleeper carriages of the Venice Simplon-Orient-Express. Waxed mirror-bright, they make up one of the longest passenger trains in Europe at slightly over 400 metres (1,320ft). Formalities are brief, before passengers are shown to their compartments in the 11 sleeping cars – the most sumptuous and spacious ever to have run in Europe.

The information booklet beside the ubiquitous, fringed Pullman lamp in your carriage lists the many and varied histories of these carriages, dating back to 1926. Unlike the carriages of Belmond British Pullman, with their exotic names, the *wagon-lits* have numbers – but their history is no less colourful. Sleeping car 3,309, built in 1926, was decorated by René Prou, and ran in the Venice Simplon-Orient-Express from 1928 to 1939, and again after the war until 1958, when it was transferred to the Sud Express. Another car, 3,425, built in Birmingham in 1929, saw service in Turkey, running in the Anatolia Express and the Aegean and Taurus expresses after the war. Also British-built, car 3,473 – typified by its 'flower garland' marquetry – ran in the famous Train Bleu between 1929 and 1937.

Shortly before 5pm the Venice Simplon-Orient-Express slips quietly away on the first portion of its journey through five European countries. Paris will be reached in around three hours. This allows ample time to familiarise yourself with your compartment, which at this stage is made up for day use,

with a couch and cushions as well as headrests. Behind the door is a cabinet within which is secreted a washbasin adorned with a hand-painted motif reflecting the marquetry decoration of the compartment.

A discreet knock at the door and your white-gloved steward introduces himself. He takes care of passport and customs formalities, ensures you are familiar with the various lighting and heating controls, and hours later reappears to convert the entire compartment into its bedtime configuration. Moments later the maitre d' is in attendance to take reservations for dinner in the *Cote D'Azur*, *L'Oriental* and *Etoile du Nord* dining cars.

By now you've left the sand dunes and marshland of the Pas de Calais behind. The forest of Crécy near Le Touquet is famous as the battlefield where King Edward III of England and his son the Black Prince overcame the might of the French in 1346. The train whizzes past farmhouses painted in faded colours and cafés with flower-filled window boxes. As you take turns to refresh and dress for dinner, the train follows the course of the River Somme – site of some of the fiercest fighting of World War I and, long before, the Battle of Agincourt in 1415 when Henry V forded the river with his army to defeat the French.

DINNER IN PARIS

The first dinner sitting is completed before the train pulls into the Gare de l'Est, which allows guests disembarking in Paris to enjoy a memorable meal, while the second sitting takes place after departing from the city. The restaurant cars await their guests in all their finery, while feverish activity goes on in the galleys. The epicurean delights of head chef Christian Bodiguel are served in the magnificent surroundings of the Salon Pullman, with its priceless Bacchanalian maiden panels by Lalique. Chilled

gazpacho with toasted pine kernels, pan-sautéed king prawns and chicken oysters followed by *mignon* of lamb with a ginger sauce are a precursor to the elaborate cheese course, which includes a signature creamy variety infused with Calvados. All choices on *Le Menu* are included in the fare, while a superb collection of fine wines are additional, as is the small *à la carte* selection.

Those awaiting the later sitting can enjoy cocktails in 3674 Bar Car – recreated from a first-class restaurant car dating from 1931. The immaculate interior, with small stools and convenient tables, is dominated by the baby grand piano adjacent to the curved bar.

As the train negotiates the loop line around Paris, the dome of Sacré Coeur reflects the setting sun and the Eiffel Tower pricks the evening sky. A bevy of anonymous Corail trains act as chaperones to their elegant older sister nudging into the Gare de l'Est. Those who dined at the early sitting take this opportunity to stretch their legs. As

Orient Express personel.

the train is stationary for almost 40 minutes there's even the chance to visit the station buffet, although their evening dress looks somewhat incongruous among the backpackers.

Departing at 9.40pm from this terminus, the train makes a sprightly escape through inky-black Parisian suburbs. At Romilly, the line joins the Seine and follows the river upstream as far as the medieval town of Troyes.

By now the Bar Car is in full swing. The pianist is playing familiar melodies from Broadway and West End musicals; this party often continues into the small hours. At whatever time you go to bed, you'll find your sleeping car has been converted to its nightime configuration. The profusion of linen and blankets deadens noise from the tracks and a relaxed sleep usually ensues.

BREAKFAST IN THE ALPS

Early risers are rewarded as the long, narrow **Zürichsee** is unravelled from the tissue of mist. Winterthur, Romanshorn and Rorschach, archetypal Swiss towns one and all, start to come to life; neat, freshly-mown lawns, flower beds ablaze with colour, quaint shop windows, not a curtain out of place, nor a graffiti inscription in sight.

Sargans comes into view with its 11th-century castle on top of one hill, a church on the other. Moments later the train swings into the frontier station of **Buchs**. It's time for breakfast – served in the privacy of your cabin by the ever-attentive steward. Croissants that came on board a couple of hours ago, Colombian coffee to kick-start the day and freshly-squeezed orange juice to assuage the excesses of the night before.

With the snow-capped peaks of **Liechtenstein** looking down on the right-hand side of the train, you strain skywards to catch a glimpse of this tiny principality's capital of Vaduz, with its castle. A few miles further, there's another neck-craning moment; you had better get used to looking out of both sides of the train, as from now on the scenery can only be described as sensational.

Mighty Schattenberg Castle towers above the Austrian border town of Feldkirch, then the fortified town of **Bludenz**, with a 15th-century church, comes into view. Climbing ever more steeply through the Vorarlberg you pass high pastures dotted with immaculate, slope-roofed chalets. Such is the incline, the train now requires not just two locomotives in front, but one behind as well, to ensure a smooth journey up the precipitous track towards the **Arlberg Tunnel**.

Opened in 1884, the third longest tunnel in Europe at 10.2km (6.3 miles) separates the Vorarlberg from the Tyrol. The summit – at 1,802 metres (5,945ft) – is reached inside the tunnel. After being plunged into darkness for seven minutes the train emerges into an amphitheatre of snow-capped mountains. At the famous alpine resort

Champagne is served.

of **St Anton** you can see the filigree ski lifts stretching up the mountain on the left-hand side of the train during its brief pause.

Gathering speed, the descent towards Innsbruck crosses the mighty, single-span Tressana Bridge, past Landeck with a massive fortified castle standing sentinel to the Inn Valley. A 30-minute stop at **Innsbruck** allows time to stretch your legs before lunch. The Tyrolean capital was a favourite with Emperor Maximilian in the 1500s, and remains a popular base for touring Austria's beautiful Tyrol region.

Another reversal of the train and another ascent, this time towards the **Brenner Pass**, whose summit is at 1,375 metres (4,357ft). A gourmet lunch is enjoyed as the train criss-crosses the spectacular alpine roads heading south, gliding past the cars and lorries backed up at the border customs post. High above the serpentine roads, castles perch like eyries as the train negotiates tight twists and turns through the rocky crags of the Dolomites.

DESCENT INTO ITALY

Soon the conifers of the higher elevations are replaced with an increasingly gentle scene of patchwork vineyards and orchards. There are little villages with attractive, ancient churches, and medieval towns with famous names like Fortezza and Bolzano. The picture-postcard moated castle, former residence of the ruling Prince Bishops, signals your arrival at **Trento**, capital of Trentino. Now the railway line follows the Adige River downstream towards Rovereto.

The setting for the ill-fated romance between Shakespeare's tragic lovers, Romeo and Juliet, the Etruscan city of **Verona**, with its attractive tiled roofs, can be seen in the distance. Some passengers alight here, especially during July, when spectacular open-air performances of Verdi's operas are held in the Roman amphitheatre, the Arena.

As the train glides across the **Veneto**, ripe and burnished by the afternoon sun, a decadent afternoon tea is served in your compartment. The vineyards of Soave and

Grand Suite Istanbul on the Venice Simplon-Orient-Express.

Alpine scenery from the Venice Simplon-Orient-Express.

⊙ Essentials

European Rail Timetable no. 61

Distance: 1,678km (1,042 miles)

Duration of journey: 40hrs

Frequency of trains: 1 per day (change at Bucharest)

Valpolicella stretch out to the horizon. Ochre-hued **Vicenza** – home to Palladio, the great Renaissance architect – precedes the city of **Padua**, which will always be inextricably linked with Galileo (1564–1642), the great astronomer who was professor of mathematics at the city's university.

JOURNEY'S END

Shortly before 5.30pm the train finally crosses the long causeway that connects Mestre, on the mainland, with the island setting of **Venice**, that unique Italian contribution to civilised city life. To the right you can glimpse several *campanile* (bell towers) rising skyward from a profusion of terracotta dwellings abutting the open reaches of the Guidecca – the large sea lane that so many cruise ships follow during their visit to the city of Titian, Tintoretto, Tiepolo and, perhaps the greatest exponent of the Venetian scene, Canaletto.

The main station, Santa Lucia, houses a frenzy of porters ready to whisk your baggage to waiting motorboats that will take you to see the sights of the city or deliver you to your hotel.

LONDON OR PARIS–ISTANBUL

It is still possible to retrace the route of the Orient Express from one side of Europe to the other, from London or Paris to Istanbul, in four days and nights of travel on ordinary scheduled, non-luxurious trains. Beware though: there is no such thing as the authentic route of the Orient Express: it ran on a variety of routes according to circumstances and convenience and you will need to make similar choices.

There are two main routes, via Budapest and Bucharest or via Belgrade and Sofia. Both have charm and history and converge at Kapikule on the Turkish border, before continuing to the outskirts of Istanbul. This book uses the route that passes through Budapest and Bucharest.

This is a long trip that takes a minimum of four days and nights each way, but is better spread out over a fortnight for the return journey which will give you time to see sights on the way and take an enjoyable detour on a narrow-gauge rail line in Bulgaria (see page 89).

You should plan your cross-continental journey carefully. It's a good idea to use a ticket agency to make sure you get the best connections. You will need to book sleepers and couchettes to suit your preference and budget, or hotel rooms if you intend to make overnight stops, which we recommend. It is wise to take food and bottled water when you get on long-distance trains, just in case there is no buffet car.

It is essential to check visa and currency requirements before you travel as you will be crossing out of the EU on the last leg of the journey. The stages of the route in Western Europe up to Budapest are described elsewhere in the book (see page 309); if you are planning to start from Paris, take the Eurostar from London.

Exiting Venice's Santa Lucia station.

For passengers on the Orient Express the exotic east began with Budapest. Travellers from the West still get a sense of leaving familiar territory behind as they pull out of the Hungarian capital on a train bound for the Balkans and that most indefinable of cities, Istanbul.

The shortest cross-continental rail route used to take trains from Budapest to Istanbul, through Belgrade and Sofia. However, years of political instability in the former Yugoslavia, and decreased personal security for train passengers, made the alternative route (through Romania) a more attractive option; although it is again perfectly viable to travel via Serbia, the Romania route is more convenient and faster. As a bonus, the trip through Transylvania and northern Bulgaria has far more of interest both in terms of scenery and of places to stop en route.

ROMANIAN EXCURSIONS

It is possible to travel from Budapest to Istanbul without breaking one's journey, spending two nights on the same train: a sleeper is preferable to a couchette for this, but requires a change of carriage at Bucharest. It may be better, however, to do the journey in stages. The fastest trains from Budapest to Brasov and Bucharest go via **Arad** (from where it is worth making a short detour south to Timişoara, often described as "Little Vienna"). But the most interesting route is to the north, crossing from Hungary into Romania at **Oradea**, which has a handsome city centre of Baroque and Art Nouveau architecture.

Across the Western Carpathians from Oradea, the train reaches the Transylvanian plateau and the Romanian-Hungarian city of Cluj Napoca. This being Transylvania, there is no getting away from its most famous undead inhabitant. Most of the Dracula locations peddled by the Romania tourist authorities are spurious but it can

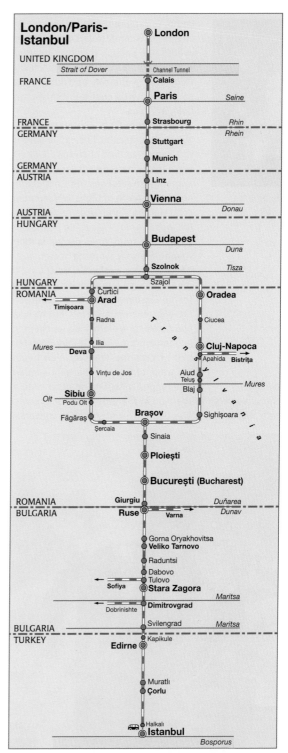

Clock tower in the citadel of Sighișoara.

Wood-burning locomotive of Mocanita, Bucovina, Romania.

be fun to explore them. In the opening chapter of Bram Stoker's book, written in 1897, the English solicitor, Jonathan Harker, takes a train on the branch line from Cluj to Bistrita en route to the vampire count's castle in the 'Borgo' (Bârgau) Pass.

Trains from Cluj also go northeast along a spectacular line to Suceava in the Romanian part of Moldavia where there are monasteries decorated inside and out with frescoes. Another scenic line heads north to Sighetu Marmatiei, centre of the Maramures region. From the wood yards of Viseu de Sus (a bus or taxi ride from Viseu de Jos station) Romania's only working steam train hauls forestry workers over 40km (25 miles) into the forest, ending up close to the Ukrainian border. Passengers are welcome on this train, but no special comforts are provided for them.

Soon after leaving Cluj the main line climbs onto the Transylvanian heath, an area of bleak, sparsely-settled, flat-topped hills. On the other side of them lie Aiud and Teiufl. Shortly before Blaj the north and south Transylvanian routes join and the line passes through the **Tarnave** wine-growing region.

To the south, easily reached by a change of train at Teius or Alba, is **Sibiu**, whose preserved city centre of cobbled streets, squares and ramparts led to it being described as one of Romania's best-kept secrets, until it became the European Union's Capital of Culture in 2007. Moreover, as it has the country's best railway museum (the other one is in Bucharest station), and stands at the hub of a mini-network of unelectrified, scenic lines, Sibiu has the potential to become a steam centre akin to Poland's Wolsztyn.

After Mediafl the main line reaches **Sighișoara**, the Transylvanian town par excellence that no one should miss. A brisk 10-minute walk uphill from the station takes you to the walled old town, the birthplace of the 15th-century ruler of Wallachia, Vlad the Impaler, the inspiration behind Bram Stoker's 1897 novel *Dracula*.

After Sighișoara, the track winds along the wooded valley of the meandering River Olt. Here and there are several villages with defensive walls and churches with stout, fortified towers, recalling a time when Transylvania, then under Hungarian sway, was settled by German-speaking people who had to defend their lands against incursions by Tartars, Mongols and Turks. Archita, Homorod, Cata and Feldioara are especially worth a look.

Brașov is Romania's second biggest city, a place to change trains or to make your base for excursions to other parts of Transylvania. The station is in the modern part of town but a taxi ride takes you to the old quarter, which is a pleasant place to stroll around. Its chief monuments are the 14th- to 15th-century Gothic Black Church and the remnants of medieval walls and gateways. Almost every visitor makes the bus trip to Bran Castle which is tenuously associated with Vlad the Impaler.

After Brașov, the main line has to squeeze between the two main parts of the Carpathian Mountains, southern and eastern. It climbs steeply out of Transylvania through woods to the 1,057-metre (3,468ft) Timis-Predeal pass between the Bucegi and Baiului Mountains. Predeal is the highest ski resort in Romania.

Sinaia, another ski resort, is the next place worth getting off the train. The first Orient Express, in 1883, made a detour here so that passengers could traipse up a muddy path in the rain to pay their respects to the king and queen of Romania. The extravagantly decorated 19th-century royal summer palace of Peleș Castle is now one of the country's top tourist attractions.

The line gradually drops down from the hills onto the great plain of Wallachia that forms the south of Romania. In between the mountains and Bucharest is **Ploiești**, the centre of what remains of an oil industry that was once so important that saboteurs were sent to disable it in World War I and US

Liberator bombers to do the same in World War II.

There is little else of interest before arriving at the Romanian capital of **Bucharest**, which, like almost everywhere else on this route, should not be judged by its station (where the whole population of the city seems to congregate) or by its immediate surroundings.

The line from Bucharest travels straight and level across the Wallachian plain to the frontier town of **Giurgiu**, where there is a long halt for passport and customs checks. Slowly the train draws near the Danube to cross the 3km (2-mile) -long double-decker bridge (the main road runs above the railway), built in 1954 and still the only fixed link between Romania and Bulgaria.

INTO BULGARIA

The line sweeps around **Ruse**, yet from the train nothing can be seen of the pleasant Danube port, which has a cosmopolitan and cultural history and deserves a visit. The town flourished in the late 19th century when it had the

Veliko Târnovo.

⊘ VELIKO TÂRNOVO

Built on a series of hills curving around a loop of the River Yantra, Veliko Târnovo is Bulgaria's most picturesque town as well as being the country's former capital.

The partially ruined citadel of Tsarevets sprawls over an impregnable site all but surrounded by the river and entered by a causeway. The best of the town's many restored churches are in the Asenova quarter beneath it. From the citadel gate the old town creeps west along a ridge and down to the edge of a cliff that fringes the river. One characteristic building is the so-called House of the Monkey, set slightly back from the main street. There is a pleasant downhill walk along cobbled Gurko Street, where No. 88 is a museum that preserves the furnishings of a typical, 19th-century bourgeois house.

first newspaper, bookshop and public pharmacy in Bulgaria. The country's first iron ship was built in Ruse and the first motion picture was screened here. In 1866 Bulgaria's first railway station was built near the bank of the Danube as the western terminus of the Balkans' first railway, which ran to the Black Sea town of Varna. The station is now a Transport Museum displaying antique rolling stock and steam engines.

The passengers of the very first Orient Express took the Varna route. Without a bridge across the Danube in those days the luxurious Wagons-Lits cars could only get as far as Giurgui, from where the passengers were ferried across the river and put on a chartered train from Varna, from where they would ship to Constantinople (Istanbul). Henri Opper de Blowitz, a journalist on board the train, described 'a countryside of most barren and melancholy monotony. The fields appeared untilled; we saw only stunted underbrush and sandy soil. Here and there was a little hamlet with a few miserable cottages, hovels built of mud and timber, many riddled with bullet holes – reminders of some past skirmishes of war and bandit attacks'. On the way to Varna is **Madara** where an 8th-century figure of a horseman is carved in the hillside.

From Ruse the north–south main line crosses Bulgaria and winds its way through the Balkan ranges via Gorna Oryakhovitsa, Veliko Târnovo, Dryanovo, Tryavna, Raduntsi, Dabovo (between these last two it climbs in two spirals) and Tulovo, to reach the city of Stara Zagora before meeting the Sofia–Istanbul line at Dimitrovgrad and continuing to the border at Svilengrad.

There are several possible detours to be made in Bulgaria. The easiest is to **Veliko Târnovo** (see page 89), the country's most picturesque town, which is reached by train or minibus from Gorna Oryakhovitsa. A trip east takes you to Varna and the Black Sea; west to the capital of Sofia. If you want to explore Bulgaria's railways further it is worth catching a train on the narrow-gauge railway from Septemvri to Bansko (see page 92) – although you'll need to allow time as it is a slow journey. Another scenic line runs southwest from Sofia to Kyustendil through the gorge of the River Struma.

When you have finished exploring, there is a direct train from Sofia to Istanbul, passing through the rail junction of Plovdiv, where the old quarter is well worth visiting. The line from Sofia and Plovdiv converges with the one from Ruse and Stara Zagora at Dimitrovgrad and as one they head for the Turkish border. Svilengrad is the last station in Bulgaria. Engineers on the Orient Express must have been relieved when they crossed a frontier and left Bulgaria because two of that country's monarchs, Ferdinand I and his son Boris III, often insisted on driving the train themselves when it was crossing their kingdom.

The Venice Simplon-Orient-Express ready to depart from Ruse train station.

TURKEY AND ISTANBUL

Kapikule, across the Turkish border, is the only frontier town on the journey between Budapest and Istanbul where you have to get off the train – in this case to buy a Turkish visa. The delay can seem interminable but once the train is moving again, time 15 minutes then look out for **Edirne**, where the old quarter is crowned by a famous mosque, designed by Sinan, imperial architect of the Ottoman 'Renaissance'. The mosque comes into view five minutes before the train arrives at the station. From here, it's a fast, straight journey across the farmlands of Thrace, planted with maize and rice.

The stretch of line between Muratli and Corlu features twice in railway history because disasters befell the Orient Express here on two different occasions. On 31 May 1891, the train was held up here and partially derailed, and its passengers politely robbed. Then, in the severe winter of 1929, the Orient Express ground to a halt in an ever-increasing snow drift where it was lost to the world for five and a half days. At first the impeccable Wagons-Lits service was maintained, but before long water, food and fuel for heating had to be rationed.

Sadly, the very last part of the route into **Istanbul** has been affected by major construction work, aimed at improving the metropolis's transport infrastructure. The train now halts at Halkali, in the city's western suburbs, from where a bus service (line BN1) continues to the original destination of Sirkeci Station. Eventually, there will be a new urban train link from Halkali to the city centre.

The bus doesn't follow the train route exactly but you can still get some sense of the excitement of approaching the city by rail along the coast of the Sea of Marmara. The city proper begins when you pass through the Theodosian Walls, a double barrier built of alternating tile and limestone,

that protected Byzantium then Constantinople (before it was renamed Istanbul), until the city fell to the Ottomans in 1453. The walls are guarded by Yedikule Castle at southern end.

Shortly after on the left is the historic hilltop district of Sultanahmet, where you will do most of your sightseeing. Standing proudly above a mass of wooden Ottoman houses, many of which have been restored, you'll see the unmistakeable Blue Mosque and Hagia Sophia. Immediately next to the old railway line on the left is the 6th-century church of SS Sergius and Bacchus, together with fragments of the Great Palace of Byzantium, on the right of the tracks.

The bus, like the train, rounds Seraglio Point and passes underneath the walls of the Ottoman sultans' Topkapi Palace. Across the water on your right is Istanbul's Asian side on which stand the landmarks of Hydarpasa Station, the Selimye Barracks, and Leander's Tower, which stands on an islet.

The Bosphorus, the Golden Horn and Galata Tower can all be seen as the bus approaches Sirkeci Station, which was

Tram on Istiklal Street, Istanbul.

Leander's Tower, Istanbul.

built in 1890 to welcome passengers on the early journeys of the Orient Express.

SEPTEMVRI TO DOBRINISHTE ON A NARROW-GAUGE RAILWAY

A picturesque narrow-gauge railway ascends into the mountains of southern Bulgaria from **Septemvri** station (on the main line between Sofia and Plovdiv). Five trains a day serve the bottom half of the line as far as Velingrad but there are only four daily trains to the upper stations of Razlog, Bansko and Dobrinishte, the first leaving at 2.45am. The track begins by climbing up the wooded valley of the River Cepinska, passing through a series of tunnels and almost doubling back on itself to gain height. Leaving the valley behind, the train follows the edge of a plateau to arrive at the spa of **Velingrad**. After Tzvetino station it crawls through a series of looping tunnels to reach the highest station in the Balkans, **Avramovo**, at 1,267 metres (4,156ft).

From here the line descends again, crossing over itself once more, before coming to Yepha Mecta station. The

The narrow-gauge railway to Bansko.

towns along the upland valley her have minarets protruding into the sk and tobacco drying under plastic awn ings in the farmsteads of their out skirts – signs of Bulgaria's minorit Muslim community, which produce one of the country's most importan industrial crops.

After Razlog, the train reaches th penultimate station of **Bansko**, whic is a better place to stay overnight tha the end station of **Dobrinishte**. Th only out-and-back journey possibl in one day is 9.05am from Septem vri, returning at 8pm. Located at th meeting point of the Rila, Rhodop and Pirin mountains, Bansko is a cen tre for winter sports and mountai hiking in the **Pirin National Park**. has a range of hotels and is know for its *mehanas* or inns, many of them old stone buildings standing in cob bled streets. In the Rila Mountain to the north, Bulgaria's highest, i the famous Rila Monastery. Despit its relative proximity to Bansko, how ever, the monastery is more easil accessed from Sofia.

⦿ ONWARDS TO ASIA

Moscow is a rail hub extraordinaire, with links to China and Japan via the Trans-Siberian express, and Central Asia on the 'Turk–Sib' line.

There are in fact three Trans-Siberian trains, all of which head east from Moscow, out over the Urals (where the line crosses into Asia) and across the forests of Siberia. To the east of Irkutsk and beautiful Lake Baikal, the Trans-Mongolian route splits off from the main Trans-Siberian line, cutting south to the Mongolian border, and passing through the Mongolian capital of Ulan Bator on its way to Beijing. The Trans-Manchurian branches off further to the east, heading south across Manchuria to Beijing. The Trans-Siberian itself continues eastwards until it reaches the Pacific at Vladivostok, where ferries operate to Nakhodka in Japan.

The Turk–Sib route runs southeast from Moscow, across the steppes to Kazakhstan and Uzbekistan, where it stops at the capital, Tashkent. From Tashkent there are easy connections to the stunning Silk Road cities of Samarkand, Bukhara and Khiva. Trains also run to the Kazak city of Almaty, from where it is possible to catch a train across the Chinese border to Urumqi and from there to other parts of China.

PARIS-MOSCOW

In the days of the Cold War, travelling on the Ost-West express from Western Europe right into the heart of the Soviet bloc was one of Europe's most daunting rail experiences. Passengers were officially warned by the British Foreign Office against travelling on what was considered one of the most dangerous train routes in Europe at the time. Buying tickets in Britain, nervous travellers were presented with a British Rail International caveat that read: 'Standards on this service may not be as high as those normally associated with European train travel'. The old Ost-West express officially ran from Paris to Moscow's Belorusskaya station, but in reality it gathered passengers and carriages from all over Western Europe with connections from London Victoria, the Belgian ferry port of Ostende, and Paris. The engine and the majority of the carriages were Russian stock, as were the guards and train crew.

Many things have changed since the Cold War days, but the rail journey from Paris to Moscow is still of great interest to rail enthusiasts, or indeed anyone of an adventurous nature. The pan-European route opens up a swathe of great cities and sweeping countryside, as you venture from the comfort of Western Europe into the old Eastern Bloc and beyond.

ROUTE OPTIONS

The high-speed line from London St Pancras to makes it more feasible than ever to take the train east. In fact, these days it is possible to travel from London to Hong Kong by rail, with just three changes (in Paris, Moscow and Beijing), over ten or eleven days.

Please note that you will need a transit visa to cross Belarus (see http://mfa.gov.by/en). Alternatively, you can travel from Nice to Moscow

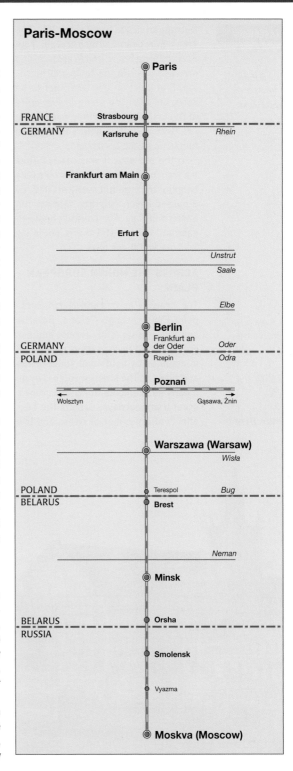

Paris-Moscow

- Paris
- **FRANCE** — Strasbourg
- **GERMANY** — Karlsruhe — *Rhein*
- Frankfurt am Main
- Erfurt
- *Unstrut*
- *Saale*
- *Elbe*
- Berlin
- **GERMANY** — Frankfurt an der Oder — *Oder*
- **POLAND** — Rzepin — *Odra*
- Poznań
- ← Wolsztyn — Gąsawa, Żnin →
- Warszawa (Warsaw) — *Wisła*
- **POLAND** — Terespol — *Bug*
- **BELARUS** — Brest
- *Neman*
- Minsk
- **BELARUS** — Orsha
- **RUSSIA**
- Smolensk
- Vyazma
- Moskva (Moscow)

Essentials

Distance: 3,450km (2,144 miles)

Duration of journey: 42hrs (1 day, 2 nights)

Frequency of trains: 1 weekly

Brest station, Belarus.

(European Rail Timetable 25). The Trans-European Express travels from Paris to Strasbourg and Frankfurt, and arrives in Berlin the following morning. Frankfurt an der Oder, not to be confused with the shiny skyscrapers of the megalopolis further west, is the last German station before Poland and functions as the border stop.

In the old days it was always after the train had pulled out of Berlin's Ostbahnhof that the fun really started, as it passed beyond the Iron Curtain into Eastern Europe. The contrast between east and west is still there, but is far less marked these days.

ACROSS THE NORTH EUROPEAN PLAIN

The scenery across the North European Plain through Poland, Belarus and into Russia is an almost endless procession of thick, dark-green forest, punctuated by fields and small towns and villages. The Moscow route is by no means as scenic as many of Europe's great train journeys, despite the best efforts of a number of rivers and low lying hills, but it is the sense of history and the feeling of riding across the political map of Europe that forms a large part of the attraction.

A couple of hours after entering the vast rural expanse of Poland, the train reaches the first major Polish city, Poznań. The area around Poznań is a true rail buff's paradise. Old Polish steam locomotives – the last regular scheduled steam trains operating in Europe (see page 312) – run the 60km (38 miles) southwest to the town of Wolsztyn.

Northeast of Poznań, a totally different rail experience awaits you. The Biskupin Railway is a perfectly preserved narrow-gauge railway that trundles across the Wielkopolska countryside. It originates in the town of **Gasawa** and rumbles on to **Znin**. This line is very much geared towards tourists, who provide the necessary money to keep the narrow-gauge trains running. There is also a network of narrow-gauge trains that connects small communities throughout the Wielkopolska region that few visitors ever take the time to discover.

Around 3.5 hours after leaving Poznań the train arrives in **Warsaw**. The train stops again at Warsaw Wschodnia, on the other side of the River Wisla, before travelling onwards to Belarus.

BORDER BREAK

Belarus is one of the few former Soviet countries that chose to stay with Mother Russia, and harbours no intention of joining the European Union (EU). The remote Belarussian border town of Brest outpost still retains some of its Cold War chill. Passengers should be wary at this stop of taking too many photos or getting off and on the train, as this often riles the border guards, whom it is best to avoid. These days, the atmosphere at **Brest** is far less threatening and the main interest is

he changing of the train bogies (an ndercarriage component) that is ecessary for travelling on the wider Russian-gauge tracks. The whole rocess of changing the bogies takes round two hours as each carriage has o be done individually. Travellers who ave taken the Trans-Siberian Express cross Russia to China or Mongolia vill be familiar with this operation; he uniquely wide Russian-gauge is a egacy of the paranoia of the former oviet leadership, who were concerned bout the possibility of foreign armies sing the rail network to invade from he West.

Once fitted with the correct bogies, he train rolls on towards Moscow nd the Belarussian capital of **Minsk**, vhich sprawls across the banks of he Svisloch and Nerniga rivers, and s somewhat unappealing on first ight. Minsk is Soviet-era planning n a grand scale with most build-ngs having been erected since 1945. Delving beyond the concrete facades, he tragic story emerges of a city hat had 270,000 inhabitants in 1941 ut just 40,000 by the end of World Var II, losing 80 percent of its build-ngs too. It is this story that fires the magination, with a number of muse-ums given over to the war years, rom heroic martyr displays to simple laces that recall personal suffering. o delve into this forgotten aspect of World War II, and for a unique insight nto what life was like behind the Iron Curtain, Minsk is well worth a one or wo-day stop.

SMOLENSK TO MOSCOW

The first Russian city en route is **Smolensk**, which is approached hrough a sprawl of goods yards vhere engines can be seen shunt-ng around freight and passenger arriages. Smolensk suffered cata-trophically during World War II when ts entire Jewish population and all ut 300 of its houses were obliterated

by the Nazis. The city had long been on the front line, with German, Pol-ish, French and Russian forces vying for control over the centuries. Today much of Smolensk's architecture is a throwback to Soviet times, but the city is worth exploring to unravel the layers of its eventful history. High-lights include the impressive town walls, the 17th-century Uspensky Cathedral and a monument to Gen-eral Kutuzov, the brilliant strategist and field marshal who distinguished himself in the 18th-century wars against Turkey and commanded the Russian opposition to Napoleon.

The final run from Smolensk and on to **Moscow** seems to take an eter-nity as the train crawls through the Stalinist-era housing estates and numerous suburban rail stations before it rolls into Moscow's impres-sively grand Belorusskaya station. With some careful advance plan-ning, you can continue your journey to Beijing or Hong Kong by rail with only two changes of train, Lhasa with three changes.

Belorusskaya station, Moscow.

The Trans-Siberian Express passes though Udmurtia, Russia.

The Jacobite steam train on the Glenfinnan Railway Viaduct in Scotland.

Train in the snow near Mussenden Temple, Northern Ireland.

GREAT BRITAIN AND IRELAND

Britain's railway heritage is second to none, and there is no shortage of attractive journeys – from the bucolic delights of the Shrewsbury to Swansea route to the scenic splendour of the West Highland line

Britain gave railways to the world. Crude wagons had been used on trackways using wood, stone and iron for rails since at least the early 17th century, but it was the work of Richard Trevithick and George and Robert Stephenson in the first quarter of the 19th century that made possible the successful application of steam power to the railway.

The opening of the Stockton and Darlington and the Liverpool and Manchester railways, in 1825 and 1830 respectively, are two of the most portentous events in modern history. Britain's railway network grew rapidly, from 9,734km (6,084 miles) in 1850 to 24,901km (15,563 miles) in 1880, reaching its greatest extent in 1926 with 32,427km (20,267 miles). A combination of sensible pruning and foolish amputation has since whittled the network down to little over 16,000km (10,000 miles).

A COLOURFUL HERITAGE

A visit to the National Railway Museum at York or one of the heritage railways with a good stock of older locomotives gives an insight into how colourful Britain's railways were until the 1920s. Few other countries invested so much money and effort into making sure that their locomotives, in particular, were an aesthetic pleasure. Yet with

the 1922 grouping of 120 railway companies into four, followed by nationalisation in 1948, variety and colour diminished.

For the past 70 years railway managers have had other concerns. Myopic governments and Treasury parsimony have presided over decades of underinvestment in the method of transport of most value in a densely populated country. Today, Britain's railways compare unfavourably with other European networks, with passengers paying higher fares for an inferior service.

Main attractions

Glasgow: Buchanan Street, St Mungo Cathedral,
York: York Minster, Jorvik Viking Centre, National Railway Museum,
Edinburgh: The Castle, The Royal Mile, National Gallery, New Town
Dublin: Temple Bar, Trinity College Library, National Gallery.

Maps on pages 100, 103, 116, 118

Driver on the Swanage Railway.

Great Britain and Ireland

0   100 km
0   100 miles

N

ATLANTIC

OCEAN

Shetland

Yell   Unst

Mainland

Foula

Lerwick

Fair Isle

Westray

Mainland

Orkney
Islands

Stromness

Hoy   South
Ronaldsay

Thurso

Lewis

Stornoway

Wick

Helmsdale

Outer Hebrides

The Minch

Ullapool

Achnasheen

Harris

Moray Firth

North
Uist

Skye

Dingwall

Elgin

W. Highlands

Inverness

Huntly

Scotland

40

Aberdeen

South Uist

Kyle of
Lochalsh

Barra

Rum

Ben Nevis

Aviemore

Eigg

1344

Mallaig

Fort William

Pitlochry

Grampian

Montrose

Mountains

Coll

Inner Hebrides

Tiree

Mull

Crianlarich

Perth

Dundee

Firth of Lorn

Oban

NORTH

SEA

Stirling

Firth of Forth

North Berwick

Jura

Greenock

10

Weymss
Bay

2

Edinburgh

Berwick-upon-Tweed

Largs

Glasgow

Islay

Arran

Carstairs

Ayr

Southern   Uplands

UNITED   **KINGDOM**

Portrush

Coleraine

Dumfries

Lockerbie

Morpeth

Londonderry

Ballymena

Larne

43

Newcastle upon Tyne

Donegal

Northern

Antrim

L. Neagh

Hexham

Durham

Carlisle

The Pennines

Middlesbrough

Enniskillen

Ireland

Bangor

Whitehaven

Penrith

Darlington

Whitby

Ballina

Sligo

Portadown

Belfast

Scafell
Pike
977

Newry

Isle of
Man

Windermere

Kendal

33

Scarborough

Carrick-on-
Shannon

Dundalk

35   36

26

Settle

**Barrow-in-
Ferness**

Lancaster

Bridlington

Westport

L. Corrib

Castlebar

Longford

Drogheda

IRISH

SEA

18

5

York

Preston

21

Leeds

**Kingston
upon Hull**

IRELAND

Athlone

Dublin

Anglesey

Llandudno

16

Blackpool

Manchester

Liverpool

4

Doncaster

Grimsby

Galway

Lough
Derg

Portarlington

Kildare

Wicklow
Mtns

Wicklow

Holyhead

Chester

Sheffield

Skegness

Snowdon 1085

**Stoke-on-
Trent**

14

Ennis

Thurles

Kilkenny

Carlow

Arklow

Blaenau
Ffestiniog

28

13

30

Nottingham

King's
Lynn

32

Gre
Yarmou

Limerick

Pwllheli

19   46

6

Crewe

Derby

21

Peter-
borough

12

Tralee

Tipperary

Clonmel

Enniscorthy

Cardigan
Bay

42

Wales

47

Shrewsbury

Leicester

7

31

Norwich

Killarney

Mallow

Wexford

Aberystwyth

45

Birmingham

37   44

Coventry

Ely

1

Lowesto

Carrantouhill
1038

Cobh

Rosslare

Cambrian
Mtns

Worcester

Stratford-
upon-Avon

**Milton
Keynes**

Cambridge

Waterford

Cork

Fishguard

St George's Channel

22

Hereford

15

Gloucester

20

Oxford

Watford

Colchester

Ipswic

Chelmsford

Milford
Haven

Carmarthen

11

Newport

Reading

London

Southend

Swansea

48

Bristol Channel

Cardiff

Bristol

Swindon

Basingstoke

3

Guildford

Marga

Barnstaple

Taunton

17

Salisbury

29

Gatwick

8

Maidstone

25

CELTIC

Bournemouth

Southampton

Brighton

Dov

Hastings

Folkesto

SEA

Exeter

23

Portsmouth

Eastbourne

Newquay

9

Weymouth

Isle of Wight

41

Truro

39

34

Torquay

Penzance

Land's
End

Falmouth

Plymouth

English Channel

Dieppe

Isles of
Scilly

1   Museums and
Heritage Lines

Fécamp

FRANC

Featured route

Cherbourg

It was hoped that the re-privatisation of the railways in 1994 would generate the sustained levels of investment necessary for Britain's railways to reach continental standards. The benefits are debateable. Today, the track and infrastructure is managed by a utility company, Network Rail, and the rolling stock operated by 24 private companies – although the railways are still subsidised. In 2007 a new high-speed line opened between London St Pancras and the Channel Tunnel. A second high-speed line (HS2) between London and Birmingham is due to be completed by 2026.

Despite many problems for the railways, Britain's chronic traffic congestion means that train travel is usually faster than the alternatives, much safer and generally less stressful. The ambience for railway passengers has improved as billions of pounds-worth of new trains have been introduced. As one would expect from a network with over 20 different train operating companies, standards and procedures across the network vary, but efforts are continuing to make the network seamless to the user.

SCENIC HIGHLIGHTS

There is no shortage of delightful journeys to add to those described in detail in the following pages. Away from the industrial areas, it is difficult to find a train journey in Scotland that is not a pleasure to the eye. South of the border, the historic line between Carlisle and Newcastle follows the only gap between the north Pennines and the foothills of the Cheviots, twice crossing the route of Hadrian's Wall and serving a series of attractive market towns, some with names dating back to Roman times.

For miles travelled beside the sea, few lines can hold a candle to the Carlisle–Barrow–Carnforth journey, which is seldom out of sight of water once the train has reached Maryport, with

its 18th-century coal port and planned town. Both Maryport and Whitehaven have much of maritime and architectural interest to detain the visitor. The only competitor for sea views is the Dovey Junction–Pwllheli section of the railway west of Shrewsbury, which also serves Aberystwyth. For miles the railway is cut into a ledge in the cliff face, and Britain's longest timber viaduct across the Mawddach estuary provides a magnificent view of Cader Idris.

The narrow-gauge Ffestiniog Railway links the Pwllheli line at Minffordd with one of Wales's last rural branch lines, a cross-platform interchange at Blaenau Ffestiniog allowing passengers to head north along the beautiful Conwy valley to Llandudno Junction on the Holyhead–Chester line. Also offering continual sea views, this main line along the north coast of Wales has two of Britain's finest engineering structures, the Conwy and Menai bridges.

The other two groups of branch lines that should be considered for a rail-based tour of Britain are in East Anglia and in the West Country. In East Anglia

The narrow-gauge Ffestiniog Railway.

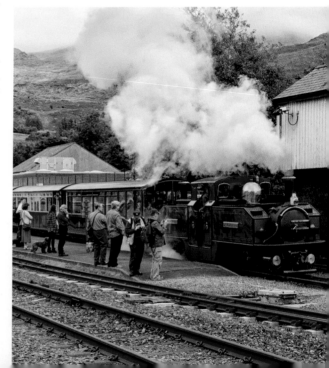

⊙ Essentials

European Rail timetable no. 218

Distance: 425km (264 miles)

Duration of journey: 5hrs 15 mins

Frequency of trains: 3–4 per day (direct)

Serenaded as you board the Belmond Royal Scotsman.

is the East Suffolk line from Ipswich to Lowestoft, from where it is possible to take a train through the Norfolk Broads to Norwich. If time permits, savour the all-too-rare experience of changing trains at a country junction by stopping at Reedham to catch a train to Great Yarmouth and reach Norwich via Acle.

Devon and Cornwall used to be a warren of branch lines serving the numerous seaside resorts. Today it is still possible to leave a London to Penzance train to take a branch to Exmouth, Barnstaple, Gunnislake, Looe, Newquay, Falmouth and St Ives. All the area's secondary cross-country lines have gone except for Bristol–Bath–Weymouth service which links some of Britain's loveliest market towns.

THE GOOD OLD DAYS

Britain is rich in railway history, which feeds a peculiarly British nostalgia. Although the last regular steam services were phased out in 1968, there are plenty of heritage lines running today to satisfy the enthusiast, with highlights including the West Somerset Railway, the Vale of Rheidol Railway in mid-Wales, and the Bluebell Railway in Sussex. The Golden Age of luxury travel is remembered in the form of the *Royal Scotsman* (see page 106) as well as in numerous specialist services using original rolling stock. A full listing of heritage railways and railway museums appears on page 124.

THE WEST HIGHLAND LINE

Standing in the bowels of Glasgow's subterranean Queen Street Station, it comes as no surprise to learn that the old steam trains had to be cable-hauled up the Cowlairs Incline (the slope leading out of the station) by stationary steam engines. This is only the first of many challenging ascents on the West Highland Line, 'The Iron Road to the Isles', an epic rail adventure that takes travellers through some of Europe's most beautiful landscapes. The sedate pace – trains take over five hours to cover the 264km (164 miles) – allows time to appreciate the majestic mountain scenery.

ECHOES OF THE PAST

The first hour of the journey is spent trying to shake off the sprawling suburbs of Glasgow and the debris of its industrial past. While the city may have gone through something of a renaissance over the last decade or so, the journey from Queen Street to Helensburgh tumbles through the rusting remnants of an era when many of the world's great ships were Clyde-built. In those days many of the world's finest engineers were Scots, a tradition of excellence carried over into the construction of the West Highland Line.

The line was built to serve two main industries – tourism and fishing – shuttling tourists between central Scotland and the Western Highlands and bringing them back along with the marine cargo.

Originally the rails only extended as far as the old garrison town of Fort William, which was reached in 1894. It was not until 1901 that the railway finally made it to the open sea at the bustling fishing port of Mallaig.

Just after Helensburgh at Craigendoran Junction, the West Highland Line splits off from the main line and begins its ascent into the Highlands. The old piers and urban clutter are soon replaced by the peaceful shores of Loch Long, Loch Goil and the Gare Loch as the train struggles up the first gradients. The most impressive loch of them all is **Loch Lomond**, the largest stretch of fresh water in Britain, which the line skirts for 16km (10 miles), winding through the wooded slopes with occasional glimpses across the cold waters. This is Rob Roy country, where the legendary outlaw evaded the authorities among the ramble of glens and lochs, a tale immortalised by 19th-century novelist Sir Walter Scott.

The train climbs more than 150 metres/yds in just 8km (5 miles) before arriving at **Crianlarich**, where it divides; two carriages head west for the town of Oban, gateway to the

islands of Mull and Islay. The remaining two carriages edge further north as expansive views of the mountains and Caledonian forests open up. One of the most dramatic set pieces of the West Highland Line is the **Horseshoe Viaduct**, a sweeping curve and small viaduct that were only built as a cash-saving measure. Journey times would have been reduced if the glen had been crossed by a single, much larger viaduct, but financial limitations meant that this glorious loop took shape between the solid masses of Beinn Odhar and Beinn Dorain.

In contrast to the winding track and steep gradients of much of the route, **Rannoch Moor** is a wide, open plateau that the train rolls across with seemingly little effort. This illusion belies the difficulty of laying a track across the sodden, inhospitable moor that Robert Louis Stevenson so dramatically immortalised in his novel *Kidnapped*. The initial attempt to lay solid foundations was a disaster as the bog swallowed up all the spoil laid on it. The eventual solution was to 'float' the

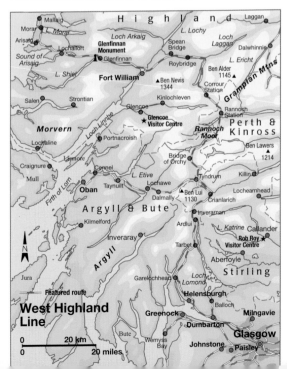

West Highland Line

0   20 km
0   20 miles

● Featured route

track across, to lay it directly on top of the sodden moor.

REMOTE RANNOCH

Rannoch station stands in spectacular isolation, a tiny dot in a bleak nether-world, miles from the nearest human settlement. In summer this is a great jumping off point for walkers, ramblers and climbers; in winter the dramatic surrounding mountains are a place for serious and experienced mountaineers only, as the regular call-outs for mountain rescue services testify.

Soon after Rannoch, at **Corrour**, the West Highland Line reaches its highest point. This is the station where the four protagonists from Irvine Welsh's *Trainspotting* decamped with the idea of doing some Highland walking, but were quickly deterred by Leum Uileim's imposing slopes.

Impressive mountains shadow the West Highland Line for much of its journey, but the granddaddy of them all is **Ben Nevis**, Britain's highest peak at 1,344 metres (4,406ft), which looms over the town of **Fort William**.

Corrour station, the UK's most remote railway station.

Ben Nevis's sturdy shape manages to disguise its height from many angles on the approach from Corrour, but the snow that usually cloaks its upper reaches indicates its lofty altitude. Travellers with time to spare could take a room in one of the many bed-and-breakfasts and hotels in Fort William and make their own challenge on the summit. Reaching the top is possible even for relatively inexperienced walkers on a good day, but it should always be approached with caution, as the weather can change from fair to atrocious in seconds.

Heading out of Fort William the train hugs the shores of **Loch Linnhe**, a sea loch that is the first sign that we are now close to the open sea. The track now struggles through the demanding terrain of the West Highland Line Extension, which celebrated its centenary in 2001. The 62-km (39-mile) route is a major feat of railway engineering, necessitating a mass of rock cutting and drilling, the building of 11 tunnels and five major viaducts. In summer the Jacobite steam

⊘ EATING AND SLEEPING IN THE HIGHLANDS

Glenfinnan station is a shining testament to what a group of enthusiasts can do for the love of the golden age of the railways. In 1991 the station was bound for dereliction until a charitable trust took it on and turned it into a facility to welcome railway tourists.

The station now incorporates a museum, a bunk house – a sleeping car that has been converted for use as comfortable self-catering accommodation for travellers – and a beautifully restored dining car serving food and its own real ale brew. The sleeping car is open all year round, is heated during the winter and has cooking and washing facilities (www.glenfinnanstationmuseum.co.uk; tel: 01397 722295).

Elsewhere on the West Highland Line there is another railway hostel, at Tulloch (www.stationlodge.co.uk). The original station building has been impressively revamped in Swiss chalet style. The bunk house also has a dining room and a small shop. The surrounding area is good walking country with a number of easily accessible munros (the name given to a Scottish peak in excess of 915 metres/3,000ft).

Railway-themed dining in the region continues with the Station House Restaurant at Corrour (www.corrour.co.uk), which also has accommodation in an old lookout tower and the Station Tearoom in Crianlarich (www.crianlarich-station-tearoom.co.uk).

Corrour
An Coire Odhar

train runs along the extension line all the way from Fort William to Mallaig and back, serving up large helpings of nostalgia along with its day-trip refreshments. While more casual tourists admire the views from the old carriages and buy a video souvenir of the journey, the rail enthusiasts crane their necks out of windows to snap photos of the steam engine pummelling its way seawards.

BREATHTAKING GLENFINNAN

The most stunning section of the extension, and arguably the greatest rail vista in the British Isles, is at **Glenfinnan**. Here the train squeals around the 21 arches of Glenfinnan Viaduct, one of the finest examples of engineering from the great golden age of Britain's railways. Initial objections that the viaduct would spoil the breathtaking beauty of Glen Finnan quickly dissolved when it became obvious that the curl of the viaduct only enhanced the dramatic scene. The viaduct appears in the Harry Potter films, carrying the Hogwarts Express. At the foot of the glen the viaduct snakes around as the River Finnan runs down in search of the salt waters of Loch Shiel, a shadowy sea loch that itself is dwarfed by the towering Highland massif. At the centre of it all is a **monument to Bonnie Prince Charlie** and his brave Highlanders who advanced as far as Derby in 1745 on their Jacobite quest, before they were finally forced to retreat north, only to be massacred on the brutal moor of Culloden.

After the overwhelming drama and sense of history of Glenfinnan the landscape now opens up with the first views of the 'Small Isles' – **Rum**, **Eigg** and **Muck** – which hang tantalisingly close offshore, and tease in and out of view on the run seawards to Mallaig. This part of the line includes the Leachabhuidh Tunnels, the Gleann Mama Viaduct and the impressive **Borrodale Viaduct**, as the train slides through rock cuttings and around hillsides. In a final scenic flourish before Mallaig the white sands of **Morar** and **Arisaig** twinkle into view, impossibly starched against the clear blue waters on a sunny day. Morar is another great stopping-off point, with impressive beaches ideal for bracing strolls, as well as Scotland's shortest river, the Morar, and deepest loch, Loch Morar. Local legend holds that Loch Morar has its own monster, Morag, who has so far attracted none of the tourist hype of her famous sibling in Loch Ness.

Journey's end is reached at **Mallaig** with the squawk of seagulls and the tang of salty sea air. The busy fishing harbour bustles with life as visitors set off on forays to unspoiled islands and fishermen tuck into 'fish suppers' they helped catch. It all feels a million miles away from the big city life and post-industrial residue of Glasgow, but soon the train will be turning tail and heading back over the tracks on one of the world's most spectacular railway journeys.

Monument to Bonnie Prince Charlie, Glenfinnan.

ROYAL SCOTSMAN

You can take stopping trains to see the best of Scottish scenery but an alternative is to take a guided tour in a luxury hotel on rails: the Royal Scotsman.

Since its inaugural run in 1985, the *Royal Scotsman* (now operated by Belmond) has redefined luxury train travel in Britain. From April to October, guests assemble at Edinburgh's Waverley station as a kilted bagpiper sets the scene. Drawn up like guards on parade, the *Royal Scotsman*'s nine gleaming carriages, resplendent in purple livery and gilt lettering, evoke the sense of a truly grand occasion. This is home for the next few days, whether you choice a journey between two or seven nights

Once settled on board, Champagne and *hors d'oeuvres* are served as you mingle in the Observation Car. Seating all 40 passengers in comfortable, two-person sofas and roomy, upholstered armchairs in muted tones of green, this carriage contains an open veranda.

The Royal Scotsman's observation lounge.

The ambience is truly luxurious. The two dining cars convey a wonderfully old-fashioned character, and the harmonious combinations of local Scottish produce, varied during the tour to satisfy eye and taste buds alike, are worthy of a Michelin star. Stewardesses in tartan skirts and nattily-attired stewards ensure that the country house party atmosphere never dips.

The theme continues in the off-train arrangements at the periodic stops to see the sights, where the team of well-informed guides, as well as the train's own liveried motor coach, form an integral part of this encounter with centuries of heritage and tradition.

The state sleeping cars are the most stylish accommodation to be found within the limits imposed by European railway carriages. Originally Pullman day cars, they have since been completely rebuilt in the style of the Edwardian era. The beds are all lower berths and there is an en-suite bathroom with shower, washbasin and toilet.

TOURING THE HIGHLANDS

Slowly and sedately this most regal of trains makes its way onto the scenic West Highland Line. Loch Long, Loch Lomond and Rannoch Moor offer a magical mosaic of mountains, lochs, pine and birch-wood forests.

At the Inverawe Smokehouse you will see how a range of locally-caught fish are smoked to perfection before they are dispatched to Harrods. Ballindalloch Castle, home of the Macpherson-Grant family since 1546, affords the chance to have a close encounter with a herd of Aberdeen Angus cattle, as golden eagles fly high in the sky.

At Kyle of Lochalsh, after a visit to the mystical Isle of Skye, traditional Gaelic melodies are played on the *clarsach* during an after-dinner recital in the Observation Car. During the coming days, Scotland's highest mountain, Ben Nevis, offers an impressive backdrop to the Caledonian Canal; Eilean Donan, the most romantic of all Scottish castles, appears straight off a calendar cover; while at the Dalmore Distillery you learn the art of whisky blending.

As the train returns south via the ancient Scottish capital of Perth, the magnificent Highland scenery gives way to gentler terrain. Crossing the Forth Railway Bridge, it is just a few more miles to journey's end at Edinburgh.

INVERNESS–KYLE OF LOCHALSH

The Inverness to Kyle of Lochalsh line takes passengers through some of Scotland's most rugged and spectacular scenery. The Skye Railway, as it is better known, stretches from the chilly waters of Scotland's east coast and the nation's newest city, Inverness, right up over the Highland mountains, and down to the west coast waters of Kyle of Lochalsh, where the Isle of Skye lies just across the water.

Originally the Dingwall & Skye Railway Company, the enterprise behind building the line, intended to extend the track all the way from Inverness to Kyle, but when it opened on 10 August 1870, financial problems meant it only went as far west as Strome Ferry. It was not until 1897, when competition from the newly opened West Highland Line forced the successor Highland Railway to extend the line, that trains ran the 132km (82 miles) between Inverness and Kyle.

ALONG THE MORAY FIRTH

After the train leaves Inverness station it spends the next half hour winding through the growing suburbs and towns that dot the banks of the **Moray Firth**. The flats of the Firth are home to grey herons, swans and geese, and there is also a colony of bottlenose dolphins that the eagle eyed may be lucky enough to spot. The line also crosses the **Caledonian Canal**, a feat of engineering on a similarly impressive scale to the Skye Railway, forming a link between Inverness and the old garrison town of Fort William at the other end of the Great Glen, 97km (60 miles) away. In summer boats can be seen queuing up to use the Ocean Lock that connects the canal to the North Sea.

Soon after the town of **Dingwall**, supposed birthplace of Macbeth, the Skye Railway finally shakes off the companion Far North Line, which breaks away in search of the top of mainland Britain. This is where the impressive scenery really starts as the North Sea is left behind for good and voluminous mountains start to loom on the horizon. There are four lochs to negotiate on this stretch: Garve, Luichart, Auchuillin and Achanalt, and also the chance to spot herds of wild red deer.

The diesel engines face hard work as the line struggles up towards **Achnasheen**, the highest station on the route at 197 metres (646ft), marking the watershed between the Atlantic and the North Sea. In summer this is a popular jumping-off point for walkers and climbers. Even in July and August there is often snow on the highest peaks, while a journey in winter takes the train through a snowy wilderness that frequently overworks the snow plough fitted to the front of the train.

Achnasheen is one of the many romantically named stations en route, translating as 'The Field of Storm'. The names of the stations themselves, many of them signposted in both Gaelic and English, give an insight into the

Train approaching Achnasheen.

complex and tumultuous history of the Highlands. There is the French-named town of Beauly, Attadale ('Valley of Fighting' in Norse) and the Gaelic Loch Luichart ('Loch of the Holly Tree') and Achnashellach ('Field of Willows'). The Gaelic name for Kyle of Lochalsh translates as 'Narrows of the Rolling Waves'.

The scenery starts to change markedly once again as the line drops down and around the west coast sea lochs. The route is at its most spectacular on the 16-km (10-mile) Strome Ferry–Kyle extension, which took four years and £250,000 to build – a fortune by 19th-century standards. The train scythes through a series of rock cuttings (some as deep as 24 metres/yds) and tunnels as it skirts the loch edge. The views are stunning, as island-dotted sea lochs shimmer on the right-hand side of the train and shadowy peaks loom in the background.

PICTURESQUE PLOCKTON

Soon after the treacherous tidal Strome Narrows, the picture-postcard village of Plockton appears. This dreamy collage of whitewashed houses and multi-coloured boats rests right on the waterfront and makes an ideal stop, with a couple of hotels, a sprinkling of bed-and-breakfasts and the odd loch-side pub to serve the needs of rail travellers. The most appropriate place to stay for train passengers is the station itself which has been converted into exquisite self-catering accommodation (www.plocktonstation.co.uk; tel: 01599 544306): choose your bedroom between the Ladies Waiting Room and the Station Master's Office.

From Plockton the line cuts through swathes of rock and heather as it flirts with views of the islands that dot the west coast. Soon the horizon in the west is filled with the craggy peaks of Skye's Cuillin mountains. Journey's end comes as the train slips into Kyle of Lochalsh station. A concrete bridge across the narrow channel to Skye, opened in 1995, has done little to tame the wild beauty of what many rate as Scotland's most attractive island, a fittingly dramatic end to

Plockton.

a rail journey that eases passengers through some of Scotland's most impressive scenery.

LONDON–INVERNESS–WICK

This 1,181-km (734-mile) journey to the northernmost reach of the British mainland requires at least two days. London to Inverness takes a little over eight hours on the fast day-time train, but a more relaxed schedule would allow exploration of some outstanding cities. The journey requires a change of train at Inverness.

KING'S CROSS TO PETERBOROUGH

The journey starts at **King's Cross** station, perhaps the most austere of London termini, with only the Italianate clock tower embellishing the functional brick façade to the twin-span roof of the train shed. Opened in 1852, it is in marked contrast to St Pancras next door, the most ornate railway terminus in Britain. The line north through Gas Works and Copenhagen tunnels used to be a smoky, noisy business in steam days, as locomotives struggled up the steep bank on rails often wet from flooding. The north London suburbs flash past the window for the first miles. Soon the train is racing through undulating Hertfordshire farmland; the East Coast main line, as the route is known, was built for speed, helped by the relative flatness of much of the countryside through which it passes.

In winter, **Hatfield House** can be seen on the hill beyond the tower of the parish church; the 16th-century house was home to Robert Cecil, 3rd Marquess of Salisbury who was three times prime minister in the 19th century. **Welwyn Garden City** was one of the low-density 'garden cities' advocated by Ebenezer Howard around 1900. Just to the north, a 40-arch viaduct built with 13 million bricks provides a grandstand view over the Mimram valley.

Once past the original garden city of Letchworth, the line leaves Hertfordshire for Bedfordshire and miles of market gardens. Approaching **St Neots** and the pinnacled church tower of St Mary's, the line passes the water-meadows of the River Ouse to the west and skirts the Fens to the east, 'where sky and Lincolnshire and water meet' as the poet Philip Larkin put it. The major junction of **Peterborough** is preceded by a bridge across the River Nene and a view east of the Barnack-stone cathedral; largely built in the 12th century, it is one of the country's finest Norman buildings.

BUILT FOR SPEED

North from Peterborough the line climbs towards **Stoke Summit**. It was on the southbound descent from Stoke Tunnel that the world record for steam traction was set in 1938 by the streamlined Pacific Mallard, which can be seen in the National Railway Museum in York.

The well-wooded landscapes for much of the way to Grantham are the

⊙ Essentials

European Rail timetable nos. 180 (London–Edinburgh); 223 (Edinburgh–Inverness); 226 (Inverness–Wick)

Distance: 1,181km (734 miles)

Duration of journey: London–Inverness 8hrs 5 mins; Inverness–Wick 4hrs 15 mins

Frequency of trains: London–Inverness 1 direct day train and 1 direct night train from Euston station (The Caledonian Sleeper, see www.sleeper.scot); Inverness–Wick 3–4 per day

Interior of King's Cross train station.

most pleasing between London and York. **Grantham**'s skyline is dominated by the graceful spire of St Wulfram's, a largely 13th-century creation with a later library of chained books above the porch. The flat landscape still has the feel of the Fens as the train reaches **Newark**, with a magnificent market square and the castle where King John died in 1216. A long stretch of woodland precedes the major railway junction of **Doncaster**, chosen by the Great Northern Railway for its locomotive, carriage and wagon works, although most people know the town for its racecourse and the St Leger race, inaugurated in 1778. A succession of murky river and canal crossings and some of the country's largest coal-fired power stations do little to relieve the landscape until **York** comes into view.

The station befits the city; its 1870s curving, four-span roof with the elegantly dec-orated supporting ironwork is a masterpiece. Outside is the Royal Station Hotel, which retains some of its original features. The station is only a short walk from the River Ouse and the city centre, which is compact enough to explore on foot.

Passing the National Railway Museum on the left, trains quickly accelerate along the straight stretch of line along the Vale of York to Darlington with the growing outline of the Hambleton and Cleveland hills to the northeast. On the right, just before **Thirsk**, is a sign marking the midway point between London and Edinburgh. Further north, **Durham** is entered by a 10-arch viaduct that offers a fine view of the Norman castle and cathedral and the River Wear.

More industrial scenes are passed on the way to one of the great moments on the journey, the crossing of the River Tyne by the **King Edward VII Bridge**, which the monarch opened in 1906. From it six other bridges can be seen, most notably Stephenson's High Level Bridge of 1849. It is Grade I listed, as is John Dobson's glorious classical station and train shed at **Newcastle-upon-Tyne**, regarded by some as the finest station in the country. The nearby Museum of Science and Engineering has plenty of information on the Stephensons' works.

As the distance between railway and coast narrows, gorgeous snatches of white sandy beaches and castles flash by. There is a lovely view of the small town and harbour at **Alnmouth** and later of Holy Island, topped by the outline of Lindisfarne Castle. The 28-arch Royal Border Bridge was the last link to be opened between London and Edinburgh, in 1850. **Berwick-upon-Tweed**, on the north bank, retains the most unusual Italian-designed fortifications, built during the late 16th century.

NORTH OF THE BORDER

The line passes a string of enticing sandy beaches as it crosses into Scotland, before turning inland to skirt the Lammermuir Hills. Bypassing the station at the former garrison town of **Dunbar**, the line regains the coast near

National Railway Museum in York.

Longniddry with occasional views over the Firth of Forth. The volcanic rump of Arthur's Seat overlooks the railway as it works its way through suburbs to arrive at **Edinburgh Waverley**, one of the best-sited major stations in Britain, conveniently placed in an inconspicuous trench between the old and new towns.

Trains for Perth take an inland route rather than crossing the Firth of Forth on the spectacular Forth Bridge. Passengers are compensated by a run through the lovely valley between the Ochil Hills in the east and southern outliers of the Grampians to the west. First stop is **Stirling**, where the largely 15th-century castle towers over the town on an immense rock. Beside the farms of Strathallan the railway makes its way to **Gleneagles**, famous for its golf course and former railway hotel, and into Strathearn for **Perth**, where the kings of Scotland used to be crowned.

The route of the old Highland Railway cuts right through the Grampians, reaching the highest summit of a British mainline railway at **Druimuachdar** (452 metres/1,484ft). Lowland farms gradually give way to forests and heather-covered moors and granite-grey rock. Even in driving rain, it is country that stirs the soul of all but the incorrigibly unromantic. There is plenty to detain those with the time to savour the small towns and villages linked by the railway: **Dunkeld & Birnam** for the ruined cathedral and the wood made famous by Shakespeare's *Macbeth*; **Pitlochry** to see the salmon pass at a dam, the theatre and Queen's View of Loch Tummel; **Blair Atholl** for the castle; **Kingussie** for the Highland Folk Museum; **Aviemore** for the Strathspey Railway.

At Aviemore the Cairngorms are seen in the distance before the train tackles the climb to the last summit before Inverness, at Slochd (401 metres/1,315ft). Dropping down across the viaduct over the Findhorn River and the 28-arch structure over Strath Nairn, the line passes west of the infamous battlefield where in 1746 the last hopes of the Jacobites were crushed

On the Strathspey Railway.

Edinburgh Waverley station at night.

Dunrobin Castle.

ScotRail train in the highlands near Kildonan.

without mercy at Culloden, the last battle fought on British soil.

Views over the Moray Firth precede arrival at the unusual, triangular station at **Inverness**, where the fine museum nearby provides a good introduction to most facets of the Highlands. There are three trains a day between Inverness and Wick/Thurso, with trolley refreshments. This is a much-underrated journey, and offers a variety of landscapes: Beauly Firth with the Black Isle on the northern shore following departure from Inverness; Cromarty Firth after leaving the junction for Kyle of Lochalsh at **Dingwall**; the climb through increasingly wild country to the sheep sale centre of **Lairg**; the gentler section beside the coast through **Dunrobin**, where the castle of the railway's great patron, the 3rd Duke of Sutherland, can be visited; the turn inland at **Helmsdale** to pass up the gloriously beautiful Strath Kildonan; the desolation of the inhospitable moors between the bird-watching centre at **Forsinard** and Britain's most northerly junction at **Georgemas**;

followed by the final sections through pastoral fields to Caithness's only towns of **Wick** and **Thurso**.

LEEDS–SETTLE–CARLISLE

Ask 10 railway buffs to nominate the most scenically dramatic railway journey in England and there would probably be a unanimous response: the Settle & Carlisle line. The reason is simple: no other route can match the grandeur of the Pennine landscapes through which the railway forced a passage.

It is a railway of ironies. It should never have been built in the first place: it was proposed by the Midland Railway (MR) as a way of relieving delays to its Anglo-Scottish traffic on the West Coast line, owned by the rival London & North Western Railway (LNWR), which had a policy of making things awkward for MR traffic. However, alarmed at the prospect of losing business to the new line, the LNWR became more cooperative. In light of this improvement, the MR was on the point of deciding against building such an obviously costly route. But Victorian railway politics intervened, ever eager for more competition, and Parliament forced it to proceed.

Once the die was cast, the Midland Railway proceeded to build one of the best-engineered mainline tracks in the country, despite the inhospitable terrain. When the Settle & Carlisle (S&C) opened to passengers in 1876, it had cost the then prodigious sum of £3.8 million. But there was little in the way of passenger traffic, and it is a final irony that it took the threat of closure in the 1980s to boost traffic figures to levels unknown for many decades.

Today the railway is in good health. Its value as a diversionary route to the West Coast main line has been properly recognised, large volumes of freight traffic are routed over it, hundreds of walkers use it on sunny weekends, and it is a popular route for steam-hauled

xcursions. Stations have been reo-
ened and restored, some by the
riends of the Settle & Carlisle Line,
hich played a major part in the suc-
essful fight against closure proposals.

EEDS TO SETTLE JUNCTION

he northbound journey on the Settle &
arlisle begins at Leeds station, where
he imposing 1938 North Concourse
as been brought back into use. As far
s Skipton, S&C trains share the line
hrough Airedale with electric stopping
rains; the S&C proper begins at Set-
le Junction, where Leeds to Lancaster
rains turn west to the sea. Between
eeds and Skipton, S&C trains stop
nly at Shipley and Keighley, but there
s much to see en route.

After the triangular junction at **Ship-
ey**, the train passes through **Saltaire**,
he model town built around a huge
nohair and alpaca mill by the enlight-
ned entrepreneur Sir Titus Salt. Part
f the mill now houses the largest col-
ection of paintings by Bradford-born
rtist David Hockney. **Keighley** is the
unction for the mostly steam-operated

Keighley & Worth Valley Railway, which
climbs into Brontë country at Haworth
and on to Oxenhope. The once important junction town of **Skipton** has a
well-preserved medieval castle and
attractive main street.

Pausing today at the restored, Grade
II-listed station of **Hellifield**, where the
line from Blackburn trails in from the
southwest, it is hard to believe that this
station once had a uniformed staff of
60 with first- and third-class refreshment rooms. After passing the signal
box at Settle Junction the S&C begins,
and the line almost immediately starts
to climb. It is not so much the gradient – 1 in 100 is not too severe – as
the length of the climb that earned the
24km (15 miles) to Blea Moor Tunnel
the nickname of 'the long drag'. For
the fireman of steam days it meant an
almost continuous shovelling of coal.

SETTLE TO CARLISLE

As the train approaches the first station, **Settle**, the green dome of Gig-
gleswick school chapel can be seen
to the west. An attractive market town

*Gresley steam
locomotive approaches
Settle Junction.*

Walkers at Ribblehead station.

with a couple of local history museums and some good vernacular buildings, Settle is easily explored on foot from the station. Continuing north through a narrow, wooded valley, the line enters the Yorkshire Dales National Park and, near the village of Stainforth, crosses twice in quick succession a loop in the River Ribble.

The valley broadens on the approach to **Horton-in-Ribblesdale**, allowing extensive views across dry-stone-walled fields to the northeast and the jelly-mould outline of Pen-y-ghent. All of the stations in the National Park offer access to good walking, and though most are unstaffed, a telephone is provided to check that trains are running to time (in case you don't have mobile coverage) – a welcome facility in poor weather when a wait in a local pub would be preferable to a station shelter.

The country becomes steadily wilder with only the occasional farm building and wind-blown tree rising above the moorland that displaces the pasture. To the west is the 724-metre (2,375ft)

Ribblehead Viaduct at sunset.

summit of Ingleborough, reache by a series of distinctive steps ar crowned by an Iron-Age fort with pa of the walls still standing. A terrac of quarry workers' cottages herald the approach to **Ribblehead**, the bes known place on the S&C, thanks to th **viaduct** to the north of the station, th longest on the railway at 405 metre yds.

Today the station has a visitor cent and provides access to the Dales Wa which passes underneath the viaduc The station was once a focal point life for the isolated community th used it; from 1880 to 1956 the boo ing hall was used for church service stone was dispatched from the adj cent sidings until the mid-1980s, an from 1938 the stationmaster had to fil an hourly weather report from 7am 9pm.

Looking north from the station driv it is hard to imagine that the hollo now filled by the viaduct was once wh served as home to about 2,000 navvie who toiled on the viaduct and on Ble Moor Tunnel. Batty Moss camp, as

was known, was in existence for seven years and had a post office, library, school, mission house, hospital and public houses, augmented by carts supplying milk, meat and vegetables.

The double track becomes single to pass over the spectacular 24-arch stone viaduct, which was the principal reason for the closure proposals in the 1980s: British Rail said it would take between £4.25 and £6 million to repair the structure; in the end it cost £3 million. Wind speeds of over 145kmh (90mph) have been recorded by the anenometer at Ribblehead; motorcars have been blown off trains, and railway workers have been forced to cross on their hands and knees to take advantage of the shelter provided by the parapet.

On the east side of the railway as the train leaves the viaduct is the lonely signal box of Blea Moor, almost a mile from the nearest road. The sight of the deepening cutting that precedes Blea Moor Tunnel was a relief to those working on the steam engines, for the line levels off soon after entering the tunnel and then begins to fall towards the northern portal. Every inch of the 2,404-metre/yd tunnel had to be blasted, so solid was the rock, and its cost was about one-third of the total for the entire line.

BRITAIN'S HIGHEST STATION

Emerging from the tunnel, the line crosses the 10-arch Dent Head Viaduct and hugs a shelf along the flank of Great Knoutberry Hill, with magnificent views to the west over Whernside. A glimpse can be had of lovely **Artengill Beck** to the east as the train crosses the eponymous 11-arch viaduct on the approach to **Dent**, the highest mainline station in England, at 350 metres (1,150ft) and now serving as self-catering accommodation (www.dentstation. co.uk; tel: 07824 665266).

To the south stands a row of stone cabins that once housed snow-clearing

gangs; during the arctic winter of 1947, it was conditions around Dent that prevented the line being used as a through route for almost two months. The best views are also to the west as the train leaves Rise Hill Tunnel, to Baugh Fell and along Garsdale. One of the few sections of level track on the line allowed the building of water troughs to replenish the tanks of steam locomotives; the only set on the S&C, they had to be steam-heated to prevent them freezing in winter. There are hopes that **Garsdale** could again become a junction: a scheme exists to rebuild the railway through Wensleydale that closed in 1959.

As at Ribblehead, the waiting room at Garsdale was used for church services, while a library occupied the ladies waiting room and the base of the water tower formed what was probably Britain's most bizarre community hall. Just north of the station the train crosses the 12-arch Moorcock Viaduct with the historic Moorcock Inn below the line to the east. This was the scene of an annual cattle and sheep fair as

Waiting to depart Garsdale Head, Cumbria.

well as a welcome and rare place for refreshment for those crossing the moors by horse or mountain pony.

AIS GILL AND WILD BOAR FELL

A few miles north of Garsdale the line crosses the northern boundary of the National Park as it nears the last summit at **Ais Gill**, situated under the lowering bulk of **Wild Boar Fell**. From here the line is on a falling gradient nearly all the way to Carlisle, first winding along the pastoral Eden Valley to the market town of **Kirkby Stephen**. Although the landscapes here may lack the scale and bleak beauty of the higher stretches of the line, the countryside is still delightful, and there are views to the west that extend on a clear day as far as the Lake District peaks.

The former county town of Westmorland, **Appleby** is dominated by its 12th-century castle, now a major attraction for visitors that incorporates a rare breeds farm. The final highlight of the line is the picturesque, wooded gorge north of the villages of **Lazonby** and **Kirkoswald**, which can be best

appreciated by walking through it to the next station at **Armathwaite**.

After a final view of the River Eden from one of the S&C's largest embankments, the line veers away from the river and reaches the border city of **Carlisle**. Visits to the castle and Tullie House Museum and Art Gallery are the best way to appreciate the town's role during the years of constant cross-border raiding.

SHREWSBURY–SWANSEA

This 196-km (122-mile) journey on the Heart of Wales line passes through some of the most unspoilt scenery in Wales. Now a branch line with only four trains a day, the Heart of Wales line once had through coaches from London Euston, Liverpool, Manchester and York to serve a string of fashionable spas.

The route begins at the grand, Grade II-listed station in **Shrewsbury**, its three-storey mock Tudor façade of 1848 resembling a university college. For the first 32km (20 miles) trains share a double track line with services bound for Hereford and Cardiff, passing through **Church Stretton** with views over the Long Mynd to the west and Wenlock Edge to the east. At **Craven Arms**, Heart of Wales services leave the Hereford line and curve sharply southwest over a single line, with a view of Stokesay Castle to the left. Running through sparsely populated rolling hills of pasture and coniferous and deciduous woodland, the train passes the halts at **Broome** and **Hopton Heath** and draws up beside the handsome stone building at **Bucknell** with its triple-gabled porch.

BORDER COUNTRY

The 8th-century Offa's Dyke and a long-distance footpath run through the market town of **Knighton**; nearby are some earthworks thought to have been raised by the 1st-century British king, Caractacus. A stop at **Knucklas**

Shrewsbury-Swansea

0   20 km
0   20 miles

N

Vyrnwy
Shrewsbury
Welshpool
Shropshire
Church
Stretton
P o w y s
ENGLAND
Aberdyfi
Newtown
Cardigan
Bay   Aberystwyth
Llanidloes
Hoptonheath
Craven Arms
Knucklas
Bucknell
Llangunllo
Knighton
W A L E S
Dolau
Ceredigion
Llandrindod
Wells
Leominster
Aberaeron
Builth Road
Herefordshire
Cilmery   Builth Wells
Lampeter
Llanwrtyd Wells
Llangammarch
Wells
Hay-on-
Wye
Hereford
Llandovery
Eppynt
Carmarthenshire
Mynydd   Usk   Brecon
Black
Mountains   Kilpeck
Llandeilo
Brecon Beacons
Carmarthen
Pen-y-Fan ▲885
National Park
National
Botanic   Ammanford   Merthyr
Tydfil   Abergavenny
Garden
of Wales   Pontardulais   Aberdare   Rhymney   Monmouthshire
Llanelli   Neath Port
Talbot   Rhondda   Pontypool
Torfaen
Swansea   Treherbert   Cynon   Caerphilly   Newport
Maesteg   Taff   Pontypridd
Gower   Port Talbot   Bridgend
Rhossili
Featured route   Bridgend   St Fagans   Cardiff   Severn

allows passengers to admire the magnificent 13-arch Knucklas Viaduct (see page 39) just to the south as the train curves towards it. There is a stiff climb through rock cuttings to the tunnel, summit and station at **Llangunllo**, the highest point on the line at 299 metres (980ft) above sea level and overlooking the village. Extensive views can be had along the valleys of the River Lugg and Cwm Aran as the train drops down through **Llanbister Road**, flowerbedecked **Dolau** and **Pen-y-Bont** halts.

Although the Romans probably knew of the waters at **Llandrindod Wells**, their exploitation was facilitated by the opening of the railway in 1865 and the town grew tenfold in the 50 years after 1861, becoming a popular spa attracting up to 80,000 visitors a year. The county town of Powys has the National Cycle Museum and the local museum has a collection of Roman antiquities from nearby Castell Collen. At the once-busy interchange of **Builth Road** the railway crosses over the remains of an equally lovely north–south journey between Brecon and Three Cocks and Moat Lane junctions, the latter on the Shrewsbury–Aberystwyth line.

Crossing the River Wye, the train pauses at **Cilmery** where Llewelyn the Last (the last indigenous prince of Wales) was killed in a skirmish in 1282. The reputed spot is marked by a monument on a hill to the right which is visible from the train. After **Garth** and two crossings of the River Irfan, the railway reaches the next spa at **Llangammarch Wells**, the only place in Britain that offered a source of barium chloride to those with cardiac and rheumatic complaints. In 1912 the German Kaiser and his family came here, travelling incognito. Today the pump house is silent. The smallest town in Britain, **Llanwrtyd Wells**, has successfully adapted from a spa to a centre for outdoor holidays. It has an historic clothing factory dating from the 1820s which reopened after World War I to employ men disabled in the war. The Cambrian Woollen Mill still functions on similar lines.

The wild moorland scenery continues during the climb up to the 914-metre/yd Sugar Loaf Tunnel, named

⊙ Essentials

European Rail timetable no. 173

Distance: 183km (114 miles)

Duration of journey: 2hrs 45 mins

Frequency of trains: 7 per day.

Train on the Sugar Loaf.

⊙ Essentials

European Rail timetable no. 146

Distance: 196km (122 miles)

Duration of journey: 3hrs 45 mins average

Frequency of trains: 4 per day (2 on Sun)

after the strikingly shaped mountain through which it burrows. The tunnel emerges onto a shelf in the hillside with dramatic views to the southeast, soon taking in the Black Mountains. From here the line drops sharply at a gradient of 1 in 60 across the curving 18-arch Cynghordy Viaduct to **Llandovery**. The railway then follows the course of the River Tywi through much flatter country with little of interest until **Llandeilo**, where the National Trust estate of Dinefwr Park can be seen to the west. Within the grounds landscaped by 'Capability' Brown is a 17th-century house with a Gothic façade and a deer park with the famous Dinefwr White Park cattle.

It is easy to detect increasing evidence of former industrial activity as the train passes **Ammanford**, the area once home to tin-plate and other heavy engineering works. Soon after **Pontardulais** the railway comes alongside the sandy expanses of Loughor estuary which has been a source of cockles since the Romans established a station here on a strategic site later chosen by a Norman lord for his castle. At the industrial town of **Llanelli**, trains reverse and retrace their route beyond Loughor to **Swansea**.

MIDDLESBROUGH–WHITBY

Standing at Middlesbrough station, it is hard to believe that this is the start of a rural railway journey. The townscape is a scene of chemical works, factory estates and dock cranes as well as the town's most famous landmark, the transporter bridge, with its 174-metre (190-yd) span across the River Tees. Before leaving, spare a moment to admire the station's elegant ticket hall with its hammer-beam roof resting on stone corbels, constructed in 1877.

Yet within 10 minutes of leaving Middlesbrough station the train for Whitby has entered the North York Moors National Park. Before it does so, it pauses at **Marton** where Captain James Cook was born in 1728 – this is the first of several links with the great explorer that you'll find at various points along the line. As urban housing gives way to pasture, the vaguely volcanic outline of Roseberry Topping comes into view. Its craggy western side was caused by a collapse into iron workings beneath; the splendid views the summit offers of the coastline can be reached by a short walk from **Great Ayton** station. The village has a small museum devoted to Cook in the school he attended, and the obelisk that hoves into view to the east was erected to mark the centenary of his birth.

A sharp curve to the west brings the train into what is left of the country junction of **Battersby**, once a conduit for iron ore from the mines of Rosedale to the south. There are few scars to suggest that over half a million tons of ore was extracted each year from

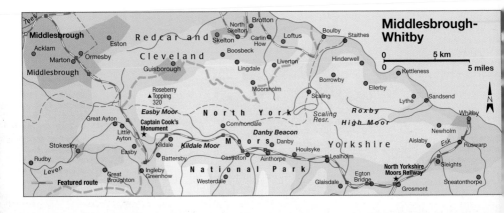

the green hills above the junction, but a pretty route up the old incline takes walkers up to join the Lyke Wake Walk, which follows part of the old mineral railway.

ALONG THE ESK VALLEY

The train reverses at Battersby and heads due east along the Esk Valley, criss-crossing the course of Sleddale Beck and then the broadening River Esk down to the sea at Whitby. Grazing land gives way to bracken, gorse and heather as the valley slopes steepen. In common with all stations on the line, **Commondale** offers a choice of various footpaths across the hills, some following routes taken by the trains of ore-laden pack-ponies that preceded the railway.

One mile from the stone houses and station at **Danby** are the remains of the palace fortress of the Latimer family where Henry VIII is believed to have courted Catherine Parr, his sixth and last wife. The cricket field beside the line at **Glaisdale** was once the site of three blast furnaces, although their fires were extinguished in 1876 and only photographs survive to convince sceptics that such an idyllic spot could once have been an ironworks.

River and railway are hemmed together by steep valley sides, restrained by massive masonry walls, as the train descends to **Egton**, famous locally for its gooseberry show, and the junction of **Grosmont**. Here the steam trains of the North Yorkshire Moors Railway (see page 126) begin their steep climb south, across the heart of the moors to Pickering.

As the train leaves Grosmont, an impressive gorge can be seen to the north. Curves so sharp that wheel flanges squeal herald arrival at **Sleights**, where the river becomes broad and placid, with rowing boats moored to the banks. The train weaves its way around the hills and suddenly the immense form of Larpool Viaduct comes into view. This Grade II listed, 13-arch viaduct towers 37 metres (120ft) above the Esk and used to carry what was then the coastal line north from Scarborough. Today, it carries

Steam train on the North York Moors, Yorkshire.

Essentials

European Rail timetable no. 211

Distance: 56km (35 miles)

Duration of journey: 1hr 30 mins

Frequency of trains: 4 per day

Whitby Abbey.

the Dover–John O'Groats route of the National Cycle Network.

WHITBY

Passing underneath the viaduct and with the Esk estuary on the right, the train rolls into **Whitby** station, a fine stone building dating from 1847, with a five-arched porte cochère on the street. The tourist information centre occupies part of the station, which is perfectly sited to explore the most delightful town on the northeast coast. Its harbour is surrounded by tiers of red-tiled buildings, reaching up to the West Cliff and some of the most elegant townhouses, while the East Cliff is dominated by the imposing remains of **Whitby Abbey**, reached by a flight of 199 stone steps. Originally founded in 657, the abbey was destroyed by the Danes in 867 but refounded in 1078, and most of the remains date from the 13th and 14th centuries.

The respect James Cook developed for the products of Whitby's shipyards while he was apprenticed to the coastal and Baltic trades encouraged him to buy a collier originally built here. The ship was rechristened the Endeavour and was made famous by Cook's first major voyage in 1768–71, carrying the Royal Society expedition to Tahiti. The house where he lodged in the attic when he was an apprentice is now the **Captain Cook Memorial Museum**.

Whitby is synonymous with jet ornaments and jewellery and also has a number of artistic and literary connections. A century after Cook's famous voyage, a local portrait photographer, Frank Meadow Sutcliffe (1853–1941), began to create what became perhaps the finest contemporary photographic record of any coastal town in Britain. Whitby is also renowned for inspiring Bram Stoker (1847–1912) with the idea for Dracula, and a stroll along Whitby Sands may evoke a picture of the walrus and the carpenter, since Lewis Carroll (1832–98) is said to have been inspired to write the poem while he was here. You could also follow the White Rabbit Trail, a walk devised by the Whitby Civic Society.

So popular is the Magpie Café fish-and-chip restaurant that you may have to queue to find out why it is so highly regarded. The white-fronted house overlooking the harbour has been a café since the 1930s and serves a wonderful variety of locally caught fish.

IRELAND

The fact that the whole of Ireland was part of the United Kingdom when the railways were built means that the system developed along British lines. The first line, from Dublin to the port of Dunleary (later Kingstown and now Dun Laoghaire), opened to passengers in 1834 and was constructed to the British-gauge of 1,435mm (4ft 8 1/2in). Subsequent main lines were, in general, laid down at the 1,602mm (5ft 3in) gauge. Towards the end of the 19th century numerous rural lines (often at the side of roads) were built to a 914mm (3ft) gauge; all of these are now closed but something of their atmosphere can be gained by a ride on a short reconstructed

stretch of the Cavan & Leitrim Railway at Dromod, immediately adjacent to the Irish Rail station on the line to Sligo.

As in much of Western Europe, the heyday of the Irish railways was coming to an end in the years after World War I; line closures were underway around 1930. The amount of track in the country has dropped by more than half, from 5,632km (3,500 miles) in the early 20th century to around 2,230km (1,385 miles) today.

To get the best overall view of Ireland the route described from Dublin to Tralee is superb, but there are other scenic lines. Belfast to Londonderry skirts the north coast for some miles, while the Dublin to Wexford line runs high above the sea south of Bray, weaving in and out of tunnels through the headlands, followed by lush river scenery. Other lines have good views of distant mountains, which look so much better with the clear Irish air giving tones of purple and green according to the season.

⊘ Essentials

European Rail timetable no. 245

Distance: 207 miles (333 km)

Duration of journey: 4hrs 25 mins

Frequency of trains: 1 per day (direct)

Train line between Londonderry and Coleraine, near the Atlantic.

Heuston Station in Dublin.

The DART passing Killiney beach.

DUBLIN-TRALEE

Since the 1930s closures of the beautiful lines through the mountains of the west to Kenmare, Dingle, Valentia, Clifden, Killybegs and Burtonport, it is the Dublin–Tralee route that gives the best overview of the timeless Irish landscape. Tralee itself makes an excellent base from which to explore County Kerry. This is the longest journey on one train in Ireland, with one through train every day and extras on Friday and Sunday, plus other opportunities involving a change at Mallow. There is no main line electrification in Ireland (just the suburban coast railway in Dublin) and trains to and from Tralee are thus diesel hauled with USA-built locomotives, named after Irish rivers. The carriages are comfortable with the provision of a good restaurant car.

The journey passes through so much that is typical of Ireland, following the double track main line to Cork as far as Mallow (232km/144 miles) where it branches off to the west through mountainous country to Tralee. Speeds, by European standards, are not fast, bu at a leisurely 112kmh (70mph) there is plenty of time to take in the countryside.

DUBLIN TO LIMERICK

Trains depart from Heuston station in **Dublin**, about 1.6km (1 mile) or so west of the city centre (the tram runs frequently from Connolly Station which is on the DART electric suburban railway and the terminus for trains from Belfast and Sligo). Heuston station (known as Kingsbridge in earlier days) has a magnificent classical frontage, built in 1844 by the English architect, Sancton Wood, with good modern shopping and catering facilities inside.

The train climbs steeply out of Dublin, then through miles of expanding suburbs (served by a suburban train service to Kildare) but soon levels out. The line is then essentially straight as far as Mallow. On the left are huge granite milestones indicating the mileage travelled from Dublin. Out in the

open country, there are glimpses of the Grand Canal, with an especially fine aqueduct at **Monasterevan** (57km/36 miles).

For much of the first part of the journey the train travels through lush countryside, with good views of the distant Wicklow Mountains. At **Kildare** (the 30 Milestone is on the platform) the old cathedral is visible, with a magnificent round tower adjoining it to the left. These towers are still common in Ireland; with their doors mounted well clear of the ground they were easy to defend.

Soon the train is moving across the central plain of Ireland, an area of poor soil with large tracts of countryside where the terrain is mostly bog. In these marshy regions the turf (peat) is dug commercially, and small railways were often utilised to get the produce to its destination – sometimes to specially built power stations.

The railway passes numerous small towns such as **Portarlington** (with a magnificent station, recently restored), Portlaoise, Ballybrophy and Thurles before arriving at **Limerick Junction** (171km/107 miles), the changing point for the city of Limerick. Most of these small backwater towns have little in the way of 'sights', but they are pleasant places to stroll and experience the Irish way of life, which, despite huge changes in the last 20 years or so, still continues at an unhurried pace.

Castles are a feature of this area, with many of them located close to the railway. These structures were often fortified homes rather than national defences and therefore have far more window openings than are usually found in castles. From **Thurles** onwards, the track runs increasingly close to the mountains and, after especially fine views of the distant ranges around Thurles (on the right), the scenery becomes more majestic until it reaches the Killarney area, set in the midst of grand landscapes.

MALLOW TO TRALEE

After Mallow, the train travels at a more leisurely pace with much wilder scenery until, at Killarney, the highest range of mountains in Ireland come into view. MacGullycuddy's Reeks, as they are called, lie to the southwest, with Carrauntouhill (at 1,038 metres/3,408ft) being the highest in Ireland. Killarney is a popular stopping-off place and there are numerous hotels to accommodate visitors, including the luxurious Great Southern (once owned by the railway company). This was built in Victorian times and stands proudly just outside the station entrance.

At Killarney, the train reverses and then sets off up the continuation of the line above the town. Tralee is reached in about 35 minutes. This final section again has wonderful mountain views and the clear air gives a rare atmosphere if you are lucky enough to come here on a sunny summer evening.

Walkers in Killarney National Park.

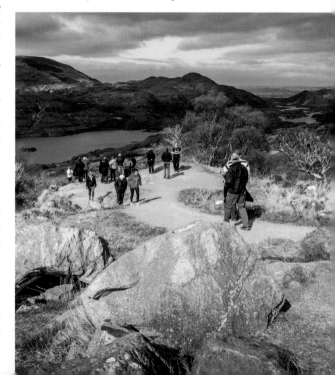

MUSEUMS AND HERITAGE LINES

No country in the world can match Britain for the density of its heritage railways and museums or for the intensity of their operating seasons. The numbers relate to the map on page 100.

MUSEUMS

Bressingham Steam Experience ❶
Thetford Road, Diss, Norfolk IP22 2AB
Café, shop, museum, carousel
Open: Apr–Oct daily
10.30am–5.30pm
Features: three narrow-gauge lines run through lovely gardens
Nearest station: Diss
Tel: 01379 686900
www.bressingham.co.uk

Riverside Museum Pointhouse Place ❷
Glasgow G3 8RS
Café, shop
Open: daily 10am–5pm, Fri and Sun open from 11am
Features: collection of Scottish locomotives and artefacts
Nearest station: Kelvin Hall (Underground)
Tel: 0141 287 4350
Glasgowlife.org.uk

London Transport Museum ❸
Covent Garden, London WC2E 7BB
Café, shop
Open: daily 10am–6pm, Fri 11am–9pm
Features: collection of London's over- and underground trains
Nearest station: Covent Garden (Piccadilly Line)
Tel: 020 7379 6344
www.ltmuseum.co.uk

Museum of Science & Industry ❹
Liverpool Road, Castlefield, Manchester M3 4FP
Café, shop
Open: daily 10am–5pm
Features: collection of Manchester-built locomotives
Nearest station: G-Mex (Metrolink from Manchester Piccadilly or Victoria)
Tel: 0161 832 2244
www.msimanchester.org.uk

National Railway Museum ❺
Leeman Road, York YO2 4XJ
Restaurant, shop, bookshop, video theatre
Open: daily 10am–6pm
Features: one of the world's great railway collections
Nearest station: York
Tel: 03330 161 010
www.railwaymuseum.org.uk

HERITAGE LINES

Bala Lake Railway ❻
(Llanuwchllyn–Penybont)
Llanuwchllyn, Bala, Gwynedd LL23 7DD
Café, shop
Open: Apr–Sept daily except some Mon and Fri
Features: lake views
Nearest station: Ruabon (bus link)
Length: 7.2km (4.5 miles)
Gauge: 600mm (1ft 11 1/8in)
Tel: 01678 540666
www.bala-lake-railway.co.uk

Battlefield Line Railway ❼
(Shackerstone–Market Bosworth–Shenton)
Shackerstone Station, Shackerstone, Nuneaton, Leicestershire CV13 6NW
Café, shop, museum
Open: Easter–Oct weekends and some weekdays
Features: Shenton adjacent to battlefield of Bosworth
Nearest station: Nuneaton
Length: 8km (5 miles)
Gauge: 1,435mm (4ft 81/2 in)
Tel: 01827 880754
www.battlefieldline.co.uk

Bluebell Railway ❽
(Sheffield Park–Kingscote)
Sheffield Park Station, Uckfield, East Sussex TN22 3QL
Restaurant, pub, café, shops, museum
Open: May–Oct daily; weekends all year
Features: outstanding stations, period coaches, dining trains
Nearest station: East Grinstead
Length: 14.1km (9 miles)
Gauge: 1,435mm (4ft 8 1/2 in)
Tel: 01825 720800
www.bluebell-railway.co.uk

Bodmin & Wenford Railway ❾
(Bodmin Parkway–Bodmin–Boscarne)
Bodmin General Station, Bodmin, Cornwall PL31 1AQ
Café, shop
Open: June–Sept daily; various weekends and weekdays
Features: woodland walks from Colesloggett Halt
Nearest station: Bodmin Parkway
Length: 10.4km (6.5 miles)
Gauge: 1,435mm (4ft 8 1/2 in)
Tel: 01208 73555
www.bodminrailway.co.uk

Bo'ness & Kinneil Railway ❿
(Bo'ness–Birkhill)
Bo'ness Station, Union Street, Bo'ness, West Lothian EH51 9AQ
Cafés, shop, museum
Open: Mar–Oct most weekends; early July–Aug daily
Features: Birkhill Clay Mines
Nearest station: Linlithgow
Length: 5.6km (3.5 miles)
Gauge: 1,435mm (4ft 8 1/2 in)
Tel: 01506 822298
www.srps.org.uk

Brecon Mountain Railway ⑪
(Pant–Pontsticill)
Pant Station, Dowlais, Merthyr
Tydfil CF48 2UP
Cafés, shop, workshop
Open: Apr–Oct almost daily
Features: overseas locos
Nearest station: Merthyr (bus to
Pant Cemetery)
Length: 5.6km (3.5 miles)
Gauge: 603mm (1ft 11¾in)
Tel: 01685 722988
www.bmr.wales

Bure Valley Railway ⑫
(Wroxham–Aylsham)
Aylsham Station, Norwich Road,
Aylsham, Norfolk NR11 6BW
Restaurant, café, shop
Open: Easter–early Oct daily; other
weekends
Features: combined train and boat
excursions on Broads
Nearest station: Wroxham
Length: 14.4km (9 miles)
Gauge: 381mm (15in)
Tel: 01263 733858
www.bvrw.co.uk

Churnet Valley Railway ⑬
(Leekbrook–Kingsley & Froghall)
The Railway Station, Cheddleton,
Staffordshire ST13 7EE
Café, shop, museum, flint mill
Open: Mar–Oct Sun; Apr–Sept Sat
and various other days
Nearest station: Stoke-on-Trent
Length: 8.4km (5.25 miles)
Gauge: 1,435mm (4ft 8 1/2 in)
Tel: 01538 750755
www.churnetvalleyrailway.co.uk

Crich Tramway Village ⑭
Crich, Near Matlock, Derbyshire
DE4 5DP
Restaurant, shop, bookshop, picnic
areas, video theatre, museum
Open: Apr–Oct daily; other days and
weekends
Features: one of the world's great
operating tram collections in period
setting over a 1-mile (1.6-km) line
Nearest station: Whatstandwell
Tel: 01773 854321
www.tramway.co.uk

Dean Forest Railway ⑮
(Lydney Junction–Parkend)
Forest Road, Lydney,
Gloucestershire GL15 4ET
Café, shop, museum
Open: Mar–Oct and Dec, various
days
Features: riverside walk, forest trail
Nearest station: Lydney Junction

Length: 6.8km (4.25 miles)
Gauge: 1,435mm (4ft 8 1/2 in)
Tel: 01594 845840
www.deanforestrailway.co.uk

East Lancashire Railway ⑯
(Heywood–Bury–Rawtenstall)
Bolton Street Station, Bury,
Lancashire BL9 0EY
Café, shops, museum
Open: weekends and Bank Holidays
all year; various weekdays
Features: walks from stations, wine
and dine trains
Nearest station: Bury
Length: 19.2km (12 miles)
Gauge: 1,435mm (4ft 8 1/2 in)
Tel: 0333 320 2830
www.east-lancs-rly.co.uk

East Somerset Railway ⑰
(Cranmore–Mendip Vale)
Cranmore Railway Station, Shepton
Mallet, Somerset BA4 4QP
Café, shop, museum
Open: Mar–Oct most weekends,
some weekdays
Features: exhibition of David
Shepherd paintings
Nearest station: Castle Cary/Frome
Length: 4.4km (2.75 miles)
Gauge: 1,435mm (4ft 8 1/2 in)
Tel: 01749 880417
www.eastsomersetrailway.com

**Embsay & Bolton Abbey Steam
Railway** ⑱
(Embsay–Bolton Abbey)
Bolton Abbey Station, Bolton Abbey,
Skipton, North Yorkshire BD23 6AF
Cafés, shop
Open: Sun all year; Apr–Oct Sat;
mid-July–Aug daily
Features: specialist collection of
industrial locomotives
Nearest station: Skipton (bus link)
Length: 7.2km (4.5 miles)
Gauge: 435mm (4ft 8 1/2 in)
Tel: 01756 710614
www.embsaybolton abbeyrailway.org.uk

Ffestiniog Railway ⑲
(Porthmadog–Blaenau Ffestiniog)
Harbour Station, Porthmadog,
Gwynedd LL49 9NF
Cafés, shops, museum
Open: mid-Mar–Oct daily
Features: glorious scenery, walks
from stations, slate museums
Nearest station: Porthmadog/
Blaenau Ffestiniog
Length: 21.6km (13.2 miles)
Gauge: 597mm (1ft 11 1/2in)
Tel: 01766 516024
www.festrail.co.uk

**Gloucesteshire Warwickshire
Railway** ⑳
(Toddington–Cheltenham)
The Station, Toddington,
Cheltenham, Glos GL54 5DT
Café, shop, narrow gauge railway
Open: Mar–Nov weekends, various
weekdays
Nearest station: Cheltenham (bus
link)
Length: 16km (10 miles)
Gauge: 1,435mm (4ft 8 1/2 in)
Tel: 01242 621405
www.gwsr.com

Great Central Railway ㉑
(Loughborough–Leicester North)
Loughborough Central Station,
Great Central Road, Loughborough,
Leicestershire LE11 1RW
Cafés, shops, museum
Open: weekends and Bank Holidays
all year; May–Sept some weekdays
Features: double track section,
dining trains
Nearest station: Loughborough
Length: 12.8km (8 miles)
Gauge: 1,435mm (4ft 8 1/2 in)
Tel: 01509 632323
www.gcrailway.co.uk

Gwili Railway ㉒
(Bronwydd Arms–Llwyfan Cerrig)
Bronwydd Arms Station, Bronwydd
Arms, Carmarthenshire SA33 6HT
Café, shop
Open: Mar–Oct, various days
Nearest station: Carmarthen (bus
link)
Length: 4km (2.25 miles)
Gauge: 1,435mm (4ft 8 1/2 in)
Tel: 01267 238213
www.gwili-railway.co.uk

Isle of Wight Steam Railway ㉓
(Smallbrook Junction–Wotton)
Haven Street, Ryde, Isle of Wight
PO33 4DS
Café, shop, museum
Open: June–mid-Sept daily; various
other days
Features: period coaches
Nearest station: Smallbrook Jct
Length: 8km (5 miles)
Gauge: 1,435mm (4ft 8 1/2 in)
Tel: 01983 882204
www.iwsteamrailway.co.uk

Keighley & Worth Valley Railway ㉔
(Keighley–Oxenhope)
Haworth Station, Keighley, West
Yorkshire BD22 8NJ
Cafés, shops, museums
Open: weekends and Bank Holidays
all year; July–Aug daily

Features: walks from stations,
Brontë Museum nearby
Nearest station: Keighley
Length: 7.6km (4.75 miles)
Gauge: 1,435mm (4ft 8 1/2 in)
Tel: 01535 640464
www.kwvr.co.uk

Kent & East Sussex Railway ㉕
(Tenterden Town–Bodiam)
Tenterden Town Station, Tenterden,
Kent TN30 6HE
Café, shop, museum
Open: Apr–Oct weekends; end July–
early Sept daily
Features: Bodiam Castle, dining
trains
Nearest station: Ashford (bus link)
Length: 16.8km (10.5 miles)
Gauge: 1,435mm (4ft 8 1/2 in)
Tel: 01580 765155
www.kesr.org.uk

Lakeside & Haverthwaite Railway ㉖
(Haverthwaite–Lakeside)
Haverthwaite Station, Nr Ulverston,
Cumbria LA12 8AL
Café, shop, museum
Open: late Mar–early Nov daily
Features: steamer connections at
Lakeside
Nearest station: Ulverston
Length: 5.6km (3.5 miles)
Gauge: 1,435mm (4ft 8 1/2 in)
Tel: 01539 531594
www.lakesiderailway.co.uk

Llanberis Lake Railway ㉗
(Llanberis–Penllyn)
Gilfach Ddu, Llanberis, Gwynedd
LL55 4TY
Café, shop
Open: Easter–May, Sept Sun–Fri;
June–Aug daily; Oct Sun–Thur
Features: mountain scenery, Slate
Museum, Country Park
Length: 4km (2.5 miles)
Gauge: 597mm (1ft 11 1/2in)
Tel: 01286 870549
www.lake-railway.co.uk

Llangollen Railway ㉘
(Llangollen–Carrog)
The Station, Abbey Road,
Llangollen, Denbighshire LL20 8SN
Cafés, shops
Open: May–Sept daily; Oct–Apr
many weekends and other days
Features: beautiful scenery, lunch
and dining trains
Nearest station: Ruabon (bus link)
Length: 12km (7.5 miles)
Gauge: 1,435mm (4ft 8 1/2 in)
Tel: 01978 860979
www.llangollen-railway.co.uk

Mid-Hants Railway ㉙
(Watercress Line)
(Alresford–Alton)
The Railway Station, Alresford,
Hampshire SO24 9JG
Cafés, shops, museum
Open: Jan–Oct weekends; many
weekdays in summer
Features: real ale trains
Nearest station: Alton
Length: 16km (10 miles)
Gauge: 1,435mm (4ft 8 1/2 in)
Tel: 01962 733810
www.watercressline.co.uk

Midland Railway Centre ㉚
(Hammersmith–Riddings Junction/
Pye Bridge)
Butterley Station, Ripley, Derbyshire
DE5 3QZ
Cafés, shops, museum, park
railways
Open: most weekends, various
weekdays
Features: country park, farm
museum, canal, dining trains
Nearest station: Derby (bus link)
Length: 5.6km (3.5 miles)
Gauge: 1,435mm (4ft 8 1/2 in)
Tel: 01773 570140
www.midlandrailway-butterley.co.uk

Nene Valley Railway ㉛
(Wansford–Peterborough)
Wansford Station, Stibbington,
Peterborough PE8 6LR
Café, shops, museum
Open: Easter–Oct weekends,
various weekdays
Features: many continental
locomotives, country park adjacent
to Orton Mere station
Nearest station: Peterborough
Length: 12km (7.5 miles)
Gauge: 1,435mm (4ft 8 1/2 in)
Tel: 01780 784444
www.nvr.org.uk

North Norfolk Railway ㉜
(Sheringham–Holt)
Sheringham Station, Sheringham,
Norfolk NR26 8RA
Cafés, shops, museum
Open: Apr–Oct most days
Features: sea views
Nearest station: Sheringham
Length: 8.4km (5.2 miles)
Gauge: 1,435mm (4ft 8 1/2 in)
Tel: 01263 820800
www.nnrailway.co.uk

North Yorkshire Moors Railway ㉝
(Grosmont–Pickering)
Pickering Station, Pickering, North
Yorkshire YO18 7AJ

Cafés, shops, museum
Open: mid-Mar–early Nov daily
Features: beautiful scenery, walks
from stations, dining trains, trains
to Whitby
Nearest station: Grosmont
Length: 29km (18 miles)
Gauge: 1,435mm (4ft 8 1/2 in)
Tel: 01751 472508
www.nymr.co.uk

Paignton & Dartmouth Railway ㉞
(Paignton–Kingswear)
Queen's Park Station, Paignton,
Devon TQ4 6AF
Cafés, shop
Open: Easter–Oct daily
Features: sea views
Nearest station: Paignton
Length: 11km (7 miles)
Gauge: 1,435mm (4ft 8 1/2 in)
Tel: 01803 555872
www.dartmouthrailriver.co.uk

Ravenglass & Eskdale Railway ㉟
(Ravenglass–Eskdale Green)
Ravenglass, Cumbria CA18 1SW
Cafés, shops, museum, mill
Open: late Mar–early Nov daily;
other weekends
Features: glorious scenery, walks
Nearest station: Ravenglass
Length: 11km (7 miles)
Gauge: 381mm (15in)
Tel: 01229 717171
www.ravenglass-railway.co.uk

**Romney Hythe & Dymchurch
Railway** ㊱
(Hythe–Dungeness)
New Romney Station, Kent
TN28 8PL
Cafés, shops, toy and model
museum, model railway
Open: late Mar–early Nov daily;
other weekends and days
Features: observation coaches
Nearest station: Folkestone (bus
link)
Length: 21.6km (13.5 miles)
Gauge: 381mm (15in)
Tel: 01797 362353
www.rhdr.org.uk

Severn Valley Railway ㊲
(Kidderminster–Bridgnorth)
Railway Station, Bewdley,
Worcestershire DY12 1BG
Cafés, shops, model railway
Open: every weekend; early May–
early Oct daily
Features: Kidderminster Railway
Museum, lunch and dining trains
Nearest station: Kidderminster
Length: 26.4km (16.5 miles)

Gauge: 1,435mm (4ft 8 1/2 in)
Tel: 01562 757900
www.svr.co.uk

Snowdon Mountain Railway ㊳
(Llanberis–Summit)
Llanberis, Gwynedd LL55 4TY
Cafés, shops
Open: mid-Mar–early Nov daily
Features: glorious scenery, walks
from stations
Nearest station: Betws-y-Coed
(Snowdon Sherpa bus)
Length: 7.6km (4.6 miles)
Gauge: 80mm (2ft 7 1/2in)
Tel: 01286 870223
www.snowdonrailway.co.uk

South Devon Railway ㊴
(Buckfastleigh–Totnes)
Buckfastleigh Station,
Buckfastleigh, Devon TQ11 0DZ
Café, shop, museum
Open: Apr–Oct daily
Features: adjacent butterfly and
otter farm
Nearest station: Totnes
Length: 11km (7 miles)
Gauge: 1,435mm (4ft 8 1/2 in)
Tel: 01364 644370
www.southdevonrailway.org

Strathspey Railway ㊵
(Aviemore–Broomhill)
Aviemore Station, Dalfaber Road,
Aviemore, Inverness PH22 1PY
Cafés, shops, museum
Open: mid-Mar–Oct weekends;
early June–Sept daily
Features: osprey viewing
Nearest station: Aviemore
Length: 16km (10 miles)
Gauge: 1,435mm (4ft 8 1/2 in)
Tel: 01479 810725
www.strathspeyrailway.co.uk

Swanage Railway ㊶
(Swanage–Norden)
Station House, Swanage, Dorset
BH19 1HB
Cafés, shops, museum

Open: Apr–late Oct daily; most
weekends and various weekdays
Features: Corfe Castle
Nearest station: Wareham
Length: 9.6km (6 miles)
Gauge: 1,435mm (4ft 8 1/2 in)
Tel: 01929 425800
www.swanagerailway.co.uk

Talyllyn Railway ㊷
(Tywyn–Nant Gwernol)
Wharf Station, Tywyn, Gwynedd
LL36 9EY
Cafés, shops, museum
Open: mid-Mar–early Nov daily
Features: scenery, walks
Nearest station: Tywyn
Length: 11.6km (7.25 miles)
Gauge: 686mm (2ft 3in)
Tel: 01654 710472
www.talyllyn.co.uk

Tanfield Railway ㊸
(Andrews House–East Tanfield)
Marley Hill Engine Shed, Marley
Hill, Gateshead, NE16 5ET
Café, shop
Open: Jan–Nov Sun and Bank
Holidays; summer Wed–Thur
Features: Causey Arch, 1854 engine
shed, period carriages
Nearest station: Newcastle
Length: 4.8km (3 miles)
Gauge: 1,435mm (4ft 8 1/2 in)
Tel: 07508 092365
www.tanfield-railway.co.uk

Tyseley Locomotive Works ㊹
670 Warwick Road, Tyseley,
Birmingham B11 2HL
Café, shop, museum, frequent
steam excursions; open weekends
Nearest station: Tyseley
Tel: 0121 7084960
www.vintagetrains.co.uk

Vale of Rheidol Railway ㊺
(Aberystwyth–Devil's Bridge)
The Locomotive Shed, Park Avenue,
Aberystwyth, Cardiganshire SY23
1PG

Cafés, shops
Open: late Mar–Oct almost daily
Features: scenery, walks
Nearest station: Aberystwyth
Length: 18.8km (11.75 miles)
Gauge: 597mm (1ft 11 1/2in)
Tel: 01970 625819
www.rheidolrailway.co.uk

Welsh Highland Railway ㊻
(Caernarfon–Porthmadog)
Harbour Station, Porthmadog,
Gwynedd LL49 9NE
Café, shop
Open: mid-Mar–early Nov daily
Features: locos from South Africa
Nearest station: Bangor (bus link)
Length: 21km (12 miles)/40km (25
miles)
Gauge: 597mm (1ft 11 1/2in)
Tel: 01766 516024
www.festrail.co.uk

Welshpool & Llanfair Light Railway
㊼
(Welshpool–Llanfair Caereinion)
The Station, Llanfair Caereinion,
Mid-Wales SY21 0SF
Cafés, shops
Open: Easter–Oct weekends, daily
in school holidays
Nearest station: Welshpool
Length: (13km (8 miles)
Gauge: 762mm (2ft 6in)
Tel: 01938 810441
www.wllr.org.uk

West Somerset Railway ㊽
(Bishops Lydeard–Minehead)
Railway Station, Minehead,
Somerset TA24 5BG
Cafés, shops, museum
Open: Apr–Oct almost daily
Features: longest heritage railway
Nearest station: Taunton (bus
link)
Length: 32km (20 miles)
Gauge: 1,435mm (4ft 8 1/2in)
Tel: 01643 704996
www.west-somerset-railway.co.uk

Antheor railway viaduct, Alpes-Maritimes, Cote d'Azur, France.

*Le Train Bleu restaurant,
Gare de Lyon, Paris.*

FRANCE

France was the pioneer of high-speed trains in Europe, but the country also has an extensive network of quiet rural railways winding through memorable mountain scenery

It was in 1827, three years after the first public rail service in Britain, that the first railway opened in France, from St-Etienne to Andrézieux. This and other lines built to Lyon and Roanne by 1836 were designed to transport coal to the Loire and Rhône rivers. Carrying passengers, who were initially accommodated in coal wagons, was a mere by-product. By 1837 the first Parisian suburban railways had opened, to be followed in 1841 by the Strasbourg to Basel line. This was not only the first French long-distance line, but also the first international railway in Europe. Today's national railway museum, the Cité du Train, at Mulhouse (see page 158) is situated on this historic route.

The French government encouraged the development of a wider rail network by granting longer concessions and financial aid, and dozens of small companies were created to build and operate isolated lines. But by 1860, seven large networks dominated the scene – the Nord, Est, Paris-Lyon-Méditerranée (PLM), Paris-Orléans (PO), Ouest, Midi and the state-run Etat. This was the situation that applied until the network was nationalised on 1 January 1938, when the Société Nationale de Chemins de Fer Français (SNCF) was formed.

While today's rail network was largely complete by 1870, the government of 1879 agreed on the construction of numerous minor lines, often built to metre-gauge, with little or no economic justification. These limped on with massive state aid until the formation of the SNCF, after which a closure programme took the network back to something like that of 1870. Traces of these narrow-gauge railways remain all over France, mainly in the form of preserved lines.

Many railways running along borders, especially the German border,

Main attractions

Marseille: Vieux Port, Opéra, Notre-Dame de la Garde
Nîmes: Roman arena, Maison Carrée, Musée des Beaux Arts
Nice: Vieux Ville, Château, Promenade des Anglais, Musée Matisse
Corsica: Bonifacio, Maison Bonaparte, Ajaccio, Palais Fesch.

Maps on pages 132, 137, 152, 154

The steam train of Cévennes.

UNITED KINGDOM

Newquay
Gunnislake
Exeter
Southampton
Brighton
Dover
Dover
Calais
Dunkerque
Gent

Truro
Torquay
Exmouth
Weymouth
Portsmouth
Hastings
Eastbourne
Boulogne-sur-Mer
Lille
Béthune
Lens
Douai

Land's End
Penzance
Falmouth
Plymouth
Isle of Wight
Étaples
Abbeville
le Tréport
Amiens
Beauvais
Douai
Aulne
Ayme
St-Quen

English Channel

C. de la Hague
Pte de Barfleur
Cherbourg
Fécamp
Dieppe
Abancourt
Tergnier

Guernsey
Channel Islands
Jersey
Bayeux
Dives-Cabourg
le Havre
Rouen
Seine
Paris
Châte
Thierr

Lisor
St-Lô
Lisieux
Elbeuf
Évreux
Versailles
2

Roscoff
Lannion
Paimpol
Granville
Vire
Caen
Argentan
Dreux
Chartres
Étampes
Moret
Veneux
Sens
Ro

I. d'Ouessant
Morlaix
St-Brieuc
St-Malo
Avranches
Surdon
Alençon
13

Brest
Guingamp
Dol
Laval
Sablé-sur-Sarthe
le Mans
Courtalan
Orléans
Auxerre

Carhaix
Quimper
Loudéac
Rennes
Loir
Vendôme
Gien

Pte du Raz
Lorient
Châteaubriant
Angers
Blois
Tours
FRANCE

Pte de Penmarch
Vannes
Redon
Savenay
Loire
Saumur
Chinon
Loches
Vierzon
Bourges
Corbi
Nevers

Carnac
Quiberon
Belle-Ile
le Croisic
St-Nazaire
Pornic
Nantes
Clisson
Cholet
Châtellerault
Indre
Châteauroux
Luçay-le-Mâle
Cher
St-Amand-Montrond
Moulins

I. de Noirmoutier
I. d'Yeu
St-Gilles-Croix-de-Vie
les Sables-d'Olonne
la Roche-sur-Yon
Bressuire
Poitiers
Vienne
Creuse
Montluçon

I. de Re
la Rochelle
Niort
Montmorillon
Busseau-sur-Creuse

I. d'Oléron
Rochefort
St-Sulpice-Laurière
Limoges
Felletin
Clern
Ferra

Bay of Biscay

Royan
Pointe-de-Grave
Saintes
Saillat
le Mont Dore
Puy de Sancy 1885
Arv

Jonzac
Angoulême
Meymac
Mass

Museums and Heritage Lines
Featured route

Coutras
Périgueux
Brive-la-Gaillarde
Aurillac
le en-

France

Libourne
Bordeaux
Bergerac
Sarlat
Figeac
le Monastier

0   50 km
0   50 miles

Arcachon
Dordogne
le Buisson
Lot
Cahors
Rodez

Golfe de Gascogne

Morcenx
Marmande
Agen
Montauban
Millau

Bassin Aquitain
Mont-de-Marsan
Tessonières
Albi
Tarn
Mont

Llanes
Santander
Laredo
Dax
Auch
St-Sulpice
Mazamet
Béziers

Torrelavega
Picos de Europa 2648
Reinosa
Bayonne
Orthez
Pau
Portet-St-Simon
Toulouse
Carcassonne
Narbonne

Bilbo/Bilbao
Baracaldo
Irún
Biarritz
11
PYRÉNÉES
Perpigr

SPAIN
Donostia/San Sebastián
Hendaye
Oloron-Ste-Marie
Tarbes
St-Gaudens
Foix
Ax-les-Thermes
Aude
Quillan
Port-Ve

Osorno la Mayor
Gasteiz/Vitoria
Miranda de Ebro
Logroño
Iruña/Pamplona
Canfranc
Lourdes
9
Bagnères-de-Luchon
Latour-de-Carol
Villefranche-de-Confluent
Portb

Burgos
Ebro
Jaca
Mte Perdido 3355
Pico de Aneto 3404
ANDORRA
Andorra la Vella
Ribes de Freser

Palencia

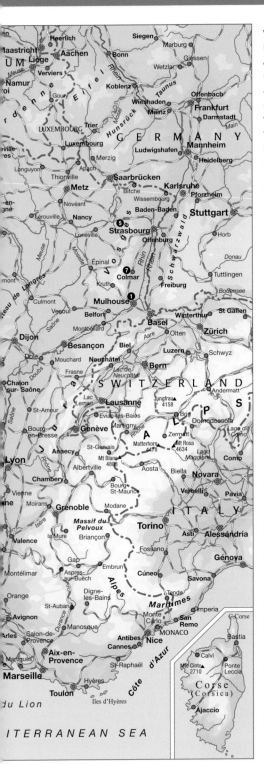

were built for strategic reasons; the lines in Alsace-Lorraine ended up in German territory after the Franco-Prussian War in 1871. Railway buildings here are very Germanic – the station at Metz is a superb example – and operating practices are different from those in the rest of France. Trains still run on the right instead of the left, so there are flyovers near the old border to allow trains to change sides.

RECONSTRUCTION AND SPEED

After World War II, massive reconstruction of the railways was necessary, and SNCF embarked on a programme of main line electrification. Around 85 percent of all traffic today is electric, the main exceptions being on cross-country routes, especially in the Massif Central. Then, from the early 1950s, came the quest for speed. While trains struggled to maintain speeds of 120kmh (75mph), new electric locomotives were gradually taken beyond 200kmh (124mph) and in an astonishing week in March 1955, two locomotives reached 331kmh (206mph) in the Landes region south of Bordeaux. The trials nearly ended in disaster as track started to deteriorate, but the record stood until the 1980s.

The Pau Funicular.

A TGV Duplex high-speed train.

Trials gradually translated into higher service speeds – 160kmh (100mph) became the norm in the 1960s, while expresses to Bordeaux and Toulouse were cranked up to 200kmh (124mph) by the end of that decade. During the 1970s, SNCF realised that the only way to go even faster, and beat increasing air competition, was with purpose-built, high-speed lines: the Train à Grande Vitesse (TGV) was born. The first high-speed line, from Paris to Lyon, opened in 1981, with trains running at 270kmh (168mph), halving the 4-hour journey time. The network is still expanding and over three-quarters of SNCF's long-distance passengers now travel by TGV – some services of which are branded inOui.

All French rail services are still operated by the public company SNCF – with the exception of one line in Brittany from Paimpol to Guingamp and Carhaix – but rail unions fear that the government's ultimate plan is privatisation. A long series of strikes was staged in the spring and summer of 2018 in opposition to proposed 'reforms' and the possible deterioration in standards of service for passengers. For now at least, travelling by train in France remains a mostly agreeable experience. Trains are very punctual and connecting services are usually held when a train is a few minutes late. Cancellations are almost unheard of, except in the Paris suburbs where trains are, anyway, very regular.

SCENIC LINES

If you take the time and the trouble to explore away from the mainlines you will find that the country still has many slower, scenic lines with time to enjoy superb views of mountain, river, forest, plain or coast. Apart from those described in this book, any line through the Massif Central, the Pyrenees, the Alps or the Jura turns up beautiful vistas. There are also a number of funicular railways, the shortest and cutest being in the city of Pau (in southwest France), which shuttles people from the railway station up to the city centre.

PARIS–MARSEILLE BY TGV

The Train à Grande Vitesse is a high-speed train that regularly attains speeds of 320kmh (200mph) and on existing railway lines. All TGVs consist of a power car – a single-ended locomotive – at each end and (for lower weight and better stability) a set of articulated coaches between. The latest generation are the double-decker **TGV Duplex** sets, which mainly operate on this route. When booking your seat, ask for the top deck for a better view. Although incredibly fast, TGVs are also very safe – no passenger has been killed as a result of a TGV crash in almost 4 decades of operation. On the high-speed lines, drivers do not observe signals but are told at what speed to drive, taking into account the state of the track and the other trains on the line.

A GRAND STATION

Before boarding the TGV, cast an eye around the **Gare de Lyon**, built at the height of the Belle Époque. Aside from the fine clock tower, the station has one of the best restaurants in Paris, the Train Bleu, a listed monument, with walls and ceiling decorated by artists of the time.

The TGV leaves Paris behind and slowly builds up speed, passing many of its sister trains being cleaned in the depot to the west. After seven minutes, the train swings east onto the high-speed line and starts to accelerate. By the time it leaves the tunnel, it has reached over 160kmh (100mph) and has left the suburbs behind. At Crisenoy the line is joined by the motor-way to the east and the train reaches 300kmh (186mph); despite the speed, the ride remains astonishingly smooth. The line runs across the plain of **Brie**, famous for its cheese but also a major cereal-producing area, crossing the **River Seine** at Montereau, an industrial town to the west.

We now enter **Burgundy**, although few of the vineyards that make the region famous throughout the world are visible. Soon after Montereau the distant 12th-century cathedral of **Sens** is visible to the west. The terrain gradually becomes more wooded and around an hour from Paris the cereal-growing region blurs into an area of pasture with buff Charolais cattle grazing peacefully between villages of warm brown stone. To the west, is **Cluny**, a centre of pilgrimage with its octagonal-spired Romanesque church and ruined abbey dating from 1088.

At this point it is possible to sense how hilly the railway line is, as it climbs to the Col du Bois Clair parallel with the local highway. The TGV makes light work of the steep gradient, which allowed the engineers to avoid building expensive tunnels. Around 1 hour and 30 minutes from Paris there is a glimpse of Mâconnais vines as the train rushes past **Mâcon-Loché** station, crosses the River Saône and turns southwards along its flood plain towards Lyon. The line turns east-wards, avoiding this superb Roman city, and after a tunnel emerges to cross the Rhône Valley railway, the *autoroute* (motorway) and the river itself.

There may be a pause at **St-Exupéry** station (serving Lyon's airport) with its magnificent, winged station building designed by Spanish architect, Santiago Calatrava. Just a couple of hours from Paris, orchards start to appear as the climate is now warm enough for peaches and apricots. Passing through **Valence** TGV station, the limestone Vercors area of the Alps forms a rugged background to the east while to the west lie the foothills of the Ardèche.

APPROACH TO THE MEDITERRANEAN

The train passes close to **Montélimar**, famous for nougat made from local almonds. The vegetation becomes Mediterranean as the line climbs over the *autoroute* and into the valley

⊙ Essentials

European Rail timetable no. 350

Distance: 750km (466 miles)

Duration of journey: 3hrs 20 mins on average

Frequency of trains: 16–18 per day

St-Exupéry station, Lyon.

of the Rhône, which will be crossed four times. This is an important wine-producing area, with stout Côtes-du-Rhône and Châteauneuf-du-Pape reds produced around the Roman town of **Orange**.

After a brief climb out of the valley, there is a superb view of **Avignon** and the Papal palace to the north, before the train plunges downhill on a magnificent double bridge back over the Rhône into the Avignon TGV station. The line now follows the river Durance to **Cavaillon**, famous for its melons, then cuts through limestone hills near **Vernègues**, a village completely razed by an earthquake in 1909.

The TGV crosses the line's longest viaduct (1,733 metres/yds) at **Ventabren**, then the **Roquefavour Aqueduct**, built in 1847, is briefly visible to the south. To the north, beyond Aix-en-Provence, is the wedge-shaped **Montagne Ste-Victoire** immortalizeed by Cézanne in many of his paintings.

We pass through **Aix-en-Provence** station, then plunge into the longest railway tunnel in France (7,834 metres/

yds). As the TGV emerges, there's a brief glimpse of the port, the Frioul islands and the Château d'If before we reach **Marseille**'s St-Charles station.

CLERMONT FERRAND–NÎMES

As an alternative to the 3-hour dash by TGV from Paris to Marseille described earlier, you may want to take the slow route through the centre of France. Le Cévenol used to depart each morning from Paris for Marseille, but its route has been reduced to the most scenic part of it, from Clermont Ferrand to Nîmes. The scenery through the Cévennes Mountains between Clermont and Nîmes is worth anyone's time. To get to Clermont Ferrand from Paris takes about three and a half hours (direct by Intercité).

Clermont Ferrand is capital of the Auvergne region and home of Bibendum, the plump Michelin man made of tyres – you'll find everything you need to know about him in the company's visitors' centre, L'Aventure Michelin. The city's 13th-century cathedral is a fine Gothic pile with double spires, and the only French cathedral built out of black volcanic rock. Clermont Ferrand is overlooked by the perfect volcanic dome of the Puy-de-Dôme, which is ascended by a rack railway.

ALONG THE RIVER ALLIER

After passing through the suburbs of Clermont, the railway joins the valley of the River Allier, which it follows, almost to its source, for the next 180km (112 miles). At this point, there are ancient volcanic plugs (puys) on both sides of the valley. To the west is the **Plateau de Gergovie** where Julius Caesar was beaten back by Vercingétorix, king of the Gauls, in 52 AD, while to the east is the **Puy St-Romain**, rising to 779 metres (2,556ft). In its shadow lies **Vic-le-Comte** (6km/3.5 miles from the station), a little town founded by Benedictine monks in the 8th century. The railway now winds

⊙ LE PUY-EN-VELAY

Le Puy-en-Velay is perhaps the most astonishing natural site in France. In a depression in the Velay plateau, two volcanic plugs (puys) rise out of the surrounding earth. On the summit of the steep-sided St-Michel puy, the Romanesque chapel of St-Michel d'Aiguilhe was built in the 11th century, probably replacing a temple to Mercury. You have to climb 268 steps to visit the chapel. The second puy, Rocher Corneille, which is less abrupt, is topped by a 16-metre (53ft) cast-iron statue of the Virgin and Child, Notre-Dame de France, which was erected in 1860. The statue is hollow and it is possible to climb to the crown for a superb view of the surrounding countryside.

The buildings of this ancient city tumble down the sides of the Rocher Corneille, while the Romanesque 12th-century Cathédrale Notre-Dame, which has Byzantine influences in its architecture, stands at its foot. For hundreds of years pilgrimages have been drawn to Le Puy to venerate a statue of a Black Virgin. Beside the cathedral is a cloister with many exquisitely carved medieval capitals.

The area is also well known for its exquisite lace; a tradition that is lovingly maintained to this day.

There are three daily direct trains to Le Puy from Clermont Ferrand, taking just over 2 hours, and six from Paris (4 hours 20 minutes) involving one change in Lyon.

along the narrow Allier valley to **Issoire**, a small town with one of the biggest Romanesque churches in the Auvergne region. Issoire is the first of many towns and villages along this route associated with the struggle between Protestants, whose French stronghold is still in the Cévennes, and Catholics. Issoire suffered badly in the Wars of Religion, when the Protestant fanatic Captain Merle led an orgy of torture and demolition of church towers in 1575, before the Catholic Duke of Anjou retook the town two years later, sacking and burning the houses in the process.

Soon after Issoire the 856-metre (2,808ft) **Puy d'Ysson** is visible to the west and above **Le Breuil sur Couze**, the remains of Nonette Castle dominate a bend of the Allier. The line then leaves the river behind to reach the ancient town of **Brioude** whose Basilique St-Julien is the largest Romanesque church in the area. The church owes its name to a Roman legionnaire, converted to Christianity, who was martyred here in 304 AD.

The railway now joins the Senouire Valley, rejoining the Allier just before **Langeac**. Shortly before this, the Le Puy branch splits off at St-Georges d'Aurac (see panel). Langeac itself is an old town nestling on a hillside at the start of the Allier Gorge, whose snaking curves the train is obliged to follow for the next 85km (53 miles). The river here is subject to unpredictable floods and no road or settlement has been built in the valley. Construction of the railway, which involved 12,000 workers, was extremely problematic; on the 67km (42-mile) section to Langogne, there are 64 tunnels, 12 large viaducts and many retaining walls. In many places there are wires to detect rock falls onto the line. Just before the plunge into the gorge, the village of **Chanteuges** has an imposing Romanesque church and the remains of an abbey to the east. There follows a series of villages – **Prades**, **Monistrol d'Allier** – shoe-horned into the valley, while the line avoids some tight river bends by tunnelling through promontories. At

⊘ Essentials

European Rail timetable no. 333

Distance: 303km (188 miles)

Duration of journey: 5hrs 5 mins

Frequency of trains: 1–3 per day (direct)

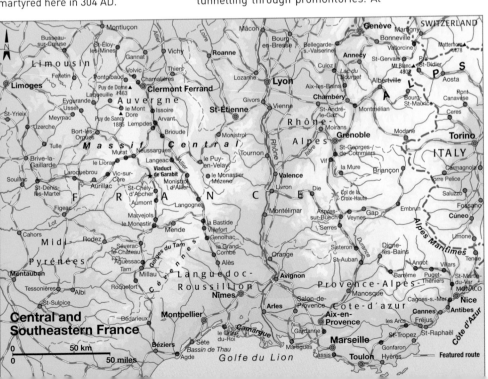

Central and Southeastern France

Chapeauroux, the railway curves on a 28-arch viaduct through the beautifully situated village.

The next town is **Langogne**, a small centre but an important one, given the sparse local population. Here, houses were built in a circle around the church in medieval times. The railway line is nearer the summit of a plateau now and views expand over greater distances until **Luc** where the Allier Valley closes in again. At **La Bastide**, the summit of the line (1,023 metres/3,356ft) is reached. The Allier rises just east from here on the watershed that separates rivers flowing into the Atlantic at Nantes and Bordeaux and into the Mediterranean.

THE STAIRWAY OF GIANTS

For the train, it is all downhill from here, on what is known as the 'Stairway of Giants', with the track clinging to hillsides as it slowly descends towards the coastal plain. First the tracks cut through a forest, mainly in tunnel, before reaching **Prévencheres**

with its 12th-century bell tower, and heading across the artificial Lac de Rachas on the Altier Viaduct. This was a massive 72 metres (236ft) high when built, but over half is now hidden by water. The train passes through more tunnels before skirting the Lac de Villefort and stopping at **Villefort** itself. Apart from the attractions of the lake, the town is a centre for visiting the Chassezac Gorges and the Cévennes National Park. The railway continues to twist and turn, passing the red-roofed village of **Concoules** to the west, before halting at **Genolhac**, a pretty town decked with flowers in summer.

The sun often appears at this point as the line leaves the Cévennes and approaches the Mediterranean, passing through a thickly forested area, before crossing the Luech valley on the **Chamborigaud Viaduct**. This is 47 metres (154ft) high, has 41 arches and describes a near semi-circle. The train then passes through the line's longest tunnel before reaching **Ste-Cécile d'Andorges** and entering

A TGV crosses the Cize–Bolozon railway viaduct in the Ain département.

the Gardon Valley. The line quickly runs into an area of abandoned coal mines, with settlements strung along the valley to **La Grand-Combe**. As the train leaves the industrial area, there is a little more savage beauty before the large town of **Alès**, which grew up on the back of the silk and, later, coal industry. For the rest of our journey, the countryside opens out, and the railway roughly follows the Gardon and crosses vineyards producing Costières du Nîmes. The city of Nîmes is known as 'the French Rome' for its classical architecture, most notably an amphitheatre.

NÎMES–BÉZIERS

To extend the trip, or to link with the next journey, a different route back to Clermont Ferrand you might want to travel this Mediterranean line that initially passes through vineyards then runs close to the coast with views of the sea. Thirty minutes from Nîmes is **Montpellier**, capital of the Languedoc – not as old as neighbouring towns from the Roman era, but with a great deal of charm all the same. As well as many superb old buildings in the city, there is the Musée Fabre, an art museum with a rich collection of paintings.

From Montpellier, the railway nears the coast, with views over several *étangs* – stretches of salt water enclosed by long sand spits. The largest is the **Bassin de Thau**, to the north after Sète, where oysters and mussels grow fast in the warm water. **Sète** itself is an attractive old fishing port, famous for its 'nautical jousting' in which jousters with 3-metre (10ft) lances try to knock each other off the bows of opposing rowing boats.

Béziers is a centre of wine production founded by the Romans around 35 BC on the banks of the River Orb. Today, the fortified cathedral of St-Nazaire, dating back to 760 AD, dominates the river and presents a fine sight from the Pont Vieux. The town has three museums, including one devoted to wine, which has examples of Greek, Etruscan and Roman vessels for carrying the valuable liquid.

Water-jousting in Séte.

⊘ PROTESTANTISM IN THE CÉVENNES

Away from the German border region, the hills of the Cévennes are traditionally the most Protestant area of France. The ideas of Luther and Calvin started to gain ground here early in the 16th century. Just a few decades later and conflict was widespread in the area, with churches burned down and whole families massacred.

The Edict of Nantes in 1598 brought greater tolerance. However, following its revocation in 1685, the conflics were reignited. Consequently, the richest Protestants fled to Switzerland or Germany. Those who remained launched a major rebellion know as the War of the Camisards (1702–04), a nickname taken from the shirts worn by Protestant rebels.

⊘ Essentials

European Rail timetable no. 332

Distance: 394km (245 miles)

Duration of journey: 6hrs 25 mins

Frequency of trains: 1 per day (direct)

BÉZIERS–CLERMONT FERRAND

This line is one of the most spectacular in France, crossing some of its wildest territory, with very little in the way of settlements – in places the population density is a mere 14 people per square kilometre. The largest town, Millau, has just 22,000 inhabitants. Unlike the Clermont–Nîmes route (see pages 136), where the tracks climb almost continuously from either direction to La Bastide, the Béziers line is a switchback ride of successive climbs and descents.

VINEYARDS AND ORCHIDS

Leaving **Béziers**, wine production is much in evidence for the first half hour of the journey. The Languedoc region produces more wine than anywhere else in France – and although much of this is decidedly *ordinaire*, there is quality, too; Côteaux du Languedoc and Faugères are the local specialities. The train then cuts through hills to reach **Bédarieux**, in the Orb valley. Following the river to Le Bousquet d'Orb, the line

twists through the Monts d'Orb, passing through a short tunnel at the Col de l'Homme Mort (Dead Man's Pass). We then descend onto the **Causse de Larzac**, which give the line its nickname the *Ligne des Causses*, the first of several bare, arid, limestone plateaux in this region, known to naturalists for their unique ecosystems; orchids thrive in this environment.

Just after **Tournemire** station, the village of **Roquefort** hugs the ridge to the west, on a hillside created by the collapse of a limestone plateau riddled with caves used to age the village's famous, blue, ewe's milk cheese. The railway soon descends to the Tarn Valley to reach **Millau**, passing the magnificent viaduct, the world's highest – but, sadly, for road traffic only. The town dates back to the 1st century AD when it was a thriving market and pottery centre; it is now more famous for making gloves from local sheepskin. The local museums display both skills and the old town is pleasant for a stroll. Millau makes a good base for exploring the Grands Causses and the gorges of the Tarn and other rivers.

The tracks now run north along the Tarn Valley then turn northwest at **Aguessac** to climb to 839 metres (2,750ft) before dropping down to **Séverac-le-Château**, a village of superb old houses, dominated by a rock on which stand the ruins of the eponymous castle. Here lived Louis d'Arpajon, a national military hero who disgraced himself by murdering his son and wife out of jealousy. The train continues its tortuous descent over the **Causse de Séverac** before dropping into the valley of the Lot near **Banassac-La Canourgue**, close to the beautiful old village of La Canourgue. Continuing alongside the Lot, then north along the Colagne Valley, we reach **Marvejols**, a centre for health cures. The village still has three ancient gates and a statue representing the 'beast of Gévaudan' (see page

⊘ STEVENSON AND THE BEAST

In September 1878, the writer Robert Louis Stevenson embarked on a 12-day tramp through the Cévennes. Starting from Le Monastier-sur-Gazeille, 20km (12 miles) south of Le Puy, his route criss-crossed the Clermont–Nîmes railway at Langogne, Luc and La Bastide. The line was under construction at the time. Indeed, Stevenson met engineers engaged on the project and swore they were the most civilised people he encountered on his trip. There is now a Stevenson Historic Trail following his eventful journey.

After spending a night in Langogne, Stevenson was forced to bed down in a wood the following night as no-one would open their doors to him, being petrified of the 'beast of Gévaudan'. The Cévennes region was still imbued with tales of a massive beast that had first spread terror throughout the Gévaudan area over a century earlier. In three years in the 1760s, the beast was purported to have killed over 100 people and injured hundreds more. When eventually shot, however, the 'beast' turned out to be a wolf of modest size – a 'Napoleon amongst wolves' according to Stevenson. Yet fears persisted; there were reports of another large beast killing 20 people in nearby Limousin around 1815, while 'rabid wolves' prowled the mountain forests at the time of Stevenson's visit.

140). The obsession with this animal has led to the establishment of the Parc du Gévaudan, famous for its wolves, 4km (2.5miles) north of the town. Wolves were eliminated from this wild region long ago, and attempts to reintroduce them have been resisted by local farmers. However, bison and vultures have both been reintroduced here recently, with great success.

The line now climbs continuously due north through wild uplands, the 1,179-metre (3,868ft) **Roc de Peyre** visible to the west before **Aumont-Aubrac**. The Aubrac area, to the west, is volcanic and covered with woods or open pasture punctuated by rocks and stone walls. To the east is the granite mass of the Margeride. Soon after St-Chély d'Apcher, the train reaches the highest point on the line at 1,053 metres (3,454ft), then crosses the Truyère River on the line's *pièce de résistance*.

The **Garabit Viaduct** (see page 40) was built in 1884 and designed by Gustave Eiffel. The 448-metre/yd central section rests on a single arch carrying the railway 123 metres (405ft) above the river. In order to visit the viaduct, you must continue to St-Flour from where a special train runs in summer. **St-Flour** itself is a lovely village perched on top of a hill overlooking the River Ander, with a 15th-century Gothic cathedral dominating the site. The train crosses another harsh plateau before arriving at **Neussargues**, where it meets the line from Aurillac (see page 143) and joins the route from Nîmes (see page 139) at Arvant. It continues north into Clermont Ferrand.

CLERMONT FERRAND–LIMOGES/BRIVE–AURILLAC (CIRCUIT)

With some careful timetable reading, and much patience, it is possible to do a circular tour of two historic scenic regions of the Massif Central – the Auvergne and Limousin – spread over two or three days, involving changes of train. This route does the tour anti-clockwise but you can reverse it if that suits you better.

Depart from Clermont Ferrand station through the northern suburbs, not far from the Michelin factory. The train's first stop is the historic city of Riom, once a rival to Clermont Ferrand. The line travels northeast to the town of Gannat, a relative stone's throw from Vichy, then swings northwest and cuts across the last of the Massif Central uplands to reach **Montluçon**, on the Cher River, which is dominated by the chateau of the Dukes of Bourbon.

From here, take the line west into the Limousin region that is renowned for its chestnut-coloured beef cattle. The route meanders across farmland, stopping at small village stations, and with views of various chateaux, ruined or preserved. There are not many stops worth making except **Moutier d'Ahun,** which is regarded as one of the prettiest villages in France and also has an

Garabit Viaduct, spanning the Truyère.

Essentials

European Rail timetable
nos. 329, 303, 310, 311
and 331

Stages:

1) Clermont–Ferrand to
Monluçon 108km (67
miles), 1hr 40 mins, 4
trains daily

2) Montluçon to Limoges,
156km (97 miles), 2
hours, 2 direct trains
daily

3) Limoges to Brive 99km
(62 miles), 1hr 20mns, 16
trains daily

4) Brive –Aurillac 102km
(63 miles), 1hr 40mins,
4-5 trains daily

5) Aurillac–Clermont
Ferrand 168km (104
miles), 2hrs 20 mins, 6-8
trains daily

Turenne, Corréze.

abbey with famous 17th-century wood sculptures.

The main halt on this line is **Gueret**. Although the capital city of the Creuse *département*, it has less than 14,000 inhabitants, which gives an idea of how sparsely populated this part of France is. Just outside of Gueret there is what claims to be the biggest permanent hedge maze in the world, with 4.5km (2.5 miles) of paths to get lost on.

If you want to break the next part of the journey, get off at Marsac and visit the nearby town of **Bénévent-l'Abbaye** which, as its name suggests, is built around a 12th-century abbey church.

After skirting around the edge of the Monts d'Ambazac the train draws into Limoges-Bénédictins station. **Limoges** is a historic city renowned for its porcelain and enamel (displayed in two fine museums that are well worth taking time to visit). The station is north of the city centre and the main sights, especially the cathedral, are an easy walk away.

The Paris–Toulouse main line whips through Limoges and takes you swiftly south first to **Uzerche**, where a heritage walking tour takes you to the abbey church and various other ancient buildings. The next stop, where you need to change trains, is Brive-en-Gaillard.

Brive-la-Gaillarde is the largest town in the Corrèze *département*, a centre for the local fruit and vegetable industry and home to a strong rugby team. There are many local trips to be made from this busy centre, the most striking, perhaps, to the village of **Collonges-la-Rouge** – the suffix refers to the local red sandstone which brings harmony to this picture-book village.

There is a scenic railway line from Brive back to Clermont Ferrand but for some years a section of it has been cut and you can only take the train as far as Ussel, passing through a gorge of the River Correze to get there. From Ussel the journey continues by bus.

BACK TO CLERMONT FERRAND

The return to Clermont starts off due south, the line cutting through a ridge in a tunnel before following the River Tourmente. The station at **Turenne** lies

some distance from the ancient village, crowned by a ruined castle; this was once the fiefdom of Huguenot Henri de la Tour d'Auvergne. After **St-Denis-lès-Martel**, a three-way junction, the line to Aurillac turns due east, following the wide valley of the Dordogne, and past **Bretenoux-Biars** it plunges into the narrow Cère Valley, criss-crossing the river through the gorge to reach **Laroquebrou**.

At **Aurillac** another change of train is necessary; this large town has an historic centre but it mostly serves as a hub for visitors exploring the surrounding countryside. The railway twists through the town then runs along the foot of the Monts du Cantal. At **Polminhac**, a castle dominates the village and **Vic-sur-Cère**, with its spring and waterfall, has many picturesque old houses. From here, the Cère Valley again closes in and the scenery becomes increasingly spectacular, with the Puy Griou and Puy Mary to the north and 1,858-metre (6,096ft) Plomb du Cantal to the south. **Le Lioran** is a modern ski resort at over 1,100 metres (3,600ft). From here the train follow the gorge of the Alagnon, amid thick pine forests. The gorge opens out from **Murat** to **Neussargues** then closes in again and the line follows it to **Lempdes**. At the miniscule **Arvant**, the branch joins the main line from Nîmes and the train heads north to reach Clermont Ferrand. An option for a last stop for sightseeing is Issoire, with a renowned 12th–century Romanesque abbey church.

MARSEILLE–GRENOBLE–GENEVA

Enjoying the wonderful Alpine scenery on the Marseille–Geneva route was once an easier proposition than it is today; since the inception of the TGV Mediterranean line, direct services between the two cities now only operate over high-speed lines via Lyon. To follow the old route via St-Auban and Grenoble involves two changes of train, at Veynes and Grenoble, but this scenic line makes it worth the effort.

The train takes the same route between Marseille and St-Auban as the return from Digne (see page 150), following the Durance Valley for much of the way. The valley narrows in the Défilé de Mirabeau then opens out again before arriving at **Manosque**, with its attractive old centre. **Sisteron** is situated in a remarkable defile cut by the Durance through a mountain ridge, and is dominated by a citadel to the west and a chapel to the east. Settlement here dates back 4,000 years. From Sisteron, the railway branches northwest along the Buëch Valley, where the landscape becomes increasingly rocky – the village of **Serres** is a lovely sight with its colourful houses clustered around the Pignolette rock peak. Alight at Veynes and wait for the Grenoble train.

VEYNES TO GRENOBLE

From Veynes the train turns north to **Aspres-sur-Buëch**, then starts

Grenoble cable cars.

⊙ Essentials

European Rail timetable
nos. 362/364

Distance:

(1) Marseille–Veynes
206km (128 miles)

(2) Veynes–Grenoble
109km (68 miles)

(3) Grenoble–Geneva
165km (103 miles)

Duration of journey:

(1) 3 hrs 5 mins

(2) 2hr 10mins

(3) 2 hrs 15 mins

Frequency of trains:

(1) 3–4 daily

(2) 6 daily

(3) 2 daily

Swimming in Lac du Bourget.

to climb along the narrowing Grand Buëch Valley following the river and main road as the mountains become increasingly wild and grandiose. At **La Rochette**, a ridge cut into teeth by erosion juts into the valley and the remains of a feudal castle can be seen to the east. At **Lus-la-Croix-Haute**, the landscape opens out into an amphitheatre of rolling alpine country surrounded by peaks, and to the the northwest is the astonishing **Mont Aiguille**, a flat-topped mountain towering to 2,086 metres (6,843ft), where climbers, possibly under the influence of local mushrooms, have claimed to see angels' clothes. From Lus the line makes the last climb to the pass at **Col de la Croix Haute** (1,167 metres/3,828ft), past houses built to withstand severe weather. Snow fences are increasingly evident. After the tunnel, the line descends gradually, hugging the mountain slopes above a profound valley. This opens out to reveal an alpine plain studded with glacial *roches moutonées*.

More amazing views of the Mont Aiguille are to be had at **Clelles-Mens**, then the train crosses to the other side of a depression at **Monestier-de-Clermont**. The line slowly descends the mountainside and follows a double loop in order to drop quickly to **Vif** before arriving at **St-Georges-de-Commiers**, where the **Chemin de Fer de La Mure** begins.

The industrial suburbs we pass next means we are coming into **Grenoble**, a high-tech city with a superb location at the foot of the Chartreuse mountains where the Drac and Isère rivers meet. The best way to see the city is to take the bubble-like cable cars from the old town across the river to the Fort de la Bastille, 500 metres (1,540ft) up the mountainside. The city has an excellent modern art museum and it is possible to visit the home of the writer, Stendhal (1783–1842), who was born in the city.

NORTH TO GENEVA

The Geneva-bound train out of Grenoble follows the Isère Valley northwards between the Chartreuse mountains to the west and the Belledonne chain to the east. This corridor, known as Grésivaudan, was cut by a glacier and is sheltered enough to be a major fruit growing area. As the line turns west at Montmélian, it passes vineyards producing the local Chignin white and Mondeuse red wine, before arriving in **Chambéry**, the old capital of Savoie, a region that once extended well into the Italian Alps. The old town includes a 15th-century cathedral and an 18th-century castle. Following the valley, the train arrives at **Aix-les-Bains**, a spa town dating back to Roman times, with one cold and two hot springs. A few Roman remains can be seen, as can elegant hotels from the 19th-century boom in health cures.

Aix lies on the shore of the **Lac du Bourget**, which the train now skirts. On the opposite shore stands the

Abbaye de Hautecombe, where 42 of the Savoie royal family are buried. Usually calm, France's biggest and deepest inland lake can become very stormy. Above the lake stretches a wild upland area, the Bugey, where lynx, originating from Switzerland, are successfully re-establishing themselves.

At Culoz, the line crosses the Rhône then joins its valley and heads north towards Switzerland. After the industrial town of Bellegarde, at the exit to a tunnel, the river and railway push between the Montagne du Grand Colombier to the west and the Montagne du Gros Foug to the east before the landscape opens out as the line enters Switzerland. Geneva itself, birthplace of Calvinism, sits in a superb site between mountains and lake, where the city's symbol, the Jet d'Eau fountain, the highest in the world, springs 145 metres (476ft) into the air. The city has a wide variety of old and new buildings, world-class museums and enough lakeside parks to rest the weariest traveller after this long journey.

CHEMIN DE FER DE LA MURE

The La Mure metre-gauge railway was opened in 1888 to carry anthracite from the mines around La Mure to the standard-gauge line at St-Georges-de-Commiers. The line follows a tortuous route (the two villages are 16km/10 miles apart as the crow flies; the track runs for almost twice that distance) of tight curves, viaducts and tunnels, and became a tourist attraction after the last mine closed in 1988. From St-Georges, there is a steep ascent to 875 metres (2,870ft). After Notre-Dame-de-Commiers, the line hugs the mountainside with a splendid view over Lac de Monteynard, some 300 metres (1,000ft) below, formed by damming the River Drac. Above the lake, the train makes a stop to allow passengers to admire the breath-taking view.

The line then turns north and climbs by means of loops, including two parallel viaducts on different levels at Loulla. After a halt at La Motte d'Aveillans station, where a museum of bee-keeping has been established, is the 'tunnel mystérieux' where pictures projected by lanterns on the tunnel wall describe the work of the now-closed coal mines. Finally, before the descent to La Mure, La Pierre Percée, a rock through which a hole has been cut by erosion, is visible to the north.

Sadly in October 2010, a huge landslide destroyed parts of the line at La Mure. Thankfully, no-one was killed, but the railway was closed indefinitely. In 2017, however, it was announced that it would re-open in 2020, after extensive repairs. For more information, see www.trainlamure.com.

MARSEILLE–NICE–MONACO

The writer Somerset Maugham once called the French Riviera a 'shady place for shady people' and nowhere is this more true than at Marseille's St-Charles station. The blue riband TGV

Marseille St-Charles railway station.

⊙ Essentials

European Rail timetable no. 360

Distance: 241km (150 miles)

Duration of journey:
2 hrs 40 mins (Marseille–Nice), 20 mins (Nice–Monaco)

Frequency of trains:
18 per day to Nice; numerous local trains operate between Nice and Monaco

Train on the Corniche de l'Esterel.

extension line may cater for journey times from Paris to Marseille of just three hours, but the station remains a raffish affair – colourful, vibrant, but still on the shady side.

HILLS AND FISHING VILLAGES

After leaving the suburbs, the train passes through **Aubagne**. The countryside around here was made famous by Marcel Pagnol, whose books *Jean de Florette* and *Manon des Sources* were turned into successful films. The train turns south to **Cassis**, a beautiful little fishing port (2km/1 mile from the station), once popular with artists such as Matisse and Dufy. The limestone coast to the west is cut with superb coves known as *calanques*, popular with hikers, divers and rock climbers.

A few minutes later, the train arrives at **La Ciotat station**, where the Lumière brothers, pioneers of cinema, made one of the first motion pictures (of a train arriving) in 1895. The coast is now fleetingly in view as we pass through **St-Cyr-sur-Mer**, where a 1st-century AD Roman villa has been turned into

a museum, and **Bandol**, an attractiv port frequented by writers Thoma Mann and Katherine Mansfield in th early 20th century. Both the Cassis an Bandol areas produce good wine.

After a glimpse of the fort at **L Seyne**, the train reaches **Toulor** France's premier military port, situ ated on a fine natural harbour. Whil the rocky coast stretches eastward to such famous places as St-Tropez the railway now turns inland toward the rugged, forested mountain range of the Massif des Maures, follow ing a wide valley full of olive groves fruit trees and vines. These produc Côteaux Varois and Côtes de Provenc wines, for which the village of **Les Arc** is the centre, while **Gonfaron** produce corks. The Massif itself is composed c oddly-shaped, orange-hued hills, dr and dusty in comparison to the spir of the Maritime Alps that runs furthe to the north. The Massif looks mor like the landscape of the Grand Can yon than anything else on the Frenc Riviera, with thinly-forested slope only heightening the barren feel of th landscape.

ALONG THE CORNICHE

The twin resort towns of Fréjus an St-Raphaël bring respite from th harshness of the hinterland, paint ing the archetypal Riviera scene c bronzed bodies lazing across th sands, seas of parasols as far as th eye can see, with swathes of pave ment cafés lining the streets. Lik many of the towns in this part c France, though, a richer past is bur ied beneath the tourist gloss of toda **Fréjus** was settled by the Massiliot before Julius Caesar's men swep into town in 49 BC, leaving behin extensive ruins. The old Roman por is now occupied by the gardens see shortly after the station, with remain of the town walls, an arena, an aque duct and a theatre, glimpsed jus before the station.

Fréjus's beach leads to **St-Raphaël**, a modern resort with a wide, sandy beach. The most eventful period of St-Raphaël's history occurred during World War II, when this was one of the main landing beaches for Allied troops, in August 1944. Today the jumble of wartime wrecks is very popular with scuba divers, with the highlight being the well-preserved American minesweeper that lies just off the St-Raphaël coastline.

The railway hugs the coast east of St-Raphaël, giving superb views along the **Corniche de l'Esterel** at every twist and turn, as well as inland, where the **Massif de l'Esterel** is formed of pink rock partially covered with *maquis*, cork-oaks and pines. At **Agay** and **Anthéor**, viaducts curve round bays, giving plunging views of sandy beaches. After passing a series of creeks, the line heads through a tunnel to reach **Théoule-sur-Mer**, a small resort at the start of the Golfe de la Napoule – the Bay of Cannes.

FESTIVAL CENTRES

Cannes is a superb resort, famous for its film festival each spring. A walk along the Boulevard de la Croisette is a must, for its elegant hotels, restaurants, boutiques and luxurious cars. But do not miss the old port, the superb villas and the view from the Cap de la Croisette. The railway continues along the coast, now largely built up, but with some excellent views of the sea, through the legendary names of **Juan-les-Pins**, famous for its jazz festival, and **Antibes**, which has conserved an historic old town and fort as well as hosting a museum devoted to Picasso in the old Château Grimaldi, visible from the station.

From Antibes, the railway skirts the long, straight beach before reaching **Cagnes-sur-Mer**, a long-established artists' colony; one of its most famous residents was Renoir, whose home, just east of the town, is now a museum.

Nice dates from Greek occupation, four centuries before Christ, and has a wonderful array of attractions – Roman remains, no fewer than six art museums, a wonderful market and enough other sights and sounds to occupy several days.

The city makes a great base for exploring the region as it is well-equipped with hotels in all price ranges as well as tour companies, car hire firms and large shops. The pebble beach may not be as impressive as some others on the French Riviera, but a stroll along the **Promenade des Anglais** at sunset is still a quintessential Riviera experience. Nice was once home to many of Europe's finest modern artists with such luminaries as Marc Chagall, Henri Matisse and Pablo Picasso flocking here to seek inspiration from the unique qualities of the local light. Today their legacy lingers in the cluster of first-rate art galleries in town, making a stop here essential

Seafront at Nice.

A Chemins de Fer de la Provence train in Digne-les-Bains.

Porte Royale, entrance to Entrevaux.

for anyone with even a passing interest in art.

Rail buffs are well catered for, too, with Les Chemins de Fer de la Provence offering a popular day trip from Nice, with two-carriage diesel trains leaving the Gare du Sud bound for the Provençal town of Digne-les-Bains (see page 150).

MILLIONAIRES' ROW

It is only a short journey up the line to the principality of **Monte Carlo**, with its glittering capital of **Monaco**. This glamorous oasis for Europe's rich and famous offers a tax-free haven for those who can afford the high cost of living. The state-of-the-art rail terminal feels more like a slick airport than a railway station, but it is well worth leaving the train and spending a day in this enclave. Accommodation is expensive, and almost impossible to find during the annual Grand Prix, but there are plenty of inexpensive places to eat along the seafront, where the most popular pastimes are people-watching and posing. The best view

of Monaco is from the terrace of the Grimaldi Palace, which rests on a steep promontory to the west of the main city. One unusual attraction is the public swimming pool, which is open to visitors. It is one of the few egalitarian places in town where it is difficult to differentiate between cash-strapped backpackers and the ultra-rich residents of one of the world's wealthiest playgrounds.

NICE–DIGNE-LES-BAINS: TRAIN DES PIGNES

The magnificent Nice–Digne-les-Bains line is one of the few remaining metre-gauge railway lines in France. It is also one of even fewer that is privately operated, by the appropriately named Chemins de Fer de la Provence (CP). Trains leave from the unassuming modern CP station, 10 minutes' walk north from Nice Ville.

NICE TO ENTREVAUX

The CP train clatters out of Nice, snaking between buildings and stopping at traffic lights guarding level crossings before climbing through pretty suburbs until it turns north after **Lingostière** to reach the valley of the River Var. The line then works its way northwards for 20km (12 miles) between the wide, stony Var and a dual carriageway, serving shopping centres and dormitory villages. After **St-Martin-du-Var**, the valley starts to close in, and after **La Vésubie**, the line crosses the river from the deep Gorge de la Vésubie and enters the equally deep **Défilé de Chaudan** with the surrounding crags becoming increasingly dramatic. Next there is a long tunnel, then the line turns northwest, still following the Var, with remarkable rock strata in view.

Villages cluster on the steep valley sides; one of them is **Villars-sur-Var**, a haven of peace (because cars are banned) surrounded by vineyards. Ten minutes later, we come to

Touët-sur-Var, a tiny village hugging a rock face, where the church is built on an arch over a torrent. Touët is also the starting point for exploration of the monumental **Gorges du Cians** to the north.

About 10 minutes from Touët is **Puget-Théniers**, an important market centre, where an attractive old town hides behind the less appealing modern district. A joyous statue of a plump nude – *L'Action Enchaînée* – caused a conflict between church and anti-clerical opinion. Dedicated to the revolutionary, Blanqui, the statue had to be removed from its place in full view of the church after protests from clerics. Puget-Théniers is the starting point for the **Train des Pignes** steam (see box below).

After a further five minutes, the train arrives at the delightful village of **Entrevaux**, which huddles at the foot of a rock in a meander of the Var. On top stands a citadel, perched 156 metres (512ft) above the town and reached via a slope that zigzags 800 metres (2,624ft) up the rock face, passing through no fewer than 20 gates on the way.

FLOOD DAMAGE

Back on the train, the line continues to follow the Var. The river was almost the undoing of the CP in 1994, when violent floods washed much of the railway embankment and even a major bridge away. Repairs were certainly not justified on economic grounds alone but it is a vital lifeline to many villages. Reconstruction took a whole year. A few minutes from Entrevaux, the line turns southwest to thread the narrow valley of the Coulomp, which joins the Var at Pont de Gueydan where the view is now ruined by quarry workings. Around this point olive groves start to give way to hay meadows and stands of sweet chestnuts, as the climate becomes harsher. After exiting a short tunnel, the train passes the **Pont de la Reine Jeanne** to the south, a bridge dating back to Roman times but rebuilt after floods in 1682.

After another five minutes we arrive in **Annot**, a village surrounded by

⊘ Essentials

European Rail timetable no. 359

Distance: 166km (103 miles)

Duration of journey: 3hrs 15 mins

Frequency of trains: 4 per day

See: tourisme. trainprovence.com

Le Train des Pignes, alongside the Var river.

⊘ SUMMER STEAM

Puget-Théniers is the starting point for steam train trips to Annot. It was steam that gave the line its name. Pignes means pine cones in Occitan and it is said that these replaced coal as fuel when times were hard.

A non-profit-making association now operates steam trains on summer weekends from May to the end of October along the most scenic part of the line. There are connections by modern trains from Nice.

Trains are formed of restored coaches dating back to between 1888 and 1912. They are pulled by a black E-211 locomotive, an unusual 'Mallet' 2-4-0 + 0-6-0 tank designed to provide good traction on mountain lines.

The association offers apprenticeships for would-be train drivers. For more information see www.gecp.asso.fr and www.traindes-pignes.com

enormous sandstone outcrops. The line now starts to climb even more steeply, needing two horseshoe curves to gain height near **Le Fugeret**. To the east, the line passes **Méailles**, a village just visible on a limestone outcrop known for its caverns, then cuts through the mountain in a long tunnel and turns southwest along the Verdon Valley. **St-André-les-Alpes** is situated between peaks at the north end of the Lac de Castillon, just visible to the south, a lake created behind a dam in 1947 in order to tame the wild Verdon River.

ALONG THE ROUTE NAPOLÉON

At Barrême the line joins the Asse Valley and the N85 road, better known as the **Route Napoléon**, which comes up from the southeast. This was the route taken by Napoléon (avoiding the Rhône Valley) as he marched north after his escape from the Isle of Elba on 1 March 1815.

Barrême station itself contains an interesting exhibition of fossils, reflecting the fact that the mountains to the west are a geological reserve. The train now snakes between outcrops of

limestone at the Clue de Chabrières, then reaches journey's end at **Digne-les-Bains**. As its name proclaims, Digne is a spa town, beautifully located at the confluence of three valleys in an area famous for its pungent lavender. The town has retained the elegance of a spa resort.

Although plans exist to extend the CP line to meet the Marseille–Veynes SNCF line at Château-Arnoux-St-Auban, it hasn't happened yet, so at present a bus ride is necessary. Nice–Digne–Marseille–Nice circuits (also Nice–Marseille–Digne–Nice) are possible in summer – in winter there are fewer trains running between Marseille and St-Auban.

ST AUBAN TO MARSEILLE

If you don't want to return to Nice from Dignes-les-Bains, an alternative is to take a bus to the SNCF station at Chateau-Arnoux- St-Auban and take the train either to Marseille or to Grenoble, following the previous route. Heading south, the SNCF line follows the wide valley of the River Durance for 45 minutes. The Durance has been systematically dammed and tapped to irrigate local orchards, with canals branching off at several points. After crossing the river on a long bridge just before Meyrargues, the line cuts through a forest then nears Aix-en-Provence with the Montagne Ste-Victoire, often painted by Cézanne, omnipresent to the east.

Aix-en-Provence dates back to the third century BC and was once the capital of Provence. Aix has retained much of the elegance of the past in its avenues, fountains and buildings, and is now classed a World Heritage Site by Unesco. The city has such a collection of beautiful buildings, squares and museums that half a day at least is required to explore all of its corners.

The train now becomes a suburban commuter shuttle, trundling through the altogether different industrial town of Gardanne before descending slowly

The Mount Blanc Express.

but surely through the rather ugly northern suburbs of Marseille.

AROUND MONT BLANC

SNCF mainline services from Lyon and Paris reach St-Gervais-les-Bains, a health spa and ski resort at the foot of Mont Blanc, giving access to three beautiful lines at the heart of the Alps. Fantastic scenery on all three is a given.

THE WORLD'S STEEPEST RAILWAY

The metre-gauge Ligne de Savoie was built by the Paris-Lyon-Méditerranée railway to reach Chamonix in 1901 and was then extended to Argentière and – passing under the Aiguille Rouge mountain range via a tunnel to reach Le Buet – Vallorcine. At Vallorcine, on the Swiss border, it meets the Martigny-Châtelard railway (MC) end on and, some services run all the way from St-Gervais-les-Bains to Martigny. The best way to travel this line is on the Mont Blanc Express, which has observation cars to maximise the views.

The line leaves St-Gervais, passing an ugly aluminium plant before climbing steeply from Chedde to Servoz, where it gains 381 metres (1,250ft) in height in only 9km (5 miles). This necessitates a 1 in 11 gradient – the steepest in the world worked by trains without rack equipment (while the Swiss part relies on racks to help climb the steep gradients, the SNCF does not). On this section, the little train is dwarfed by a massive but elegant motorway viaduct that takes traffic through the Mont Blanc road tunnel into Italy. The line then follows the pretty Arve Valley between towering mountains to Chamonix. At Les Bossons, the Bossons glacier can be seen to the south as it reaches right down to the roadside.

One of the world's foremost mountaineering centres, **Chamonix** itself is a pleasant town nestling in the valley and is the point from which travellers can experience another world record – the world's highest cable car, which at times hangs 500 metres (1,640ft) above ground on its way to the Aiguille du Midi, a 3,842-metre (12,600ft) peak extending the Mont Blanc range. It is also the terminal for the Chamonix-Montenvers line.

The Mont Blanc Express continues to Martigny, following the Trient valley. On the way it crosses the Swiss border and passes through wild gorges, beside silent forests and beneath towering peaks.

One popular way to extend this excursion is to continue from Martigny along the shores of Lac Léman (Lake Geneva) through Montreux and Lausanne to Geneva (see page 145). From Geneva's Eaux Vives station, it is possible to return to St-Gervais on an SNCF service.

TRAMWAY DU MONT-BLANC

Cross the station forecourt at St-Gervais-les-Bains and you are at the start of the Tramway du Mont Blanc (TMB). This is France's highest railway, climbing from 584 metres (1,916ft) to the

⊘ Essentials

European Rail timetables nos. 572/397

Mont Blanc Express: www.mont-blanc-express.com

Tramway du Mont-Blanc and Montenvers/Mer de Glace: www.montblancnaturalresort.com

Climbers on Mount Blanc.

Nid d'Aigle (Eagle's Nest) terminus at 2,372 metres (7,782ft). The line first runs through the streets of **Le Fayet**, a spa resort where people still come to take the waters at the famous baths. The line then becomes a true rack railway, the cogs on the small electric train engaging in the teeth of the rail between the tracks.

The line traverses a wood and emerges onto alpine meadows where the air is full of jangling cow bells. From Bellevue station, over the final 2km (1 mile), the line climbs 600 metres (1,970ft) along narrow ledges and through tunnels hewn in the rock. The Nid d'Aigle terminus was reached in 1914; it was meant to be temporary, but the funds were never found to continue to the Bionnassay glacier on the north face of Mont Blanc and the Aiguille du Gouter, just under the summit. For now, the only solution is to continue on foot. You can, should you wish, hike back down to Bellevue station. Note that you should always keep to marked trails and it is forbidden to walk along or even near the tram rails. Do not, of course, walk anywhere in the Alps if the weather is bad or if you are not properly equipped or you are uncertain of your ability to negotiate a particular route.

CHAMONIX–MONTENVERS

Just over the footbridge from Chamonix station is the terminus of the Montenvers line, whose little red trains climb from the base station at 1,042 metres (3,417ft) to the terminus at **Montenvers** (1,913 metres/6,275ft). This rack rail line, built in 1909, climbs through forests, two major tunnels and innumerable avalanche shelters that allow it to operate all year round. There are departures every 30 minutes most days and the journey takes around 20 minutes.

At the top there are tremendous views over the 200-metre (660-ft) thick **Mer de Glace**, a vast sea of ice where the Leschaux, Tacul and Talefre glaciers meet to form the second biggest glacier in the Alps. The ice slides downhill at a rate of just over 8mm per hour. A cable car carries passengers from the station down to the edge of the ice from where a tunnel has been cut into the glacier. It is an enjoyable hour-long walk back to Chamonix from here.

ROUTES IN THE FRENCH PYRENEES

Main lines cross the border on at either end of the Pyrenees. In the east you can now travel at high speed between Perpignan and Figures but you won't see anything of the mountains. To best enjoy scenery from a train window you need to go inland. Two options are covered here. Another idea is to take the train from Toulouse to Latour-de-Carol (see page 154). A promising prospect for the future is to travel on the magnificent Pau to Canfranc line, which runs up a beautiful valley the middle of the range to a tunnel crossing the frontier. It was closed by an accident in 1970 and is currently only open as far as Bedous but there are plans to reopen the whole thing one day.

Eastern Pyrenees

LA RHUNE

La Rhune, the westernmost peak of the Pyrenees, can be ascended by an old-fashioned cog railway that sets off from a mountain pass, the Col de St-Ignace (169 metres/554ft), between Ascain and Sare. The lower station is connected by bus with St-Jean-de-Luz on the coastal main line.

An alternative to the round trip is to take the train to the top of the mountain and follow the marked footpath down (allow at least two hours). Either way, wear warm clothing as the train doesn't have glass in the windows and conditions on the mountaintop can be changeable.

The four wooden trains are shunted up 25-percent (1-in-4) inclines by an electric locomotive. The trip takes about 35 minutes each way, with the train jerking along at only 8kmh (5mph). The first part of the route is an abrupt ascent, pushing you back into your seat. Half way up the mountain the track levels, divides to let trains cross and goes into another steep incline, passing the tree line to reach the summit. On the way up you have good views back over the French countryside and towards the resorts of the Atlantic coast. The slopes beside the track are grazed by wild ponies, and vultures can often be seen soaring above.

The summit of La Rhune (905metres/2,969ft) is a curious no-man's land. You disembark from a French railway, climb some steps and arrive at three Spanish bar-restaurant-souvenir shops after crossing an invisible international frontier. On a clear day you have a 360-degree view from here, stretching to horizons some 100km (60 miles) away and taking in a large sweep of the Basque Country.

LE TRAIN JAUNE

Le Train Jaune (the Yellow Train) runs along 63km (39 miles) of narrow-gauge track from Villefranche-de-Conflent (connected by bus to Perpignan) to Latour-de-Carol on the Pyrenean plateau of the Cerdagne. There are three through trains all year plus extra services to Fort Roman in July and August.

◷ Essentials

www.rhune.com

Distance: 4.2km (3 miles)

Duration of journey: 35 minutes (allow two hours for the return trip)

Frequency of trains: varies with demand; every 40 mins average

La Rhune cog railway.

⏱ Essentials

European Rail timetable no. 354

Distance: 63km (39 miles)

Duration of journey: 3hrs

Frequency of trains: 4–5 per day (June–Sept); 2–3 per day rest of the year. Bus replacement frequent in winter

Most of the 20 stations en route are request stops *(arrêts facultatifs)* but they are only worth getting off at if you intend to go hiking. Mont Louis is a good place to wait for a return train if you are travelling with children and don't want to go too far. Continuing to the less interesting Bourg-Madame, however, gives you an opportunity to see more of the Cerdagne countryside. It's only really worth going on to Latour de Carol, an international station with three gauges of rail (French, Spanish and the Yellow Train's narrow-gauge), if you are a real train buff. The best views are to be had from the open carriage, which kids love, but on busy summer days you need to arrive at Villefranche early in order to get a place and you should be armed with plenty of suncream and a hat.

The first part of the route is up the steep-sided Têt Valley. Shortly after **Thuès-les-Bains** station you will see below you the spa of the same name which has the hottest naturally-heated waters in France (over 80°C/175°F). Pulling out of the next station, Thuès-Carança, look left for a glimpse of the picturesque **Gorges de la Carança**. A few minutes further on, the line strides across the Têt Valley on the granite Séjourné Viaduct. After Sauto station the train goes through a series of tunnels before crossing the Têt again by way of the **Gisclard Suspension Bridge**, which is 80 metres (262ft) high.

An hour out of Villefranche the train climbs out of the Têt Valley and onto the upland plateau of the Cerdagne. The landscape is suddenly quite different: forest and scrub give way to lush pastures filled with Pyrenean wild flowers. The next halt is **Mont-Louis-La Cabanasse**, protected by the highest fort in France. The line continues to climb and reaches its zenith at the inconspicuous **Bolquère-Eyne**. At 1,593 metres (5,226ft), this is the highest SNCF station in France. Leaving **Font-Romeu-Odeillo-Via** station you can see the back of the **Four Solaire d'Odeillo/Font-Romeu**, a solar oven powered by a bank of mirrors, that is used for scientific research.

Immediately after Estavar station there is a tight bend with views over **Llívia**, an island of Spanish territory marooned in France by an accident of history. The frontier town, **Bourg-Madame**, has little to offer except a walk over the River Rahur for coffee in the outskirts of its Spanish counterpart, Puigcerda. The train continues for 15 minutes to **Latour-de-Carol**, a route node at 1,231 metres (4,038ft) where lines of three different gauges meet. From here you can take a mainline train to either Toulouse or Barcelona.

CORSICA

Corsica's metre-gauge railways form a lopsided 'Y', with the branch from Calvi in the northwest meeting, at Ponte Leccia, the main line from Bastia in the northeast, to force a dramatic passage through the mountains to Ajaccio. The lines were built with immense difficulty – which is, of course, part of the reason for their appeal to travellers today: the

main line has 32 tunnels and 51 major bridges or viaducts, yet was built with a skill and speed that is a tribute to their 19th-century engineers.

State-sponsored construction began at various points between Bastia and Corte in 1883, opening five years later, and today's 232-km (145-mile) system was completed by 1894. Only one branch, running along the east coast from Casamozza near Bastia to Porto-Vecchio, was a protracted business, opened in stages from 1888 to 1935. Sadly, it was so badly damaged during World War II that it never reopened.

Apart from the modern diesel engines that operate all services, little has changed since construction: the station buildings are still mostly original, and even the water towers and columns for steam locomotives remain, almost half a century after the last whistle was heard.

The idiosyncratic delays to Corsica's trains described by some guidebooks are largely a thing of the past, and travelling by rail is an excellent way to gain an impression of the island and to visit some of its principal attractions. Even where a parallel road exists, it is generally at a lower level, with diminished views. During the summer months, trains are well patronised, and passengers should not arrive at the last minute expecting to get a seat.

BASTIA–CORTE

Located only a few minutes' walk from Place St-Nicolas, **Bastia** station is conveniently sited for a walk through the old streets around the harbour and the various places of interest within Terra Nova (or Citadelle). Once on the train, the passage through the suburbs and beside a busy dual carriageway is uninspiring, but once past the railway's workshops at **Casamozza**, the scenery improves dramatically as the railway swings west. It climbs through woods, rock cuttings and a series of short tunnels up the valley of the River Golo, crossing the crystal clear waters three

times on substantial viaducts, the first offering a glimpse of the picturesque remains of a Genoese bridge.

The characteristic location of Corsican villages soon becomes apparent: most were built high up on hillsides to escape the malarial mosquito (eliminated just after World War II), but were seldom positioned on the ridge itself. A well still stands beside the station at **Ponte Nuovo**, close to the bridge where Corsican nationalists were heavily defeated by the French in 1769.

On the approach to the island's only railway junction at **Ponte Leccia**, the train crosses the River Asco and runs alongside the Calvi line for the last 500 metres/yds into the station. An adventure tourism company occupies a redundant railway building, its clients often joining the train to reach one of the more remote stations in the mountains. From Ponte Leccia the valley broadens as the train presses south, with more signs of agriculture than on any other stretch of line, even if these are sometimes cows sheltering from the sun on the verandas of abandoned farmhouses or barns.

Open-air carriage on Le Train Jaune.

En route to Calvi.

The line soon starts to climb, and after **Francardo** the railway describes the first of many horseshoe-shaped loops. Ahead can be seen a viaduct at a higher level, giving a graphic idea of the gradient. The slopes are covered by the *maquis* for which the island is famous, an aromatic and varying mix of arbutus, heather, juniper, laburnum, lavender, myrtle and rosemary that gave its name to French resistance fighters during World War II (because they often hid out in such terrain). Remains of neglected terracing bear witness to the rural depopulation that has affected Corsica, while ruined towers are reminders of the centuries of Genoese rule. The line reaches its summit in a tunnel under the Col de San Quilico before dropping down to the old capital of **Corte**. It is less than 10 minutes' walk from the station up to the old town, and access by train obviates the struggle for parking space in a town disfigured by traffic in high season. The labyrinth of narrow streets and cobble-stepped alleys below the citadel is best explored on foot.

Pont du Vecchio, Corsica.

MOUNTAIN PARADISE

Leaving Corte, the climb resumes, affording wonderful views over unbroken forest as the train twists endlessly round a confusing series of loops and disorienting tunnels before arriving at the well-sited station at **Venaco**. Flying buttresses brace the arched stone walls of a deep cutting as the train briefly descends towards the **Pont du Vecchio**, the stone and steel girder bridge designed by Gustave Eiffel that spans the River Vecchio at a height of 80 metres (262ft). There is hardly time to appreciate the structure before the train dives into an unlined tunnel. Soon after emerging, the track ahead can be seen high up on the right, with the twin water towers at the station of **Vivario**; the line describes such an immense loop to reach it that a straight line between kilometre posts 91 and 98 measures just 200 metres (656ft).

There follows the most spectacular part of the journey as the train weaves a course through the mountains, with dizzying views down into the gorges of the Vecchio and Manganello

vers and over to Monte Rotondo
,622 metres/8,602ft) in the distance.
glimpse may be had of the extensive
emains of Fort de Pasciolo above the
ne. After **Savaggio** there is a long
ection of Larico pine woods and fern-
lled cuttings before the train reaches
attone, one of several places where
re crews are stationed in summer to
eal with the frequent forest fires.

The climb is over as the rail-
ay attains a summit of 906 metres
,974ft) at **Vizzavona** station, where
here is a restaurant and bar catering
or the many walkers who use the sta-
on. Immediately to the south the train
nters a dead straight tunnel, the long-
st on the system at 4km (2.5 miles).
he village at **Bocognano** can be seen
elow long before the train reaches
, and further ahead is a viaduct at a
uch lower level. Descending through
orests of chestnuts the railway joins
he valley of the River Gravona and fol-
ws it all the way to the sea and along
he front to the terminus at **Ajaccio**,
hich is the administrative centre of
he southern département of Corsica.
he town is famous as the birthplace
f Napoleon Bonaparte in 1769, and his
amily home is open to visitors.

ONTE LECCIA–CALVI

part from the two trains a day that run
he entire stretch of line, there is also an
lmost-hourly summer service between
alvi and Ile Rousse to serve the resorts
nd beaches along the coast. Leaving
he junction at Ponte Leccia the rail-
ay turns away from the Bastia line
nd follows the Navaccia Valley through
arren, sandstone countryside almost
evoid of habitation or trees. Although
till operating, the station at **Pietralba**
natches the terrain in its dereliction.
nce through the summit tunnel there
s a magnificent view across to **Novella**
tation, which has been converted into
 gîte, and the terraces around the vil-
age. The line passes the derelict station
uilding at **Palasca** and through a deep

rock cutting towards the strangely-
named station of **PK79 + 800** where
extensive views open up over the coastal
plain and its occasional splashes of irri-
gated green in summer. Emerging from
one of the many rock cuttings, there is
a panorama over the sea and the popular resort of **Ile Rousse**, named after
the causeway-linked island that glows
red in the evening sun. The train runs
beside the beach, past the old town
and through the old wall to the station.
From here to Calvi the line is seldom out
of sight of the sea, as the train rattles
around the headlands and past the tiny
beach-side halts served by the 'Tramway de Balagne' railcars. Corsican
pines fringe the beaches and shelter
the many campsites to the south of the
railway. A glimpse can be had of the
Foreign Legion base at Camp Rafelli
opposite **Calenzana-Lumio**.

Passing hundreds of sizzling, sun-
soaked bodies, the train runs past the
sands towards the distinctive outline of
the Genoese-built citadel around which
huddles the station and lovely old town
of **Calvi**.

⊘ Essentials

European Rail timetable
no. 369

www.cf-corse.corsica

Distance:

(1) Bastia–Corte
152km (94 miles)

(2) Ponte Leccia–Calvi
73km (45 miles)

Duration of journey:

(1) 3 hrs 45 mins

(2) 1 hr 45 mins

Frequency of trains:

(1) 4 per day

(2) 2 per day

*Algajola beach, near
Calvi.*

MUSEUMS AND HERITAGE LINES

France has around 40 preserved railway lines operated mainly by associations of volunteers using a variety of rehabilitated rolling stock. Most are open in summer only. The numbers relate to the map on page 132. A novel experience is to explore a disused line by velorail – a pedal powered vehicle (see www.veloraildefrance.com for details).

MUSEUMS

Cité du Train – Musée Français du Chemin de Fer ❶
2 rue Alfred de Glehn, Mulhouse
Open: daily 10am–6pm; Oct–Mar closes 5pm
Restaurant, shop
Features: France's national railway museum, claimed to be the largest rail museum in Europe.
Nearest station: Mulhouse Ville
Tel: 03 89 42 83 33
www.citedutrain.com

Musée du Chemin de Fer de Longueville ❷
AJECTA, Dépôt des Machines, Rue Louis Platriez, Longueville
Open: May–Oct 10am–6pm, Oct–Apr 1–6pm.
Features: museum in old roundhouse depot, 1 hour from Paris; open day with live steam in mid-September
Nearest station: Longueville
Tel: 01 64 60 26 26
www.ajecta.org

HERITAGE LINES

Chemin de Fer de la Baie de Somme ❸
La Gare, BP 80031, 80230 St-Valéry-sur-Somme (Noyelles-sur-Mer–Le Crotoy, Noyelles-sur-Mer–Cayeux-sur-Mer)
Features: shop, coastal views, nature reserve
Nearest station: Noyelles-sur-Mer
Length: 27km (17 miles)
Open: Apr–Sept daily; Feb–Mar & Oct–Nov weekends
Gauge: 1,000mm (3ft 3 3/8in)
Tel: 03 22 26 96 96
www.cfbs.eu

Chemin de Fer du Vivarais ❹
Avenue de la Gare Tournon-sur-Rhone (Tournon–Lamastre)
Café, shop at Lamastre
Features: superb gorge scenery
Nearest station: Tain l'Hermitage (20 minutes' walk)
Length: 33km (20 miles)
Open: May–Sept daily; Mar–Apr & Oct–Nov check times
Gauge: 1,000mm (3ft 3 3/8in)
Tel: 04 75 08 20 30
www.trainardeche.fr

Chemin de Fer Forestier d'Abreschviller ❺
2 Place Prévot, Abreschviller (Abreschviller–Grand Soldat)
Souvenir shop
Features: steam, forest scenery
Nearest station: Sarrebourg
Length: 6km (4 miles)
Open: July–Aug daily; Apr–Oct most weekends
Gauge: 700mm (2ft 3 9/16in)
Tel: 03 87 03 71 45
www.train-abreschviller.fr

Chemin de Fer Touristique de la Vallee de l'Aa ❻
CFTVA, 3 rue des Cuvelots, Bayenghem-les-Seninghem (Arques–Lumbres)
Café, restaurant
Features: access to canal boat lift and V2 rocket museum
Nearest station: St-Omer
Length: 15km (9 miles)
Open: Apr–Oct various weekends but not all & holidays
Gauge: Standard
Tel: 03 21 93 45 46
www.cftva62.com

Chemin de Fer Touristique du Rhin ❼
26 rue des Cordiers, Andolsheim (Volgelsheim–Sans Souci)
Features: line along River Rhine, possible boat trips
Nearest station: Colmar
Length: 12km (7.5 miles)
Open: May–June & Oct Sun; July–Sept Sat–Sun
Gauge: Standard
Tel: 03 89 71 51 42
www.ried-express-cftr.fr

Chemin de Fer Touristique du Vermandois ❽
St Quentin (St-Quentin–Origny Ste-Benoîte)
Restaurant car
Features: cathedral town, valley scenery
Nearest station: St-Quentin
Length: 23km (14 miles)
Open: Mar–Dec selected weekends
Gauge: Standard
Tel: 03 23 64 88 38
www.cftv.fr

Petit Train d'Artouste ❾
Adminstrative office, Avenue Messier, Iseste (La Sagette–Lac d'Artouste)
Shops, restaurant, cafés
Features: climb through Pyrenees to mountain lake; highest panorama in Europe at over 2,000 metres (6,500ft)
Nearest station: Pau (38km/24 miles)
Length: 9km (6 miles)
Open: mid-May–mid -Sept daily
Gauge: 500mm (1ft 7 11/16in)
Tel: 05 59 05 36 99
www.train-artouste.com

Petit Train de la Haute Somme ❿
APPEVA, Amiens
(Froissy–Dompierre)
Shop, bar
Features: steam on former
narrow-gauge railway serving
Allied trenches in World War I, plus
museum
Nearest station: Albert
Length: 7km (4 miles).
Open: July–Aug Tue–Sun; May, June
& Sept Sun
Gauge: 600mm (1ft 11 5⁄8in)
Tel: 03 22 83 11 89 www.appeva.org

Petit Train de La Rhune ⓫
(see page 153)
Col de St-Ignace, Sare
Shop, restaurant
Nearest station: St-Jean-de-Luz
Length: 4.2km (2.5 miles)
Gauge: 1,000mm (3ft 3 3⁄8in)
Open: Mar–Nov daily
Tel: 05 59 54 20 26
www.rhune.com

Train à Vapeur des Cévennes ⓬
CITEV, Place de la Gare, Anduze
(Anduze–St-Jean du Gard)
Shops, bar
Features: mountain terrain,
bamboo forest
Nearest station: Alès

Length: 13km (8 miles)
Open: July–Aug daily; Apr–June &
Sept–Oct certain days
Gauge: Standard
Tel: 04 66 60 59 01
www.trainavapeur.com

Train à Vapeur de Pithiviers ⓭
AMTP, Musée des Transports de
Pithiviers, rue Carnot, Pithiviers
(Pithiviers–Bellébat)
Shop
Features: narrow-gauge line and
museum
Nearest station: Malesherbes
Length: 4km (2.5 miles)
Open: May and Oct Sun, July–Aug
Sat–Sun; Apr–June & Sept Sun &
holidays
Gauge: 600mm (1ft 11 5⁄8in)
Tel: 02 38 30 48 26
www.amtp-pithiviers.wifeo.com

Train Touristique du Cotentin ⓮
Agon-Coutainville
(Carteret–Portbail)
Features: fishing port, coastal
views
Nearest station: Carentan
Length: 10km (6 miles)
Open: July–Aug Tue, Thur, Sat, Sun;
Jun, Sept Sun and holidays
Gauge: Standard

Tel: 02 33 04 70 08
www.train-touristique-du-cotentin.com

**Train Touristique des Monts du
Lyonnais** ⓯
18 Place Sapéan
(L'Arbresle–Ste Foy l'Argentière)
Features: scenic ride near Lyon
Nearest station: L'Arbresle
Length: 20km (12.5 miles)
Open: June–Sept Sun and holidays
Gauge: Standard
Tel: 06 07 27 88 42
www.train-touristique-monts-lyonnais.
com

Train Touristique Livradois-Forez ⓰
AGRIVAP, Train Touristique, La
Gare, Ambert
(Courpière–Sembadel)
Features: ride through regional
park, paper and tractor
museums, abbey at La Chaise
Dieu. Includes 17 tunnels and 18
bridges and viaducts.
Nearest station: Thiers
Length: 96km (64 miles)
Open: July–Aug weekends.
Reservations online.
Gauge: Standard
Tel: 04 73 82 43 88
www.agrivap.fr

Vélorail from Condé-sur-Vire to Gourfaleur.

High-speed RENFE train travelling through Castilla La Mancha.

SPAIN AND PORTUGAL

A massive investment programme has brought Spanish railways to the forefront of Europe's high-speed network, but there are also slower, scenic routes to explore both here and in Portugal

Spain's first line, from Barcelona to Mataró on the Costa Brava, opened in 1848. Seven years later, the Railway Bill stipulated that the only tracks that could be laid were those that began or ended in Madrid; this has resulted in the awkward radial nature of the network still evident today. Another lasting problem has been the gauge size, which is broader than that used in the rest of Europe. Nevertheless, by 1867 a basic network running to 4,649km (2,889 miles) of track had been laid. The state-controlled rail company RENFE was founded in 1941.

In recent decades the network has been transformed by the addition of high-speed lines connecting Madrid with Seville, Córdoba, Malaga, Valencia, Barcelona and other cities. A cross-border line runs through the Pyrenean foothills from Barcelona to Perpignan. New lines under construction will reach Galicia and the Basque Country.

While Spain does fast and comfortable intercity services exceptionally well, it is less well equipped with scenic lines but they do still exist. The best are covered in this chapter, but there are others that fill in the spaces between the high-speed lines that are worth exploring.

Oriente station, Lisbon.

PORTUGUESE RAILWAYS

The Portuguese have had a railway since 1856. By 1877 there was a rail link between Lisbon and Porto, its highlight the laced-metal bridge designed by Gustave Eiffel, spanning the Douro River. The Companhia dos Caminhos de Ferro Portugueses came into being in 1951, and now operates a network totalling 3,100km (1,940 miles).

Trains reach smoothly across the country – north to Valença and Spanish Galicia, south to the Algarve coast,

Main attractions

Bilbao: Guggenheim Museum, Casco Viejo (the old town),
Córdoba: Sinagoga, Alcázar de los Reyes,
Seville: Catedral & Giralda, Alcázar
Madrid: , Plaza Mayor, Parque del Retiro.
Porto: Sé (Cathedral), Cais de Ribeira area, Port lodges.

Maps on pages 164, 175, 176, 179

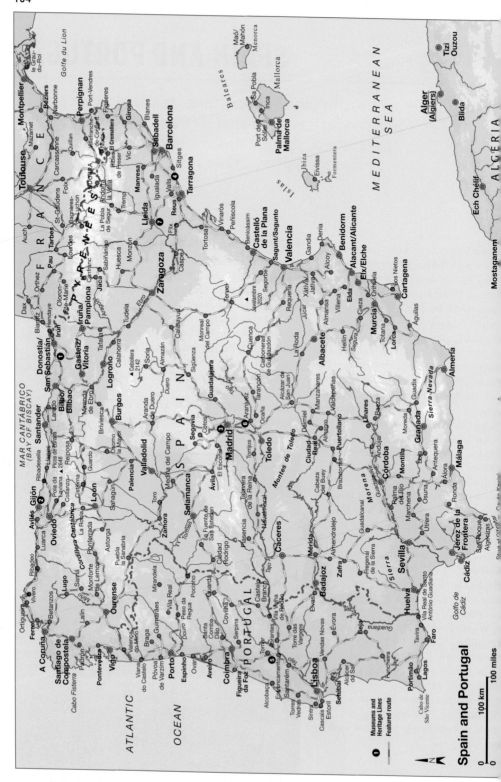

Spain and Portugal

0   100 km

0   100 miles

N

1   Museums and
Heritage Lines

   Featured route

across the Alentejo plains to the wonders of Évora. From Lisbon an electric train runs west alongside the Tagus River to Estoril and Cascais; at Belém station there are grand sights relating to the Age of Discovery. Other discoveries, as you travel, might include the fascinating variety of stations – the little tiled ones along the northern rivers, the mock-Manueline façade to Lisbon's Rossio station and the stunning architecture of the ultra-modern Oriente station in the Parque das Nações, a major transport hub east of the city.

THE TRANSCANTÁBRICAN ROUTE

Spain's northern coast, beside the Bay of Biscay, stretches for hundreds of kilometres from the border with France to eventually reach Spain's 'Land's End': Cape Finisterre (Cabo Fisterra). This long coastline sees far fewer holiday visitors than Spain's warmer Mediterranean shores, yet it fronts a fascinating and varied region, full of history and with some of Europe's most delightful countryside where the slopes of the Cordillera Cantábrica run down towards the sea.

A metre-gauge railway runs almost the entire length of the Biscay coast; known as the Transcantábrican line, this is one of Spain's most memorable rail journeys. Even at its fastest the run takes three days, transporting the traveller through a variety of landscapes and cultural traditions; however, each section of the journey is worth savouring rather than rushing straight through, and a week is not too long to set aside for the whole route.

Travelling east to west, the Transcantábrican journey starts at Hendaye on the French frontier, takes in San Sebastián, Bilbao, Santander and Oviedo along the way and eventually makes its way to the port of Ferrol on the distant coast of Galicia. This route was once a linked system of independent railway companies whose names can still be seen on some station buildings, but today it is run by two companies: Euskotren a public corporation responsible for transport in the Basque Country and the state-run, light railway group FEVE. The cheerfully painted stations, modern trains and helpful staff all combine to make the journey a real pleasure.

ALONG THE BASQUE COAST

Hendaye, where we meet the easternmost extremity of the Transcantábrican route, is just within France, across the Bidasoa estuary from Spain. Our journey starts on a suburban electric train which will take us across a bridge over the border and then rattle along through numerous stations and even more numerous tunnels to San Sebastián (Donostia in Basque), 22km (15 miles) along the coast. The Hendaye–San Sebastián line has been electrified since its inception and the rolling stock consists of blue, two-carriage units. Because of all the tunnels, the service is nicknamed El Topo (The Mole).

⊙ Essentials

European Rail timetable nos. 686/687

For the first part of the trip see http://euskotren. eus;

for the second part see www.renfe.com/EN/viajeros/ feve

Distance: 780km (485 miles)

Duration of journey:

(1) Hendaye–San Sebastián 35 mins

(2) San Sebastián–Bilbao 2 hrs 35 mins

(3) Bilbao–Santander–Oviedo 8 hrs 10 mins

(4) Oviedo–Ferrol 7 hrs 15 mins average

Frequency of trains:

(1) every 30 mins (2) hourly (3) 1–2 daily (change at Santander) (4) 2 daily direct

The Hendaye–San Sebastián train.

San Sebastián, a city of 200,000 people, is the capital of Guipuzcoa, a stylish seaside resort that merits at least one night's stop. The Euskotren terminus, Amara station, is on the left bank of the River Urumea. The old town, with a plethora of restaurants and bars, is about a kilometre's walk to the north. While there are several places on the Transcantábrican route that pride themselves on their gastronomy, San Sebastián is second to none. The city has its own funicular railway, up Monte Igeldo on the western end of the beach, the Playa de la Concha. It serves an amusement park at the top but you may want to take it just for the views.

From San Sebastián, hourly trains run along the coast towards Bilbao, 111km (70 miles) away, taking just over 2 hours 30 minutes. The trains are three-carriage electric units in blue and grey livery with a good turn of speed between stations, although their spartan interior reflects their original role in short-haul suburban services.

A run of 27km (17 miles) along the built-up coastal strip brings us to at Zumaia, which has a picturesque, half-timbered station building; there is a bus connection here for the Basque Railway Museum at Azpeitia in the hills to the south. The train speeds through attractive rolling countryside with occasional glimpses of the Bay of Biscay, until Deva, where the line turns inland. From here to Durango the railway heads southwards, away from the coast, winding uphill into the mountains along narrow valleys lined with plane trees, stopping here and there at busy industrial towns with factory chimneys protruding among the wooded hills.

GERNIKA AND BILBAO

At Amorbieta, some two hours west of San Sebastián, a branch line heads north to Bermeo, a colourful port where the train comes to a halt beneath the prows of the fishing craft. However, it is Gernika (also spelled Guernica), the largest town on this line, which makes it really notable. This is

Pintxos at a bar in San Sebastián.

⊘ LA ROBLA RAILWAY

At Aranguan junction, outside Bilbao, La Robla line diverges from the Transcantábrican route and heads off southwest towards the mountains. This metre-gauge railway, opened in stages before 1915, weaves to and fro through the heart of the Cordillera Cantábrica, at times in sight of the Picos de Europa, eventually reaching León and La Robla on the Castilian side of the mountains.

A fleet of modern railcars provides one service per day in each direction – trains depart Bilbao Concordia station at 2.30pm and arrive at León at 22.03pm. With only one train a day you can't get off anywhere for a walk around unless you are prepared to spend the night in some out-of-the-way place and continue your journey the next day. (European Rail timetable No. 683).

the same Gernika that was razed by the 1937 blitzkrieg by the Condor Legion during the Spanish Civil War (1936–39), the market-day massacre commemorated by Picasso's famous painting. A visit to the traditional parliament building is a thought-provoking experience.

Back on the route to Bilbao, the line – double track now – winds on from Amorbieta through wooded hills. On either side we pass numerous examples of the *caserio*, the characteristic Basque country farmhouse with an enormous gabled roof, very much a hallmark of the region. Soon the railway begins the descent to Bilbao, entering the suburbs after the long tunnel at Usansolo.

Bilbao is a fascinating city from many points of view. The Guggenheim Museum put it on the international map and marked its transition from a centre of steelmaking to one of the most vibrant, arty places in Spain. It has acquired some stunning architecture along the way in contrast to the preserved old quarter, which has an endless choice of tapas bars and restaurants. The public transport network is complex: four rail termini, two funicular railways, metro and tram systems, and a 19th-century transporter bridge – a metro ride down river from the city centre.

The train from San Sebastián arrives at **Atxuri** station, a stone building designed for the Vascongados line by Manuel Smith in 1912 in the style of a medieval Basque tower-house: look out for the huge roof beams in the vast, spotless booking hall. Atxuri is a terminus, but it is less than a 2-km (1-mile) walk to **Concordia** station on the other side of the Ria Bilbao (there is no good public transport link), where we pick up the Transcantábrican route again. Concordia, with its superb 19th-century iron and glass façade, is no less impressive than Atxuri, although in a quite different architectural style. It still proclaims the name of its original owners, the FC Santander-Bilbao company, over the entrance. The booking hall is at street level, the trains on the floor above in an elegantly pillared

Bilbao Concordia station, built in a unique Modernist style in 1902, also known as Santander station.

La Robla train.

train shed. Between the platforms upstairs stands a preserved 0-4-0T steam engine, and in the lively Café FEVE early-morning travellers mingle with home-going night-clubbers.

WEST TO CANTÁBRICA

The next leg of the Transcantábrican line is more like a serious cross-country journey than the trip on the busy inter-urban route from Hendaye and San Sebastián. The FEVE diesel railcar waiting at Bilbao Concordia is well equipped and comfortable but it lacks a buffet: bring your own food and drink for the journey.

The Santander train – usually made up of several carriages coupled together – roars away from Bilbao Concordia in spirited fashion, first through a tunnel under the city and then along the river for a couple of kilometres before heading into the hills. Beyond **Aranguen**, the junction for the La Robla route (see page 166), the train starts to climb into the wooded upland country that divides the Basque region from the region and province

of Cantábria. The growl of the diesel power unit deepens as the gradient starts to bite: the route must have been a real challenge to the drivers of the small steam engines, 4-4-0 tank locos built in Glasgow in the 1880s, that ruled the roost before diesels first arrived in the 1950s.

A succession of tunnels takes the train over the line's summit and into **Cantábria**. As the line starts to wind downhill, meadows fill the valley on either side and rocky crags rise in the background; this is an enchanting tract of country, especially in the spring when the fields are ablaze with wild flowers. Progress is unhurried, with the train making frequent stops at the red-roofed villages, their stations' old-fashioned brick or stone buildings smart with FEVE's yellow paint: the leafy station at **Limpias** is especially picturesque.

The hills fall back as the train approaches the coast, and three hours after leaving Bilbao it arrives at Santander's centrally-located metre-gauge terminus, alongside the RENFE

El Transcantábrico between Candás and Luarca, Asturias.

station. **Santander**, a modern port and resort as well as the provincial capital, has excellent sandy beaches; walk up the Península de la Magdalena to admire the view of the city across the bay, framed by the green Cantabrian Mountains.

ASTURIAS

The journey from Santander to the city of Oviedo is another good day's run. The Cordillera Cantábrica is a continuing presence to the south, the track itself keeping to the coastal strip for the first two hours and serving a string of coves, fishing villages and seaside towns. The station gardens along this section are full of rose bushes, lemon trees and palms, sometimes all of them together. The seaside resort of **Llanes**, almost two hours out of Santander, has a pretty harbour and makes a good stop if you want to break the journey for lunch. A short way inland from here is the massif bulk of the Picos de Europa Mountains.

Half an hour further on, at **Ribadesella**, the train turns away from the sea and heads inland along another wooded valley. In the old days, the steam locomotives of the Económicos de Asturias railway were renowned all over Europe for their immaculate paintwork and polished brass. They must have looked splendid racing through the landscape on the route up to Oviedo.

At **Norena**, shortly before Oviedo, the line makes a 90-degree flat crossing with the Langreo metre-gauge route heading down to the coast at Gijon. The vast hangars in the angle of the two lines house FEVE workshops.

Like Bilbao, **Oviedo** is a formerly industrial city with an improved image: both the 14th-century cathedral and the stone *palacios* in the old squares are superb. The best sights however are the city's exquisite pre-Romanesque churches. For lunch, try a traditional Asturian *fabada* (bean stew) in one of the many excellent restaurants. Oviedo is a convenient centre for visiting the Gijón Railway Museum, 33km (21 miles) north, with a large collection of steam engines (see page 181).

THE COSTA VERDE AND GALICIA

Oviedo's main RENFE station at the end of the Calle de Uria caters to the metre gauge lines as well as the broad-gauge. The FEVE side has its own buffet above the platforms, which is a good place to stock up with provisions for the journey in another of the modern railcars, to the seaport of El Ferrol. This will be the final leg of our journey, a run out to the far northwest of Spain along the Costa Verde, the aptly named Green Coast.

This is another long run, lasting over six hours. The train starts by taking what was until recently a broad-gauge line along to **Trubia**, then heading through the populous Asturian hills towards the sea. The stretch after **Pravia** is the most scenic part of the entire journey. For kilometre after kilometre

Steam locomotives at the Gijon Railway Museum.

EL TRANSCANTÁBRICO

One of the legendary train journeys of Spain is across the green landscapes of the north, from the French border and the Basque Country to Galicia.

Luxury land-cruise trains are an established feature on several of Europe's standard-gauge rail networks, but it has taken the FEVE railway along Spain's Biscay coast to adapt the concept to the slimmer metre-gauge, with its successful El Transcantábrico operation. The rake of the blue and white coaches of the luxury Transcántabrico train is a familiar sight on the tracks that snake along between the coastline and the Cantabrian Mountains.

What El Transcantábrico offers is essentially a well-furnished mobile hotel that serves as a base for excursions during the day. The route runs either from León via Bilbao to Ferrol, then on to Santiago de Compostela by coach, or does the same journey in

Welcome aboard El Transcantábrico.

reverse. The countryside lends itself to this sort of upmarket touring – green valleys and mountain vistas, eminent museums and historic towns, fine food and famous restaurants. The Transcantábrico melds these facets of Cantabria, Galicia and the Basque country in the course of its eight-day, seven-night run.

Hauled by a powerful diesel engine, the train makes its way out of the historic Castilian city of León after lunch on Saturday and heads northeast through the Cantabrian Mountains towards Bilbao. The first night is spent at Cistierna, the passengers retiring to their two-bed or single-suite rooms. Next morning it's breakfast in the dining car. After excursions to Saldaña and the caves at Sotoscueva, Bilbao is reached on Monday. Passengers spend the morning here – most want to see the Guggenheim Museum – before the train departs for Santander, where it stops for the night.

This blend of nights on the train, days touring the countryside and splendid meals in picturesque surrounding, carries travellers on for five more days and nights.

VISITING THE SIGHTS

The next day, starting at **Santander**, provides three highlights: the wonderful neolithic paintings in the caves at Altamira; the medieval village of Santillana de Mar; and dinner in the historic town of Cangas de Onís.

The coach trip from Arriondas station high up into the Picos de Europa National Park makes a particularly memorable day, as does the run along the coast west of the Asturian capital of Oviedo, where the railway glides across estuaries and inlets on high viaducts. Very pleasant in summer, Oviedo is located on the north side of the Cantabrian mountain range and is approximately 24km (15 miles) from the coast, a gateway to both beach and skiing resorts. The line's highlights include the picturesque fishing village of Cudillero, the port of Ribadeo with its steep cobbled streets, and the walled town of Vivero. Ferrol is the end of the line; from here a coach runs the final 80km (50 miles) to the pilgrimage centre of Santiago de Compostela, with its marvellous cathedral. Alternative itineraries to the one described are 4 days and 3 nights from Santander to León and 5 days and 4 nights from Santander to Santiago de Compostela.

the view is constantly changing; there are deserted beaches with surf crashing on the shore, sweeping vistas across a wide estuary from a high viaduct, shafts of sunlight illuminating an eucalyptus forest, people working in the fields next to tiny, red-roofed hamlets. All these images occur and recur. The fishing ports of **Ribadeo** and **Vivero** are both picturesque little spots to break the journey.

At last, after a final hour where the railway switchbacks through glades of chestnuts and gum trees, the train arrives at the spacious terminus of El Ferrol. The city of Santiago de Compostela, a pilgrimage site since the Middle Ages, is only 80km (50 miles) further on, and many travellers will choose to take the bus or RENFE broad-gauge train to Santiago and finish their journey there.

ALGECIRAS–RONDA

The Algeciras to Ronda *ferrocarril* was built by the Algeciras (Gibraltar) Railway Company Ltd in 1892, and it remains a useful – and scenic – gateway to the hinterland from the coast. A century ago, the journey took a full day and could be highly dangerous, with highwaymen hiding out in the hills; nowadays the only danger is likely to be heatstroke; temperatures in July and August can be around 40°C (104°F), although there is air-conditioning of sorts on most trains. The trains have only two or three carriages and are usually full of local people as well as a few tourists.

SAN ROQUE

The track follows the course of four rivers all the way from the coast up to Ronda. Algeciras is an ugly sprawl best avoided; a more pleasant starting point is **San Roque**, a short distance inland. The station is 6km (4 miles) below the ancient town itself, which is dramatically set in the foothills of the Sierra Bermeja. It has a beautiful old centre, with steep streets lined by houses with iron-work balconies.

Shortly after leaving San Roque the train pulls into **Almoraima**, where the hills are covered in cork-oaks; cork is a major business in these parts. Further on, cypresses and wild flowers cover deep ravines. The atmospheric remains of the once-grand castle that gives its name to **Castellar de la Frontera** is reached by a narrow climbing road.

RURAL IMAGES

The train lurches off again with a blast on the horn, and before long it is announcing its arrival in **Jimena**. From the station you can see a Moorish tower, and white houses spilling down the hillside. The train makes its way through countryside of densely wooded hills and valleys; fields of golden wheat and the ever-present slopes of cork- and dwarf-oak trees.

Tiny stations with lacy clapboard trimmings follow one another: San Pablo, Gaucín, Cortes de la Frontera, Jimera de Líbar, Benaoján, Morales,

⊘ Essentials

European Rail timetable no. 673

Distance: 106km (66 miles)

Duration of journey: 1hr 50 mins

Frequency of trains: 5 per day

Castle at Jimena.

Arriate – the names chug along to the rhythm of the engine. It shuttles through a dozen or so tunnels, giving passengers fleeting glances of oddly shaped mountains and a vast, blue firmament as well as brief respite from the heat. The train enters a viaduct for several kilometres, with each archway a nano-second window onto the gully. Bushes of pink blooms grow in profusion beside a river that is little more than a stream in places.

Each station is pretty and each village worth a brief visit – if only to walk in the fields and enjoy a cooling drink at the local bar.

THE CAVE OF THE CAT

At **Benaoján**, you can visit the nature study information centre behind the station, where you will find directions to the **Cueva del Gato** (Cave of the Cat), a couple of kilometres away via a path through fields and olive groves. Although the cave is only accessible to experienced potholers, the site is out of this world, with gushing waterfalls and the craggy Sierra de Grazalema

towering above. The Cueva de la Pileta (Pileta Cave, guided visits only), about 4km (2.5 miles) south of Benaoján, was discovered by a local farmer early last century and has fabulous stalactites and stalagmites, as well as Palaeolithic animal paintings dating from around 25,000 BC. The view from the entrance, over undulating valleys, is itself worth the trip.

Shortly after Benaoján, **Ronda** appears to the left of the train. A rocky escarpment shoulders the town, 180 metres (600ft) above the Guadalevín Valley. The river cleaves the escarpment in two, with the 18th-century Puente Nuevo (New Bridge) spanning the cleft. The old town sits on the southern side of the bluff, the new town is perched on the northern side. There is another, older bridge further upstream which has Moorish origins. Ronda was the capital of an independent Muslim sovereignty until 1485, when Isabela and Ferdinand, the Catholic monarchs, reclaimed the area for Christianity. Churches and monasteries began to make an appearance after the Reconquest, many converted from or built on the sites of existing mosques. Only one 14th-century Moorish tower remains in the town. This is now an integral part of a church – albeit with the Moorish architectural influences that created the style known as Mudéjar.

There are beautiful Moorish baths, ancient palaces and ramparts, museums, gardens and churches, but the star of Ronda is the ravine itself.

SEVILLE–MADRID ON THE AVE

Seville's impressive Santa Justa station is the starting point for this journey aboard RENFE's pride and joy: the Alta Velocidad Española (the acronym, AVE translates as 'bird' in Castilian).

In the early 1990s, the Spanish Government was keen to keep up with the rest of Europe in modernising its

The Puente Nuevo (New Bridge) spans the 120 metre (393-ft) -deep chasm of the Guadalevin River that divides Ronda.

railway network. With Madrid as an obvious departure point, Seville was chosen as the destination for the first high-speed line – the city was due to host the huge trade fair of Expo '92.

The latest AVE trains (series 103) consist of eight units: an engine at each end producing 8,800 kW of power, a club car, a preferential class car, a buffet and four tourist class carriages. They are 200m (656ft) in length and can carry 404 passengers at a speed of 350km/h (220mph). The deluxe club class buys you a driver's view of the rails and a fully rotating seat.

The Spanish high-speed network now stretches for 3,152km (almost 2,000 miles), of which 2,514km (1,562 miles) are European-standard-gauge of 1,435mm, 567km (352 miles) are conventional Iberian-gauge (1,668mm) and 71km (45 miles) are a combination of the two gauges.

At Santa Justa station, you'll pass through security before emerging on the platform where the long, sleek, aerodynamic AVE awaits. At the appointed departure time to the

second, it purrs into life and glides – there is no other word for it – into the northeastern suburbs of Seville as a steward's voice comes over the tannoy welcoming everyone aboard, in both Spanish and English.

STYLE AND COMFORT

Even in tourist class, the seats are comfortably upholstered, the aisles are wide and thickly carpeted and the toilets spacious, with shiny chrome 1950s-style soap dispensers. In the buffet car there is an ergonomic free-standing bar with plenty of standing space in which to enjoy a pizza, sandwich or beer.

The ride is silent and smooth as stewards hand out headphones for the film about to be shown. Air-conditioning is, of course, paramount in a country where summer temperatures regularly exceed 35°C (95°F). In no time, the train is sliding through the countryside, with grand *cortijos* (farm estates) dotting the flat, buff-coloured plains and far-off mountains colliding with a big sky. The landscape becomes

⊙ **Essentials**

European Rail timetable no. 660

Distance: 471km (293 miles)

Duration of journey: 2hrs 20 mins–2hrs 50 mins

Frequency of trains: roughly every hour

Botanical garden inside Madrid's Atocha train station.

hillier, with undulating fields of cereal unfurling into the distance and dry riverbeds flash by in a blur.

The train streams into **Córdoba**'s modern station 45 minutes later. All is orderly and calm on the glossy platforms and there are security officials weaving their way among passengers, ensuring that everything is running smoothly.

Once out of the station, more suburbs whizz by, in no time reaching the heart of the *campo* (countryside) once again. Hostesses hand out *caramelos* (sweets) to combat ear-popping as the altitude rises. There are glimpses of retreats shaded by pine trees and the play of light on water between hillocks covered in silvery olive trees. This is tunnel time on the AVE, as it rushes through and around the majestic **Sierra Morena**, negotiating several viaducts en route.

ONTO THE *MESETA*

The sierra is left behind and the meseta, Spain's vast central plateau, is reached, where the landscape

becomes drier and emptier. The train speeds past the town of Villanueva de Córdoba, surrounded by holm-oak woods. Gradually, the gentle hills become more jagged as the train enters the foothills of the Sierra de la Alcudía to the west and the Sierra Madrona to the east, and the AVE crosses a beautiful viaduct. North of here are grassy yellow plains fringed by the far-off Puertollano Mountains as the line passes through the Valle de Alcudía. This will be the view all the way to the capital, enlivened by a couple of towns: at Puertollano there is a glut of disused red-brick industrial buildings. Ugly electricity generators mar an otherwise pleasant, red-earthed and craggy landscape, along with the ubiquitous olive groves. Nearer the capital, rows of huge jarras (pitchers once used for storing oil or wine) lie on their sides beside boggy marshland.

The AVE speeds into the outskirts of **Madrid**, where lines of washing are strung across balconies and tower blocks are shuttered against the heat. Within minutes, the train is gently

El Cremallera railway in Vall de Núria.

raking as it enters beautiful **Atocha** tation. Built 1889–91, it was modern-ed when this high-speed link was eeded for Seville's Expo '92. There is ow a lush tropical garden in its spa-ious atrium.

L CREMALLERA

he rack railway affectionately known s El Cremallera ('The Zip') climbs om the town of Ribes de Freser to he Santuari de Núria in the Catalan yrenees. The line was opened in 1931, naking it the last of Europe's rack rail-rays to be built. **Ribes Vila** station is he best departure point if you arrive y car, but if you are coming by rail, the tation at the bottom, **Ribes-Enllaç** onnects with the mainline RENFE rain from Barcelona. There are nine lue and white trains each way a day 11 at weekends) powered by 1500 volts om overhead cables. Choose a seat n the right-hand side of the train for he best views.

The entire line is only 12.5km (7.75 niles) long, and the toothed middle ail only starts after 5km (3 miles) just efore the mid-way station of **Quer-lbs**. Thereafter the severe gradients egin and you climb quickly above the alley. Just in case it is not obvious hat you are ascending to almost 2,000 netres (6,560ft), a series of small sign-oards beside the track give compara-le altitudes in other parts of Spain and urope.

Shortly after Queralbs, the track nters the attractive gorge of the River lúria, which is here a series of gush-ng waterfalls. In spring and early ummer, if you look carefully among he trees you will see the bright yel-ow flowers of the Yellow Turk's-Cap ily *(Lirium pyrinaicum)*, which is used s the symbol of this area, the Vall de lúria.

PAIN'S HIGHEST STATION

he train emerges from the ninth tun-nel into a bowl in the mountains which

has a double role – this is one of Cata-lonia's most holy places as well as being a magnet for hikers and climb-ers. **Núria** is the highest station in Spain at 1,964 metres (6,444 ft), fully 1,000 metres (3,280ft) higher than your starting point. From the train you step into a visitor complex that includes a shop, bar, restaurant and hotel. There are also exhibitions about the Cre-mallera train itself, and the wildlife in the Vall de Núria. The nucleus of the complex is a church dedicated to the Virgin of Núria, which attracts pilgrims all year round – it was the main reason for building the railway up here in the first place.

From spring to autumn Núria is a hiking and outdoor leisure centre, and in winter it's a ski resort. A series of summits (rising to over 2,700 metres/ almost 9,000ft) screens Núria to the north and forms the border with France. You can gain a little more height yourself by following one of the hiking trails up from the town, or by taking a ride on the cable car (which is included in the price of the train ticket).

⊙ Essentials

European Rail timetable no. 658

Distance: 12km (7.5 miles)

Duration of journey: 40 minutes

Frequency of trains: 6 to 12 per day

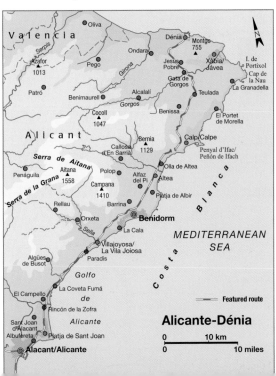

Alicante-Dénia

⏱ Essentials

European Rail timetable no. 667

See also tramalicante.es

Distance: 94km (58 miles)

Duration of journey: Alicante–Benidorm 72 mins; Benidorm–Denia 1 hrs 40 mins

Frequency of trains: Alicante– Benidorm every half hour; Benidorm–Denia hourly.

There are only two ways down from Núria: the train, or a beautiful walk down through the gorge to Queralbs station (allow two or three hours for this).

In the south of Catalonia, a pair of rack railways run to the spectacular monastery at Montserrat, which can also be reached via a vertigo-inducing cable car.

ALICANTE–DÉNIA

The resorts of the Costa Blanca are linked by a picturesque narrow-gauge railway built by a French company in 1914–15 to transport fruit, vegetables, wine and fish from Dénia to Alicante and return with imported guano (fertiliser), grain and flour. The line is now part of the Alicante tram network. Alicante–Luceros station to Benidorm is tram line 1 and Benidorm to Denia is tramline 9.

For the first few kilometres out of Alicante the tram-train runs adjacent to the beach; at Palmeral, Carrabiners and Sant Joan the sand is only separated from the track by a main road.

The resort of **El Campello** is the firs major halt. Following the coast, th line crosses a long, iron girder bridge the first of seven viaducts, to reac **Villajoyosa**, after which it swing inland under the shadow of Pu Campana (1,410 metres/4,626ft), an back towards **Benidorm**, giving goo views of the skyscraper resort. Fron Benidorm station the Limón Expré a tourist train with antique woode carriages, sets off five days a week fo Gata de Gorgos.

Drawing into **Altea**, the old town ca be seen gathered around the blue an white dome of the church. The trai runs beneath the town via two tunnel before climbing steeply through luxu riant vegetation. It then edges along corniche, passes through a tunnel an emerges above the clear green se Another tunnel feeds the line abruptl onto a metal bridge, which, at 10 metres (345ft), is the highest on th line. There is only a second to take i the precipitous **Mascarat gorge** befor the train disappears into yet anothe tunnel.

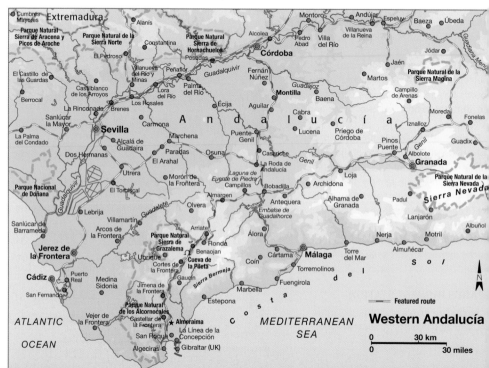

For the next few kilometres there are views of the **Penyal d'Ifac**, the mighty rock which rises from the sea in great vertical cliffs; the nearest station is Calp. Leaving Calp, the line turns away from the coast and rattles around a large curve and over another high viaduct. This is the most scenic stretch of line, and the track is fringed with wild flowers. In every ravine there are reeds and oleanders, thirsty century plants keel over on embankments while thistles, chicory and valerian poke out of the grass. After Teulada the train crosses the River Jalón and comes to **Gata de Gorgos** where the station is a minute's walk from the town centre and five minutes from numerous craft and souvenir shops specialising in wicker, raffia and basket work. It is only a short distance through the orange groves to the terminus of **Dénia**. The station here is close to the bars and restaurants of the harbour and the attractive town centre. The only forward connection is by bus, the nearest mainline station being Gandía.

PALMA-SÓLLER

The antique electric train from Palma de Mallorca to Sóller departs from the fin de siècle station on Palma's Plaça d'Espanya and climbs over the mountains to descend into the lovely Sóller Valley. The narrow-gauge line opened in 1912 and has changed little since. The scenery is still wonderful, and the train itself a delight – the rolling stock is original, and the electric power units date back almost as far (the line was initially steam operated).

Palma is a small city, worth exploring in its own right. Most worth visiting is the Gothic cathedral. Leaving the station, soon the train is amid the olive groves of the gently sloping plain, a riot of wild flowers in spring (beginning in late January). Before long the land begins to rise and the craggy peaks of the Serra de Alfàbia (part of the larger range of the Serra de Tramuntana) appear. The train stops at tiny stations, many of which were built to service the *possessiós* (country estates) visible across the fields. By the time it arrives at **Bunyola** it is approaching the main

⊘ Essentials

European Rail timetable no. 674

See trendesoller.com

Distance: 28km (17 miles)

Duration of journey: 55 mins

Frequency of trains: 5-6 per day

Soller's historic tram passing Sant Bartomeu church.

⊘ GREENWAYS

The closure of an unviable branch line does not have to spell the end of its usefulness. Railways often run through beautiful countryside and they can be given a new life in the cause of recreation.

Spain has 2,400km (1,500 miles) of abandoned railway lines which in recent years have been converted into surfaced cycle or hiking tracks known as *vías verdes* – 'greenways'.

There are 117 such itineraries all over the country, the longest being 190km (120 miles). All are flat and easily accessed, some even by wheelchair users. They are so popular they even have their own television series.

Some *vías verdes* have evocative titles such as the Vía Verde del Aceite (olive oil) in the Córdoba and Jaén provinces of Andalucia, which used to be the main cargo of the line. The Vía Verde del Tren de 40 Días, meanwhile, recalls the legend that this line was built in 40 days during the Spanish Civil War to relieve Madrid, which was being besieged by the rebel army of General Francisco Franco.

Their accompanying buildings have not been neglected: 98 former stations have been converted into cafés and restaurants, rural hotels, information offices or museums.

All that are missing are the rails and the trains – but you can supply these with your imagination.

To find about more about Spain's greenways see www.viasverdes.com.

ridge of the Tramuntana. Bunyola is a pleasant little town, a base for hikers, and has a fine example of Modernist architecture in the Villa Francisca, whose tall yellow spire can be seen from the train.

ACROSS THE MOUNTAINS

Much of the steep section leading to the summit of the line is negotiated in a series of tight curves and tunnels, one of them almost 2.876km (1.7 miles) long. In 7km (4.5 miles) the train gains 199m (650ft) of altitude. After a few minutes the train emerges onto the northern side of the ridge and a tremendous panorama of Sóller, its valley, and the mountains beyond – including the bare crags of Puig Major, at 1,445 metres (4,740ft) the highest on the island. The 10.50am departure from Palma stops for 10 minutes at the **Mirador del Pujol den Banya** to allow time to enjoy the view. Be warned that this train is very popular, and it can be difficult to get a seat.

Gradually the track descends into the valley, with more beautiful views and glimpses of the sea. Once on the valley floor the train passes through the famous Sóller citrus groves and pass small town gardens to reach **Sóller** railway station on the Plaça d'Espanya. From here you can either walk the block or two into the picturesque town centre, or take the open-carriaged *tramvia*, similar to the train in its wood-panelled low-tech charm, from its starting point in front of the station to **Port de Sóller** a short distance away. The gauge is the same as the railway line – 914mm (3ft). Three of the engine units and two of the carriages were built in 1913. Soller makes a good base from which to explore the sights of the northwest coast, especially Santuari de Lluc, Sa Calobra and Deià.

OTHER ROUTES IN SPAIN

In addition to the high-speed arteries of the AVE lines, there are many less well known rail routes in Spain to explore if you have time to study timetables. In some cases you may have to fill a gap in the network with a bus journey.

The train from Barcelona to Tour de Latour de Carol in the Pyrenees (European Rail Timetable 656) links up with

⊘ THE TRAMS AND FUNICULARS OF LISBON

The old-fashioned rail-borne transport systems of Lisbon are one of the delights of the city for any traveller.

The hilly terrain inspired three funiculars to be built at the end of the 19th century as well as one extraordinary lift – counted as an honorary vertical railway for the purpose of this book. All of these have been classified as National Monuments. Two of the funiculars originally used a rack rail, cable and water counterweight; the other was steam powered. All were electrified in the 1910s.

The Bica funicular (built in 1892) is Lisbon's best-known and most picturesque route. It runs from Sao Pedro de Alcantar to Largo Calhariz. Almost equally well-loved is the Gloria funicular (1885), running from Praça Restauradores to Bairro Alto (São Pedro de Alcântara Belevedere) via Calçada de Glória. The third route is the Lavra funicular (1884) from Largo da Anunciada to Rua Camara Pestana. Not to be missed is the cast iron vertical lift, the Elevador de Santa Justa (1902) which raises passengers from Largo do Carmo to Rua do Ouro.

Lisbon's five tram lines have non-consecutive numbers (12, 15, 18, 24 and 25) and carry 57 vehicles. Some of these are modern articulated trams but the most touristy routes are equipped with historical yellow trams (actually reconstructions, but they still look good) complete with old-fashioned bells.

You can catch the No. 12 tram in Praça da Figueira. It runs on a circular route through some of the picturesque neighbourhods and hills in east Lisbon. It takes in the Miradouro das Portas do Sol, the Miradouro de Santa Luzia and the cathedral.

The No. 28 is probably the one you will see most and want to photograph. It runs between Graça and Prazeres, passing palaces and the cathedral, climbs up to Chiado and Estrela and terminates in Campo de Ourique.

If you want to sit with locals rather than tourists, a better bet is the No. 25, which operates the route between Prazeres and Campo das Cebolas. It pass under the flyover at Campo de Ourique, goes through Estrela, descends (or climbs, depending on the direction of travel) to Lapa and then runs parallel to the river from Santos to São Paulo, Cais do Sodré and Praça do Comércio until stopping in Campo das Cebolas, in front of the Casa dos Bicos.

Porto and Sintra also have heritage tram routes between them.

he Yellow Train in France but can also be a leisurely and scenic way to get to Toulouse.

Lleida to La Pobla de Segur is another Pyrenean route that can be done by regular train or on a rail heritage trip.

On the east coast, there is a little-known 20-km (12-mile) long narrow-gauge railway between Los Nietos on the Mar Menor and the naval city of Cartagena, which offers a trip through industrial archaeology (see www.renfe.com/EN/viajeros/feve).

The trip from Granada to Almería (European Rail Timetable 673) goes via the cave town of Guadix and then across Europe's only region of desert, the Desierto de Tabernas.

The short line from Málaga to Bobadilla (see www.renfe.com) is worth doing just for the brief stretch in which it passes through the gorge of La Garganta del Chorro. A precarious footpath has been fixed to the side of the gorge and walking it is one of the highlights of visiting Andalucia. The railway line provides brief tantalizing views.

Zaragoza to Madrid (European Rail Timetable 670) is a route not many people do for pleasure but it passes through several places associated with the Mudejar culture of Spain – the Mudejars being the Muslim habitants of Spain who stayed on after the Reconquest.

To visit the magnificent monastery of Montserrat (www.montserratvisita.com)

is an agreeable's hour's train ride followed by either an ascent by cable car or by rack railway. The RENFE website (www.renfe.com) has a very useful section on tourist trains: themed journeys or along picturesque routes. Depending on your interests you can take a medieval train, a Cervantes train, a geological train, five different wine tours by train, or make a pilgrimage journey to Santiago de Compostela without having to leave your seat.

PORTUGAL: THE DOURO VALLEY

The most popular rail excursion for visitors to Portugal is down the Douro valley from Porto. The only downside is that there is no onward connection and there is nothing to do when you get to your destination, except ride the same train back again. It's served by few trains, but it is still possible to make it there and back in the same day although you may prefer to break your journey overnight. There used to be three narrow-gauge railways emanating from the valley but sadly they have all disappeared for reasons of cost-cutting.

Porto, the departure point for the Douro line is the only large city in northern Portugal. **São Bento station** makes a grand *entrada* to any journey. Built on the site of an earlier monastery, it was completed in 1916 and beneath its soaring ceilings is a feast of blue and white *azulejos* (painted tiles)

⊘ Essentials

European Rail timetable no. 696

Distance: 175km (109 miles) (Porto–Pocinho)

Duration of journey: 3hrs 30 mins or 3hrs 50 mins (one change at Régua)

Frequency of trains: 4 per day

Mosaic at Pinhão train station.

Passing the Croft Winery, Douro Valley.

by artist Jorge Colaço. Three arches of stained glass lead to the platforms.

The first part of the journey after leaving Porto is equally delightful. The train plunges into a series of tunnels, only to re-emerge high above the town. Below is the gleaming river, the travellers' companion throughout the Douro journey, spanned by Gustave Eiffel's famous bridge and, among others, the graceful two-tier Ponte de Dom Luís I, designed in 1886 by Teófilo Seyrig, who took his inspiration from the Eiffel bridge.

Little happens between Porto's Campanhã and **Livracão**, a typically attractive two-storey station, with a long shaded platform. Continuing east, the train enters the longest tunnel in the valley. Climbing steadily, it emerges from the darkness into sparkling sunlight and a relatively steep descent towards **Mosteirô**. Keep your eyes firmly to the right for the most exhilarating sight of the trip: a view of a town far below beyond the mighty Douro River, washing flapping and a wedding often in progress. From this point, the river is a constant, a fat, grey ribbon dancing and curving in sinuous moves. At times the train runs along the river, at times parallel with the road above.

Régua (also called Peso da Régua) is a big town but is not of much interest except if you are visiting on a weekend between June and October when it is the departure point for steam-hauled services to Tua.

From Régua to **Pocinho**, the Douro runs so close to the track that the only things visible are water and the river bank opposite, with steep, vine-covered terraces dotted with port warehouses and handsome *quintas* (manor houses). If you don't want to spend all your time sitting on a train you can get off at the small station of **Pinhão**, one of the most attractive in Portugal, with a handsome façade lined with large panels of hand-painted *azulejos*. Alternatively, continue to Pochino, the terminus, and return from there. Depending on the time of year, you will be heading west in the most westerly country in mainland Europe as the sun sets over the Douro River.

MUSEUMS AND HERITAGE LINES

There are few heritage railway lines in Spain, and none at all in Portugal; there are, however, several excellent railway museums. The numbers relate to the map on page 164.

MUSEUMS

Museo Vasco de Ferrocarril ❶
(Eusko Burnibide Museoa/) Julián Elorza 8 Azpeitia, Guipuzcoa
Tel: 943 150 677
Open: Tue–Fri 10am–1.30pm, 3–6.30pm, Sat 10.30am–2pm, 4–7.30pm, Sun 10.30am–2pm
Features: rich collection drawn from the region's railway heritage. The tall, imposing station building houses the museum office and small exhibits; spacious sheds and hangars outside contain the full-size exhibits: locomotives, coaches and tram cars. The museum also operates steam trains (Sat 12.30 and 6pm and Sun 12.30pm) on 5km (3 miles) of relaid metre-gauge track as far as Lasao station on the old route north towards Zumaia.
Nearest station: Zumaia (bus link)
www.bemfundacioa.org

Museo del Ferrocarril de Asturias ❷
Plaza de la Estación del Norte, Gijón
Tel: 985 181 777
Open: Tue–Fri 9.30am–6.30pm, Sat & Sun 10am–6.30pm
Features: large collection of steam engines in the old Gijón North station. Themed displays explore the social, political and economic history of the local railways.
Nearest station: Gijón
www.museos.gijon.es

Museo del Ferrocarril de Madrid ❸
Paseo de las Delicias 61, Madrid
Tel: 902 22 88 22
Open: Mon–Fri 9.30am–3pm; Sat & Sun 10am–7pm; closed afternoons in winter
Features: housed in the 1880 Delicias station, the museum has collections of steam, diesel and electric locomotives and period carriages as well as rooms dedicated to model railways, railway equipment and clocks.
Nearest station: Delicias. Atocha is within easy walking distance to the north.
www.museodelferrocarril.org

Museu del Ferrocarril de Catalunya Vilanova i la Geltrú ❹
Plaça Eduard Maristany Vilanova i la Geltrú (45km/28 miles southwest of Barcelona)
Tel: 938 158 491
Open: Tue–Sun 10.30am–2.30pm; Sat also 4–7.30pm;
Features: located in a historic locomotive depot, the museum has one of the best collections of steam locomotives in Europe. There are steam-hauled trips every first Sunday in the month.
Nearest station: Vilanova i la Geltrú (RENFE)
www.museudelferrocarril.org

Museu Nacional Ferroviario ❺
Complexo Ferroviário do Entroncamento Rua Eng Ferreira de Mesquita No. 1 A Estrada Nacional No. 3 Entroncamento
Tel: 249 130 382
Open: Tue–Fri 1–6pm, Sat and Sun 10am–6pm
Features: Portugal's national rail museum located in Entroncamento northeast of Lisbon.
Nearest station: Entroncamento
www.fmnf.pt

HERITAGE TRAINS

Tren de la Fresa ❻
(Madrid–Aranjuez)
The train, run by the Museo Ferrocarril in Madrid, departs from Madrid's Atocha station. The line once ferried strawberries from Aranjuez to the capital. There are five ticket types available depending what you want to visit in Aranjuez. If you want to go as you please, choose "fresas al natural".
Operates: Runs 32 times between Apr–Oct, departures from Atocha at 9.50am
www.ffe.es

Tren dels LLacs ❼
Tel 93 366 45 53
For more details, ask at the information office in any Barcelona station, or at Lleida
Historical diesel engines pull old fashioned rolling stock into the Catalan Pyrenees.
Operates: certain days from April to Oct
www.trendelsllacs.cat

The Brienzer Rothorn steam-powered cogwheel train in the Bernese Oberland, looking down over Lake Brienz.

Crossing the river Inn, near
Cinuos-chel-Brail.

SWITZERLAND

Switzerland offers some of the world's most spectacular train journeys, on a user-friendly railway system that is run with clockwork efficiency

Swiss public transport is among the best in the world, and for many visitors its quality and ease-of-use are a revelation. Trains are clean and punctual, stations have a good range of facilities, and information systems are exceptionally clear. But the key to the success of the system is the way each mode of transport is integrated to provide seamless connections and to avoid wasteful and damaging competition between bus and train.

Almost every line, whether operated by Swiss Federal Railways (Schweizerische Bundesbahnen/SBB) or one of the many other operators, has a minimum of a train an hour for at least half the day. The smaller railways run their trains to connect with SBB, and buses, funiculars and lake steamers are almost invariably timed to meet trains or each other. Timekeeping is exemplary, and there is a range of passes for visitors that offer remarkably good value. Couple these factors with the necessity of using mountain railways or cable cars to reach many of the country's finest sights (because there are no roads) and the case for using the Swiss Travel System is overwhelming. It is no wonder that the Swiss people use their railways more than any other nation in Europe. SBB offers many added-value services, some aimed specifically at tourists,

such as the Fly-Rail system, by which checked-in cases are not seen again until you reach your station in Switzerland. Luggage can also be sent separately by train. Bicycles can be hired from over 80 stations, and returned to a different station, allowing advantage to be taken of favourable descents.

MOUNTAIN CHALLENGES

With its abundance of steep terrain, Switzerland makes extensive use of rack railways when gradients become too steep for reliance on the normal

⊘ **Main attractions**
Geneva: Cathedral of St-Pierre, International Red Cross and Red Crescent Museum
Zurich: St Peter's Square and Church, Fraumünster, Grossmünster
Luzern: Swiss Transport Museum (Verkehrshaus), Art Gallery, Museum of Art & Concert Hall.

Map on page 186

Enjoying lunch at Kleine Scheidegg.

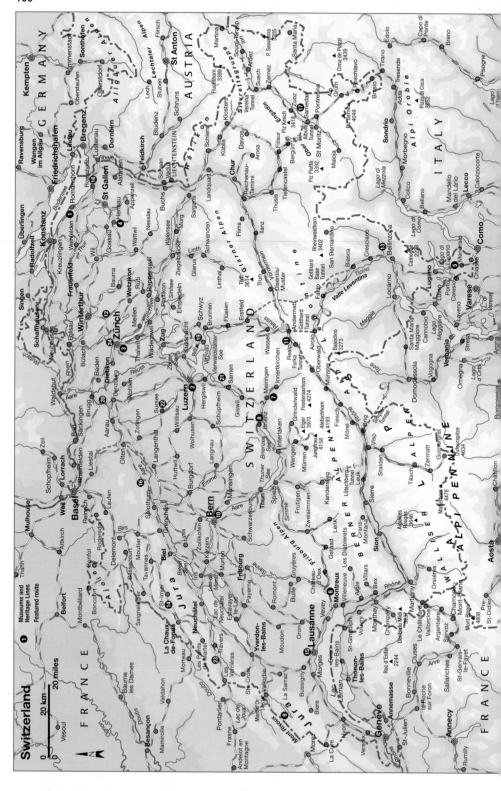

adhesion of steel wheel on steel rail. There are several different types of rack system, each named after its inventor, but all rely on a cogwheel fitted to the train engaging a slotted metal bar fitted centrally between the rails. This both allows the train to climb when the conventional wheel would simply slip and helps the train's braking systems on the descent.

Switzerland has several truly spectacular railway journeys – in fact it is almost impossible to find one that does not offer something to the visitor: even the commuter lines of Zürich take one into pleasant countryside, or up the city's local mountain, the Uetliburg. The speed and frequency of trains means that the country can be traversed easily: St Gallen to Geneva is only 4 hours and Basel to Chiasso under 4.5 hours. With a Swiss Pass, offering unlimited travel over much of the Swiss Travel System, it is easy to explore the country if one wishes to see as much as possible in a short time.

GENEVA–MILAN

It takes just under 4 hours to travel across the Alps from Switzerland's most cosmopolitan city to Italy's industrial capital. Yet speed is almost a handicap to enjoying this journey, and the larger windows of conventional trains allow a wider panorama of the splendid views over Lake Geneva (Lac Léman) and the Alps. The route links a dozen places that deserve a day or more to appreciate.

Geneva has accepted exiles and refugees for centuries, from English regicides to Russian anarchists, and the many international organisations based here continue this cosmopolitan tradition. Today almost a third of the population is non-Swiss. This spirit, coupled with the scenic splendours offered from the north side of the lake, has encouraged the rich and famous to make their homes along the lake shore between Geneva and Montreux (see

box on page 189). Even the railway line you travel on was built by a foreigner, the Irishman Charles Vignoles.

The exit from Geneva is a delight, passing the Botanical Gardens and the wooded grounds surrounding the venerable mansions of the city's early élites. Before long the trees thin out to reveal the sickle-shaped Lake Geneva, which is seldom out of view to the right until it comes to an end at Villeneuve. Vineyards cover many of the northern slopes along the lake and along the Rhône Valley to Brig.

Nyon, with its five-towered castle, was founded by Julius Caesar in 45 BC and is now the junction for the narrow-gauge line to La Cure, serving the closest ski resorts to Geneva. Another fine castle guards the shoreline at **Morges** and today houses the military museum of Canton Vaud.

LAKESIDE VISTAS

Lausanne has proved a productive setting for many writers including Edward Gibbon, Charles Dickens, Arnold Bennett and T.S. Eliot, and it still has a

⊙ Essentials

European Rail Timetable nos. 82/590

Distance: 379km (235.5 miles)

Duration of journey: 3 hrs 58 mins

Frequency of trains: 4 per day (direct)

The Pilatus railway, built in 1889, is the steepest cogwheel railway in the world.

Charlie Chaplin statue, Vevey.

Amongst the vineyards on the banks of Lake Geneva.

thriving artistic life, reflected in the many galleries and museums. The town has a 12th- to 13th-century cathedral that many regard as the finest Gothic building in the country, as well as the Olympic Museum, celebrating the movement and the work of the International Olympic Committee, based here since 1915. The streets tumble down to the lake at so steep an angle that the city has Europe's steepest metro, and it is on leaving the station at Ouchy that passengers enjoy some of the best views of the French Alps and the string of lakeside villages on the southern shore. Their piers are served by the lake's mix of screw-steamers and paddle-steamers, some of which have been restored to steam propulsion.

The metro descends to the lakeside to pass the small harbour at **Cully**, sharing the foreshore with vines and tiny private gardens built on headlands that are reached by footbridges across the tracks. The lakeside towns of **Vevey** and **Montreux** are excellent centres for walking, and the start of other great railway journeys. Charlie Chaplin lived in Vevey for the last 25 years of his life, commemorated in the museum, Chaplin's World; while Montreux is known for its jazz festival, held in the first half of July. For railway buffs, it is one of the world's few stations with three different track gauges. The railway and the lovely lakeside footpath between Vevey and Villeneuve both run past the walls of one of the world's most famous and romantically situated castles, the Château de Chillon, immortalised by Byron's poem *The Prisoner of Chillon*.

INTO THE RHÔNE VALLEY

Once past **Villeneuve**, formerly an important staging post for the road over the St-Bernard Pass, the character of the landscape changes dramatically as the lake ends and the railway enters the Rhône Valley, its northern slopes covered in vines and the valley floor home to the occasional heavy industrial plant. **Aigle** is a centre of the wine industry, and the magnificent late 15th-century castle to the north of the line houses a wine museum.

he station marks the start of three delightful narrow-gauge railways serving resorts in the surrounding mountains, and a fourth line, to the ski resort of Villars, begins at Bex.

The train races along the valley to **Martigny**, once the Roman capital of the region. Though little remains of the 5,000-seat amphitheatre, the nearby Pierre Gianadda Foundation is an astonishing art gallery and museum for such a small town, hosting exhibitions in conjunction with the likes of the Metropolitan Museum of Art in New York. A spectacular narrow-gauge line heads southwest from Martigny to Chamonix and St-Gervais in France.

The Rhône, accompanied by the railway, now swings round to the east. The modern appearance of **Sion** from the railway belies its interesting old centre, with a pair of finely sited castles, one containing what is claimed to be the oldest playable organ in the world, built in the 14th century, on which occasional concerts are given. The town is a great centre for walking, with numerous bus routes into surrounding valleys, many of which are threaded by ancient *bisses* (irrigation channels). Some of these have been incorporated into the 7,000km (4,375 miles) of footpaths in the region. Europe's largest underground lake, discovered only in 1943 at St-Léonard, can also be reached by bus from Sion.

VISP, BRIG AND THE SIMPLON TUNNEL

As the railway nears the junction of **Visp**, it is joined by the line from the new Lötschberg Base Tunnel and the southern ramp from the old Lötschberg Tunnel can be seen descending the northern flank of the valley. At Visp the narrow-gauge line from Zermatt joins the formation for the last few miles to **Brig**, a good place to break the journey. The town itself is a pleasure to walk around, its most notable building being the Stockalper Palace, which was Switzerland's largest private building when owned by its creator, Kaspar von Stockalper, in the mid-17th century. Around the arcaded courtyard are storerooms and accommodation

☉ FAMOUS RESIDENTS

There can be few areas of the world that have attracted as many famous foreign residents as Geneva and the northern shore of Lake Geneva. In the 1550s, the Scots reformer John Knox chose the city as his home, becoming its first British pastor. Several of those who signed Charles I's execution warrant fled here in 1649. Geneva was later home to French philosopher Jean Jacques Rousseau (who was born here in 1712). The Enlightenment writer, Voltaire, spent many years in and around the city in the mid-18th century, and composed his satirical tale, *Candide*, here.

Countless writers, composers and artists have since found peace and inspiration for their work in the area: Goethe, Byron, Corbet, Dickens, Dostoyevsky, Tolstoy, Tchaikovsky and Stravinsky being among the most famous. More recent celebrities have included the artist Oscar Kokoschka, soprano Dame Joan Sutherland, Charlie Chaplin (when his political sympathies forced him to leave America), Sir Nöel Coward, actors Richard Burton and Peter Ustinov, and rock star David Bowie.

In the 1990s the German magazine *Stern* ran an article claiming that Geneva had more millionaires than unemployed people – for every two people out of work, there were three millionaires. Quite the record.

and three tall towers topped by onion domes.

Leaving Brig the train enters the famous **Simplon Tunnel**, Europe's fifth-longest railway tunnel at 19.8km (12.5 miles) with the Swiss/Italian border at roughly the halfway point. It was opened in 1906, completing the Simplon railway to Italy. The railway emerges into daylight for the pleasing, isolated station of **Iselle di Trasquera** before plunging into a spiral tunnel down Val Divedro to **Domodossala**, junction for the Centovalli line to Locarno. The railway follows the valley of the River Toce to **Verbania-Palanza** and the start of the final scenic delight of the journey, the long stretch beside Lago Maggiore through **Stresa** and **Arona**.

ZÜRICH–CHIASSO

The most important north–south railway in Switzerland carries a staggering amount of traffic, passenger trains sharing the route with hundreds of freight trains a week. It is also the route of various international expresses running between variou points in northern Europe and Italy.

Once the train has threaded th maze of tracks outside Zürich Haupt bahnhof, it passes through almos continuous suburbs to **Thalwil** (o takes the tunnel to Baar), with view overlooking Lake Zürich to the left. tunnel leads to **Sihlbrugg** – the bridg across the Sihl – and a pleasant stretcl beside the broad river. Nothing to b seen from the railway would tempt on to explore **Zug**, but its old town, clos to the lake, is delightful, with severa streets of shuttered houses with pro nounced eaves and linear ribbons o colour in their window boxes.

The railway continues along th hillside, with views across Zuger Se towards Mt Rigi before reaching th junction of **Arth Goldau**, the start of th second rack line up Rigi. After curv ing around tiny Lauerzersee, the lin passes **Schwyz**, which gave the coun try its name in 1315. Appropriately, th Swiss Federal Archives, with all th charters of the Confederacy from 1291 are located here.

The Gotthard Panorama Express at Flüelen.

Unfortunately for travellers, much of the railway beside the Urner See (the southern extension of Vierwaldstättersee, or Lake Luzern) is in tunnel, but passengers gain sufficient glimpses of the lake to appreciate its beauty, enhanced by the sight of one of the five sleek and beautifully maintained paddle-steamers that ply its waters. The lake ends at **Flüelen**, where a transfer between boat and train takes place as part of the Gotthard Panorama Express journey (formerly the William Tell Express) from Luzern to Lugano/Locarno.

The train enters the broad valley of the Reuss, passing **Altdorf** where, according to the legend, William Tell shot the apple from his son's head. **Erstfeld** became a railway town because it is here that the northern ascent of the famous Gotthard begins – and needed assisting locomotives in steam days. The railway has to climb a vertical height of 634 metres (2,080ft) in just 28km (17.7 miles), requiring a spiral tunnel and two horseshoe curves to gain height before reaching **Göschenen**. Situated in a narrow defile, the lonely station here is a junction for the short rack line up to Andermatt through the Schöllenen Gorge. Andermatt is on the route of the Glacier Express.

Just south of the station the train enters the 15-km (9.2-mile) long **Gotthard Tunnel**, dead straight but for a slight curve at the southern end where the line emerges at **Airolo** in Ticino, the Italian-speaking part of Switzerland. It takes 10 minutes to pass through the tunnel; before it opened, it took a whole day to travel from Göschenen to Airolo. On the left, near the station buildings, is a monument to the 177 men who died during construction work.

Although the southern descent from the Gotthard Tunnel is less severe than the northern climb, it still calls for some impressive bridge-work and two pairs of spiral tunnels, the first just north of Faido, the second to the south. Shortly after the lower spirals, the picturesque village of Giornico and its two fine churches can be seen from the railway. The best way to appreciate the extraordinary ingenuity of the railway builders – and to see the 15th-century frescoes of San Nicolao – is to hire bicycles at Airolo station and freewheel down to Biasca station via the old road and farm tracks, which are almost traffic-free.

SOUTHERN SLOPES

As the train arrives at **Biasca**, look up to the left to see a waterfall pouring over the cliff face. It is a fast, straight run along the broadening valley to the capital of the Ticino at **Bellinzona**, a magnet for anyone interested in medieval military architecture since the town has no fewer than three remarkably intact castles, and they are all open to visitors. Shortly after leaving Bellinzona, the Locarno line veers off to the west, while the Chiasso line

⊘ Essentials

European Rail Timetable no. 550

Distance: 220km (137 miles)

Duration of journey: 3 hrs 26 mins

Frequency of trains: 8 per day (direct)

The Montebello castle, Bellinzona.

climbs along the contours to the lakeside resort of **Lugano**.

Besides its enviable position and the mild, sunny climate (nearby Agra is the sunniest place in Switzerland), Lugano is noted for its modern buildings, especially those of local architect Mario Botta. A funicular links the station with the pedestrianised heart of the town, and there are several good museums and galleries such as the collection of local painters at the Giovanni Züst Cantonal Art Gallery. Funiculars take visitors up Lugano's two mountains, San Salvatore and Bré, and boats serve 14 piers at villages around the lake.

Leaving Lugano, the train quickly descends to run along the lake shore and crosses a man-made causeway to reach **Capologo-Riva San Vitale**; Switzerland's oldest surviving ecclesiastical building can be found in the latter village, the baptistry dating from around 500 AD. Immediately beyond the railway yards at **Chiasso** is the tunnel that marks the frontier with Italy; Milan is just 40 minutes away.

ZERMATT–ST MORITZ ON THE GLACIER EXPRESS

The Glacier Express is Switzerland's best-known train, and deservedly so. Although it takes 8 hours to cover the 290km (181 miles) between the famous resorts, the marvellous landscapes that roll past the window are constantly changing, the observation cars allow panoramic visibility and the freshly-cooked lunch is surprisingly good. Yet the train is a double misnomer: it is definitely not an express, and it no longer offers passengers sight of the glacier after which it was named. From its inauguration in 1931 until 1982, trains ground their way past the Rhône glacier on the ascent to the Furka summit; now they rush through the Furka Base Tunnel, and anyone intent on seeing the shrinking glacier from a train window will have to take the preserved Dampfbahn Furka Bergstrecke railway from Realp (see page 212). But neither of these facts detracts from a journey that would be in the top 10 of a pantheon of the world's great train journeys.

The Matterhorn.

ZERMATT TO BRIG

The journey begins in **Zermatt**, a remote village that grew to be a town because of its proximity to the Matterhorn and the macabre fate of the first party of climbers to reach the summit, in 1865. Human nature was little different then from now, and tourists in their thousands flocked to see where Edward Whymper's party came to grief. Zermatt remains one of the most popular Alpine resorts, offering skiing until later in the spring than most others. The number of visitors would have destroyed the character of the place but for the enlightened decision to ban cars; electric vehicles ferry luggage and passengers between station and hotel, and parts of the town still have a rustic character.

The railway north to Visp follows the Matter Vispa River, and the susceptibility of the Mattertal to avalanches is apparent as soon as the train glides out of Zermatt and enters the first of many shelters that protect the line. The sheer scale of the Alps is immediately evident through the tinted roof-glass of the panoramic coaches, giving a worm's eye view of the mountains on either side. It's best to keep looking upwards as the train passes **Täsch**: the place is a vast coach- and car-park for Zermatt, with shuttle trains ferrying back and forth between the two.

There are plenty of views of the river as the railway switches banks, while grazing cows and barns on staddle stones are reminders of the principal activity of these Alpine valleys before the growth of tourism in the 19th century. **Stalden-Saas** is the station for frequent buses to the well-known winter sports resort of Saas-Fee, which is another car-free zone. The railway continues its rack-braked descent to the floor of the Rhône valley at Visp, where it turns east to follow the Geneva–Milan main line into **Brig** (see page 189). Visp station has been rebuilt to become the junction station for trains using the Lötschberg Base Tunnel from Bern/Spiez and the main line from Geneva as well as the narrow-gauge Matterhorn–Gotthard-Bahn.

TO THE FURKA BASE TUNNEL

From Brig the railway climbs to its first summit at the entrance to the base tunnel under the Furka Pass at Oberwald. It is a measure of the difficulty faced by the construction engineers that this section of railway was one of the last significant lines in Switzerland to be finished, finally opening in 1926. At that time, it proved impossible to keep the line up to the original Furka Tunnel open between October and April because the costs of snow clearance and avalanche protection could not be met in the days before winter sports gained mass appeal. The winter weather on the section between Oberalp and Realp was so severe that it even had a bridge that could be dismantled every autumn.

The gradients are not too steep for adhesion working until **Betten**, where

⊙ Essentials

European Rail Timetable no 575

Distance: 290km (180 miles)

Duration of journey: 7 hrs 47 mins

Frequency of trains: 2 per day summer, 1 per day winter; no serve mid-Oct to early Dec

The Glacier Express on the Oberalp Pass.

the first rack section is announced by the characteristic clunking sound of the rack being engaged by the cog wheels under the train. Here the railway crosses the Rhône, which has seldom been out of sight since Brig, and at **Grengiols** the train crosses the highest viaduct on the FO just before entering a tunnel that spirals inside the mountain to emerge at a higher level, looking down on the viaduct and the confluence of the Rhône and Binna rivers.

For one of the finest vantage points over the **Aletsch Glacier**, Europe's longest at about 24km (15 miles), it is worth breaking the journey at **Fiesch**. Five minutes' walk from the station is the cable car to Eggishorn, from where you can get an excellent impression of the size of the glacier. The train canters past a succession of pretty villages along the broadening valley, the white-towered churches surrounded by dark-wood chalets and some centuries-old agricultural buildings. **Niederwald** was the birthplace of César Ritz, who managed the Savoy Hotel in London before building the Ritz in Paris and giving hi name to the famous London hotel.

The mountains begin to crowd in a the train approaches **Oberwald** and the start of the **Furka Base Tunnel**. From Oberwald the railway used to climb continuously on the rack for almos 9km (5.2 miles) up past the Rhône gla cier to a summit tunnel underneath the Furka Pass. This closed in 1982 when the Furka Base Tunnel opened, allow ing year-round operation of through trains. Oberwald is the starting poin for two spectacular bus journeys, ove the Gotthard Pass to Airolo in Ticin and over the Grimselpass to Meiringen

ANDERMATT AND THE OBERALP PASS

The train emerges from the 15-km (9.2-mile) tunnel at **Realp** to a land scape of gorse-covered hills. Soon after passing a 12th-century towe at **Hospental**, it arrives at the resor of **Andermatt**, junction for the rack line through the Schöllenen gorge t Göschenen (see page 191). There fol lows one of the most spectacular sec tions of the journey as the line climb at 1 in 9 through a succession of fou half spirals, three of them in tunne at the elbow bends, which increase the sense of disorientation. Before the train turns east again, you can look down on Andermatt and back along the Urseren Valley towards Realp.

The line continues to climb, though at gentler gradients, towards the highest point on the Matterhorn–Got thard-Bahn at **Oberalp Pass** (2,03 metres/6,670ft), the boundary betwee Uri and Graubünden cantons. The landscape is desolate – tussock gras and bog, broken by only the occasiona farm building. In winter the train i sometimes in a sheer-walled canyo of snow, and sections of the railwa are protected by avalanche and snov shelters. **Oberalppasshöhe** is the star of a walk to the source of the Rhin at Toma Lake – where you can jum

The Aletsch Glacier.

across the stream – and the beginning of the steep descent towards Disentis. The long tunnel is often the opportunity for the train's head waiter to demonstrate his skill at pouring grappa from a bottle several feet away from the glass, while the steepness of the descent makes diners appreciate the necessity of the angled stems on the wine glasses (which can be bought as souvenirs).

Twisting down the valley of the Vorderrhein, the train passes a branch line leading to the tunnel workings of the AlpTransit project, which is building a new railway tunnel under the Alps. The town of **Disentis** is dominated by the great Benedictine monastery of St Martin, thought to have been founded around 700 AD by an Irish monk. Here the Matterhorn–Gotthard-Bahn ends and a Rhätische Bahn (RHB) locomotive takes over for the rest of the journey to St Moritz.

ALONG THE VORDERRHEIN

The countryside becomes more pastoral and wooded as the line follows the broadening Vorderrhein to the historic town of **Ilanz**, with a fortified church and some 15th-century houses. Beyond Valendas-Sagogn is the bizarre **Flims Gorge**, its towering white cliffs contorted into such peculiar shapes that it would have made a perfect set for filming Star Wars. The line to St Moritz trails in on the right just before the Vorderrhein meets the Hinterrhein to become the Rhine. Some Glacier Expresses continue through the junction station at **Reichenau-Tamins** to the attractive cantonal capital of **Chur**. An important town since Roman times, Chur was the birthplace in 1741 of portrait painter Angelica Kauffmann, who emigrated to England in 1766 and became a founder of the Royal Academy. An art gallery in Grabenstrasse has some of her paintings.

The Glacier Express for Davos continues east, while the main part of the train reverses direction at Reichenau-Tamins before turning south along the valley of the Hinterrhein. After the scenic delights of the route so far, it is hard to believe that this final stage will

> **⊙ Tip**
>
> For the best view of the Matterhorn without donning crampons, you should take the Gornergrat Bahn from Zermatt, which climbs 1,484 metres (4,868ft) in just 9.4km (6 miles) to a hotel and verandah opposite the peak.

Chur, the capital of the canton of Graubunden.

⊙ Tip

For an awe-inspiring view of the Rhône Glacier, take the preserved Dampfbahn Furka Bergstrecke line from Realp to Gletsch.

not be an anti-climax; but it proves just as varied and interesting as the rest of the journey, and the climb to the Albula Tunnel is regarded as one of the railway wonders of the world.

THE LANDWASSER VIADUCT

Several castles guard the flanks of the valley as the train climbs to **Thusis** where the Via Mala can be seen briefly to the right. This 15th-century road passes through a narrow gash in the earth – 'the most sublime and tremendous defile in Switzerland' according to Murray's Handbook, and painted several times by Turner. Beyond the pretty village of **Tiefencastel** the valley becomes wilder, the thickening forests allowing occasional glimpses of waterfalls. After Alvaneu stands one of the world's best-known railway bridges, the **Landwasser Viaduct**, which is approached alongside the river of the same name. It is not so much the structure itself that impresses, though the curving masonry bridge of 5-and-a-bit arches is handsome enough, but arailway crosses the incomplete arch

The Landwasser Viaduct.

and dives straight into a tunnel in a sheer wall of rock.

The few hotels in the attractively sited village of **Filisur** are a good base for walkers: a footpath leads back to the Landwasser Viaduct and another follows the river and railway along the beautiful valley towards Davos. But it is to explore the footpath leading to the **Albula Pass** that many people break their journey: the path is punctuated by boards explaining how the railway climbs a vertical height of 416 metres (1,364ft) in just 13km (8 miles) without any rack assistance. It does this by a series of loops and spirals with 14 tunnels and 8 viaducts, making the section even more disorienting to the passenger than the climb out of Andermatt.

Once through the 6-km (3.75-mile) **Albula Tunnel**, the railway begins its descent to the junction with the line from Scuol-Tarasp (see page 198) before Bever, where the railway joins the broad valley of the upper Engadin. Leaving Samedan there is a delightful view to the left of a picturesque church set amid trees on a low hill.

The last station before journey's end, Celerina, is near the foot of the Olympic bobsleigh track and the famous Cresta run, built in 1884 by three Englishmen.

After a short tunnel, the Glacier Express draws into the world-famous resort of **St Moritz**. Although the spa here has been used since at least the 16th century, it was only during the second half of the 19th century that it became a popular winter resort, when the enterprising hotelier, Johannes Badrutt, offered a group of British tourists free accommodation to prove how delightful the area could be during the winter months. It convinced them, and thousands followed.

Winter sports apart, St Moritz makes a good base for walking, with excellent public transport by train, bus or cable car to the start of many valley or mountain walks. It is also the start of a delightful cycle route beside the River Inn through the Engadin to Innsbruck, in neighbouring Austria. Although the town's status inevitably means higher prices, there are still some excellent hotels, full of character, away from the centre.

The Palm Express postbus journey to Lugano is one of the finest in the country, passing the village of Sils-Maria, where the Giacometti family (Alberto being the most famous member) lived and worked. A museum commemorates them, with examples of their sculpture and paintings. St Moritz is also the start of two other scenic railway journeys, to Scuol-Tarasp and Tirano in Italy.

ST MORITZ–SCUOL-TARASP

It is difficult to define what makes a landscape pleasing, but the gentle valley of the Inn between St Moritz and Scuol-Tarasp, close to the Austrian border, is an unending delight, punctuated by attractive villages where buildings are often decorated with the painted graffiti decoration characteristic of the region. The railway itself was a major civil engineering achievement, with 17 tunnels and 72 bridges, some of great elegance. Its cost was originally justified by the expectation that it would become part of a through route from Austria to Italy.

ATTRACTIVE STATIONS

The journey from St Moritz entails a change of train at **Samedan** as trains for Scuol now start at Pontresina. From **Bever**, they keep to the north flank of the valley for most of the journey. The first station at **La Punt-Chaumes** is, like most stations on the line, a pleasure to look at, with attractive round-topped doors, and windows decorated with colourful window boxes. Some of the larger farm buildings combine houses with barns and other agricultural functions, an arrangement typical of the Engadin region and much of eastern Switzerland.

At the large village of **Zuoz** the distinctive three-storey tower of the once-influential Planta family home can be seen from the train. Surprisingly for

⊙ Essentials

European Rail Timetable no. 545

Distance: 57km (35.5 miles)

Duration of journey: 1hr 21 mins

Frequency of trains: hourly

Steam train crossing the river Inn near Brail.

⊙ **Tip**

Europe's longest floodlit toboggan run is from Preda station on certain winter nights when the road down to Bergün is closed to traffic. The railway obligingly ferries passengers and toboggans up the hill, and the 6-km (3.7-mile) road is lit with lanterns.

such a well-protected country, Switzerland has only one national park (straightforwardly named **The Swiss National Park**); access to its western end can be gained from S-chanf station. At **Cinuos-chel-Brail** the valley narrows and the railway crosses the Inn by a single-span bridge over a deep gorge. The railway describes a large loop to diminish the gradient down to **Zernez**, where there is an exhibition about the park in the National Park House. The uniform character of the houses in the village is the result of a decision to rebuild to a common plan after fire swept through the village in 1872.

After **Susch** is the junction for the Vereina Tunnel line through to Davos, which has reduced the journey time between Zürich and St Moritz/Scuol-Tarasp for those who don't mind missing the scenic pleasures of the Albula Pass route. The villages of **Guarda** and **Ardez** have both received awards for the way they have conserved their architectural heritage and are a pleasure to explore on foot.

When the sound of the train indicates the end of the long Tasna Tunnel, look to the right: as it crosses the highest bridge on the line before diving into another tunnel there is a magnificent glimpse of one of Switzerland's most romantic castles, at Tarasp. There is also a good view of the castle from the station at **Ftan**, situated so far below the village that the latter has a bus service from Scuol.

SCUOL-TARASP

The station at **Scuol-Tarasp** is also slightly above the spa town – a legacy of a proposed link with Austria – and a shuttle bus meets trains throughout the working day. There are two parts to Scuol: the upper part is the older, and many houses have deeply recessed windows splayed through the massive walls like gunports; the lower is the more recent, where buildings designed to exploit the 'champagne of the Alps', as Scuol's waters are known, were built during the 19th and 20th centuries. The water's health-giving properties have been recognised for centuries, and there is an old fountain in upper Scuol, on La Plazzetta, that offers ordinary water, and reddish, iron-rich water. An even greater variety of water used to be on offer at the Trinkhalle, built in the 1840s beside the river, each type accessible through a separate arched opening.

The town has one of the most attractive spas in Switzerland: the Bogn Engiadina was built in the 1990s, using marble of different colours and other high-quality materials, to produce a centre that is visually exciting as well as restful. One of the pools leads outside, allowing bathers to enjoy the beauty of the surrounding mountains, and computer-programmed whirlpools complement personal advice on preventive medicine and diet.

In common with the whole of the Engadin, Scuol offers some of the best walking in Switzerland, with thousands

Ardez in winter.

of kilometres of footpaths that can be accessed using the railway or postbuses. Postbus is also the best way to reach the enchanting village of **Tarasp**, which would be popular even without the attraction of its 11th-century castle.

TARASP CASTLE

Built by the lords of Tarasp, the castle was for centuries owned by Austrian families before it was taken over by the canton of Graubünden after the Napoleonic Wars. The cost of upkeep prompted its sale, but a succession of irresponsible owners allowed it to deteriorate and its contents were gradually sold. In 1900 it was bought by Dr Karl Linger, the German inventor of a popular mouth freshener. On his death the castle was offered to a grandson of Queen Victoria, Grand Duke Ernest Ludwig of Hesse. Now under new ownership, the castle is open for guided tours of a number of rooms, including the dining room which has been used for concerts and has some rare, early 16th-century stained glass.

ST MORITZ–TIRANO

Few railway journeys as short as the 2 hours and 30 minutes of the **Bernina Express** between St Moritz and Tirano can encompass such an extraordinary transition – from glaciers to palm trees. The highest rail crossing of the Alps is made even more spectacular in summer by open-air carriages, which enable photographers to take panoramic pictures of the stupendous landscapes that open up with every twist of this sinuous railway. In figures, this translates into a climb from 1,778 metres (5,833ft) at St Moritz to 2,256 metres (7,401ft) at Bernina, followed by an ear-popping descent to 429 metres (1,407ft) at Tirano in Italy. What is astonishing is that this fall of 1,524 metres (5,000ft) in less than 40km (25 miles) is accomplished without any rack assistance – the Bernina railway

overcomes by adhesion a greater vertical distance than any Swiss rack railway.

As with all the Swiss journeys, a week or more could be spent exploring the villages the stations serve, walking up some of the valleys and taking cable cars or funiculars up some of the surrounding peaks.

ST MORITZ TO ALP GRÜM

The Bernina line leaves **St Moritz** on a different alignment from the Chur/Scuol-Tarasp routes, passing through the line's longest tunnel to race across the lovely triangle of land at the upper Engadin. Passing the 1720-built chalet station of **Celerina Staz** (a rare instance of an older building being adapted for railway use) and **Punt Muragl Staz** (change for the nearby funicular up to Muottas Muragl), the train reaches the junction of **Pontresina**. The town has an Alpine Museum with reconstructed rooms as well as various themed displays.

From **Morteratsch** there is a 'climate trail' to illustrate the hastening retreat

☉ Essentials

European Rail Timetable no. 545

Distance: 61km (38 miles)

Duration of journey: 2hrs

Frequency of trains: 11 per day

The Bernina Express bus provides a link between St Moritz and Tirano.

No other country in the world can match Switzerland for the number and variety of passenger-carrying narrow-gauge railways. Narrow-gauge lines are preferred for mountainous or remote areas with low population densities, because the difficulty and/or expense of building a standard-gauge railway does not merit the investment.

Some of the longer and best-known narrow-gauge railways are described in detail in this book, but visitors to Switzerland should not miss the chance to ride on other equally impressive, if shorter, lines. Most remain lifelines for the communities they serve, especially in winter when roads are

In Centovalli, between Locarno and Domodossola.

treacherous, or closed. Some are rack railways, and all have a distinctive character.

Martigny–St-Gervais-les-Bains This international route linking the Geneva–Brig main line with Chamonix and the SNCF line to Annecy traverses the breathtaking gorge of Le Trient, with vertiginous drops of 426 metres (1,400ft) to the valley floor.

Bex–Villars–Col-de-Bretaye Notable for the sheer variety of landscapes and the extraordinary contrast between the start of the journey in the Rhône Valley and the tranquillity of the Alpine meadows at Col-de-Bretaye.

Aigle–Les Diablerets The most interesting of the three narrow-gauge railways that start at the wine centre of Aigle, it loops around the town's magnificent castle before forging up the lovely valley of the Grand Eau.

La Chaux-de-Fonds–Glovelier/Tavannes The network of lines serves the Jura Mountains, one of the least visited parts of Switzerland. An area of woods and heathland, it offers good walking and unrivalled country for riding.

Yverdon-les-Bains–Ste-Croix After twisting through foothills planted with sugar beet, the train suddenly climbs steeply through woods and along the dramatic Gorges de Coratanne to the world capital for the manufacture of music boxes and mechanical music, with a museum to prove it.

Locarno–Domodossola The international railway through the glorious scenery of the Centovalli has the most striking steel viaducts of any railway in the country, crossing the many tributaries of the Melezza River.

St Gallen–Gais–Appenzell–Herisau–Gossau The Appenzellerbahn serves this eponymous area of the country, noted for its cycling and walking, particularly in the mountains around the Ebenalp and Säntis, which dominate the landscape.

Luzern–Engelberg This busy railway passes through the historic town of Stans (for the quaint funicular up the Stanserhorn) on its way to the resort of Engelberg. Most people come to take the cable car up Mt Titlis, but there is also an important Benedictine monastery which is open to visitors.

Chur–Arosa The winter and summer resort of Arosa could hardly have a better approach than the railway, high up on a ledge above the Schanfigg Valley with its pretty villages and farms. The line crosses the Langweis Bridge, the longest reinforced concrete span in the world when opened in 1914.

of the glacier, which can be seen from the train as it describes a loop on its climb towards Bernina Diavolezza. The **Morteratsch Glacier** is a classic example of a by-product of global warming that afflicts the entire Alps – glacial retreat. When the station opened in 1908, Edwardian tourists could walk the 150 metres/yds to the tongue of the glacier in a few minutes; today it is a 3-km (2-mile) hike. More than half the ice in Alpine glaciers has melted since 1850. The thaw of the permafrost imposes huge costs: it acts as a glue to prevent rock avalanches, so measures have to be taken to protect vulnerable settlements, as well as transport infrastructure and winter sports facilities.

A cable car ascends from here to Diavolezza where there is what Baedeker describes as 'a view of surpassing grandeur' over the Bernina range. The terrain becomes desolate as the train approaches the summit of the line and skirts the pale-green waters of Lago Bianco, once four separate lakes until dammed for hydroelectric power. Walkers often disembark at the summit station of **Ospizio Bernina**, which looks as though it has been built to withstand being buried in snow. Some take the 2-hour walk down to **Alp Grüm**, where there is a hotel and terraced restaurant by the station with a magnificent view over the Palü glacier.

A DRAMATIC DESCENT

There follows one of the world's steepest descents of an adhesion railway, the line dropping at an almost continuous gradient of 1 in 14. To achieve this it loops repeatedly back and forth, with tunnels or viaducts at many of the elbows, so passengers are quickly disoriented when they emerge from a tunnel with the hill rising on a different side. Trees cover many slopes, but they periodically break to give glimpses of Val Poschiavo.

As the train leaves Cadera Tunnel, the flange-squealing eases and

speed picks up as the train makes for **Poschiavo**, where the workshops of the Rhätische Bahn are passed. Well worth exploring, Poschiavo has a main square with some fine patrician houses and a Spanish quarter, built in 1830 with the savings of returning emigrants. Running along the road on grooved rails embedded in the tarmac, the train reaches Lago de Poschiavo at **Le Prese** and skirts the water to the southern end of the lake at **Miralago**. Looking north, there is a good view of the mountains through which the train has passed.

A variety of crops begins to appear in the fields as the train descends more steeply, with the Poschiavino River on the western side, past the emphatically Italian campaniles at **Brusio** and on to the last engineering flourish of the railway – the nine-arched curved viaduct by which the line spirals under itself. Three modern sculptures have been placed inside the circle of this unusual feature.

Once through the last station in Switzerland at **Campocologno**, the

Lago Bianco in winter, at Ospizio Bernina.

⊙ Essentials

European Rail Timetable nos. 561/564

Distance: (1) Luzern–Interlaken 74km (46 miles); (2) Interlaken–Jungfraujoch 32km (20 miles)

Duration of journey:
(1) 2 hrs

(2) 2 hrs (change trains at Lauterbrunnen or Grindelwald, and Kleine Scheidegg)

Frequency of trains: both routes have half-hourly services

Paddleboat on Lake Lucerne.

valley broadens and joins the Valtellina. After trundling through orchards and past market gardens, the train again behaves like a tram and clatters along the road into Tirano alongside the standard-gauge railway that can take passengers on to Lago di Como and Milan.

LUZERN–INTERLAKEN–JUNGFRAUJOCH

In tours that try to cram as much of Europe as they can into a fortnight, the Swiss element is most likely to be a train journey up to **Jungfraujoch**, famous primarily because it is the highest railway station on the Continent, at 3,454 metres (11,333ft). It is also a spectacular journey, with views better than from the summit itself. The cost of maintaining a railway like the Jungfraubahn is prodigious, so it is not surprising that the otherwise all-encompassing Swiss Pass entitles holders only to a discount on the high fare. Consequently it is worth checking that there is a good chance of clear visibility before setting off (most likely

in the morning); warm clothes and sunglasses are essential at any time of year.

The round trip from Luzern can easily be done in a day, perhaps even using a steamer on Brienzer See for part of it. The line between Luzern and Interlaken is the only metre-gauge railway operated by Swiss Federal Railways (SBB). The scenery is so good that there are panorama coaches with swivel armchairs on some trains.

LUZERN AND ITS LAKE

Luzern is one of the best holiday bases in Switzerland, with excellent rail links, a host of places to visit via the magnificent fleet of steamers on the lake (five of them paddle-steamers), exceptional museums and galleries for a town of its size, one of Europe's finest concert halls, and a good range of hotels, many of outstanding quality and character.

Interlaken-bound trains soon meet the edge of Lake Luzern, sharing tracks with trains for Engelberg as far as the junction and lakeside resort of

Hergiswil. A tunnel masks the transition to the shore of the Alpnachersee and **Alpnachstad** where the world's steepest rack railway begins its ascent of Mt Pilatus. Monumental cliffs rearing out of the lake give way to rolling farmland as the train makes for **Sarnen**, capital of Obwalden canton, where the oldest account of the inception of the Swiss Confederation, written around 1470, is kept in the town hall.

More water comes into view to the west (right-hand side) as the railway skirts the lake of Sarnen, its surface often broken by brightly coloured sailing boats. The pretty village of **Sachseln** on its shore has many fine houses, some dating from the 17th century. The surrounding hills gain in height as the train pauses at **Giswil**, start of the rack-assisted ascent to the Brünig Pass and broadening views back over Sarnersee and then over the turquoise waters of Lungernsee, now a reservoir.

Passing through a delightfully unspoilt valley, with only a few farm buildings amid the trees and fields, the final section of the climb reaches the summit at **Brünig-Hasliberg**. This station is used by hikers who then gain access, by postbus and cable car, to numerous dramatic walks along the ridge. The descent to the floor of the Aare Valley is even steeper than the ascent, breaks in the trees affording a glimpse of the river and railway heading west to Brienzer See.

MEIRINGEN MERINGUES

The train reverses direction at **Meiringen**, which gave its name to the meringue, devised by a local *patissier*. The town is also famous for its association with Sherlock Holmes, since it was the setting of the nearby Reichenbach Falls that Sir Arthur Conan Doyle chose for the fatal struggle with Professor Moriarty. The connection is commemorated in an imaginatively-designed museum in the basement of the English Church. Besides a funicular to the

falls, there is an astonishingly narrow gorge, wide enough only for a footpath, to the east of Meiringen.

The line runs through orchards along the flat valley floor to the eastern end of Brienzer See, of which there are enchanting views as the railway takes the northern shore to reach the woodcarvers' village of **Brienz**. A connecting bus takes visitors to the 80-ha (198-acre) **Swiss Open-Air Museum** at Ballenberg, an outstanding collection of rural buildings rescued from demolition and re-erected in an authentic setting. Opposite the station is the foot of the rack railway up Mt Rothorn; most of the trains are steam-operated, some with locomotives built in the 1990s. The pier at Brienz gives passengers the option of making one leg of the journey to or from Interlaken by boat. The lake has one paddle-steamer, the 1914 Lötschberg.

Interlaken Ost is the interchange between the Brünig line, the standard-gauge (with direct trains from places as far afield as Frankfurt and Hamburg), and the Bernese Oberland

Museum of Transport, Luzern.

At the Swiss Open-Air Museum, Ballenberg.

Railway (BOB). The boat pier is also close by. The yellow and blue carriages of the bob take passengers for the Jungfrau as far as Lauterbrunnen. It is important to be in the correct part of the train, since BOB trains divide at Zweilütschinen; almost invariably the front section goes to Lauterbrunnen, the rear to Grindelwald.

The train curves round the perimeter of an airfield to reach **Wilderswil**, junction for the rack railway up Schynige Platte and, curiously, the burial place of two daughters of Schumann and one of Mendelssohn. Just before the junction of **Zweilütschinen** the railway crosses the Black Lütschine, shortly before its confluence with the White Lütschine, which the railway follows up a narrowing valley towards **Lauterbrunnen**. As the village is flanked by two remarkably sheer walls of rock, it is no surprise that there are 72 waterfalls of varying size along the valley, the most famous and spectacular of which are the Staubbach and Trümmelbach.

At Lauterbrunnen there is a cross-platform change to the connecting train of the Wengernalpbahn, which in a rare display of lack of Swiss foresight, was built to a different gauge from the BOB and the Jungfraubahn, necessitating two changes. As there are no roads that climb above the valley, everything has to be transported by train, with wagons for supplies and large quantities of luggage.

LAUTERBRUNNEN TO KLEINE SCHEIDEGG

Leaving Lauterbrunnen there is a good view of the Staubbach Falls to the right while to the left the massif of the Männlichen, Tschuggen and Lauberhorn towers above the line. Gradually the village of Mürren comes into view, situated on a dramatic shelf above a vertical slab of rock. The railway divides, the 'old' line now used for goods traffic continuing to the right, while the 'new' line (opened in 1910) bears to the left on slightly gentler gradients. The two meet just before the railway reaches the car-free resort of **Wengen**.

The clean air and peace of the compact village are a tonic, and for some

⊘ BUILDING THE JUNGFRAUBAHN

The construction of a railway to Jungfraujoch was first mooted in the 1870s, but encountered local opposition from farmers who feared it would frighten their cattle, while horse-drawn-carriage operators saw their livelihoods under threat. Despite the opposition, various plans were drawn up and duly rejected, in part due to exorbitant costs. At least one proposal failed because the speed at which it transported passengers to the 3,454-metre (11,330-ft) summit would allow insufficient time to acclimatise to the altitude. In 1893, Adolf Guyer-Zeller came up with the idea of starting the railway at the newly finished summit station of the Wengenbahn at Kleine Scheidegg rather than down in the valley. A breakthrough was the concept of building the line in stages, which could be opened for business one at a time, thereby generating funds for the continuing construction further up the line.

The railway Guyer-Zeller began to build in 1896 was much as he originally envisaged. The first stretch up to Eiger Glacier opened just two years later. The entire system was finally completed in 1912 (nine years later than planned), after many vicissitudes, including the explosion of a gunpowder store that was reputedly heard as far away as Germany.

a revelation of how pleasant places can be without traffic. Electric vehicles are available to shuttle luggage between hotels and station, or carry those with disabilities. A cable car ascends the Männlichen, from where there is a panorama of the various valley systems that form this part of the Bernese Oberland. From the summit there is a walk along the ridge to Kleine Scheidegg.

The views from the train above Wengen become progressively more spectacular as it climbs closer to the adjacent peaks of the Eiger, Mönch and Jungfrau. It is no wonder that Byron found the inspiration to write Manfred while staying at **Wengernalp**; even today there is nothing but the station and one of the most peaceful hotels in the world to distract one from the awe-inducing view. Tchaikovsky, Mendelssohn and Wagner were also guests here.

A REMOTE INTERCHANGE

Situated on a saddle of rock linking the Lauberhorn and the Jungfrau massif, the remote Kleine Scheidegg station is full of activity. Trains from Lauterbrunnen and Jungfraujoch exchange passengers and a Grindelwald line feeds in from the north.

Shortly after the station and restaurant at **Eigergletscher**, where the huskies that haul sledges at the summit are kennelled, the train enters the 7,122-metre/yd tunnel. Stops are made at **Eiger Wall** and **Eismeer** for passengers to de-train and walk along a passage to a viewing window in the side of the mountain before continuing to the underground station at **Jungfraujoch**.

It is advisable to walk slowly on leaving the train as most people feel some effect from the altitude. Lifts ascend to the various levels for restaurants, an audio-visual programme about the mountain and the railway (with English as well as German commentary), exhibition area, sledge rides, open-air verandas and winter garden. A weather station and Europe's highest grid-connected solar power plant also share the mountain.

Jungfraubahn passes passes by Jungfrau, Bernese Oberland.

⊙ Essentials

European Rail Timetable
no. 566

Distance: 75km (46.5
miles)

Duration of journey:
2hrs 10 mins

Frequency of trains:
hourly

MONTREUX–ZWEISIMMEN–LENK

The metre-gauge Golden Pass Express is operated by special panoramic trains with outstandingly comfortable coaches and driving trailers that allow some passengers to enjoy a driver's eye view of the track. Reservations are not obligatory, but they are advisable in season to secure the best seats.

Famous for its jazz festival and nearby Castle of Chillon, **Montreux** makes a good base for walking and exploring the eastern end of Lake Geneva. Its station on the Geneva–Brig–Milan main line is one of the few places in the world where three different track gauges meet, the smaller two being the 800-mm (2ft 7½-in) gauge of the rack railway up Rochers-de-Naye, the larger one the metre-gauge of the Montreux–Oberland Bernois Railway that operates the trains through to Lenk.

The climb up to the 2,045-metre (6,709-ft) summit of Rochers-de-Naye begins as soon as the train leaves Montreux. There is a tremendous view at the top over Lake Geneva and the French Alps. The Swiss Pass is valid as far as Caux, with a 25 percent discount thereafter. There are some great walks from the intermediate stations at **Glion** and **Caux**, and an Alpine garden with over 1,000 species near the summit, which has a restaurant and an audio-visual display to show the views you're missing on cloudy days.

SPIRAL TUNNELS AND HORSESHOE CURVES

The journey to Lenk starts in a U-shaped tunnel that gives a foretaste of the horseshoe curves by which the train gains height to give wonderful views over the lake and into France. Chamby is one end of the Blonay–Chamby heritage railway, so a steam locomotive may be glimpsed at weekends. Beyond Les Avants, where Noël Coward lived for 14 years, the gradient reaches its steepest point, at 1 in 13.7 – an astonishing figure for a railway worked solely by adhesion.

The long tunnel under the Col de Jaman marks a complete transition of landscape, into the remote Hongrin Valley with scattered chalets and farm buildings down which the railway drops to the junction of **Montbovon**, for trains to Gruyères and Bulle. Occasionally sheltered from avalanches, the railway climbs again, forging a way through the wooded gorge of the Sarine to enter the Pays d'Enhaut. Pausing at **Rossinière** where there is a magnificently decorated chalet dating from 1754 near the station, the railway turns away from the Sarine to reach the area's principal town of **Château d'Oex**.

BALLOONING CENTRE

The association of Châteaux d'Oex with hot-air ballooning dates only from 1979 but the area's ideal atmospheric conditions have quickly made it an international centre, and the town hosts the world's leading ballooning championship in the last week of January. At other times of the year visitors can experience

Rochers-de-Naye, a cogwheel railway.

the thrill of seeing the Alps from a balloon. The town's Pay-d'Enhaut Museum is an entertaining introduction to this distinctive area and its history.

Continuing along a ledge in the hillside with broad views across the valley, the railway crosses into German-speaking Switzerland at **Rougemont**, where the 11th-century Romanesque church hosts concerts as part of the Menuhin Festival between mid-July and early September, as does the 15th-century church in **Saanen**. The train takes advantage of the last opportunity for fast running to reach the famous summer and winter sports resort of **Gstaad**, after which the line climbs in earnest. Numerous cable cars and chairlifts can be used for short-cut access to upland walks, of which there are many around Gstaad, with some of the remoter valleys, such as Lauenental, being accessible by postbus.

The line describes a semi-circle at a 1 in 25 gradient to cross an impressive three-span viaduct. The white peaks of the Diablerets group can be seen as the train climbs to the summit of the railway at Saanenmöser, after which there is a sharp descent into the Simme Valley and the junction with the standard-gauge line from Spiez at Zweisimmen. The largest village in the Simmental, Zweisimmen also has one of the longest gondola rides in Switzerland – the two-section lift up to Rinderberg, which is 5,102 metres/yds in length to gain a vertical height of 1,061 metres (3,481ft).

Pausing at **Blankenburg** with its baroque castle and covered bridge across the river, the train parallels the river as it heads for the horseshoe of mountains that rings **Lenk** and seals it from any other approaches. The panorama from the town is dominated by the Wildstrubel at 3,243 metres (10,639ft). Besides being a popular year-round resort, Lenk is also a spa, with the strongest Alpine sulphur springs in Europe. A music academy and a New Orleans Jazz Festival in July swell the summer visitors, many of whom are attracted simply by the walking and the quiet of a town without through routes.

Château de Chillon.

Semaine Internationale de Ballons â Air Chaud, Château-d'Oex.

MUSEUMS AND HERITAGE LINES

Switzerland has some of the finest heritage railways and museums in Europe. The numbers here relate to the map on page 186.

MUSEUMS

Locorama ❶
Alte SBB Lokremise, Egnacherweg 1, CH-8590 Romanshorn
Open: Apr–Sept Sun 2–5pm
Features: collection of historic locomotives and rolling stock.
Nearest station: Romanshorn
Tel: 071 460 24 27
www.locorama.ch

Verkehrshaus der Schweiz ❷
(Swiss Transport Museum)
Lidostrasse 5, CH-6006 Luzern
Open: Mar–Oct daily 10am–6pm; Nov–Feb 10am–5pm
Restaurant, shop
Features: one of the world's great railway collections
Nearest station: Luzern
Tel: 041 375 7575
www.verkehrshaus.ch

Zurich Tram Museum ❸
Forchstrasse 260, CH-8008
Open: Apr–Oct Wed–Fri 2–5pm, Sat 1–6pm, Sun 1–5pm
Shop, model tramway
Features: tram rides
Nearest stations: Burgwies (Line 11, direction Rehalp)
Tel: 044 380 21 62
www.tram-museum.ch

HERITAGE LINES

Appenzeller Bahnen ❹
Open: daily
Features: buffet car and saloon coach; occasional steam
Nearest stations: St Gallen, Gossau

Gauge: 1,000mm (3ft 3 3/8 in)
Tel: 071 354 50 60
www.appenzellerbahnen.ch

Associazione club del San Gottardo ❺
(Mendrisio–Stabio–Valmorea–Cantello–Malnate Olona)
Club del San Gottardo, Casella Postale 1250, CH-6850 Mendrisio
Open: June–Oct, first Sun of month
Features: heritage railway
Nearest station: Mendrisio
Length: 12.5km (7.8 miles)
Gauge: 1,435 mm (4ft 8 1/2 in)
Tel: 076 732 56 42
www.clubsangottardo.ch/chi-siamo.html

Chemin de Fer Musée Blonay–Chamby ❻
Open: May–early Oct weekends and some weekdays
Café, shop, museum
Features: largest working collection of historic railway locomotives and vehicles in Switzerland
Nearest stations: Blonay, Chamby
Length: 3km (2 miles)
Gauge: 1,000mm (3ft 3 3/8 in)
Tel: 021 943 21 21
www.blonay-chamby.ch

Ballenberg-Dampfbahn ❼
(Interlaken Ost–Meiringen–Giswil)
Open: steam operation on various Sundays
Café, shop
Features: bar coach, rack section
Nearest station: Interlaken Ost
Length: 45km (28 miles)
Gauge: 1,000mm (3ft 3 3/8 in)
Tel: 033 828 73 40
www.ballenberg-dampfbahn.ch

Brienz Rothorn Bahn ❽
(Brienz–Rothorn)
Open: end May–late Oct daily
Cafés, shops, summit hotel
Features: steam and diesel cog operation
Nearest station: Brienz
Length: 7.6km (4.8 miles)

Gauge: 1,000mm (3ft 3 3/8 in)
Tel: 033 952 22 22
www.brienz-rothorn-bahn.ch

Compagnie du Train à Vapeur de la Vallée de Joux ❾
(Le Pont–Le Brassus)
Open: daily; steam on various days
Features: historic carriages, café
Nearest station: Le Pont
Length: 13km (8 miles)
Gauge: 1,435 mm (4ft 8 1/2 in)
Tel: 079 434 74 63
www.ctvj.ch

Dampfbahn Bern ❿
Bernstasse 8, Konolfingen CH-3150
Open: runs on a few Sundays each year
Operates: varied excursions
Features: use of locomotives near Bern
Nearest station: Konolfingen
Gauge: 1,435 mm (4ft 8 1/2 in)
Tel: 031 302 39 68
www.dbb.ch

Dampfbahn Furka Bergstrecke ⓫
(Realp–Oberwald)
Open: late-June–early Oct Fri– Sun; early July–mid-Aug daily
Café, shop
Features: beautiful scenery, long summit tunnel.
Nearest stations: Realp, Oberwald
Length: 18km (11 miles)
Gauge: 1,000mm (3ft 3 3/8 in)
Tel: 0848 000 144
www.dfb.ch

Dampfbahn–Verein Zürcher Oberland ⓬
(Bauma–Bäretswil–Hinwil)
Open: May–mid-Oct various Sundays
Café, shop
Features: historic coaches
Nearest stations: Bauma, Hinwil
Length: 12km (7.5 miles)
Gauge: 1,435 mm (4ft 8 1/2 in)
Tel: 052 386 17 71
www.dvzo.ch

Ferrovia Mesolcinese ⑬
(Misoxerbahn)
(Bellinzona–Mesocco)
Open: June–Aug, various Sundays
Features: historic electric
vehicles
Nearest station: Castione-Arbedo
Length: 31km (19 miles)
Gauge: 1,000mm (3ft 3 3/8 in)
Tel: 079 262 39 79
www.seft-fm.ch

La Traction ⑭
(CF du Jura)
Open: steam excursions on various
days
Cafés, shops
Features: historic carriages, steam
locomotives
Nearest stations: La Chaux-de-
Fonds, Glovelier, Tavannes
Length: 74km (46 miles)
Gauge: 1,000mm (3ft 3 3/8 in)
Tel: 032 952 42 90
www.cj-transports.ch
www.la-traction.ch

LEB ⑮
(Lausanne–Echallens–Bercher
Bahn)
Features: historic carriages
Nearest station: Lausanne
Length: 23km (14 miles)
Gauge: 1,000mm (3ft 3 3/8 in)
Tel: 021 621 01 01
www.leb.ch

Oensingen–Balsthal Bahn ⑯
Open: daily; steam on various days
Café
Features: saloon and historic
coaches
Nearest station: Oensingen
Length: 4km (2.5 miles)
Gauge: 1,435 mm (4ft 8 1/2 in)
Tel: 062 391 31 53
www.oebb.ch

Rhätische Bahn ⑰
Graubünden
Open: daily
Operates: occasional
programme of steam and
historic electric excursions,
including Graubünden and
Grisons.
Features: glorious scenery
Gauge: 1,000mm (3ft 3 3/8 in)
Tel: 081 288 65 65
www.rhb.ch

RHB ⑱
(Rorschach–Heiden Bergbahn)
Open: daily; steam on various
Sundays
Café, shop
Features: rack railway
Nearest station: Rorschach
Length: 7.1km (4.5 miles)
Gauge: 1,435 mm (4ft 8 1/2 in)
www.appenzellerbahnen.ch

Rigi Bahnen ⑲
(Vitznau–Rigi)
Open: daily; steam on various days
Café, shop
Features: glorious scenery, walks
from stations, summit hotel
Nearest station: Arth-Goldau; boat
service to Vitznau
Length: 6.8km (4.2 miles)
Gauge: 1,435 mm (4ft 8 1/2 in)
Tel: 041 399 87 87
www.rigi.ch

Schinznacher Baumschulbahn ⑳
Open: late-Apr–early Oct, Sat–Sun
Café, shops, gardens
Features: spectacular narrow-
gauge railway around nursery
Nearest station: Schinznach Bad
Length: 2.5km (1.5miles)
Gauge: 600 mm (1ft 11 5/8 in)
Tel: 056 463 62 82
www.schbb.ch

Stanserhorn-Bahnen ㉑
(Stans–Kälti)
Open: Apr–late Nov, daily
Café, restaurant, shop
Features: Switzerland's most historic
funicular, spectacular scenery, with
cable car from Kälti up Stanserhorn,
Nearest station: Stans (boat from
Lucerne to Stanstaad, then train to
Stans)
Length: 1.5km (1 mile)
Gauge: 1,000mm (3ft 3 3/8 in)
Tel: 041 618 80 40
www.stanserhorn.ch

Sursee–Triengen-Bahn ㉒
Open: steam on various days
Features: saloon and historic
carriages
Nearest station: Stans
Length: 8.9km (5.5 miles)
Gauge: 1,435 mm (4ft 8 1/2 in)
www.dampfzug.ch

VVT Vapeur Val-de-Travers ㉓
(St-Sulpice–Travers–Neuchâtel)
Open: various weekends
Café, shop, museum
Features: historic carriages,
occasional longer excursions
Nearest stations: St Sulpice,
Neuchâtel
Length: 24km (15 miles)
Gauge: 1,435 mm (4ft 8 1/2 in)
Tel: 032 863 24 07
www.rvt-historique.ch/

Zürcher Museums-Bahn ㉔
(Zürich Wiedikon–Sihlbrugg)
Open: programme of steam
excursions on various Sundays
Features: historic coaches
Nearest station: Zürich Wiedikon
Length: 18.6km (11.5 miles)
Gauge: 1,435 mm (4ft 8 1/2 in)
Tel: 0848 962 962
www.museumsbahn.ch

Waiting at Milan Central station.

Train arriving at Monterosso al Mare on the Cinque Terre.

ITALY

Many lines in the Italian south and on the islands are old-fashioned and picturesque. Further north, the network connects with its neighbours using some of Europe's smoothest trains

On 3 October 1839, in the 'Kingdom of two Sicilies', the aptly-named locomotive, *Vesuviana*, steamed the 6km (4 miles) between Naples and Portico to signal the birth of rail travel in Italy. Other Italian states, not wishing to be outdone, quickly ordered tracks to be built, and by 1850 the country had some 2,000km (1,240 miles) of railway lines. With the desire to link disparate parts of the new nation, following Italian unification (completed in 1871), the network really began to take shape, encouraged by the government's offer to refund the cost of construction as soon as a new line was opened. Within four years all Italy's principal cities were inter-connected. The railways were nationalised in 1905, although there are still private-operators today. In the years between the two world wars, particularly under the dictator Benito Mussolini, who is said to have stood at Rome's railway station, stop-watch in hand, to ensure that his trains ran on time, electrification of the rail system proceeded apace, and soon Italian trains were the fastest in the world. With the development of Pendolino tilting trains, first introduced in 1988, Italy proved itself to be at the forefront of high-speed rail technology.

The system now has a total length of about 16,000km (10,000 miles) and covers the entire country, including Sicily

Local train service in Sicily.

and Sardinia. The state-owned company, Ferrovie dello Stato (FS), better known as Trenitalia, also has a basic shipping fleet comprising a variety of train-carrying ferries that ply between Calabria and Sicily (passengers and freight) and between Civitavecchia and Sardinia (freight only).

NORTH AND SOUTH

The services offered by FS and other companies are varied. They range from Le Frecce, the fastest and most luxurious trains of the fleet through

Main attractions

Verona: Roman Arena, Castelvecchio, Palazzo Maffei, Teatro Romano, Juliet's House
Rome: St Peter's and the Vatican, Pantheon, Trevi Fountain, Spanish Steps,
Naples: Castel Nuovo, Teatro San Carlo
Palermo: Palazzo dei Normanni, Via Vittorio Emanuele.

Maps on pages
214, 216, 225

214

Italy

① Museums and Heritage Lines

Featured route

| 0 | | 100 km |
| 0 | | 100 miles |

workaday Intercities to more mundane Regionale trains. On the whole, punctuality and comfort of services decrease from north to south.

Other than those routes featured in the following pages, there are numerous attractive railway journeys all over Italy. Many of the lines running across the Apennine Mountains in the centre of the country are picturesque, with mountain views and quintessentially Italian villages; Rome to Pescara, and the line from Terni to Sulmona are good examples. Other highlights include the run from Pistoia to Viareggio on the Ligurian coast, which winds through timeless Tuscan countryside; and the narrow-gauge mountain route from Catanzaro up to Camigliatello in the beautiful Sila region, a journey through one of Europe's least-known regions.

VERONA–INNSBRUCK

This is a breathtaking journey with glorious views of Alpine peaks, many of which remain snow-covered throughout the year. Narrow fast-flowing rivers run alongside the tracks, and the landscape is lush with coniferous and deciduous trees, fruit orchards and vineyards. Numerous castles are passed en route, but unfortunately few of them can be seen from the train.

INTO THE HILLS

On leaving Verona the track loops northwest along the left bank of the River Adige – the second-longest river in Italy – skirting on the right the vine-planted hillsides of **Valpolicella**, renowned for its sparkling wine. Soon, **Rivoli** and its valley is reached, followed by the wider Val Lagarina and, after 69km (43 miles), the busy railhead of **Rovereto**, at an altitude of 211 metres (693ft). Travellers are greeted by three life-sized dinosaurs, a reminder of the 1991 discovery of 200-million-year-old Jurassic footprints in the area. Eight kilometres (5

miles) beyond, the village of Calliano with the restored Castle Beseno – more of a fortified town than a castle – can be seen.

The train keeps to the left bank of the Adige and after 14km (9 miles) arrives in **Trento**, the capital of Trentino, sitting in a large natural amphitheatre surrounded by mountains. Immediately across the river from the station a cable car ascends to the lower slopes of majestic Mt Bondone. A private railway, Ferrovia Elettrica Trento-Malè, runs from its own separate Trento station northwest to Marivella at the start of the Brenta Dolomites where, with a great deal of luck, you will see brown bears – only about a score remain. Trains depart about every hour and make the 66-km (41-mile) journey in about 1 hour 40 minutes.

North of Trento, the valley narrows and the intensity of cultivation increases. The vines are strung on wide pergolas – a horizontal trellis supported on posts – a traditional method of viticulture in these parts since Roman times. This permits the

⊘ Essentials

European Rail timetable no. 595

Distance: 274km (170 miles)

Duration of journey: 3hrs 35 mins

Frequency of trains: 6–8 per day (direct)

A Trenitalia train approaching Florence.

breezes blowing up the Adige Valley from Lake Garda to circulate round the grapes, with a beneficial, cooling effect.

At this point the train abandons the River Adige and follows its tributary, the Isarco. The next stop is **Bolzano/Bozen** – from here to Innsbruck all signs are in both Italian and German. Bolzano is the capital of the bilingual province of Alto Adige/Süd Tirol, ceded by Austria to Italy after World War I. In the mountain valleys people use German rather than Italian, and favour dumplings and *schnitzels* rather than *prosciutto* and pasta. With them they drink some of the great wines that are produced in the region – it is estimated there are 40 vines for every inhabitant. Visitors to Bolzano can see the 5,300-year-old remains of 'Otzi', a human being found mummified in a glacier 10 years ago.

THE DOLOMITES

To get closer to some superb views of the **Dolomites**, whose improbably jagged peaks soar to over 3,300 metres

(10,800ft), board one of the three cable cars operating from Bolzano (turn right outside the station). Departures are at 20-minute intervals, taking you 1,220 metres (4,000ft) up the slopes of Mt Renon/Rittner to Soprabolzano/Oberbozen, from where there are stunning views stretching across to Rosengarten. Next to the cable car terminus board the electric tramway (hourly service) – with luck, antique wooden coaches will be in service – for the 20-minute journey to Collalbo/Klobenstein to view the fanciful Longomoso Pyramids, eroded earth pillars capped by stone 'hats'.

Frequent trains make the 32-km (20-mile) journey alongside the River Adige northwest to **Merano**, a renowned spa with a casino, delightful botanical gardens and splendid views of the mountains. The journey time is 40 minutes.

THE SOUTH TYROL

Back on the Innsbruck line, after a long tunnel, the track enters the Isarco (Elsack) Valley and makes a sweeping arc for the next 60km (38 miles).

Piazza delle Erbe, in the historic city centre of Bolzano.

In doing so, it is following the traditional spine of the South Tyrol which has been a major route between the Germanic and Mediterranean worlds since Roman times. At first the valley is rocky but soon becomes lush with fruit orchards, vineyards and chestnut trees. The river is narrow and fast-flowing, and at several places is crossed by flimsy, covered wooden bridges.

Ponte Gardena/Waidbruck and Castle Trobug, perched high on a crag above Gardena to the right, soon appear. This area is renowned for its wood carvers – there are reputedly 3,000 of them, many of whom speak Ladin (Romansch), a derivative of Latin that has been spoken here since time immemorial. Superb quality pieces, as well as kitsch, are on sale.

The train passes through Chiusa/Klausen, a picturesque little town 28km (18 miles) from Bolzano, before arriving at elegant Bressanone/Brixen, a popular resort with a baroque cathedral and restored royal palace. On leaving Bressanone large gun bunkers can be seen, a reminder that the Tyrol has long been a battleground. A further 11km (7 miles) takes you to Fortezza/Franzensfeste, where limestone pinnacles shoot skywards from dense pine forests.

THE BRENNER PASS AND INNSBRUCK

Soon after Fortezza, a long, narrow, wooded valley opens out into a lush green basin and the town of **Vipiteno/Sterzing**, a pretty place grouped around a street lined by typical, white Tyrolean houses with red-tiled roofs and geraniums bursting from overhanging balconies. And so to the **Brennero/ Brenner Pass**, which, at 1,375 metres (4,511ft), is the lowest route across the Alps and the only one crossed in the open by a main railway line. From here the track, hemmed in by trees, runs due north and sharply

downhill through the Sill Valley. As the train emerges from a short tunnel, the first sight of the Tyrolean capital, **Innsbruck**, is the solid, red, Baroque Stiftskirche (Wilten Abbey Church) backed by the snow-covered Nordkette slopes, rising to 2,334 metres (7,657ft).

To reach the Altstadt (Old Town) where Innsbruck's major attractions are interspersed with cafés and restaurants, stroll 300 metres down Salurner Strasse, which faces the station, and turn right into Maria Theresien Strasse, then into pedestrianised Herzog Friedrich Strasse. Here stands the 14th-century Stadtturm tower, with grand views from the top. Across the square is the Goldenes Dachl (Golden Roof), composed of 2,657 16th-century, gilded copper tiles. The interior houses a museum devoted to Habsburg emperor, Maximilian I.

NICE–ROME

For the most part, at least until La Spezia, this is a romantic corniche journey with magnificent views of the Ligurian Sea, together with the French and

⊙ Essentials

European Rail timetable nos. 90, 360, 580, 610, 611

Distance: 685km (425.5 miles)

Duration of journey: 7hrs 40 mins (Ventimiglia–Rome)

Frequency of trains:

Ventimiglia–Rome: 1 per day (direct)

Nice–Genoa: 3 per day

Genoa–Rome: 7 per day

Castle Trobug.

Italian Rivieras. Beyond Pisa, the Ligurian gives way to the Tyrrenhian Sea and the scenery gradually becomes less dramatic. Passengers who board the direct express from Ventimiglia will travel the 652km (405 miles) to Rome in under 8 hours – for those with more time it is better to travel on the not-infrequent slow trains, even if that entails a number of changes. The route is dotted with ports – Genoa, La Spezia, Livorno, Civitavecchia – from where ferries leave for the islands of Elba, Corsica and Sardinia. There is no direct train from Nice to Rome. You will need to change at Ventimiglia or take the Thello service from Nice to Genoa and change there.

NICE TO GENOA

As the train leaves **Nice** on its coast-hugging 33-km (20-mile) journey to the French–Italian frontier, the view is of the foothills of the snow-covered Alps plunging into an azure and turquoise sea. Frequently, however, the glorious scenery is blocked by millionaires' mansions and de-luxe hotels.

No sooner are you settled in your seat than the train arrives at the pretty, resort of **Villefranche**, with colourwashed houses and a station practically on the beach. Next comes the 7-km (4-mile) stretch of villas and sleek white yachts that is the principality of **Monaco**, the heart of the Côte d'Azur. The wealth continues unabated to the final French stop of **Menton**, surrounded by orange and lemon groves, where the station is just a few metres from the sea.

It's a short hop to **Ventimiglia** in Italy. From here to La Spezia (240km/150 miles), the rail route mainly follows the broad, concave sweep of the Italian Riviera. The views over the lush Riviera di Ponente are often glorious and, for the first 40km (25 miles), enlivened with cultivated flowers. On leaving Ventimiglia the train passes plantations of palms whose fronds are used, to the exclusion of all others, by the Vatican during Holy Week. The train soon arrives at **San Remo**, the ageing queen of the Italian Riviera, with elegant old hotels and a palm-lined promenade. **Alassio** heralds a series of more contemporary resorts, and the rail line clings to the sea until **Albenga**, with its medieval wall and Roman ruins. This is succeeded by the resorts of Finale Ligure, Savona and Varazza. After the attractive, prosperous town of **Genoa**, the Riviera di Ponente ends and the Riviera di Levante commences.

THE RIVIERA DI LEVANTE

The scenery becomes wilder as the train passes the elegant resorts of Santa Margherita and Rapallo. From the former it is just a few kilometres to the fashionable resort of **Portofino**. The next part of the journey is a game of hide and seek as the train pops in and out of tunnels to permit tantalising glimpses of the **Cinque Terre**, five colourful villages perched high above the turquoise sea and virtually unknown until the railway reached them. The

Portofino.

train soon arrives in **La Spezia**, set on a wonderful natural harbour whose surrounding hills are dotted with old Genoese castles.

After La Spezia the frontier between Liguria and Tuscany is quickly crossed. This stretch of coast, the Riviera della Versilia, is jammed with disappointingly unattractive resorts, from **Carrara**, where all great sculptors from Michelangelo to Henry Moore have searched for the perfect marble block, to **Viareggio**, the largest Tuscan resort. Gradually the hinterland becomes flatter, and 15 minutes beyond, away from the sea, is **Pisa** with its improbable Leaning Tower and splendid, multicoloured, four-tiered Duomo. The next stop is **Livorno** (Leghorn), Italy's second largest port.

The track, now running across reclaimed swampland, keeps close to the sea as it passes yet another Riviera, the Etruscan, which consists of several over-built unattractive resorts. Matters improve at **Cecina**, in the vicinity of which is the World Wildlife Fund (WWF) reserve of **Bolgheri**, an important feeding ground for migrating birds. Leaving Cecina a glimpse is caught of the promontory of Populonia and of the island of **Elba**. At **Campliya Marittima**, where the track abandons the coast, the train enters the Maremma, a reclaimed coastal strip that stretches south into Lazio and as far east as Monte Amiata. In classical times this was the northern heartland of the Etruscans.

After **Follonica** the line runs round the foot of the Cape Castiglione massif before reaching Grosseto, the principal town of the Maremma. After the River Ombrone is crossed there is a splendid view of the picturesque Bay of Talamone. As the train enters the region of Lazio, the words of writer D.H. Lawrence come to mind. He described the plain and the low hills that stretch to **Rome**, over 100km (60 miles) to the south, as 'a peculiarly forlorn coast'.

NAPLES–PALERMO

This rail voyage around the Tyrrhenian Sea connects the two largest cities in the southern half of the country. The

⊘ Essentials

European Rail timetable no. 640

Distance: 702km (436 miles)

Duration of journey: 9hrs 20 mins

Frequency of trains: 2 direct trains per day and 1 overnight sleeper

The location of the first Italian railway, constructed in 1839, at the Museum of Italian Railways.

⊘ THE CIRCUMVESUVIANA

Before you set off from Naples you might want to consider two special trips. The first of these is close to Naples. The Sicily-bound train scarcely does justice to the area around the Bay of Naples. For that you are better off exploring with the private Circumvesuviana railway network that skirts the base of Mt. Vesuvius. Circumvesuviana has its own ultra-modern station on Corso Garibaldi in Naples but all trains stop at the lower level of the Stazione Centrale as well. The service is half-hourly and the journey to Pompeii takes about 25 minutes.

En route there is a constant view of the bay and its islands. Trains stop at Ercolano (for Herculaneum and Vesuvius) as well as Pompeii. To visit Vesuvius, board a No. 5 bus outside Ercolano station; this takes you to a car park at the base of the crater from where it is a gentle 40-minute walk over gravel to the rim of the crater, which still emits occasional puffs of smoke (the last eruption was in 1944). To visit the ruins of Pompeii, alight at the Pompei-Villa dei Misteri rather than the Pompeii-Sanatuario station.

The other special trip you might want to make a bit later in the itinerary is around the attractive Tropea promontory. For this you will have to eschew the direct service to Sicily in favour of stopping trains.

line stays close to the west coast of the peninsula all the way to Villa San Giovanni on the Strait of Messina, from where a ferry transports the train to Messina. Palermo is a further three hours along the Sicilian north coast.

SOUTH TO THE CILENTO

If you are going direct to **Palermo**, take a seat on the right side of the train for the best views. Leaving Naples, the train makes its way through the crowded suburbs, and before long the bulk of Vesuvius comes into view, immediately followed, on the right, by the blue waters of the Bay of Naples. The track passes the buried town of Herculaneum, followed shortly afterwards by Pompeii, before heading eastwards across the plain towards Salerno, reached in around 45 minutes from Naples.

Pulling out of **Salerno** the sea is glimpsed as you travel southeast for a short distance to Battipaglia from where a track goes off east to Taranto in the heel of Italy. The train for Palermo turns due south and crosses

the plain of Paestum, a sea of plastic hothouses, passing close to the impressive Roman temples at **Paestum** (see page 222). A little further south, past the town of Agrópoli and its ruined castle, it enters the squarish, low massif that juts out from the coast between the gulfs of Salerno and Policastro. This is the **Cilento**, a region of wild, unspoilt beauty where journeys are still made by mule and cart. The coast consists of rugged cliffs, stands of pine and small, pristine coves.

Turning inland and passing through several tunnels, the train emerges into the Alento valley, from where there are tantalising glimpses through olive groves to **Cape Palinuro**, the most beautiful part of this coast. A short distance from the cape the line turns due east, away from the sea, running through tunnels until a steep section of coast is regained at the busy rail junction of Sapri.

The track now runs through olive groves overlooking the beautiful Gulf of Policastro; to the east, sharp-peaked mountains rise to over 1,000 metres

Train tracks at the ferry port in Messina, Sicily.

(3,300ft). This tiny slice of coastline (30km/19 miles long), tucked between Campania and Calabria, belongs to Basilicata, Italy's most backward and undeveloped region. A stop is made at the fashionable resort of **Maratea**, 'city of 44 churches' where there is an unusual marble Christ, with hands outstretched.

THE TOE OF ITALY

Several tunnels later, the River Noce marks the entrance to **Calabria** – the most southern of Italy's mainland provinces. From here until it reaches the ferry at Villa San Giovanni the track clings fairly closely to the coast as it passes through a landscape of luxuriant vegetation. The first town in Calabria is **Praia a Mare**, a small resort facing the tiny, uninhabited Isola di Dino. Having passed the picturesque town of Scalea, perched on ledges of rock, and the calcified ruins of Cirella, the train arrives at **Páola**, a major junction (for fast trains this is the first stop since Salerno, 220km/137 miles to the north). St Francis of Páola, Calabria's principal saint, spent most of his life here; in a ravine near the station stands the Santuario di San Francesco.

The line now runs through an intensely cultivated area past a series of small resorts, of which **Amantea** is the largest and liveliest. Rounding Cape Suvero there are tremendous views across the great sweep of the Gulf of Sant' Eufémia, then it's a run across flatlands before we arrive at **Lamezia Terme**.

TROPEA TO THE STRAITS

From Lamezia the main route makes a beeline for Rosarno, while the historic line follows a 72-km (45-mile) arc along the coast of the **Tropea** promontory before rejoining the main line at Rosarno. To forego the latter, longer route, whose first half between Pizzo and Capo Vaticano is called the Costa Degli Dei (Coast of the Gods) is to deny

yourself a glorious journey. There are tantalising glimpses of golden sands, which are easily accessible from several stops – Tropea (known as the Capri of Calabria), Iopollo and Nicótera are three possibilities.

The track runs high above the shore where sparkling seas splash into coves and inlets and the land is a cornucopia of orange groves, prickly pears, palms and oleander. From the magnificent headland of Capo Vaticano, grand views of the Gulf of Gioia can be enjoyed, before the train enters the lush plain of Ravello and soon pulls into **Rosarno** station. All around are groves of century-old, gnarled olive trees.

Back on the main route, the track continues southwards through intensely-cultivated land, passing the beaches (many unseen) of several resorts. **Palmi**, from where the tall television mast on Sicily's northern tip is visible, marks the start of the **Costa Viola** – a name earned from the colour of the sea. A series of tunnels in quick succession blocks out views of beaches until the train emerges just

Tropea beach, Calabria.

Train tracks pass Isola Bella beach in Taormina, Sicily.

THE TEMPLE ROUTE

Italy means ancient history and archaeology. A visit to one the great excavated sites is always a highlight of any tour through the country, especially the south and Sicily.

Many Greek temples and other monuments in southern Italy and Sicily are still in splendid condition. The railway route south from Naples has several classical wonders, most notably at Paestum, reached in about 35 minutes from Naples (services hourly). Three squat, solid, well-preserved, golden Doric temples stand on a flat piece of ground. The oldest is the Temple of Hera (circa 550 BC), which retains its double row of columns, while the bestpreserved is the Temple of Neptune, To the north is the Temple of Ceres, the smallest of the trio, which served for a time as a Christian church.

The temple at Segesta, Sicily

From Palermo, a train journey through lovely countryside to the south leads to Castelvetrano (three direct trains daily), from where a 20-minute bus ride terminates at Marinella. Here, scattered over a large area of sand dunes are eight Doric temples, which, with one exception, were built in the 5th and 6th centuries BC. The temples are separated into an eastern group of three and a western group of five. Temple E in the eastern group was probably sacred to Hera and was reconstructed in 1958. Temple G, almost completely in ruins, was one of the largest in antiquity. Cross the depression, Gorgo Crottone, to reach the acropolis and the western group, which is dominated by the partially reconstructed Temple C, the oldest temple, whose renowned metopes are in the Palermo museum. Glorious views can be enjoyed from the acropolis.

THE MARVELS OF AGRIGENTO

Better known are the temples built between the late 6th and late 5th century BC, which line Agrigento's renowned Valley of the Temples. Agrigento may be reached either directly from Palermo by a train journey of a little over two hours (a dozen trains daily) across the heart of Sicily, or alternatively by bus from Selinunte, which takes the same length of time.

Enter the valley at its eastern end to see the temples of Juno Lacinia. Concord is one of the best preserved in the world; Hercules is probably the oldest of the Agrigento temples; Zeus, if it had been completed, would have been among the world's largest Greek temples; and finally the Sanctuary of the Chthonic Deities which has vestigial remains of four temples. Using these remains part of a temple dedicated to the Heavenly Twins – Castor and Pollux – has been erected.

West of Palermo, standing in chaste solitude atop a hill, is a gem: the unfinished (although this is not evident at first sight) ochre-coloured Doric temple of Segesta (c. 420 BC). It is an uphill walk of about 2km from Segesta Tempio, the unmanned station – more of a restaurant than a station, really – at which passengers alight. This is reached from Palermo by taking the train to Trapani. There are four trains daily. Theoretically, it is possible to visit Segesta and Selinunte by rail and bus on the same day – but don't depend on it.

before **Scilla**, a popular resort with an excellent long beach.

On this stretch of coast you may catch sight of small boats with disproportionately tall, ladder-like masts, on which sits one of the crew, and an equally long bowsprit (spar projecting from the bow) on whose tip sits another crew member. These are fishing boats in search of *pesce spada* (swordfish), which abound in these waters: the man atop the mast is the 'spotter', the one on the bowsprit the harpoonist.

ACROSS TO SICILY

Villa San Giovanni is the embarkation point for the crossing to Messina in Sicily. The voyage itself may take only 20 minutes, but the loading of the train onto the ferry takes well over an hour. This is because the train has to be divided up to fit on the ferry, resulting in a great amount of shunting: push the first two coaches into the ferry's innards, then back off; push the next two coaches in, and so on.

Not surprisingly, there is always talk of building a suspension bridge – the world's longest – across the Straits. However, the ever-present threat of an earthquake has so far prevented anything progressing past the drawing-board stage. In the 1908 earthquake, 84,000 inhabitants of Messina perished.

It is possible to get off the train at Villa San Giovanni while it is being loaded onto the ferry, but the town holds little of interest. However, the much larger town of **Reggio di Calabria**, 13km (8 miles) and 15 minutes to the south, has in its museum a treasure beyond belief – the *Bronzi di Riace*, two glorious 2-metre (6ft 5-inch), 5th-century BC bronze statues, which fishermen dragged from the sea in 1972. While the train is being loaded onto the ferry, risk-takers might consider boarding a train to Reggio and alighting at Reggio Marittima Stazione from where the museum is a three-minute uphill walk. Bear in mind, however, that trains in this part of Italy are not noted for reliability, so if you want to see the museum it's better to take a taxi.

From **Messina**, the undistinguished, modern, third city of Sicily, which lies on the lower slopes of the Peloritani Mountains, the train starts its westward journey to Palermo following the coast of the Tyrrhenian Sea for much of the time. Away from the coast the terrain rises slowly to the Nebrodi and, further west, Madonie mountains, both Mafia heartlands. Scattered along the entire route are numerous classical remains. Once the urban sprawl of Messina is left behind, most of the countryside is relatively lush and covered with orange and lemon trees. **Milazzo**, the first stop of note, 36km (22 miles) from Messina, is situated on a verdant peninsula, unfortunately utterly blighted by a giant oil refinery. The station is far from the port which is the starting point for ferries to the other-worldly **Isole Eolie** (Aeolian Islands), the best known of which are volcanic Stromboli and Vulcano.

⊘ THE CIRCUMETNEA

From Messina trains run south for the 3-hour journey to Siracusa. The route is a delight, with the Ionian Sea almost always in view and, for the first part of the route, fine views of the Calabrian coast terminating in Cape Sant'Alessio, a bold promontory of whitish rocks.

Landward is lush, with orange and lemon groves backed by mountains. It is not long before Mt Etna, Europe's highest and most active volcano (3,323 metres/10,966ft) comes into view. A memorable side trip around the volcano can be enjoyed by alighting from the Messina–Siracusa train at Giarre-Riposto and boarding a train of the narrow-gauge Ferrovia Circumetnea. The 114-km (71-mile) loop to Catania takes five hours.

The narrow-gauge track climbs up the slopes of the volcano, passing barren stretches of black lava from recent eruptions; there are glorious views of terraced vineyards and almond, hazelnut and orange groves. The train stops at several interesting villages – Linguaglossa, Randazzo, Bronte Adrano, Paterno. Towering above is the threatening presence of Etna. Alight in Catania at the Ferrovia Circumetnea station and take the FCE metro to the State Railway station, where you can catch a train to Siracusa or back to Messina. For timetables and more information, see www.circumetnea.it

From Milazzo to **Cefalù**, the next major stop, the line runs past many small, clean stony beaches backed by extensive citrus groves. From the main square in **Patti** buses make the short journey to Tindari and ancient **Tyndaris**. This was one of the last Greek settlements on Sicily and the beautiful ruins are predominantly Roman rather than Greek. However, what attracts most visitors is not the ruins but the Santuario della Madonna Nera, a modern building that houses a black-faced Byzantine Madonna, said to have miraculous powers.

After passing rocky Cape Calva, we come to the pleasant resort of **Gioiosa Marea**; from here, the island of Vulcano is a mere 20km (12 miles) offshore. Soon, the windswept peninsula of **Capo Orlando** and the resort of the same name, is reached. It became famous throughout Italy after its shopkeepers defied the demands of the Mafia for their infamous pizzo (protection money). **Sant'Agata di Militello** is a good place to alight for those who wish to visit the vast Nebrodi National Park, rich in deciduous trees, especiall beech, where foxes and wild cats roan and eagles soar. Unique to the park i the Fratello breed of horses, distin guished by their odd-shaped noses At **Santo Stefano di Camastra**, furthe along, some of Sicily's best ceramics with styles ranging from traditional t contemporary, may be purchased.

THE FINAL STRETCH: CEFALÙ TO PALERMO

Busy, delightful **Cefalù** is second onl to Taormina in its popularity as resort. On leaving the station the trai travels directly above the long, lovel beach; looking backwards, the town' renowned Arab-Norman cathedra can be seen. About 20 minutes beyon Cefalù is the large station of Termir Imerese, which owes its importance t the oil refinery that disfigures the land scape. Somewhat surprisingly, there i a beach here and the ubiquitous clas sical ruins.

Far more attractive is the view fron **Bagheria** station. The handsome cream-coloured, Baroque buildin that can be seen from here is one o several villas built in the 17th and 18t centuries when Bagheria was a sum mer retreat for the nobility. The Vill Palagonia, 10 minutes beyond the sta tion, is known for its menagerie of gro tesque sculptures.

Ahead, jutting out into the sea, i Palermo's limestone promontory o Monte Pellegrino, but before the cit is reached the train turns away fron the coast to enter a lush plain plante with row upon row of orange an lemon trees. This is the hill-encircle **Conca d'Oro** (Golden Basin) formerly glorious cornucopia of fruit and othe produce, but now much blighted b concrete. Palermo's Centrale statior lies just ahead.

SARDINIA

Sardinia, the second largest islanc in the Mediterranean, has two

Houses along the shoreline, Cefalú.

ailway systems: the Italian state-
wned and run railway, Trenita-
ia (FS) and ARST, owned by the
egional government, which trades
under the brand name Trenino
Verde. Whereas the Trenitalia trains
un on 1,435mm (4ft 8½in) standard-gauge tracks, the Trenino Verde
stock runs on 950mm (3ft 13/8in)
narrow-gauge. On occasions, they
share the same track, which then
consists of three lines of rail. In
some towns both share the same
station: in others each has its own.

The major regular line runs from
Cagliari in the south via Macomer to
Chilivani in the north, equidistant from
the east and west coasts. At Chilivani it
divides, with the eastern branch terminating at Golfo Aranci and the western
branch at Porto Torres, having passed
through Sassari.

However, the Sardinian pearls for
the railway buff are the Trenino Verde
routes on which a tourist service runs
during the summer months. Itineraries vary each year and you will need
to look at the schedule on the website
(www.treninoverde.com) for forthcom-
ing journeys. Mostly short trips are on
offer on the Trenino Verde (approximately 33–62km/20–40 miles) but this
route describes the longest trip possible. Please note that during your visit,
it may only be possible to do a section
of it – see the website for more details
and current schedules. This is one of
the Trenino Verde's four lines. The others are Mandas–Sorgono (a fork from
the route described below), Bosa-
Macomer–Nuoro in the middle of the
island and Sassari–Tempio–Palau in
the north.

There are two other ways to travel
on Trenino Verde trains apart from
scheduled tourist trips. Either you can
privately hire a whole train, or you can
hope for a 'last minute' opportunity
– to hop on board rolling stock being
relocated, in which case you will be
charged a heavily reduced fare.

THE CAGLIARI–ARBATAX ROUTE

The train that runs from the rudimentary station at Piazza Repùbblica in
Cagliari is a regular year-round commuter service. Leaving noisy, chaotic
Cagliari behind the track soon travels
through the pleasant rolling hills of
Trexenta, where olive and almond trees
grow in profusion. From **Mandas**, which
is reached after a couple of hours, the
train travels through the mountains for
158km (98 miles) to Arbatax. The line
was inaugurated in 1894, with the aim
of opening up the rich mineral deposits
and forests in the heart of Sardinia.

A plaque at Mandas station honours D.H. Lawrence (1885–1930), who
describes the journey from Mandas to
Sorgono in his book, *Sea and Sardinia*.
The Sorgono line, running due north
from Mandas, traverses similar rugged
scenery to the Arbatax line.

Dispel all thoughts of steam engines
bellowing smoke and pulling historic
wooden carriages. Sensible legisla-
tion forbids the use of steam in the dry
summer months, and although wooden
coaches stand at Mandas they are not

⊘ Essentials

European Rail timetable
no. 629 (scheduled
services in Sardinia)

Distance: 218km (135.5
miles)

(Cagliari–Arbatax)

Duration of journey:
6hrs 40 mins

Cagliari-Arbatax

normally used. Groups who make prior arrangements and who travel during the 'No Fires' period may try to arrange for a steam train pulling historic coaches.

Immediately after setting off eastwards from Mandas the track climbs, twists and turns; the train squawks and screeches and its whistle screams warnings to any animals on the track and to the users of level crossings. These – there are a fair number – are rudimentary affairs, consisting of chains hung across the road.

The 5-hour journey through dramatic mountain landscapes is best described as bone-shaking. So sinuous and convoluted is the route that unless you are carrying a compass you will be at a loss to know in which direction the train is travelling.

Thirty minutes out from Mandas the train halts at Orroli and then turns north. This is the region known as the **Barbagia**, the home of bandits where vendettas were part of everyday life until not too long ago. The name is of Roman origin, derived from the Latin Barbaria – a term used by th Romans for those whose culture an lifestyle differed from their own. Abou 250 well-preserved nuraghe, ancien squat, circular towers for which Sar dinia is renowned, are found in th Barbagia. One of the most famou the Nuraghe Arrubiu, is a mere 5km (miles) from Orroli. Unfortunately, non can be seen from the train.

ALONG THE FLUMENDOSA

Below Orroli, through a valley covere with fields of barley, flows the Flu mendosa, the second longest river i Sardinia. It broadens out to becom the attractive Lago dei Flumendosa, man-made lake formed by one of thre dams along the river's journey to th sea. The water remains in sight near all the way to **Esterzili**, reached aroun an hour later. The landscape is well wooded and the region is especiall known for its varieties of oak, includ ing holm- and cork-oak. Higher u the mountains chestnuts, hazelnuts maples and yews thrive.

Soon we reach the village of **Sádal** built around the 13th-century church c San Valentino, next to which gushes sparkling waterfall. As the train enter the tunnel between Sadali and the ne stop, **Seui**, it reaches, at almost 90 metres (3,000ft), the highest point c the journey. There's a break of about 1 minutes at Seui to allow the passage c the down train arriving from Arbata and this gives passengers time t make a dash for the simple station caf for a cold drink or a shot of espresso.

THE SCENTED MACCHIA

The thick, tangled, heavily-scente vegetation that is so prevalent her is called *macchia* (*maquis* in France and is not dissimilar to the vegeta tion on Scottish moors, particularl when it contains yellow-flowerin broom, gorse and heathers. Othe aromatic plants that make up the *mac chia* include rosemary, juniper, myrtle

Trenino Verde in the Sardinian countryside.

thyme, rock rose, arbutus (strawberry) trees and mastic shrubs. This is the principal source of food for pigs and goats, and also yields an oil for domestic use. The juniper and myrtle berries are used to make schnapps, and it is from the blossoms of the arbutus that bees collect nectar for the pungent, Sardinian honey, which, it is claimed, is a cure for bronchial asthma. As a result of forest fires, *macchia* is on the increase.

Anulu, the stop after Seui is the highest station in Sardinia, at 865 metres (2,838ft). All around are the Geulo mountains, dominated to the north by Mt Perdedu. For sheer dramatic beauty the next stretch of line between Seui and **Gairo**, which crosses a stone and lattice girder bridge over the San Girolamo River, is unsurpassed. The town of Gairo was rebuilt after 1951 when its predecessor, Gairo Vecchio, had to be evacuated when torrential rains resulted in a series of landslides.

Hill walkers and nature lovers will want to get off at San Girolamo, midway between Seui and Gairo, and explore the enchanting Montarbu forest to the north. From here footpaths leads to Monte Tonneri (*tonneri* are massive, limestone cliffs) where deer and mouflons (mountain sheep) live among ash, holly and yews. This is one of the best-known sections of the Gennargentu massif.

After Gairo the line turns north and enters the valley of the Flumendosa at the southern end of Lago Alto del Flumendosa. A short distance later, **Villagrande**, surrounded by reddish granite rocks and renowned for the production of *prosciutto* ham from free-range pigs, is reached. As the train turns south and passes **Arzana**, the track makes a series of sweeping curves including a complete circle, in order to get over a steep slope.

Ultimately the train arrives at **Lanuei**, perched on the eastern slopes of the Barbagia at a height of 555 metres (1,821ft) and backed by mountains. This was formerly the capital of the region and, because of its salubrious climate, a popular health resort. From here the Tyrrhenian Sea and the large, lush plain which leads to it can be seen.

DESCENT TO THE EAST COAST

The train now commences its descent to the east coast, first north and then due east around numerous curves on the steep, rocky hillside. This is the steepest gradient on the route – about 1 in 30. The untamed scenery is gradually replaced by a gentler landscape with groves of olive trees and prickly pears.

The end of the line is the attractive little station at the placid town of **Arbatax**, standing alongside one of the large new marinas that are being built all over the island of Sardinia. If you are intending to spend the night or stay longer in the region, it might be better to leave the train at **Tortolì**, which is reached nine minutes before Arbatax and is a much livelier town.

Traditional Sardinian dress.

Sardinian coastline.

THE TRAIN OF KINGS

Of all the trains that there have ever been, one stands out for its celebrity and its literary assocations that have earned it a mythical status.

On 4 October 1883, the official inaugural run of the Orient Express began from the Gare de l'Est in Paris. The passengers embarked under the impression that they would be carried without interruption to Constantinople (Istanbul). This was not to be, as the tracks were not yet built all the way through. Passengers said farewell to the Orient Express at the desolate Romanian village of Giurgiu, from which a ferry took them across the Danube into Bulgaria. From that point a decidedly non-deluxe train continued to the town of Varna, on Bulgaria's Black Sea coast, where they boarded a steam packet to complete their trip to

1920s poster for the Simplon-Orient-Express.

Constantinople. The first complete journey had to wait until 1889.

Over the years the route of the Orient Express changed with the vicissitudes of war, politics and economics. The train was largely superseded in 1919 by a new deluxe Orient Express that travelled through the Simplon Tunnel. This new, southern route was dictated by the victors of World War I, who wanted to connect Western Europe with the emerging states of Eastern Europe but bypassing Germany and Austria, their former and possible future enemies.

World War II put much of Europe's train network in the hands of the Germans, who inaugurated a sort of Nazi Orient Express from Berlin to Istanbul. Many Wagons-Lits cars were taken over by the German army to transport officers, and some cars in occupied France were used as stationary restaurants and hostels. One even served as a brothel for Nazi officials. Others were stored in the French countryside, their magnificent, risqué Lalique glass panels and intricate Prou marquetry removed and hidden from harm.

DECLINE AND REVIVAL

The Paris–Istanbul service resumed after the war, but it was no longer an all-luxury train. Through passage was also hampered by the complexities of crossing the borders of Iron Curtain countries. Air travel further diminished the appeal of international sleeper trains, and the Orient Express made its last regular run with through sleeper service to Istanbul on 22 May 1977 – a shrunken outcast of the hurry-up age.

On 8 October 1977 Sotheby's put five of the original carriages up for auction in Monte Carlo. The first two cars were sold to a decorator representing the King of Morocco, the next two cars were knocked down to James B. Sherwood.

Over the next five years he scoured Europe for 1920's deluxe Wagons-Lits and First Class Pullman cars from the same vintage that could be restored. Finally, on 28 May 1982, Sherwood stood in front of assembled Hollywood stars and socialites at Platform 8 of London's Victoria Station and declared: 'The Venice Simplon-Orient-Express is resumed.'

MUSEUMS AND HERITAGE LINES

As in the rest of southern Europe, preserved railways are few and far between in Italy, although there are several railway museums. The numbers relate to the map on page 214.

MUSEUMS

Museo Ferroviario ❶
Via Sassari 24 Presso Stazione Trenitalia, Cagliari
Open: Sat 9am–noon
Features: exhibits include equipment used by the builders of the earliest railways, a reconstruction of a typical 19th-century railway station with a line linking two stations and a section with period carriage material still in working order
Nearest station: Cagliari.
Tel: 070 679 4715
www.sardegnavapore.it or www.cagliariturismo.it

Museo Nazionale Ferroviario di Pietrarsa ❷
Stazione FFSS Pietrarsa, via Pietrarsa, Naples
Open: Thu 2am–8pm Fri 9am–4.30pm, Sat–Sun 9.30am–7.30pm
Features: one of the most important railway museums in Europe, housed in the 19th-century locomotive workshop of Pietrarsa. Displays 38 locomotives, 6 railcars and 10 coaches; of special note is the royal train built in 1929 for the wedding of Umberto di Savoia with Maria José of Belgium. East of Naples city centre on the way to Portici
Nearest station: Pietrarsa S. Giórgio a Cremano

Tel: 081 472 003
www.museodipietrarsa.it

Museo Ferroviario di Trieste Campo Marzio ❸
Stazione di Trieste Campo Marzio, via Giulio Cesare 1, Trieste
Open: currently closed until further notice for restoration work – see website for more details.
Features: housed in an early 20th-century station, documents the history of railway transport. Displays consist of tools, machinery, railway material, a number of steam, electric and diesel engines, passenger and goods coaches, horse-drawn and electric trolley-cars from Austria, Hungary and Germany. Monthly tour of the city on vintage trains
Nearest station: Trieste Centrale
Tel: 040 379 4185
www.museoferroviariotrieste.it

Museo Nazionale della Scienza e della Tecnica ❹
(National Museum of Science and Technology)
Via S. Vittore 21, Milan
Open: Tue–Fri 10am–6pm; weekends and holidays 10am–7pm; closed Mon
Features: 16th-century monastery housing steam and electric locomotives
Nearest station (metro M2): St Ambrogio (Green Line)
Tel: 02 485 551
www.museoscienza.org

HERITAGE LINES

Ferrovia Basso Sebino (Treno Blu) ❺
(Bergamo–Paratico Sarnico) Via Zanica 75, Bergamo

Open: scheduled steam and vintage electric train trips on certain days Feb–Dec
Features: links with boat trips to Monte Isola on the Lago d'Iseo
Nearest station: Bergamo
Length: 90km (56 miles)
Gauge: 1,435 mm (4ft 81⁄2in)
Tel: 338 857 7210
www.ferrovieturistiche.it

Ferrovia Val d'Orcia (Treno Natura) ❻
(Siena–Asciano–Monte Antico)
Features: a vintage train (occasionally steam-hauled) travels south of Siena in the heart of Tuscany, through the Sienese Crete (clay hills) and the Orcia Valley at the foot of Mount Amiata
Open: scheduled steam and vintage diesel train trips on certain days Mar–Dec
Gauge: 1,435 mm (4ft 81⁄2in)
Nearest station: Siena
Tel: 338 857 7210
www.ferrovieturistiche.it

Il Trenino Verde ❼
(see page 225)
Via Posada 8–10 Caligari, Sardegna (Sardinia)
Features: ARST operates four narrow-gauge lines, which are of great interest (although not strictly speaking heritage lines: (Mandas–Arbatax; Mandas–Sorgono; Macomer–Bosa; Nulvi–Tempio–Palau.
Open: runs certain days Mar–Sep; also possible to arrange specialised itineraries
Gauge: 950 mm (3ft 13⁄8in)
Tel: 070 26 57 1
www.treninoverde.com

ÖBB S-bahn in the winter.

AUSTRIA

Glorious Alpine scenery, accessed by an extensive
network of rack railways and longer runs make Austria a
favourite destination for train lovers

Austria is a far more varied country than most people imagine. The classic Alpine scenery most associated with it does not extend much beyond Vorarlberg and the Tyrol, the western spur of its territory. The area south of Salzburg has the highest mountains and is more rugged; Carinthia and Styria are lower, drier and heavily forested. The area to the north of the Danube has a distinctly central European feel, while low-lying Burgenland in the east has more in common with Hungary than with the Alps.

The first Austrian railway opened in 1837, running 20km (12 miles) north-east from Vienna to Deutsch Wagram to form the initial part of the link from the capital to the Silesian coal fields (now in Poland). The ensuing development of the railways was conceived with the grand aim of connecting the far-flung territories of the Austro-Hungarian Empire. Unlike many other European countries, Austria has largely retained its network of branch lines serving rural areas; some of these are operated by private railway companies. The major lines are run by Österreichische Bundesbahnen (ÖBB), the national rail operator.

Today the ÖBB network totals 6,123km (3,804 miles) of track, 3,523km (2,189 miles) of which are electrified. The backbone of the

network is the Vienna–Linz–Salzburg Westbahn, with a branch from Wels to Passau on the German border. Other major lines radiating from Vienna are those to Breclav in the Czech Republic, which continues north to Prague and Warsaw; to Hegyeshalom in Hungary, leading to Budapest; and the Südbahn to Bruck an der Mur, where it splits into a line to Slovenia via Graz and to Italy via Villach.

These lines are supplemented by Bruck an der Mur–Linz, Salzburg–Wörgl, Innsbruck–Bregenz and

Main attractions

Innsbruck: Goldenes Dachl balcony, Helblinghaus, Hofburg palace, Hofkirche, Salzburg: Festung Hohensalzburg (fortress), Mozart's birthplace Vienna: St Stephen's Cathedral, National Opera House, Imperial Treasury, Café Central.

Map on page 236

Graz Central station.

⊘ Essentials

European Rail Timetable
no. 951

Distance: 204km (127 miles)

Duration of journey:
2hrs 46 mins

Frequency of trains: 1 per day (direct); 9 per day with a change at Bregenz; 7 per day with a change at Feldkirch

Salzburg–Villach. Of great importance for freight traffic is the Brenner route south of Innsbruck, which runs over the Brenner Pass to Italy. The construction of railways through Austria's mountainous terrain proved a challenge for 19th- and early 20th-century engineers, and the network has more than its fair share of bridges, viaducts and tunnels, the longest being the Terfner Tunnel (10.8km/6.7 miles) on the Neue Unterinntalbahnthrough the lower Inn valley.

NARROW-GAUGE LINES

Austria is an extremely beautiful country, and the narrow-gauge lines, in particular, promise spectacular journeys. Narrow-gauge branches include Waidhofen to Lunz and Ybbsitz, Gmünd to Gross Gerungs, Litschau and Heidenreichstein, Zell am See to Krimml, and St Pölten to Mariazell. The St Pölten–Mariazell line is electrified, and is considered by many to be the most scenic narrow-gauge line in Austria. It is worked with old electrics dating from 1909.

LINDAU–INNSBRUCK

This 3-hour journey from the German border to the Tyrolean capital is one of the most scenic rail routes to enjoy in the Alps. There are several opportunities to break the journey in attractive towns, many of which have rack railways ascending into the mountains.

The journey begins on the shores of the **Bodensee** (Lake Constance) close to the point where three countries – Austria, Germany and Switzerland – converge. The German town of Lindau is situated just a few kilometres from the Austrian border, on an island linked to the mainland by a long causeway. From Lindau the line runs along the shores of the Bodensee, crossing into Austria before arriving in **Bregenz** an attractive town that is the capital of Austria's westernmost province, Vorarlberg. Bregenz enjoys a privileged location between the lake and Mt Pfänder and although the area close to the shore is fairly uninspiring, further uphill there are some lovely old buildings, including the local church, dating

Travelling through Alpine countryside with Mount Zugspitze in the background, Lermoos.

rom 1736. The town is famous for its summer performing arts festival, the stage for which has been built into the lake. Sadly, the narrow-gauge line up Bezau has been closed since 1980, and today only a short section near Bezau itself is operated as the Bregenzerwald Museumsbahn.

Leaving the Bodensee behind, the next town is **Dornbirn**, an industrial centre, and the largest town in the Vorarlberg region. A few kilometres west of the railway the Rhine marks the border between Austria and Switzerland. Huge dams have been built along the river and these are being maintained by means of a narrow-gauge industrial railway, jointly operated by the two countries. Excursions run along the river from Lustenau during the summer months.

After Götzis the main line arrives at **Feldkirch**, a major junction. From Feldkirch to Buchs in Switzerland the railway passes through Liechtenstein, one of Europe's smallest countries; this section is owned and operated by ÖBB, since Liechtenstein does not have its own railway company. Most of the Vienna–Zürich services use this route.

The line to Innsbruck continues eastwards through the mountains to **Bludenz**. At the station you can see electric railcars in yellow livery, belonging to the narrow-gauge Montafonerbahn, which connects Bludenz with Schruns, a popular resort in both summer and winter. Trains to Schruns operate approximately hourly (every half hour in late morning to early evening), taking 20 minutes.

ALONG THE ARLBERGBAHN

The railway from Bludenz to Landeck is the Arlbergbahn, built as a single line and completed in 1884; some sections have now been doubled. The Arlberg Tunnel at the summit is the heart of the line. Construction of this tunnel, at 10,250 metres (33,630ft) one of the longest in Austria, only got underway after the Gotthard Tunnel in Switzerland had opened and proved to be a success. Its construction claimed the lives of 92 workers. As one of the most important lines in the country, the

⊘ ÖTZTAL BY BIKE

The Innsbruck line follows the Inn downstream to the town of Ötztal. It has earned itself quite a reputation as a centre for road and mountain biking, with 700km (435 miles) of cycle trails for all levels of fitness and experience, and several local cycle hire shops. You can start on the cycle trail from the station, but if you'd prefer to avoid the uphill route, take the bike on one of the frequent bus services from the station up to Sölden or Obergurgl and then coast back down the valley.

The Ötztal Alpine valley is 55km (34 miles) long, and gains 700 metres (2,300ft) in height as it leads towards the glacier-covered Ötztal Alps. A short distance up the valley is the stunningly situated village of Ötz with a church dating from the 14th century. Längenfeld is the next village, followed by Sölden, an internationally popular tourist resort during both summer and winter. A few kilometres further up is Zwieselstein, where the Ötztal splits into the Vent and Gurgl valleys. The road to Vent is open in summer only, and is very narrow. Proceeding up the Gurgl valley, you reach Obergurgl – at 1,910 metres/6,266ft it's the highest village with a church in Austria, and famous for skiing. The road continues up the mountains and crossing into Italy via the Timmelsjoch Pass. South of Obergurgl this road is open from June to October only. The route through the Ötztal is classic Tyrol, with magnificent mountain views. Tourism is well developed, and there is a wide range of accommodation.

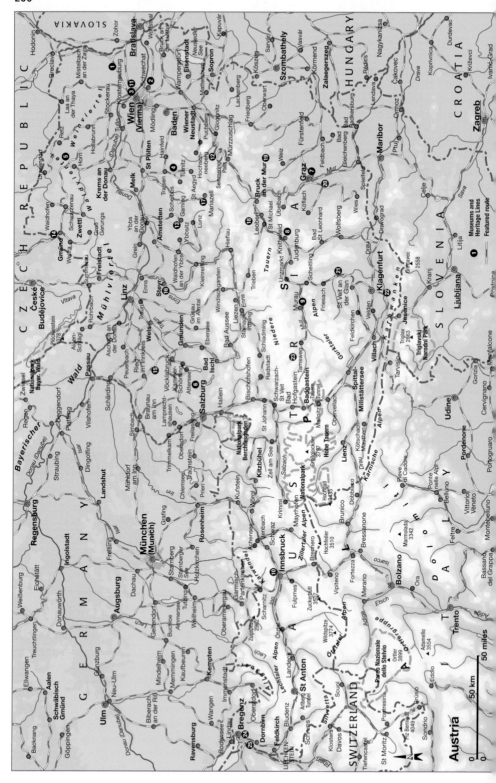

Austria

Arlbergbahn was electrified in 1925 (plans for electrification had been made in 1908 but World War I delayed the work). A few electric locomotives from bygone days have been preserved and are used on occasional charter trains.

The steep gradients demand special methods of operation, and most freight and express passenger trains require the assistance of a second locomotive at the rear of the train. During the winter, the line is threatened by avalanches; the steep slopes have been fortified with anti-avalanche equipment and detectors have been fitted to monitor the track. At times of high avalanche risk, observation posts along the line are staffed around the clock.

The view from the train is splendid, each bend revealing more mountain-tops, which often remain covered in snow until late summer. **Langen** is the last stop before we enter the **Arlberg Tunnel**. From the village a mountain road leads to Lech, a well-heeled ski resort. At the far end of the tunnel is St Anton, with its super-modern underground station, completed in 2001 for the Alpine Skiing World Championships. There are various opportunities for winter sports and many funiculars and ski-lifts give access to the surrounding mountains. The highest of these are Galzig (2,183 metres/7,162ft) and Valluga (2,809 metres/9,215ft).

INTO THE TYROL

East of **St Anton** the line drops continuously and offers more wonderful views. There is a succession of tunnels along this difficult section of track, and shelters have been built to protect the railway from avalanches and falling stones. A few kilometres west of **Pians** the line crosses a long girder bridge, which passes 80 metres (262ft) above the River Trisanna, just beyond Wiesberg castle. The valley of the Inn is reached at the large town of **Landeck**. To the south, a mountain road climbs

the Reschen Pass into Italy. During the first years of the 19th century plans were made to build a railway along this route, and work was well underway when World War I broke out in 1914; the line was never completed. From here, the track follows the Inn to reach Ötztal, with its beautiful valley running south to the Italian and Swiss borders (see box).

FROM ÖTZTAL TO INNSBRUCK, THE TYROLEAN CAPITAL

From Ötztal the railway runs along the widening Inn Valley. Just past the town of **Stams** on the right is one of Austria's finest monastery complexes, a 13th-century Cistercian abbey with a superbly restored church. At **Zirl** you can see a steep rock formation to the north – the so-called **Martinswand**, named after St Martin – with the narrow-gauge line from Innsbruck to Garmisch-Partenkirchen in Germany threading its way through tunnels beneath it. This line is of special interest since it was the first Austrian electric main line to use single phase

Skiing, St Anton.

⊙ Essentials

European Rail Timetable nos. 950, 951, 960

Distance: (1) 382km (237.5 miles) (via Zell am See);

(2) 323km (via Rosenheim)

Duration of journey:
(1) 5 hrs 14 mins

(2) 3 hrs

Frequency of trains: (1) 6 daily (change at Wörgl and Salzburg); (2) hourly

alternating current. The success of this new technique in 1912 led to the introduction of this type of electric supply to other lines. Seefeld, 25km (15 miles) from Innsbruck, is a tourist resort and was the location of the Nordic skiing competitions in the 1964 and 1976 Winter Olympics.

Innsbruck, flanked to the north by the Karwendel Mountains and to the south by the Patscherhofel Mountains, is the capital of the Tyrol, and makes an excellent base for exploring the region. Its attractions were recognised by Maximilian I, who moved his court here, and the town has managed to preserve the character of its old centre, with its arcaded and colourful stucco-fronted buildings. This is one of the crossroads of Europe, where the east–west route through Austria joins the route from Germany to Italy via the Brenner Pass.

INNSBRUCK TO FULPMES

Innsbruck has a metre-gauge tramway system and two light railway lines of the same gauge. While the line to

⊙ THE ACHENSEEBAHN

The metre-gauge Achenseebahn rack railway runs 7km (4 miles) north from Jenbach to the Achensee, at an altitude 400 metres (1,300ft) higher than the Inn Valley. Journey time is 50 minutes and there are six daily departures in summer (June–Sept), falling to three in May and October. In 1889 the railway was opened as far as Maurach. Four of the original engines are still used, making them the world's oldest cog-wheel steam locomotives in regular service.

The railway starts outside the main line station and immediately begins to climb steeply. The loco usually pushes one or two antique passenger coaches, some of which have nothing but curtains to cover the open windows. After 4km (2.5 miles) you reach Eben station, where the rack sections ends. Here the loco runs round its train and is coupled to the leading carriage and from here works as an adhesion loco. Passing Maurach, the former terminus, the train follows the line extended in 1916 to reach the boat-cruise pier. The Achensee is the biggest lake in the Tyrol, with a superb mountain setting, and is popular in summer and winter. Maurach is at the southern end of the lake while Pertisau is on the western shore. The train is usually met by a boat that takes passengers for a cruise across the lake.

Igls, just to the south of Innsbruck, has always been part of the tram system, the 21-km (13-mile) Stubaitalbahn to Fulpmes was constructed by an independent company (in 1904). The Fulpmes railway was originally operated with a/c and only switched to the d/c tram power supply in 1983. Trains to Fulpmes now start at the main railway station and pass via the tram system to Stubaital station, from where the original light railway line starts. There is also the Tiroler Museumsbahnen railway museum, and the old shed shelters some of the original a/c railcars.

En route to Fulpmes the railway climbs steep slopes which offer good views across Innsbruck and the surrounding mountains. Of these, the Nordkette to the north, have the most impressive peaks: if the view tempts you but you prefer an easy way up, a funicular climbs into the mountains from Hungerberg station in Innsbruck. The Stubaitalbahn continues to the southwest, passing through the villages of Mieders and Telfes with their 18th-century parish churches.

Fulpmes is the pleasant main village of the Stubaital valley, and a good starting point for hiking tours. It has long been known for its iron-workers, and there are still a few riverside workshops today, their hammers powered by the Plövenbach stream. Ice axes and crampons from here are highly regarded. The tradition is detailed in the Schmiedemuseum (Blacksmith Museum). From Fulpmes the road eventually reaches the enormous Stubai glacier, a year-round skiing area accessible by cable car from Mutterbergalm, reached by bus from Fulpmes.

INNSBRUCK–SALZBURG–LINZ

This route can be covered in two different ways; the shorter option heads north from Wörgl to take a short-cut through Germany to Salzburg; the scenic route stays within Austrian territory, passing through glorious countryside to Zell am See and Bischofshofen, before turning north to Salzburg. The tracks are reunited for the final stretch to Linz, which traverses the stunning region of Salzkammergut. En route there are various opportunities to take narrow-gauge branch lines into the mountains.

The line from Innsbruck to Wörgl is one of Austria's busiest since it is being used both by east–west and north–south traffic flows. Soon after leaving Innsbruck we get to **Hall in Tirol**, where salt was mined until 1968; salt water springs are still used for medicinal treatment. A few kilometres further east, near Baumkirchen, a new railway bridge crosses the River Inn; this is the Innsbruck bypass line, which is used by freight trains going directly up the Brenner Pass. After passing Schwaz the train arrives in **Jenbach**, where two scenic branch lines run north and south of the main railway.

THE ZILLERTALBAHN

While the Achenseebahn runs to the north of Jenbach, the longer 760mm (2ft 6in) gauge (and much less steep) Zillertalbahn heads south towards the majestic Zillertal Alps, departing from a separate station adjacent to the ÖBB one. Most of the trains are operated by modern diesel railcars, but certain departures are hauled by steam – these operate up to five days a week in summer.

The Zillertalbahn runs 32km (20 miles) south from Jenbach to Mayrhofen, through pristine Tyrolean scenery; the journey takes 50 minutes. The line follows the Ziller Valley, hemmed in between the Tux Alps to the west and the Kitzbühel Alps to the east. After passing Fügen and Kaltenbach the train reaches **Zell am Ziller**, centre of the lower Zillertal. Via Hippach the line reaches **Mayrhofen**, the railway's end, from where cable cars offer easy access to the mountains.

JENBACH TO ZELL AM SEE

The main east–west line continues east from Jenbach to **Rattenberg**,

Pinzgauerbahn.

☉ THE PINZGAUERBAHN

The Pinzgauerbahn narrow-gauge line from Zell am See runs for 53km (33 miles) alongside the River Salzach, and takes 1 hour 23 minutes to reach Krimml. The line is diesel operated but there is a steam-hauled tourist train, which runs twice a week during summer.

Leaving Zell am See and its picturesque lake, the Pinzgauerbahn line heads west, running close to the village of Kaprun, which is the gateway to the year-round skiing paradise of Schmiedinger Kees. You can hire bikes at Zell am See and Kaprun, and you can take them with you on the train if you don't want to cycle all the way.

Mittersill is the centre of the Pinzgau region, with two outstanding Baroque churches. The valley now begins to narrow, with good views ahead to the 3,674-metre (12,053-ft) peak of Grossvenediger. From Krimml, take a bus to get to the Krimml waterfalls, the highest in Europe and the fifth-highest in the world. The Krimml River drops about 380 metres (1,246ft) by means of three cataracts. A visit takes around three hours; follow the path through the dense forest to take in each of the seven different viewing points.

Railjet, a high-speed ÖBB train that operates at speeds of up to 230 kmh (143 mph).

Enjoying a summer's day at Lake Zell.

which has a 15th-century church and a remarkable number of houses of the same age. From the major railway junction at **Wörgl**, the Austrian main line heads to the east, while the Rosenheim and Munich line continues along the River Inn to the north. Be careful when choosing a train to Salzburg: the Innsbruck–Vienna through trains take the shorter route via Germany (ÖBB fares apply), which cuts the journey time by an hour. The line via Zell am See is used by some Innsbruck–Salzburg and Innsbruck–Graz through services and by local trains. If you have time, choose the Zell am See route, the more attractive of the two.

Leaving Wörgl, the railway climbs steadily and passes Hopfgarten and Westendorf. Just before the long-established ski resort of **Kitzbühel**, the Schwarzsee can be seen to the north. The Kitzbüheler Horn (1,996 metres/6,548ft) can be reached by a cable car, and offers excellent views all year round, and near the summit there is an Alpine flower garden with some 400 species. The railway now turns north and as it approaches S Johann you can see the mountains of the Wilder Kaiser to the northwest The line turns east again and passes Fieberbrunn, marking the start of the climb up the Griessen Pass; many trains need the assistance of an additional locomotive to get over this incline. Having passed the summit, the line drops continuously to Saalfelden To the north there is a good view of the Birnhorn (2,634 metres/8,641ft) At Saalfelden the track turns south to pass Maishofen, before running along the shores of Zeller See and arriving at **Zell am See** station.

South of Zell am See the main line again turns to the east. **Bruck** is the next major station of interest, where the mountain road to the **Gross glockner** starts. There's a bus to Franz-Josefs-Höhe, from where you can see the top of Austria's highest mountain, the Grossglockner (3,797 metres/12,457ft). From Bruck the track continues to Schwarzach-St Veit where it meets the one from Villach and on to Salzburg via Bischofshofen

The Schwarzach–Salzburg section, and Salzburg itself, are described in the Villach–Salzburg chapter (see page 245).

THE SALZKAMMERGUT

From Salzburg the main Alpine range is left behind, yet the landscape remains diverting, with smaller mountains and lakes. Several narrow-gauge lines meander south into the area of limestone peaks and lakes known as the Salzkammergut, which provided the locations for filming *The Sound of Music*.

The route passes the Wallersee close to Neumarkt and reaches Vöcklamarkt station, beyond Frankenmarkt. Here another narrow-gauge railway winds through the hills to Attersee, on the lake of the same name, which is the largest in the area at 20km (12 miles) long and 3km (2 miles) wide. The electric railway is run by a private operator, Stern & Hafferl, and connects with boat cruises across the Attersee. Trains run throughout the year, with more frequent services during the peak summer months, with journeys taking 24 minutes. Other towns of interest along the shores of the lake are Schörfling in the north, Nußdorf and Unterach in the south.

Back on the main Salzburg–Linz line, Vöcklabruck is a short distance east, from where another local railway runs south to the Attersee; this line, to Kammer-Schörfling, operates year-round, seven times a day except Sunday. While Vöcklabruck is the district's capital, nearby Attnang-Puchheim is the main railway junction. The line north leads to Schärding on the Wels–Passau main line, while that to the south connects to Gmunden and Bad Ischl, joining the main Graz–Innsbruck line at Stainach-rdning. Gmunden is a pleasant town on the Traunsee, while Bad Ischl was the summer residence of the Austrian emperors until 1918 and still preserves its imperial atmosphere.

From Attnang-Puchheim the route continues past Schwanenstadt before arriving at Lambach. The latter station has a bypass for fast trains but local trains stop and offer connections to two more local electric railways. The line to the north terminates at Haag while the southern branch ends at Vorchdorf, where you can change trains and continue on a narrow-gauge line to Gmunden.

The next major stop on the main line is **Wels**, where trains from Nuremberg and Passau join the Salzburg–Linz–Vienna line. It only takes 15 minutes on an express to complete the final leg to **Linz**, the capital of Oberösterreich province, with a major steel and chemical industry. Fortunately the plants are situated east (downwind) of the centre, and pollution has been greatly reduced in recent years. The centre can be reached easily by tram. Tram route No. 3 crosses the Danube and goes straight to Urfahr, the terminus of one of the steepest adhesion railways in the world. This electric railway goes up the Pöstlingberg, with its large pilgrimage

Bad Ischl.

⏱ Essentials

European Rail Timetable
no. 980

Distance: 372km (231
miles)

Duration of journey:
4hrs 21 minutes

Frequency of trains:
7 per day

church. The gradient is 10.5 percent and special braking equipment has been fitted for safety reasons. A visit to the Pöstlingberg is highly recommended as it offers a tremendous view across Linz and the River Danube.

VIENNA–VILLACH

Vienna to Villach trains run on the Südbahn (Southern Railway), opened in stages during the 1840s to link the capital of imperial Austria with the seaports of the Mediterranean. The line runs along the easternmost slopes of the Alps, the so-called Thermenregion (spa region), famous for its wine as well as its waters.

A major rebuilding programme saw the new Vienna Hauptbahnhof opened in 2014; by 2015 international services were running through it. Some services, including Westbahn-operated trains to Salzburg, still use the old Westbahnhof. It takes about 10 minutes for an express to emerge from the outskirts of Vienna into open countryside, with vineyards and small villages. It passes through Baden and

The Puchberg rack railway.

Bad Vöslau, both of which have hot sulphur springs, before arriving at **Wiener Neustadt**, a major junction 30 minutes from Vienna, and home of the Austrian Military Academy since the days of the Habsburg Empire.

WIENER NEUSTADT TO HOCHSCHNEEBERG

Several interesting branch lines fan out from Wiener Neustadt, east and south into the Burgenland region, and west to **Puchberg** from where a metre-gauge rack railway (the Schneebergbahn) runs up to Hochschneeberg. From Wiener Neustadt hourly departures to Puchberg head into the hills, and you can glimpse Schneeberg rising to 2,076 metres (6,811ft) ahead. Transfer to the Schneebergbahn, where most of the trains are diesel but some steam trains remain. Reservations are obligatory on all services and can be organised at any major ÖBB station or online. The track climbs steeply to an intermediate station at Baumgartner, where the steam locomotives usually stop to take on water. The final climb leads through a treeless mountain area until you reach **Hochschneeberg**, the highest station in Austria, at 1,792 metres (5,878ft), with an excellent view. The tracks climb even higher, up to the nearby hotel (Berghaus Hochschneeberg) but are only used to deliver supplies. Various shelters serving meals and drinks are scattered across the Schneeberg, and there are trails down to Puchberg if you want to make your own way back down – allow around 2 and a half hours for the walk.

THE SEMMERING PASS AND TRIALS

From Wiener Neustadt the main line continues southwest to **Gloggnitz**, the starting point of the **Semmering Pass**, over which the line gains 457 metres (1,500ft) in altitude in 29km (18 miles). When the railway reached Gloggnitz from the north in 1842 and the section from Mürzzuschlag to Bruck an der Mur was opened in 1844, it had still not been decided how to get across the Semmering. Many engineers, including George Stephenson, expressed the opinion that it would be impossible for adhesion locomotives to operate on such a steep slope; possible alternatives included rope inclines (with stationary engines positioned at the summit pulling the wagons up by means of ropes and pulleys), and horse-drawn trams. However, the engineer in charge of completing the line, Carl Ritter von Ghega, was encouraged by his study of the mountain railways of the United States and decided to go ahead with a traditional adhesion railway. Maximum gradients were restricted to 1 in 40, and a total of 16 tunnels and 16 viaducts were necessary to complete the route.

The Semmering line was officially opened on 15 May 1854. Since then the line has been electrified, but otherwise has remained unchanged. Plans to build a base tunnel have long been a subject of political dispute.

Try to get a seat on the left-hand side of the train, for splendid views of the Semmering area. The town of **Semmering** was a well-known resort until the 1930s, but never recovered from World War II. Some of the old hotels, however, have been restored and the town remains popular with skiers.

MÜRZZUSCHLAG TO UNZMARKT

From Mürzzuschlag to Villach the line runs through the Mürztal region, following the long valley of the Mürz and Mur rivers. This area was industrialised during the 19th century with the help of the railway, and steelworks and other industrial plants are in evidence all the way to **Bruck an der Mur**. At Bruck the main line splits into two, one branch leading to Graz, the capital of the province of Styria, and the other continuing to Villach and on to Italy. On the Villach line, the next stop is **Leoben**, centre of the iron industry. The branch line from Leoben to Vordernberg is now

Café Schwarzenberg, one of Vienna's famous cafés.

On the Semmering line.

closed to passenger services. From St Michael, fast trains run to Linz and Bischofshofen. Having passed Bruck, the tracks follow the River Mur through another industrial area, with steel works at Judenburg and Zeltweg, while Knittelfeld is the home of a repair works owned by ÖBB. Fans of motor racing probably already know that the Austrian Formula 1 Grand Prix takes place near Zeltweg.

A few kilometres after passing Judenburg, **Teufenbach** marks the point where the line to Villach leaves the River Mur and begins its ascent into the beautiful southern province of Carinthia. There are several castles in the vicinity of this small village, which dates from the 12th century.

ALONG THE MURTALBAHN

At Unzmarkt, a narrow-gauge railway, the Murtalbahn, runs for 65km (40 miles) along the upper Mur Valley to the town of Tamsweg, through a popular holiday area – the tourist

traffic has ensured the survival of the line. The Murtalbahn has been built to the gauge of 760mm (2ft 6in), the standard for most Austrian narrow-gauge lines, and is run by the Steiermärkische Landesbahnen, which also operates other branch lines in the province of Styria. Most trains are modern and diesel-powered, although steam trains operate in the summer months between Murau and Tamsweg. In fact, the railway has been among the Austrian pioneers of steam operations on tourist lines, and self-driving courses with steam locos are also on offer.

The upper Mur Valley enjoys a healthy climate, milder than that found further east, and its idyllic villages make an ideal base for hiking in the wooded hills. Having passed Teufenbach (see above), trains pull into **Murau** station, 45 minutes from Unzmarkt. Murau is the capital of this section of the Mur Valley, and a centre for Nordic sports. The line from Murau to Tamsweg is especially scenic, with excellent views. The main

Maria Worth, on the southern shore of Lake Wörther See.

point of interest in **Tamsweg**, one hour from Murau (steam trains take an extra 45 minutes), is the pilgrimage church of St Leonhard, with 15th-century stained glass. The railway once continued to **Mauterndorf** but it was neglected and closed down by the authorities several years ago. However, a private society has preserved the line and now operates tourist trains during the summer.

CASTLES AND CASINOS

At Friesach the main Vienna–Villach line enters Carinthia, Austria's southernmost province, with an almost Mediterranean climate in the summer. At Treibach-Althofen you can see a narrow-gauge track along the main line, the first 3km (2 miles) of which have been preserved as a museum line (the Gurkthalbahn), leading to Pöckstein castle. As you approach **St Veit an der Glan**, there are views of the spectacular Hochosterwitz Castle, perched on a rock outcrop to the left. At St Veit a secondary line heads directly to Villach along Ossiacher See.

Express trains take the geographically longer (but actually quicker) route via **Klagenfurt**, the capital of Carinthia. This town has an interesting centre with a 16th-century cathedral and the seat of local government which was built at the same time. Klagenfurt is situated at the eastern edge of the **Wörther See**, the most famous of the Carinthian lakes; the waters are particularly warm in summer, making it extremely popular for swimming. The railway runs along the northern shore of the lake, giving great views across the clear waters. Steamboat cruises operate from April to October. Resorts line the shore; **Velden** with its casino is the best known. At Velden the lake is left behind; a few minutes later, entering **Villach**, up on a hill to the right you can see the remains of Landskron Castle, which was rebuilt by Albert II in the

14th century. Most of its medieval walls survive.

VILLACH–SALZBURG

Villach is a major railway junction, located at the point where the Vienna–Venice line joins the Salzburg–Ljubljana line for a few kilometres. The journey north to Salzburg passes close to Austria's highest mountains.

The Salzburg line heads northwest from Villach, following the River Drau to **Spittal an der Drau**, where a picturesque line turns west to Lienz in the Osttirol, eventually reaching the Italian town of Fortezza on the main Innsbruck–Verona route. Spittal's town centre deserves a walkabout; the major sight, Porcia Castle, is said to be the most important Florentine-style building in Austria. Its court is used for open-air festivals. The **Millstätter See** is situated east of Spittal, and there are splendid views across the lake from surrounding mountains, although, unfortunately, one mountain hides the lake from the view of train passengers.

Essentials

European Rail Timetable no. 970

Distance: 182km (113 miles)

Duration of journey: 2hrs 32 mins

Frequency of trains: 9 (7 during the day, plus 2 during the night)

Hochosterwitz Castle.

SPITTAL TO THE TAUERN TUNNEL

Northwest of Spittal the railway leaves the valley of the Drau and starts climbing. This stretch of line began operating in 1909 as a single track, but most sections have now been doubled as far as Mallnitz-Obervellach. Near Oberfalkenstein the train crosses a wide bridge with an excellent view of the remains of Oberfalkenstein Castle. Soon afterwards it enters a tunnel, then runs across the Kaponig Viaduct, immediately after which another tunnel extends as far as Mallnitz-Obervellach. The old line via Kaponig has been abandoned. **Mallnitz**, the last station before the railway crosses the Tauern mountains on its way north, is a winter sports resort and a starting point for hiking tours in the region. For those who want to spend a day in the mountains without the effort of actually climbing them, there is a cable car – reached by a regular bus service from Mallnitz station – towards the Ankogel (3,246 metres/10,649ft). A few kilometres north of Mallnitz the train enters the 8.5-km (5.2-mile) Tauern Tunnel. Since there are no roads north of Mallnitz, ÖBB operates a car shuttle to Böckstein.

HOT SPRINGS AND SPA TOWNS

The weather is often quite different at the northern end of the tunnel, from where the line reaches the Gastein Valley, well known for its thermal springs. The therapeutic qualities of the springs have been noted since at least the 15th century. **Böckstein**, the first town north of the tunnel, has no hot springs, but in an abortive 1940s attempt to mine gold here it was discovered that the hot and humid atmosphere inside the mountain was a beneficial treatment for rheumatism. Since 1952 the mine tunnel has been used for therapy for those with rheumatic complaints. Trains run to the mine from Böckstein every two hours. The 600mm (1ft 11 5/8in) gauge line is operated by electric locos.

The most important town in the valley is **Bad Gastein**, which has been a flourishing spa for many decades and now doubles as a ski resort. The hot springs contain radon gas, again beneficial for treating rheumatic complaints. It is also possible to swim in the Felsenbad pools – both indoor and outdoor (the water is hot enough to make a mid-winter dip tolerable in the latter). As the main centre of the valley, Bad Gastein has numerous well-established hotels. A walk along the Kaiser Wilhelm Promenade is recommended for the fine views it offers across the town and its surroundings.

Further north is the modern thermal resort of Bad Hofgastein, followed by Dorfgastein, a village favoured by those who like to get away from the bustle of the spa resorts. North from here the railway descends a steep incline with stunning views over the River Salzach, to reach Schwarzach-St Veit, another

Bad Gastein during winter.

major railway junction. The line from Villach joins the Wörgl–Saalfelden–Salzburg line, the only rail track that connects the Tyrol with the central and eastern parts of Austria without running through Germany. The line via Schwarzach-St Veit is still important for freight traffic, however, and the section to Salzburg is part of the route to Villach that plays a major role in traffic from Germany to Carinthia as well as to Slovenia and Croatia.

SCHWARZACH-ST VEIT TO HALLEIN

Heading north to Salzburg the train soon reaches the Pongau region, passing the castle of Goldegg on the left before arriving at **St Johann im Pongau**, a small town with one major attraction. Just to the south of the town, the walls of the **Liechtensteinklamm** gorge extend 300 metres (985ft) but in places are only a couple of metres apart. The word 'narrow' does not do it justice. A hiking trail (which takes about 20 minutes), in places blasted through the rock, reaches into the gorge, eventually leading through a tunnel to reach a 65-metre (212ft) waterfall.

Bischofshofen, 6km (4 miles) up the line, is the next village; like many other places in the area, it functions as both a summer and winter resort. On the next stretch to Golling the railway runs through an extremely narrow section of the Salzach Valley, the so-called Pass Lueg. The spectacular castle of Burg Hohenwerfen can be seen high above the valley, near the village of Werfen. Close to the village of Golling are the impressive Gollinger waterfalls, plunging 62 metres (203ft).

SALT MINES TO SALZBURG

The next major stop is **Hallein**, right on the German border. Salt contributed to the wealth of the region for 3,000 years until mining came to an end in 1989; in the past this was one of the most valuable possessions of the archbishops of Salzburg. The entire mining area has now been converted into a museum and the railway lines inside the mountain have been retained. The mine entrance can easily be reached by means of a funicular which starts right in the centre of Hallein. The guided tour of the mines is enjoyable and informative, and takes around 90 minutes, and outside is a reconstruction of Salina, giving an idea of what life was like for the Celts some 2,600 years ago. Visitors enter the mine complex on the narrow-gauge underground railway, slide down a chute on a toboggan (popular with children), and take a boat trip across an illuminated underground lake.

From Hallein it is just 19km (12 miles) to **Salzburg**, one of Austria's major visitor attractions. It is the birthplace of Mozart (1756–91) and has a prestigious classical music festival. From the Hohensalzburg fortress there are magnificent views across the town and its many churches.

Mozart monument in Salzburg.

Outdoor cinema in Kapitelplatz during the Salzburg Festival.

MUSEUMS AND HERITAGE LINES

Austria has numerous museums and heritage lines. The numbers here relate to the map on page 236.

MUSEUMS

Eisenbahnmuseum Strasshof ❶
Sillerstrasse 123, A-2231 Strasshof (25km/15 miles northeast of Vienna)
Open: Apr–Oct Tue–Sun 10am–4pm
Features: largest Austrian railway museum, national collection
Nearest station: Silberwald (Line S1)
Tel: 02287 3027
www.eisenbahnmuseum-heizhaus.com

Eisenbahnmuseum Schwechat ❷
Schwechat station, A-2300 Schwechat
Open: May–Oct Sat 1–6pm, Sun 10am–5pm
Features: narrow-gauge line with working steam, standard and narrow-gauge railway vehicles
Nearest station: Schwechat
Tel: 01 93000 24585
www.eisenbahnmuseum.at

Wiener Tramwaymuseum ❸
Holochergasse 24, A-1150 Wien
Open: May–Oct Sat–Sun 9am–4pm
Features: shop, biggest tram museum in the world
Tel: 06991 7860303
www.tram.at

Feld- und Industriebahn-museum ❹
Maierhof 8, A-3183 Freiland
Open: Apr–Oct Sun 10am–4pm
Features: industrial railway museum with working steam on 600-mm gauge
Nearest station: Lilienfeld, then bus to Freiland

Tel: 0664 2749113
www.feldbahn.at

Waldviertler Eisenbahnmuseum Sigmundsherberg ❺
Museumstrasse 1, A-3751 Sigmundsherberg
Open: all year daily 9am–4pm
Features: standard-gauge rolling stock exhibits
Nearest station: Sigmundsherberg
Tel: 0676 3632858
www.eisenbahnmuseum-waldviertel.at

Salzkammergut Lokalbahn SKGLB Museum ❻
Seebaldstrasse 2, A-5310 Mondsee
Open: June–Sept weekends 10am–noon, 2–5pm
Features: preserved narrow-gauge steam locos
Nearest station: Salzburg Hauptbahnhof
Tel: 06232 4270
www.museum-mondsee.at

Tramway Museum Graz ❼
Mariatrosterstrasse 204, A-8044
Open: June–Sept Sun 2–6pm
Features: tram vehicles
Nearest station: Graz Hauptbahnhof
Tel: 0316 887401
www.tramway-museum-graz.at

Eisenbahnmuseum-Knittelfeld ❽
Ainbachallee 14, A-8720 Knittelfeld
Open: all year Tue–Sun 9am–5pm
Features: standard-gauge exhibits, garden railway (May–Oct Sat–Sun)
Nearest station: Knittelfeld
Tel: 0676 5440795
http://eisenbahnmuseum.bplaced.net

Club 760, Frojach ❾
P.O. Box 51, A-8850 Murau
Open: sporadically; trains run July–Aug Tue–Wed
Features: exhibition of narrow-gauge steam locomotives
Nearest station: Frojach
www.club760.at

Tiroler Museumsbahnen ❿
Pater Reinischweg 4, A-6020 Innsbruck
Open: May–Oct Sat 9am–5pm
Features: tram and light railway museum
Nearest station: Innsbruck Hauptbahnhof
Tel: 0664 1116001
www.tmb.at

HERITAGE LINES

Liliputbahn Prater ⓫
Prater 99, A-1020 Wien
Open: Apr–Oct daily; steam Sat–Sun
Features: park railway with steam and diesel locos
Nearest station: Wien Nord
Length: 3.5km (2 miles)
Gauge: 381mm (1ft 3in)
Tel: 01 7268236
www.liliputbahn.com

Museumsbahn Payerbach-Hirschwang ⓬
ÖGLB, Poschgasse 6, A-1140 Wien
Open: June–Sept Sun
Features: narrow-gauge railway with diesel and electric locos
Nearest station: Payerbach-Reichenau
Length: 4.8km (3 miles)
Gauge: 760mm (2ft 6in)
Tel: 02666 52423
www.lokalbahnen.at/hoellentalbahn

Ötscherland-Express (Bergstrecke Ybbsthalbahn) ⓭
NÖLB, Im Markt 1, A-3292 Gaming
Open: June–Sept weekends
Features: narrow-gauge railway
Nearest station: Scheibbs, then bus to Kienberg-Gaming
Length: 17.4km (11 miles)
Gauge: 760mm (2ft 6in)
Tel: 07482 20444
www.lokalbahnen.at/bergstrecke

Waldviertler Schmalspurbahnverein ⓮
Bahnhofstrasse 59, A-3871
Altnagelberg
Open: weekends and Wed, June–
Sept
Features: museum railway
Nearest station: Gmünd
Length: 38km (24 miles)
Gauge: 760mm (2ft 6in)
Tel: 0680 1253003
www.erlebnisbahn.at/wsv

Museumsbahn Ampflwang ⓯
ÖGEG, Postfach 11, A-4018 Linz
Open: May–Oct Wed–Sun
10am–5pm; trains run Sun July–
mid-Sept
Features: museum, steam and
diesel trains
Nearest station: Timelkam
Length: 10.5km (6.5 miles)
Gauge: 1,435mm (4ft 8½in)
Tel: 0664 5087664
www.oegeg.at

Steyrtal Museumsbahn ⓰
ÖGEG, as above
Open: May–Sept weekends
Features: steam operated museum
railway
Nearest station: Steyr
Length: 17km (10.5 miles)
Gauge: 760mm (2ft 6in)
Tel: 0664 5087664
www.oegeg.at

Museumstramway Mariazell ⓱
An der Museumsbahn 5, A-8630 St
Sebastian-Mariazell
Open: July–Sept weekends
Features: museum tram line to
Erlaufsee
Nearest station: Mariazell
Length: 2.5km (1.5 miles)
Gauge: 1,435mm (4ft 8½in)
www.museumstramway.at

**Museumsbahn Vordernberg –
Eisenerz ⓲**
Viktor-Zack Strasse 1, A-8794

Vordernberg
Open: July–Sept weekends
Features: museum trains
Vordernberg to Eisenerz
Nearest stations: Leoben
Hauptbahnhof
Length: 18.7km (11.5 miles)
Gauge: 1,435mm (4ft 8½in)
Tel: 0664 5081500
www.erzbergbahn.at

**Feistritztalbahn
Betriebsgesellschaft ⓳**
Hauptplatz 13, A-8190 Birkfeld
Open: mid-June–Oct various Mon,
Thu and weekends
Features: steam excursions Weiz–
Birkfeld
Nearest station: Weiz
Length: 24km (15 miles)
Gauge: 760mm (2ft 6in)
Tel: 0664 88291066
www.feistritztalbahn.at

Museumsbahn Stainz ⓴
A-8510 Stainz
Open: May–Oct weekends
Features: museum line to Preding-
Wieselsdorf
Nearest station: -Preding-
Wieselsdorf
Length: 11.4km (7 miles)
Gauge: 760mm (2ft 6in)
Tel: 0664 9615205
www.bahnerlebnis.at

**Gurkthalbahn-Kärntner
Museumsbahn ㉑**
A-9330 Althofen
Open: July–Sept weekends
Features: shop, museum line to
Pöckstein-Zwischenwässern
Nearest station: Treibach-Althofen
Length: 3km (2 miles)
Gauge: 760mm (2ft 6in)
www.gurkthalbahn.at

Ferlacher Bahn ㉒
NBiK, A-9028 Klagenfurt, Postfach
27

Open: July–Sept weekends
Features: museum line to Ferlach,
with bus trip to Historama transport
museum
Nearest station: Weizelsdorf
Length: 5.7km (3.5 miles)
Gauge: 1,435mm (4ft 8½in)
www.nostalgiebahn.at/rosentaler-
dampfzuege.html

Taurachbahn ㉓
A-5570 Mauterndorf 53
Open: July–Aug weekends
Features: museum line to St Ändra;
the highest narrow-gauge line in
Austria
Nearest station: Tamsweg
Length: 10km (6 miles)
Gauge: 760mm (2ft 6in)
Tel: 06472 7949
www.taurachbahn.at

Bregenzerwald Museumsbahn ㉔
Nr. 39, A-6941 Langenegg
Open: mid-May–early Oct weekends
Features: museum line Bezau–
Schwarzenberg
Nearest station: Bregenz
Length: 5km (3 miles)
Gauge: 760mm (2ft 6in)
Tel: 0664 4662330
www.waelderbaehnle.at

Rhein-Schauen ㉕
Höchster Strasse 4
A-6893 Lustenau
Open: May–Oct Fri–Sun
Features: electric-hauled
excursions (occasional steam) on
industrial narrow-gauge line
Nearest station: Lustenau
Length: 10km (6 miles)
Gauge: 750mm (2ft 5½in)
Tel: 05577 20539
www.rheinschauen.at

ICE train undergoing maintenance.

ICE train on the platform at Berlin Hauptbahnhof.

GERMANY

Speed, comfort and reliability are hallmarks of the
impressive German rail network, complemented on many
lines by attractive mountain, forest and river scenery

From the opening of the first railway in Germany in 1835 (between Nürnberg and Fürth), railway construction proceeded rapidly, and by the end of the century the network covered a total of almost 64,000km (40,000 miles). Three German states owned their railways from the outset – Baden, Oldenburg and Württemberg – while the private railways in the five others – Bavaria, Hesse, Mecklenburg, Prussia and Saxony – were gradually taken over by their states during the last quarter of the 19th century. The legacy of this individuality can still be seen in the variety of designs of station buildings.

The companies owned by the various states were amalgamated in 1921 to form Deutsche Reichsbahn (DR); the name was retained by East German railways after World War II, those of the West being renamed Deutsche Bundesbahn (DB). The railways had played a central role during the conflict, taking supplies over progressively extended supply routes to the front line. By the end of the war, the damage inflicted on the railways had been severe, but reconstruction and major programmes of electrification quickly restored the network.

CHALLENGES OF REUNIFICATION

Reunification in 1990 presented a huge challenge. There was an urgent need to integrate the two networks, to reinstate east–west links severed by the Iron Curtain. The formal merger of DB and DR as a federally-owned public limited company finally took place in 1994. Some privatisation has happened with the establishment in 1999 of the semi-independent division of DB known as DB Fernverkehr in 1999 (then called *DB Reise & Touristik*), which operates long-distance ICE and IC passenger trains.

The greatest changes have been in Berlin, where the separate systems

⊙ **Main attractions**

Cologne: Cathedral,
  Rathaus (town hall),
Frankfurt-am-Main:
  Römer (town city hall),
  Historisches Museum
Trier: Porta Nigra, Roman
  Imperial Baths,
Munich: Frauenkirche
  (Cathedral), Bavarian
  National Museum,
Dresden: Opera House,
  Frauenkirche.

⊙ **Maps on pages 254, 256**

Clock at Düsseldorf Airport station.

Germany

0 — 100 km
0 — 100 miles

● Museums and Heritage Lines
▬ Featured route

N

NORTH SEA

BALTIC SEA

SWEDEN

DENMARK

NETHERLANDS

GERMANY

POLAND

BELGIUM

LUXEMBOURG

FRANCE

CZECH REPUBLIC

SWITZERLAND

AUSTRIA

LIECHTENSTEIN

ad to be amalgamated. The new
interchange between north–south and
east–west routes at a new Hauptbahnhof opened in 2006 was one of the most
significant changes. Other investment
has resulted in impressive new trains
for cross-country and branch line
services.

The quality of German trains is
among the best in the world. Sleek
new InterCity Express (ICE) high-
speed trains were introduced in 1991
and quickly won traffic from air and
road. The next levels of services are
InterCity (IC) and InterRegio (IR) trains,
supplemented by local trains and tram
networks; some operate over railway
tracks and lines in city-centre streets.
Even on secondary routes trains are of
a standard that eclipses the mainline
trains of many other countries.

There are plenty of scenic journeys,
in addition to those described in this
chapter. Others include Arnstadt–Mei-
ningen (through the Thüringer Wald);
routes in the southwest around the
Black Forest; beautiful river scenery
along the Neckar (Heidelberg to Heil-
bronn); the upper reaches of the Danube (Ulm to Tuttlingen); and coastal
scenery near the Danish border (Nie-
büll to Westerland).

COLOGNE–FRANKFURT-AM-MAIN

Cologne (Köln) takes its name from
Colonia Agrippina, third wife of the
Emperor Claudius who founded a
colony here in AD 51, which later
became a prosperous religious, artistic and intellectual centre, thanks to
its position on the trade routes around
the River Rhine. The station is in the
heart of the old town, right next to the
famous cathedral.

The section of the Rhine between
Cologne and Frankfurt-am-Main is one
of the best-known stretches of river in
Europe, largely because a railway along
each bank provides a marvellous way
to appreciate the scenic splendours of

this busy waterway. As with the Mosel
between Trier and Koblenz, the sky is
constantly pricked by the spires, turrets and bartizans of real and mock
castles which can often be seen only
from the railway on the opposite bank
and are therefore described in the
'opposite' text. Many of the riverside
villages are full of delightful timber-
framed houses and inns.

The incessant barge and pleasure-
boat traffic – which includes the pad-
dle-ship *Goethe* – adds to the interest
of the journey. The area is also famous
for its wine; vineyards predominate on
the west- and south-facing slopes.

WEST BANK ROUTE
The exit from Cologne takes the train
almost underneath the broadcast-
ing tower and through unremarkable
country to the capital of the former
West Germany, **Bonn**. Following parliament's move to Berlin, the birthplace
of Beethoven (in 1770) still has some
ministries and fine museums, including the Rheinisches Landesmuseum
which provides a good introduction to
the area. The suburb of **Bad Godesberg**
is dominated by the ruins of a 13th-
century castle.

Remagen is remembered as the
place where US troops first crossed
the Rhine, over the Erpel Bridge. The
bridge collapsed but the remains
house a Peace Museum. **Brohl** is the
junction for the metre-gauge Brohltal-
bahn to Engeln, reached by a rack section further up the line, and medieval,
walled **Andernach** clusters around
the Mariendom Cathedral. There is an
impressive view of the old town to the
east as the train approaches **Koblenz**.

Just south of **Königsbach**, the River
Lahn joins the Rhine from the east,
overlooked by the uninspiring bulk
of Lahneck Castle, whose walls were
defended by the last of the Knights
Templar. The next hill is crowned by the
soaring central tower and surrounding
buildings of Marksburg Castle, the only

Essentials

European Rail Timetable
nos. 800, 914, 914a

Distance: 210km (130 miles)

(231km/143 miles East bank)

Duration of journey:
2 hrs 20 mins (some high-speed trains take 1 hr)

(4 hrs 4 mins East bank)

Frequency of trains:
hourly (direct); change at Koblenz on East bank route

⊙ Tip

The Drachenfelsbahn is Germany's oldest rack railway, opened in 1883. Take the train to Bonn Haupt-bahnhof, then tram line U66 to Bad Honnef. Alight at Königswinter Fähre, from where it is a 10-minute walk to the Drachenfelsbahn in Drachenfelstrasse.

Rhenish castle that withstood siege during the Thirty Years War.

Situated on the outer curve of a bend, Boppard has fine views of the river and is a good base for walking up the six valleys that converge on the pretty village. Just to the south, on the east bank, are the adjacent ruins of Sterrenberg and Liebenstein castles, known as the hostile brothers. To their south is Deurenberg Castle, nick-named Maus, immediately followed by Katz Castle, which can be seen as you approach the bend at Loreley with its towering mass of basalt, 132 metres (433ft) high. The treacherous currents as the Rhine rounds the Loreley cliffs are notoriously dangerous, and the river has been dredged to create safe channels.

After the attractive town of **Ober-wesel** there is a good view of ruined Gutenfels Castle, once taken by the Swedish, above Kaub on the east bank. Inside the town wall of **Bacharach** lies a gem of a medieval village and, above the town, a hostel occupies the 12th-century castle of Stahleck. Above

Niederheimbach are the remnants of the early 13th-century Fürstenberg Castle, destroyed by the French in 1689. The famous bend at **Bingen** has for a century or more been the place where passengers exchanged the train for a steamer or vice versa. The town is associated with the extraordinary Abbess Hildegard of Bingen – visionary, naturalist, playwright, poetess and composer – who spent most of her 8? years in nearby Benedictine monasteries (a Berlin–Frankfurt express was named after her). Approaching the station, the railway crosses the River Nahe; opposite the town are the twin-towered remains of Ehrenfels Castle.

Just after Bingen, a large-plinthed statue of Germania stands above the vineyards on the opposite bank. Unveiled in 1883, it commemorates the reunification of Germany in 187? following the Franco-Prussian War. The railway moves away out of sight of the river, through an area of orchards and market gardens, to Mainz, centre of Germany's wine trade. It was here that Gutenberg developed the printing process, commemorated in a museum named after him. The Romanesque cathedral and the old town are also worth visiting.

The short, remaining part of the journey to the immense station serving the country's commercial capital of **Frankfurt-am-Main** is increasingly urban, although the line skirts the forests that lie to the south of the city.

THE SCENIC EAST-BANK ROUTE

The slower east-bank route from Cologne to Koblenz reaches the Rhine at **Bonn-Oberkassel**, where only a cycle path lies between the railway and the water. Vines and orchards replace commuter housing as the train passes the attractive resorts of Königswinter and Bad Honnef. To the south of **Erpe** is the dark stone ruin of Ockenfels. The railway climbs briefly to a higher level near **Linz am Rhein**, junction for

Köln-Frankfurt/ Trier-Giessen

rack railway up to Kalenborn, but
oon returns to river level. As the train
asses **Bad Hönningen**, the imposing
astle of Rheineck can be seen above
e village of Brohl on the west bank.
Approaching the many-spired pano-
ama of **Koblenz**, the projecting spit
f land where the Mosel and Rhine
eet bears the immense, 36.6-metre
20-ft] equestrian statue of Emperor
ilhelm I, erected in 1897. At **Ehren-
reitstein**, Koblenz's principal east
ank station, is the fortress built by the
russians in 1816 on the site of a castle
at dates back to 486 and the time of
e Franks.

Shortly after **Niederlahnstein** the
ne to Giessen turns to the east and
e railway crosses the Lahn near
s confluence with the Rhine. On the
pposite bank is the first of a proces-
on of castles, the huge yellow-ochre
ulk of Stolzenfels, where Queen Vic-
oria once stayed. Now a museum, the
astle was built in 1244, destroyed in
689, then restored by Kaiser Wilhelm
in 1836–42. **Oberlahnstein** has two
astles: a small one by the station and
larger, white-walled fortress near
e river. The next section of line, fol-
wing the meander past the wisteria-
lad station at **Osterspai**, is one of the
veliest stretches of the journey, with
stone-protected and tree-lined island
the braided river.

At **St Goarshausen** there is a view of
e vast ruin of the 13th-century castle
f Rheinfels above St Goar on the west
ank, once the strongest fortress on
e Rhine. After passing a small har-
our you get a glimpse of the crenel-
ated portal of Loreley Tunnel, which
followed by Roßstein Tunnel at a
end in the river. Emerging, the multi-
urreted castle of Gutenfels looks down
n the village of Oberwesel, opposite.
For a change, the next castle is right
the middle of the river, situated on
n island at **Kaub**; the 11th-century
falz was built to collect customs tolls.
statue of Field-Marshal Blücher, of

Waterloo fame, overlooks the main
street to commemorate his crossing
of the Rhine here in 1813. The partly-
habitable castle of Schönburg, with
its large cylindrical tower, appears on
the opposite bank, south of Oberwesel, followed by the ruined castle of
Fürstenberg to the north of Niederheimbach, opposite **Lorch**. North of
Aßmannshausen and before the bend
at Bingen is Rheinstein Castle, built
on a prominent rock. Aßmannshausen
itself is a pretty village with some good
hotels. The cream and ochre-red fort
of Mäuseturm stands on an island just
north of the confluence of the River
Nahe with the Rhine at Bingen, where
both railways follow the river in its turn
to the east.

Shortly after the popular resort of
Rüdesheim the railway leaves the
river, and the hills of the Rheingauge-
birge to the north recede and become
lower, allowing the first extensive views
since entering the Rhine gorge. East
of **Hattenheim**, its handsome station
building decorated with coats of arms,
is the oldest town of the Rheingau,

⊙ Essentials

European Rail Timetable
nos. 915, 906

Distance: 229km (142
miles)

Duration of journey:
3hrs 36 mins (change at
Koblenz)

Frequency of trains:
every two hours

*Pfalzgrafenstein Castle,
known as the 'Pfalz'.*

Harvesting grapes on the steep hills along the Mosel River.

Eltville, with many 16th- and 17th-century townhouses and a castle. Vines cover the gently undulating surrounding countryside.

Trains enter the terminus at **Wiesbaden**, the capital city of Hesse, before reversing for the final part of the journey to Frankfurt-am-Main. As the royal spa town in the 19th century, Wiesbaden has numerous fine buildings associated with the thermal waters as well as a novel water-operated rack railway up the Neroberg.

TRIER–KOBLENZ–GIESSEN

The first part of this cross-country journey is on many an itinerary, starting as it does in Germany's oldest city and running through picturesque scenery close to the River Mosel. The second half, however, is one of those neglected byways that is all the more pleasing for being something of a discovery. Between Koblenz and Giessen, the railway and the River Lahn are seldom far apart, except for three large loops in the river, and the valley through which they run is exceptionally

beautiful and unspoilt. The journey involves a change of trains at Koblenz; most trains from Trier to Koblenz originate in Saarbrücken, and some continue on to Cologne.

TRIER AND THE MOSEL VALLEY

The Romans founded a military base at Trier around 20 BC and it is for those remains, rather than later noteworthy buildings, that the city has attained its Unesco World Heritage Site status. Bahnhofstrasse leads directly to Trier's most notable Roman building, the Porta Nigra, a four-storey sandstone gateway, from which it is easy to walk to all the city's other principal attractions.

Soon after leaving Trier the line crosses over the Mosel, but is then out of sight of the river for the next 40 minutes (sadly, the Moselbahn that once hugged the southern bank of the river to Bullay has closed). To the south, across farmland, are the distant hills and woods of the Hunsrück, immortalised by Edgar Reisz's epic film *Heimat*, while to the north are heavily wooded

⊘ STATIONS FOR CASTLES

Castle (bank): Station

Ehrenfels (East): Aßmannshausen
Fürstenberg (West): Niederheimbach
Godesburg (West): Bad Godesburg
Gutenfels (East): Kaub
Katz (East): St Goarshausen
Lahneck (East): Oberlahnstein
Liebenstein (East): Kestert
Marksburg (East): Braubach
Maus (East): St Goarshausen
Nollich (East): Lorch
Oberwesel (West): Oberwesel
Pfalz (East): Kaub
Reichenstein (West): Trechtingshausen
Rheineck (Wes): Brohl
Rheinfels (West): St Goar
Rheinstein (West): Trechtingshausen
Schönburg (West): Oberwesel
Sooneck (West): Niederheimbach
Stahleck (West): Bacharach

slopes, broken by the occasional church spire piercing the skyline.

After **Bengel** the first vineyards appear on the south-facing slopes beside the line, which is supported by a long, arched wall. One of the numerous meanders in the Mosel touches the railway just before it dives into Prinzenkopf Tunnel, from which the line emerges to cross the river. **Bullay** is the only junction before Koblenz, with a 10.6-km (6.5-mile) branch turning southwest to follow the northern bank of the river to a centre of the Mosel wine trade at Traben-Trarbach.

For most of the remaining journey to Koblenz, there is hardly a moment without a vine in sight and there is plenty of opportunity to admire the way the neat rows are grown on the steepest of slopes and on every available patch of good soil and sun. The beauty of the natural surroundings also made the area a popular place for those with the wherewithal to build a *schloss* on an eminence. With the river briefly to the left, a weir and loch are passed just before Neef where there's a tunnel,

followed by a return to the north side of the river.

At Ediger-Eller the railway enters the Kaiser-Wilhelm Tunnel, one of the country's longest at 4.2km (2.5 miles). In the vineyard chapel at Ediger is an unusual sculpture of Christ being crushed by a wine-press. After Cochem, railway and river run side by side all the way to Koblenz, the constant succession of passenger and cargo boats providing continual interest. Reichsburg, one of the most celebrated castles in the Mosel Valley, stands on a vine-covered, conical hill 30 minutes' walk above Cochem; the ruins were rebuilt in 14th-century style during the 19th century. Most of the villages along the opposite bank are of necessity linear in layout, hemmed in by the wooded slopes that rise behind the single street. Occasionally a turn in the river will allow a slope with a sufficiently southerly aspect to be planted with vines, but the majority of vineyards are on the same bank as the railway.

From **Moselkern** it is an hour's signposted walk beside a stream to one

Joint DB Regio and CFL train running alongside the Mosel River.

of Germany's most stunningly-sited castles. The many pinnacles around the steep roof of **Eltz Castle** rise dramatically from the surrounding forest. It has the kind of art and antiquities that only come from over 900 years of continuous ownership. Sandwiched between the railway and the Mosel near **Kobern-Gondorf** is a Gothic castle, through the grounds of which the road passes. Soaring above the line after the river and railway turn southeast is a functional motorway viaduct, impressive because of its height. The river briefly turns away from the railway before passing underneath it on the outskirts of Koblenz.

KOBLENZ AND THE LAHN

Koblenz is situated at an intersection of rivers and hills: the Mosel enters the Rhine almost opposite the Lahn at what is known as the Deutsches Eck (German Corner), and from this crossroads four ranges of hills diverge – the Hunsrück to the southwest, the Eifel to the northwest, the Taunus to the southeast and the Westerwald to the northeast. As well as its delightful riverside gardens, the city is full of historical interest and associations, not least with guidebooks, for it was here that Karl Baedeker set up his publishing business, producing his first guide (to the Rhine) in association with John Murray, in 1834.

The city's oldest building is the Romanesque church of St Castor: founded in 836, it was here that the decision was taken to divide up Charlemagne's empire. Other significant structures include the Romanesque Liebfraukirche, the 13th-century castle, and the imposing equestrian statue of Kaiser Wilhelm I at the confluence of the Mosel and the Rhine, where the Teutonic Knights established their first base, in 1216. The Rathaus (Town Hall) was a Jesuit college until 1794. Take care where you stand to admire the nearby bronze fountain of the spitting boy! On the east bank, reached by ferry, are the immense Ehrenbreitstein Fortress, the birthplace of Beethoven's mother, and the Rhine Museum, largely devoted to ships and river trade.

Ehrenbreitstein Fortress, Koblenz.

Trains for Giessen (also spelled Gießen) leave Koblenz in a southerly direction, crossing over the Rhine and turning east off the Frankfurt line at **Niederlahnstein**. Above is the rather ugly pile of Lahneck Castle. The station buildings on this section are often delightful, a good example being the part timber-framed **Friedrichssegen**. Running between valley slopes covered in deciduous woods, the railway reaches **Bad Ems**, passing some fine 19th-century industrial buildings – an age when companies were willing to spend money creating premises with some architectural merit. The station has an overall roof, recalling the time when the hydropathic facilities of Bad Ems were often the choice of royalty. It was here in 1870 – commemorated by a stone on the promenade – that Wilhelm I's response to the French ambassador resulted in the Franco-Prussian War of 1870–71. The conversation was incorporated in the crucial Ems Telegram. Murray's *Handbook* of 1886 comments that the society patronising the ballroom-equipped kursaal (the spa's social centre) was 'usually more select' than could be found at Wiesbaden or Baden-Baden.

In a striking position overlooking the railway on the approach to **Nassau** is an extraordinary pair of buildings associated with the Prussian statesman Baron Stein: the square tower with corner turrets and steeply pitched roof was built by him, and the modern-looking temple below is a monument in his memory. The castle, begun in 1101, was the cradle of the Nassau family which split into two branches in the 13th century, one producing the dukes of Nassau, the other the king of the Netherlands. Emerging from the last of three short tunnels, there is a spectacular view of the Lahn as the track crosses it just before **Obernhof**, which has a very large, dramatically sited church dating from 1359, and the Abbey of Arustein.

Vines appear on the valley slopes, which press in on the line until there is little but the river and railway between them. Above **Laurenburg** stands a chevron-shuttered tower, another home of the Nassau family. Outcrops of grey rock break up the valley sides on the approach to **Balduinstein**, where the ruins of the castle, built in 1320 by Archbishop Baldwin of Trèves, can be seen up a valley to the right. The well-preserved Oranienstein Castle stands on a rocky eminence as the train approaches **Diez**; built in 1672–84, this was one of the ancestral castles of the Nassau-Orange royal house (from which King William III of England was descended) and is now a barracks with a museum open to visitors.

LIMBURG TO GIESSEN

Dominating the skyline of the large town of **Limburg** is the Romanesque-Gothic cathedral, surrounded by attractive stone and timber-framed buildings. The character of the countryside has changed by the time the train passes the junction for

⊙ **Tip**

Quedlinburg is designated a World Heritage Site for its many streets, containing some 1,300 timber-framed houses. The medieval centre is a 10-minute walk from the railway station.

A DB cargo train crossing the Rhine near Urmitz.

⊙ Essentials

European Rail Timetable
no. 867

Distance:
(1) Nordhausen–
Wernigerode 61km (38
miles)

(2) Nordhausen–
Quedlinburg 70km (43.5
miles)

(3) Wernigerode–Brocken
34km (21 miles)

Duration of journey:
(1) 2 hrs 44 mins

(2) 2 hrs 51 mins

(3) 1 hr 41 mins

Frequency of trains:
(1) 4 daily, change at
change at Eisfelder
Talhmühle or Drei Annen
Hohne (2) 1 direct from
Nordhausen direction
only or Alexisbad (3) 6
daily

Runkel castle.

Frankfurt-am-Main at **Eschhofen**, being much flatter, with distant views to the north. But after **Kerkerbach**, railway and river again share a well-wooded valley. **Runkel** has a magnificent castle with a stone bridge leading to it, followed by an idyllic section running beside the river all the way to **Weilburg**, with its castle on the hill.

After **Löhnberg**, railway and river emerge from the valley and enter a much flatter landscape to reach **Wetzlar**, where 35mm film was invented at the Leitz factory in 1924. It was the emotions Goethe felt in Wetzlar through his unrequited love for Charlotte Buff that led to *The Sorrows of Young Werther*; Charlotte's birthplace, known as the Lottehaus after the fictional heroine, is open to visitors.

The station buildings at **Giessen** in Upper Hesse, are singularly attractive, having been redeveloped in 1904 to incorporate a tall clock tower outside the main hall. Built of red sandstone with decorative carved griffins and lions, the station is a junction on the Frankfurt-am-Main–Kassel line.

Giessen's university was founded around the 12th-century castle in 1607, two years before its botanical garden.

HARZER SCHMALSPURBAHNEN

The most extensive and scenic of the narrow-gauge railways in the former East Germany is the 140-km (87-mile) network of lines known as the Harzer Schmalspurbahn. The main line links the delightful town of Wernigerode with Nordhausen, while the principal branch line leaves the main line at Eisfelder Tahlmühle and heads east, then north to Gernrode. In 2006, the 8km (5 miles) of standard-gauge railway between Gernrode and the World Heritage Site of Quedlinburg was converted to narrow-gauge. Of the three other branches, the most important is the remarkable line up the Brocken, a mountain renowned for its literary associations and the saturnalia of Walpurgis Night. Heinrich Heine's book about the Harz made his name, and Goethe set part of *Faust* here.

A LARGE INVESTMENT

Since unification, large sums have been invested in the railway, improving the facilities and introducing such amenities as cafés and bar cars. The railway attracts hundreds of thousands of visitors to the area each year, and gives walkers access to the densely forested Harz Mountains, a prime hiking area.

The timetable requires careful reading. There are no direct Nordhausen–Wernigerode or Eisfelder Tahlmühle–Quedlinburg trains, so an easy change of train is necessary. Anyone in search of steam workings should note that the Eisfelder Tahlmühle–Stiege section is entirely diesel-operated apart from occasional special trains. Nearly all trains up the Brocken are steam-hauled.

One of the delights of the locomotive-hauled trains is the opportunity

to ride on the open-balcony coaches. Besides enjoying wider views and the cool smell of the forest, you can stand right by the chimney of a bunker-first working and hear at close quarters the stirring bark of the huge tank engine tackling the steep grades that characterise the system.

The southern terminus of the system, well served by Halle–Kassel trains, is **Nordhausen**. Large enough to have a tram system, the town was badly bombed during World War II but the church still contains much from the 14th-century, including the choir stalls. To the north of the town lies the Konzentratsion-lager-Dora, part of Buchenwald concentration camp, which supplied labour for the construction of V1 and V2 rockets in the 11km (7 miles) of massive tunnels that were carved out of the mountain of gypsum known as Kohnstein. A grim memorial is open to visitors.

NORDHAUSEN TO WERNIGERODE

Trains stop at several halts on the outskirts of Nordhausen, until after **Ilfeld**

the suburbs are left behind. The railway starts to wend its way through the wooded hills that continue all the way to Wernigerode, alternating between narrow valleys with fast-running, tree-shaded streams, beech woods, forests of generously spaced conifers and open meadows ablaze with wild flowers. At **Netzkater** there is a museum of equipment, the Rabensteiner Stollen, from mining railways and a café in the station.

Many passengers change trains at the junction of **Eisfelder Tahlmühle**, where the lines to Gernrode and Wernigerode split. Heading north to Wernigerode, the wooded station of **Benneckenstein**, 13km (8 miles) further on, has a railway museum in the goods shed, while the pretty, half-timbered building at **Elend** houses a station café/bar. In the 8km (5 miles) between **Drei Annen Hohne** and Steinerne Renne there are 72 curves and the line's only tunnel, as the track descends at gradients up to 1 in 30, providing a challenge for southbound trains. Occasional clearings in the

> ☉ **Tip**
>
> Nordhausen is on the electrified Kassel–Halle line, but connoisseurs of railway byways will not be disappointed by the DB journey between Wernigerode, Halberstadt and Quedlinburg.

Historical steam train heading up Brocken Mountain.

☉ THE BROCKEN

One of the last daily steam spectacles in Europe is provided by the succession of well-filled trains to the roadless 1,142-metre (3,747-ft) summit of the Brocken. From the junction at Drei Annen Hohne it is an almost unbroken climb at 1 in 30 to the summit, calling for delightfully demonstrative exertion from the bulky locomotives. The woods are particularly thick as the line climbs to the one intermediate station at **Schierke** for a stop to replenish the water tanks.

Climbing through boulder-strewn, thinning woodland, crisscrossed by walking trails, the line comes out of the trees near the refuge siding at Goetheweg (allowing trains to pass in summer), with views over nothing but unbroken forest for miles.

When the line is busy, descending trains are often diverted into the siding to allow an ascending train an unchecked run up the bank, affording passengers in the waiting train the fine sight and sound of the locomotive storming up the bank. A prominent ski-jump in the distance indicates the popularity of the area for winter sports. Finally, the line spirals round the summit before coming to a halt below a large building housing a restaurant, café and communications equipment.

woods give a sense of how vast an area the forest covers. **Steinerne Renne** is a halt and a passing loop in woods, from which the train drifts downhill, past the backs of houses and alongside a stream to **Wernigerode Westerntor**, where the railway's workshops are situated, and the main station at **Wernigerode**. The old town itself seems to be entirely composed of well-restored, half-timbered houses; it also has a splendidly spired 15th- to 16th-century Rathaus and a multi-turreted *schloss* dating from 1862–85 on the hill. The castle is open to visitors and can even be reached by a miniature railway from the marketplace in summer. The castle terrace offers splendid views over the Harz and the Brocken.

THE GERNRODE LINE

The line from Eisfelder Tahlmühle to Quedlinburg soon leaves the woods and climbs up to a lonely plateau of wild grassland on which the isolated junction of **Stiege** is situated. The line then ambles past a series of attractive villages, birch woods and

a willow-fringed river to the spa village of **Alexisbad**, junction for Harzgerode and its 16th-century castle. Passing through deep rock cuttings, the railway comes alongside the road near **Drahtzug** before reaching **Mägdesprung** with its large collection of old factory buildings. It was here that Prince Frederick Albert of Anhalt, who died in 1796, founded a large ironworks. Among its products were 'tasteful articles in cast iron', according to Baedeker, which could be bought from the foundry by passing tourists. Wood-fringed fields border the line before it re-enters the woods at **Sternhaus-Haberfeld** and drops down steeply to **Gernrode**. The town's most notable attraction is the 10th-century St Cyriakus, the oldest Ottonian church in Germany.

INNSBRUCK–GARMISCH-PARTENKIRCHEN–MUNICH

Passengers on the scenic line through the Arlberg between Bregenz and Innsbruck may notice on the western side of the Tyrolean capital a track

Wernigerode's old town.

climbing in a most extraordinary manner along the steep northern flank of the valley, weaving in and out of side valleys over viaducts and through tunnels. This is the start of the line that climbs into the mountains of southern Bavaria and continues to Munich (München), reached in under three hours. The southerly section between Innsbruck and Garmisch-Partenkirchen was a late addition, built as an electrified railway between 1910 and 1912; Garmisch-Partenkirchen had been reached from the north in time for the 1890 passion play in Oberammergau.

A VERTIGINOUS ASCENT

Trains for Munich leave Innsbruck in a westerly direction before turning north to cross the River Inn and start the long ascent through the wooded slopes at gradients as steep as 1 in 28. The view (best from the left-hand side of the train) steadily broadens as the train gains height, looking down across the airport to the mountains of the Tyrol and along the Inn Valley. Passengers sometimes have the unusual experience of travelling at the same height as, or even above, an aeroplane. Pausing at tiny halts and wayside stations, the train twists along its ledge and through an avalanche shelter before entering a long tunnel. Those who suffer from vertigo may be thankful that the trees mask the depth of the drop, but occasional openings reveal dizzying chasms of rock.

By **Leithen** the line has curved to the north away from the Inn Valley and reached an area of upland meadows and coniferous forest. Past **Reith**, the summit is reached and the line dips to the winter sports resort of **Seefeld in Tirol**. The importance of forestry is indicated by wagons loaded with tree trunks at **Scharnitz**, the last station before the train crosses the Austro–German border.

The first station in Germany is the year-round resort and violin-making centre of **Mittenwald**. The musical association stems from 1681 when Mathias Klotz started making violins here after studying the craft with Nicola Amati in Cremona. Prominent in the townscape is the frescoed baroque tower of the fine church of SS Peter and Paul, and the town contains a wealth of houses with *Lüftlmalerei* (elaborately painted facades). Cable cars provide access for hiking to four nearby peaks. Soon after leaving Mittenwald the line crosses the Isar Valley, flanked by the steep Karwendel range, and resumes its climb through fields peppered with small farm buildings. **Klais** has the distinction of being the highest station in Germany reached by mainline trains. Beyond it, the valley narrows and trees crowd in on the railway, which soon joins the broad valley of the River Loisach at Garmisch-Partenkirchen, the approach heralded by the ski jump built for the Winter Olympics in 1936.

⊘ **Essentials**

European Rail Timetable no. 895

Distance: 160km (100 miles)

Duration of journey: 2hrs 50 mins

Frequency of trains: hourly

On the line between between Garmisch and Farchant, with a magnificent Alpine backdrop.

GARMISCH-PARTENKIRCHEN, OLYMPIC VILLAGE

Merged from two villages for the Olympics, **Garmisch-Partenkirchen** was home to the composer Richard Strauss until his death in 1949, and there is a June festival devoted to his work. Attractively decorated houses line some of Garmisch's streets, and it is worth visiting the small pilgrimage church of St Anton for the poignant memorial photographs of soldiers killed in both world wars. To the northwest of the town, and reached by bus, is Ludwig II's jewel-like Schloss Linderhof, one of his smallest creations. Set in a remote valley, the eclectic hunting palace was the only one of his residences to be completed. The formal French gardens are surrounded by parkland in which there is a Moorish pavilion, a Moroccan timber house and a grotto of Venus. Buses from the town also serve two of Ludwig's most ostentatious castles, at Hohenschwangau and – most famously – Neuschwanstein. The area has numerous cable cars providing easy access to mountain walks, as well as the rack railway up the Zugspitze. Although the area has the best skiing facilities in Germany, it is an equally appealing summer resort. Whatever the season, it is worth taking the Ausserfernbahn, the cross-country line west from Garmisch-Partenkirchen to Kempten, as it offers exceptional scenery.

THE BAVARIAN FOOTHILLS

Leaving Garmisch, the train bowls along the broad valley of the Loisach, flanked by gully-riven mountains, to cross the river after **Eschenlohe** and climb at 1 in 45 to the junction for Oberammergau at **Murnau**. Staffelsee comes into view to the west as the contours flatten and market gardening becomes the dominant activity. You can visit the Russian House (also known as the Münter House), where Wassily Kandinsky, Russian-born pioneer of abstract art, lived from 1909 to 1914 and many of his works can be seen at the Lenbachhaus in Munich. The castle museum has exhibitions on local

DB train to Innsbruck Hbf arrvies at Garmisch-Partenkirchen during the winter.

artists and writers, and on life in the Bavarian countryside.

Reaching the outer limit of the Munich S-bahn at **Tutzing**, passengers are denied sight of Starnberger See by intervening woodland until **Starnberg** where there is a lovely view back along the lake. The waters were the scene of an event that continues to exercise a fascination for anyone interested in one of Europe's most colourful monarchs. It was near Berg Castle on the lake that Ludwig II and his physician mysteriously drowned in 1886, following his deposition. An impromptu commission had declared the king insane and unfit to rule, and it remains a mystery whether he committed suicide, and the doctor died trying to save him, or whether both were murdered.

You arrive in the Bavarian capital, **Munich**, at the large but uninspiring station built in 1963. You need a long visit to do justice to the city's many attractions. It has dozens of well-presented museums and galleries and many other places of interest reached by the excellent S- and U-bahn or tram/bus network. The best way to explore the pedestrianised centre is on foot, and for English-speakers there is a range of guided tram and walking or cycling tours. Besides architectural visits, there are tours devoted to hops and malt, political history and nature.

The major event in Munich's calendar is the 16-day Oktoberfest, beginning in late September. Dating from 1810 and the marriage of the Bavarian Crown Prince, later Ludwig I, to Therese von Saxe-Hildburghausen, the festival has become a major international event, attracting over 6 million people a year. Hotel prices cash in on the high demand, and regulars advise leaving the beer tents at 10.30–11pm, at least an hour before closing time, to avoid the crush later.

THE ZUGSPITZBAHN SCALES THE HEIGHTS

Mechanised access to Germany's highest mountain was first achieved from the Austrian side, by a cable car system opened in 1926. The metre-gauge rack railway that takes visitors most of the way up from the German side was built between 1928 and 1930, with a maximum gradient of 1 in 4. The line starts at a small station on the west side of Garmisch-Partenkirchen station. The trains are painted in Bavaria's national colours of blue and white.

From Garmisch the Zugspitzbahn parallels the scenic cross-country line to Reutte and Kempten, acting as a regular local railway and stopping at small halts. Access to walks in the hills leading up to the Alpspitze is provided by the cable car to Kreuzeck at **Kreuzeckbahn** station. Small wooden huts for hay storage litter the flower-rich grassland, and almost every chalet in the villages seems set on winning a 'Bavaria in bloom' award. An immaculately tended cemetery is passed just before the principal intermediate

Beers at Oktoberfest.

The Zugspitzbahn passes through Garmisch-Partenkirchen.

station of **Grainau**, where passengers change to a rack-fitted railcar.

Climbing through mixed woods, the railway reaches **Eibsee** and the foot of a direct cable car from the summit (a ticket allows you to travel by different routes in each direction). The lake comes into view as the climb continues, the shallows around the islands a beautiful crown of turquoise set in the dark blue of the deeper water.

At a height of 1,650 metres (5,413ft) at **Riffelriß** the line enters the long tunnel that leads to the summit station at **Zugspitzplatt** (2,590 metres/8,497ft). Here passengers transfer to the cable car for the final ascent to the summit at 2,962 metres (9,717ft), although many break their journey by walking up to Germany's highest chapel.

The cable car was rebuilt in 2017 and has the world's longest wire span with a single support tower (3,213 metres/ yds). It deposits visitors right at the summit in a warren of passageways, stairs, lifts, shops, cafés, restaurants, terraces, and an exhibition gallery,

the last of which is free to enter and chronicles the mountain summit's 200 years as a tourist attraction, including the development of the cable car and the rack railway.

OBERAMMERGAU, THE PASSION PLAY VILLAGE

The branch line to the town that performs the world-famous passion play every 10 years (next showing is 2020) is as pleasant a journey as one would wish to such a celebrated place. Distant mountains are usually in view as the train winds round the hills, through woods and farms.

The railway was just finished in time for the 1900 play, and 155,000 people arrived by train. Ten years later it was 224,000. Although the line was electrified, the electric rolling stock could not cope and many steam trains had to be hauled by three locomotives.

The railway climbs as far as **Bad Kohlgrub** and then drops down through a stream-threaded wood to the broad, flat valley that leads to **Oberammergau**. Although very obviously devoted to tourism, the town has some attractive houses; their distinguishing feature is the *trompe l'oeil* decoration known as *Lüftmalerei*. Some of the paintings are old and depict religious subjects, some are newer.

Woodcarving keeps some of the population busy between the plays, the origins of which go back to 1633, when plague in southern Bavaria led to the area being sealed off to protect itself against infection. The cordon was penetrated by a local labourer wanting to return to his family; in two days he was dead and so, within three weeks, was a quarter of the village. The survivors vowed that if the pestilence ceased they would stage a passion play every 10 years. The first was performed the following year, but some time around 1680 it was moved to what is commonly regarded as the first year of a decade.

The Zugspitze cable car.

Nearby is Ludwig II's hunting lodge, Schloss Linderhof, which can be reached by an hourly bus from the station.

MUNICH–LINDAU

The railway from Munich to Lindau is a pleasant way to reach Bodensee (Lake Constance), the second largest expanse of Alpine water after Lake Geneva, with an area of 531 sq km (205 sq miles). Direct trains run from Lindau across the border into Switzerland to St Gallen and Zürich, and further international connections are available from nearby Bregenz in Austria, reached by local trains in 10 minutes. Alternatively, this can be made into a circular day trip from Munich, proceeding on to Bregenz and Innsbruck and back to Munich via Garmisch-Partenkirchen. Off the Lindau line are numerous cross-country and branch lines, the connecting trains arriving or waiting as your train enters the junction. It is also a line well used by cyclists and walkers to reach the Allgäu Alps. The better views are to be had on the left.

MUNICH TO KEMPTEN

Exits from principal stations are seldom visual treats, and Munich is no exception, although it is surprising how quickly the train reaches coniferous forest interspersed with vast fields of cereals and neat villages with onion-domed church towers and shuttered chalet farmhouses attached to cavernous barns.

Near **Grafrath** a glimpse can be had of Ammersee to the south. The lake can be reached from Munich by the S-bahn line to Herrsching or by a branch line from Geltendorf. Three successive lines branch off the Lindau line to the north towards Augsburg (where Rudolf Diesel developed the engine that is hauling your train), the fastest being the last, from **Buchloe**. As a track trails in to the right from Memmingen, the train arrives at the capital of the Allgäu Alps at **Kempten**. One of the oldest towns in Germany, dating from the Roman occupation, Kempten has remains of the original walls, a fine Roman collection in the Zumsteinhaus in Residenzplatz, and

⊙ Essentials

European Rail Timetable no. 935

Distance: 220km (137 miles)

Duration of journey: 2 hrs 40 mins

Frequency of trains: 12 per day

Munich station.

some civic buildings dating from the 17th century. It is also the junction for the scenic line that cuts briefly through northern Austria en route to Garmisch-Partenkirchen.

IMMENSTADT TO BODENSEE

As the train leaves Kempten, the Allgäu Alps rise to the west and south. Nearing **Martinszell**, passengers can look down on a lake fringed by pretty villages to the west before the track joins the River Iller to reach the resort of **Immenstadt**, junction for the branch south to the mountain resorts of Sonthofen and Oberstdorf, once known for their sanatoria. The pedestrianised old town of Immenstadt is very close to the station: worth a visit are the Königsegg Palace, dating from 1620, the 17th-century town hall and the museum, which features the local craft of linen weaving.

The line curves round the east end of Alpsee and hugs its northern shore, the water often skimmed by brightly coloured sailing boats. The railway was obviously built to a tight budget as it obviates the need for tunnelling by curving around the hills: in only one place did the engineers find it impossible to avoid a tunnel, and that is after the **Thalkirchdorf** halt, where the line enters the 124-metre (136-yd) darkness of Oberstaufener Tunnel to reach the summit of the line at **Oberstaufen**. Noted for its cleansing dietary treatments, which are based on the ideas and research of a local physician, the town makes a good base for walking, with cable cars to assist in the ascent of the nearby peak of Hochgrat (1,833 metres/6,014ft).

After crossing the viaduct at **Röthenbach**, the train picks up speed as the line takes a straighter alignment through receding hills. Once past the junction at **Hergatz** the enormous expanse of Bodensee comes into view through the trees to the southwest, the railway descending through orchards and market gardens towards the water's edge. It reaches the station at Lindau by a narrow causeway to the island which the station shares with the old town.

Heading up to Oberstaufen, with Lake Constance in the background. On the opposite side of the lake is Bregenz (Austria).

LINDAU AND ITS ENVIRONS

Lindau is a truly delightful place, its old centre partly pedestrianised and the area around the station and hotel-ringed harbour also free from traffic. Once a Roman camp and naval base, the island was a free city of the Holy Roman Empire until 1803 when Napoleon made it part of Bavaria. The comings and goings of the lake's steamers in the picturesque setting of the small harbour, with its vaguely Moorish 13th-century lighthouse and huge lion, dating from 1856, at the end of the eastern mole, encourage visitors to linger over a coffee at the many terrace cafés. The first steamer plied Bodensee in 1824, and there is still one paddle-steamer on the lake: the *Hohentwiel*, dating from 1911.

To the west, at a point on the northern shore almost opposite Konstanz, is the small town of **Meersburg**, one of the best-preserved medieval towns in all Germany. Closer to Lindau, and quickly reached by the railway that parallels the northern shore, is the town famed for its association with the inventor of airships, Graf Ferdinand von Zeppelin. **Friedrichshafen**'s fine museum is actually an extension of the station and is notable not only for the section devoted to Zeppelin and dirigibles, but also for having the largest collection of works by the realist painter, Otto Dix (1891–1969).

DRESDEN–NÜRNBERG–FRANKFURT-AM-MAIN

Linking cities of great historical importance and interest, the route begins in southern Saxony, traverses the northern part of Bavaria known as Franconia, and finishes in Hesse. Services are operated by diesel trains because part of the line is still not electrified. There are no through trains from Dresden to Frankfurt; eight daily trains run from Dresden to Nürnberg (Nuremberg), from where there are hourly departures to Frankfurt.

DRESDEN TO NÜRNBERG

The station at Dresden has a most unusual layout, with S-bahn platforms at a higher level flanking the main terminal platforms. Before the end of the

Essentials

European Rail Timetable nos. 880, 920

Distance: 628km (390 miles)

Duration of journey: 7 hrs 12 mins (change at Hof and Nürnberg)

Frequency of trains: hourly

ICE train at Dresden station.

S-bahn and suburbia, the terminus of the 750-mm-gauge line to Kurort Kipsdorf, which still uses steam traction, can be seen to the right and at a lower level at Freital-Hainsberg. At Tharandt the railway leaves the conurbation behind and cuts through the eastern part of the forest of the same name before skirting its southern edge, with good views to the south.

After **Muldenhütten**, the railway crosses the River Freiberger Mulde by viaduct before reaching **Freiberg**, the town that was largely responsible for the historical wealth of Saxony, thanks to its silver mines. The first published book on mining was written by a citizen of Freiburg, and the world's first Mining Academy was established here in 1765.

Panoramic views open up after **Oederan**, followed by the crossing of the River Flöha by the Hertzdorfer Viaduct. On the outskirts of Chemnitz, to the right, is the half-roundhouse railway museum at **Hilbersdorf**. **Chemnitz**, formerly Karl-Marx-Stadt, was once dubbed the German Manchester on account of its heavy industry, and has a few remaining

historical buildings of note, a Renaissance town hall being perhaps the finest.

The large car factory to the left at Mosel used to produce the notorious Trabant, but now turns out Volkswagens. A few kilometres to the south is the former coal-mining centre of Zwickau, the birthplace in 1810 of composer Robert Schumann, and the house is open to visitors. The Gothic Mariendom and the early 16th-century Gewandhaus, a hall built for the drapers' guild and now used as a theatre, are also worth visiting.

There are lovely views to the west of **Reichenbach** over gently rolling farmland. To the south of **Plauen** the landscape is a painter's dream of farms and woodland stretching for tens of kilometres. Pressing due south through **Hof** before turning west again at **Marktredwitz**, the line reaches **Kirchenlaibach**, junction for nearby Bayreuth – the town synonymous with Wagner.

The final outstanding stretch is between **Neuhaus** and **Vorra**, which affords lovely views up side valleys between a succession of tunnels. The villages of

The Göltzsch Viaduct is the largest brick-built bridge in the world.

Hohenstadt and **Hersbruck** display the distinctive vernacular style of tall-roofed houses with many small windows extending into the steeply pitched gables.

NÜRNBERG TO FRANKFURT

The architectural legacy of **Nürnberg**'s medieval heyday was lost during World War II when whole areas of timber-framed houses were destroyed, but the principal public buildings and some areas around them have been painstakingly restored. The German National Museum is exceptional, having the largest collection of German art and culture, and the vast stadium where the Nazis held their rallies is now an exhibition on 'Fascination and Terror'.

The section of railway from Nürnberg to **Fürth** was the first stretch to be opened in Germany, in 1835, with a locomotive built in Newcastle-upon-Tyne. The line continues through pleasant but unremarkable farmland to **Würzburg**, a good place to break the journey to see the immense Baroque palace known as the Residenz (a World Heritage Site), the Hofkirche and the

Marienberg fortress, which can be seen from miles around. It is perched on vine-covered hills and reached from the old town by a bridge with a statue of St Kilian, patron saint of wine. The Residenz was intended as the 'palace of all palaces', and the staircase leading up to Tiepolo's frescoes is regarded as one of the most beautiful of the rococo period. Thankfully, it survived the bombs that destroyed much of the old city, which has been rebuilt.

The River Main is on the left of the line for the next 51km (32 miles), providing some delightful views as the two twist and turn. After leaving the river at **Lohr** the track continues west through forest to **Aschaffenburg**. The principal attraction here is the German Renaissance Schloss Johannisburg, but it also has a replica of a Pompei house built for Ludwig I, in the garden. The castle houses a museum exhibiting German and Dutch old masters and liturgical objects. Just beyond Aschaffenburg is the village of **Dettingen** where, in 1743, George II became the last English monarch to lead his troops into battle.

Display at the DB Museum, in Nürnberg.

A replica of Adler, which was the first train to run in Germany, in Fürth.

MUSEUMS AND HERITAGE LINES

Germany is unusual in having a number of narrow gauge railways that survived as steam-operated concerns under the GDR and continue to operate. The numbers here relate to the map on page 254.

MUSEUMS

Deutsche Dampflokomotiv-Museum ❶
Birkenstrasse 5, 95339 Neuenmarkt/Oberfranken
Open: Tue–Sun 10am–5pm
Features: in former DB depot, 30 steam locomotives
Nearest station: Neuenmarkt-Wirsberg
Tel: 092 275700
www.dampflokmuseum.de

Deutsches Museum Verkehrszentrum ❷
Theresienhöhe 15, 80339 München
Café, shop
Open: daily 9am–5pm
Features: collection of railway and transport exhibits
Nearest station: Schwanthalerhöhe (U4 and U5)
Tel: 089 2179 333
www.deutsches-museum.de

Deutsches Technikmuseum Berlin ❸
Trebbiner Strasse 9, D-10963 Berlin
Café, shop
Open: Tue–Fri 9am–5.30pm, Sat–Sun 10am–6pm
Features: trains through the ages, with 40 original vehicles on display
Nearest station: (U-bahn) Möckernbrücke or Gleisdreieck
Tel: 030 90254-0
www.dtmb.de

Eisenbahnmuseum Bochum Dahlhausen ❹
Dr C.-Otto-Strasse 191, D-44879 Bochum
Café, shop
Open: Mar–mid-Nov, Tue–Fri, Sun and holidays 10am–5pm
Features: in a former rail depot, with special trips and themed events
Nearest station: Bochum-Dahlhausen (Essen S-bahn, line 3)
Tel: 0234 492516
www.eisenbahnmuseum-bochum.de

Eisenbahnmuseum Darmstadt-Kranichstein ❺
Steinstrasse 7, D-64291 Darmstadt
Open: Sun 10am–4pm, Apr–Sept Wed 10am–4pm
Features: eight-road roundhouse and open tracks, with over 200 railway vehicles; steam and diesel locomotives on operating days
Nearest station: Darmstadt-Kranichstein
Tel: 06151 377760
www.museumsbahn.de

Eisenbahnmuseum Neustadt ❻
Schillerstrasse 3, D-67434 Neustadt (Weinstrasse)
Open: Tue–Fri 10am–1pm, Sat–Sun 10am–4pm
Features: collection of locomotives; also operates Neustadt–Elmstein on various days
Nearest station: Neustadt (Weinstrasse)
Tel: 06321 30390
www.eisenbahnmuseum-neustadt.de

Museumeisenbahn Hamm ❼
(Hamm Süd–Lippborg)
Schumannstrasse 35, 59063 Hamm
Open: Wed 6–8pm, Sat noon–6pm
Features: museum operating over local private line on various days to Lippborg-Heintrop.
Nearest station: Hamm Süd
Length: 18.7km (11.5 miles)
Gauge: 1,435mm (4ft 8½in)
Tel: 02381 540048
www.museumseisenbahn-hamm.de

Lokwelt Freilassing ❽
Westendstrasse 5, 83395 Freilassing
Open: Fri–Sun 10am–5pm
Features: steam and electric locos on 17 tracks in half roundhouse
Nearest station: Freilassing
Tel: 08654 3099320
www.lokwelt.freilassing.de

Verkehrsmuseum Dresden ❾
Johanneum am Neumarkt, Augustusstrasse 1, D-01067 Dresden
Open: Tue–Sun 10am–5pm
Features: comprehensive railway section
Nearest station: Dresden Hauptbahnhof
Tel: 0351 86440
www.verkehrsmuseum-dresden.de

DB Museum Nürnberg ❿
Lessingstrasse 6, D-90443 Nürnberg
Café, shop
Open: Tue–Sun 9am–5pm
Features: locos and rolling stock
Nearest station: Nürnberg/Opernhaus on U2
Tel: 0800 32687386
www.db.de/dbmuseum

HERITAGE LINES

Bergische Museumbahnen ⓫
(Kohlfurther Brücke–Greuel)
Strassenbahn-Museum Kohlfurther Brücke 57, D-42349 Wuppertal
Open: various days
Features: major tram museum
Nearest station: Wuppertal
Length: 3.2km (2 miles)
Gauge: 1,000mm (3ft 33⁄8in)
Tel: 0202 470251
www.bmb-wuppertal.de

Berliner Parkeisenbahn ⓬
An der Wuhlheide 189, D-12459

Berlin-Köpenick
Open: various days
Features: steam and diesel
operation around park
Nearest station: S-bahn S3
Wuhlheide
Gauge: 600mm (1ft 115⁄8 in)
Tel: 030 53892660
www.parkeisenbahn.de

Lokpark Braunschweig ⑬
Schwarzkopffstrasse 3, D-38126
Braunschweig
Open: Apr–Oct, last Sat of month
Features: steam locomotives.
Occasional operation over regional
lines
Nearest station: Braunschweig
Tel: 0531 264034
www.vbv-bs.de

Brohltal-Eisenbahn ⑭
Bahnhofstrasse 11, 56656 Brohl-
Lützing
Open: varying days mid-Apr–late
Oct
Features: Vulkan Express, steam as
far as Oberzissen (12km/7.5 miles)
on certain days
Nearest station: Brohl
Length: 17.5km (11 miles)
Gauge: 1,000mm (3ft 33⁄8 in)
Tel: 02636 80303
www.vulkan-express.de

Bruchhausen-Vilsen-Asendorf ⑮
Bahnhof 1, Bruchhausen-Vilsen,
NI 27305
Shop
Open: weekends in summer and
special days
Features: first preservation
society, opened in 1966; 6 steam
locomotives
Nearest stations: Eystrup, Syke
Length: 8km (5 miles)
Gauge: 1,000mm (3ft 33⁄8 in)
Tel: 04252 9300-50
www.museumseisenbahn.de

Chiemseebahn ⑯
Seestrasse 108, 83209 Prien am
Chiemsee
Café, shop
Open: May–late Sept
Features: links DB and steamer on

Chiemsee
Nearest station: Prien
Length: 1.8km (1 mile)
Gauge: 1,000mm (3ft 33⁄8 in)
Tel: 08051 609-0
www.chiemsee-schifffahrt.net

Dampfbahn Fränkische Schweiz ⑰
(Ebermannstadt–Behringersmühle)
Postfach 1101, D-91316
Ebermannstadt
Open: May–Oct Sun
Features: steam and diesel
Nearest station: Ebermannstadt
Length: 16km (10 miles)
Gauge: 1,435mm (4ft 81⁄2in)
Tel: 09194 725175
www.dfs.ebermannstadt.de

Dampflokfreunde Salzwedel ⑱
Am Bahnhof 6, D-19322
Wittenberge
Open: Sat 11am–4.30pm and other
days
Features: the largest rail museum
in Brandbenburg, housed in a
former depot, with turntable,
locomotive sheds, track and
locomotives
Nearest station: Wittenberge
www.en.dampflok-wittenberge.de

DBK Historische Bahn ⑲
(Schorndorf–Rudersberg and other
lines)
Geschäftsstelle, Horaffenstrasse
32, D-74564 Crailsheim
Open: various days
Features: collection of mainline
locomotives at Crailsheim
Nearest station: Schorndorf
Length: 22.9km (14.25 miles)
Gauge: 1,435mm (4ft 81⁄2in)
Tel: 0700 325 80 106
www.dbk-historische-bahn.de

Kandertalbahn ⑳
(Kandern–Haltingen)
Postfach 1128, D-79400 Kandern
Open: May–Oct, most Sun
Features: pleasant river valley
Nearest station: Haltingen
Length: 12.9km (8 miles)
Gauge: 1,435mm (4ft 81⁄2in)
Tel: 07626 972356
www.kandertalbahn.de

**Delmenhorst-Harpsted
Eisenbahnfreunde ㉑**
Postfach 1236, D-27732
Delmenhorst
Open: various Sun
Features: steam and diesel
Nearest station: Delmenhorst
Length: 22km (14 miles)
Gauge: 1,435mm (4ft 81⁄2in)
Tel: 04244 2380
www.jan-harpstedt.de

Pressnitztalbahn ㉒
Interessengemeinschaft
Preßnitztalbahn78, 09477 Jöhstadt
Open: various weekends
Features: glorious scenery, three
Saxon Meyers
Nearest station: Annaberg-
Buchholz, then bus to Wolkenstein
Length: 7.8km (5 miles)
Gauge: 750mm (2ft 51⁄2in)
www.pressnitztalbahn.de

Schwaben Dampf ㉓
Neuoffingen 3, 89362 Offingen
Open: various dates
Features: extensive programme of
steam-hauled excursions
Nearest station: Neuoffingen
www.schwabendampf.de

Selfkantbahn ㉔
Am Bahnhof 13a, 52538 Gangelt
Display shed
Open: Easter-end Sept Sun
Features: steam tram as well as
locomotives
Nearest station: Geilenkirchen
Length: 5.5km (3.5 miles)
Gauge: 1,000mm (3ft 33⁄8 in)
Tel: 0241 82369 or 02454 6699
www.selfkantbahn.de

Sauschwänzlebahn ㉕
Bahnhofstrasse 1, 78176 Blumberg
Open: May–Sept most weekends,
some Wed and Thu
Features: spiral tunnel, tremendous
scenery
Nearest station: Blumberg-
Zollhaus
Length: 25km (15.5 miles)
Gauge: 1,435mm (4ft 81⁄2in)
Tel: 07702 51300
www.sauschwaenzlebahn.de

The Oslo–Bergen train passes snow-covered cars in Gol, Norway.

The Inlandsbanan passes by Fåker, Östersund municipality.

SCANDINAVIA

The wide open spaces of Europe's northern wilderness are penetrated by a few isolated railway lines, operated by fast, comfortable trains

The railways of Denmark, Finland, Norway and Sweden are independent, although their close relationship is reflected in many international services. However, Finland is handicapped because its former status as a grand duchy of Russia bequeathed it a 1,524-mm (5-ft)-gauge compared with the normal 1,435mm (4ft 8½in), which inhibits through trains. The standard of services in all countries is high, and the quality of the long-distance trains in Norway and Sweden ranks them among the best in Europe. Networks thin out to the north, with isolated lines penetrating beyond the Arctic Circle in Norway, Sweden and Finland.

As the largest and most populous of the four countries, Sweden predictably has the largest network (9,684km/6,017 miles as of 2016), with tilting X2000 trains over its busiest southern inter-city routes. The Øresund Link (Tunnel and Bridge) across to Denmark means that it is possible to travel quickly and comfortably between Sweden, Denmark and Germany.

A CHALLENGING ENVIRONMENT

Norway is Europe's most thinly populated country, with only 4.4 million inhabitants and a mountainous topography, so financing the railway

Flåmsbana in winter.

has always been difficult. Despite these obstacles, Norway has a network of 4,209km (2,615 miles). Significant investment has gone into the construction of tunnels to eliminate particularly sinuous sections of line and improve journey times. New, high-quality trains run on main routes: the seats are exceptionally comfortable and well equipped, with a children's play area, a coffee bar and audio jacks at all seats, and premium facilities available in NSB Komfort class.

Main attractions

Bergen: Bryggen, Hanseatiske Museum Grieghallen
Oslo: National Gallery, Norwegian Museum of Cultural HistoryHelsinki: Cathedral, Kiasma (Museum of Contemporary Art)
St Petersburg: Mariinsky Theatre, Peter and Paul Fortress, Cathedral.

Maps on pages
280, 282, 293

Scandinavia

0 ——— 200 km

0 ——— 200 miles

N

● Museums and Heritage Lines
═══ Featured route

BARENTS SEA

NORWEGIAN SEA

Nordkapp

Vardø

Pečenga

Tromsø

Nikel

Murmansk

Inarijärvi

Ivalo

Monchegorsk

Murmashki

Narvik

Torneträsk

Lokan tekojärvi

Kovdor

Kebnekaise 2117

Kiruna

Kolari

Alakurti

Arctic Circle

Bodø

Fauske

Stora Lulevatten

Gällivare

Rovaniemi

Kemijärvi

Ozero Knyazero

Rognan

Jokkmokk

RUSSIA

Mo i Rana

Hornavan

Boden

Tornio

FINLAND

Ozero Srednye Kuyto

Uddjaure

Moskoen

Sorsele

Arvidsjaur

Luleå

Kemi

Oulu

Sofporog

Storuman

Jörn

Perämeri Bottenviken

Kostomuksha

Malgomaj

Grong

Vilhelmina

Lycksele

Oulujärvi

Kontiomäki

Steinkjer

Hoting

Ylivieska

Kajaani

Nurmes

Vännäs

Kokkola

Iisalmi

Lieksa

Trondheim

Hell

SWEDEN

Umeå

Pielinen

Åre

Støren

Storlien

Storsjön

Östersund

Långsele

Vaasa

Kuopio

Joensuu

Oppdal

Bräcke

Härnösand

Seinäjoki

Alavus

Pieksämäki

Vyartsilya

Andalsnes

Røros

Ånge

Jyväskylä

Mikkeli

Savonlinna

Dombås

Dovre

Sundsvall

Jämsä

Gittertind 2470

Otta

Sveg

Hudiksvall

Tampere

Lappeenranta

Vinstra

Pori

Lahti

Kouvola

Vyborg

NORWAY

Flåm

Bollnäs

Söderhamn

Hämeenlinna

Voss

Lillehammer

Elverum

Mora

Turku

Hyvinkää

Kotka

Sankt-Peterburg

Gjøvik

Malung

Falun

Gävle

Salo

Helsinki

Labyazhye

Bergen

Geilo

Eidsvoll

Hamar

Kongsvinger

Borlänge

Åland

Gulf of Finland

Oslo

Torsby

Avesta

Hanko

Narva

Drammen

Ludvika

Uppsala

Tallin

Arvika

Västerås

Sala

Arsta

Tapa

RUSSIA

Stavanger

Moss

Kristinehamn

Eskilstuna

Stockholm

Riisipere

ESTONIA

Gdov

Sandnes

Skien

Halden

Säffle

Örebro

Södertälje

Hiiumaa

Tartu

Egersund

Nelaug

Strömstad

Vänern

Katrineholm

Nynäshamn

Saaremaa

Pärnu

Viljandi

Pskovskoye Oz

Arendal

Vänersborg

Lidköping

Norrköping

Valga

Pskov

Kristiansand

Uddevalla

Skövde

Vättern

Linköping

NORTH SEA

Skagerrak

Skagen

Göteborg

Jönköping

Västervik

Gulf of Riga

Skulte

Valmiera

Vecumi

Ostrov

Hirtshals

Borås

Nässjö

Ventspils

Riga

LATVIA

Frederikshavn

Kungsbacka

Värnamo

Oskarshamn

Gotland

Jurmala

Rēzekne

Thyborøn

Tisted

Alborg

Varberg

Aseda

Saldus

Ergli

Holstebro

Randers

Halmstad

Växjö

Kalmar

Öland

Liepāja

Jelgava

Daugava

Daugavpils

Ringkøbing

Viborg

Grenå

Mažeikiai

Druya

Nørre Nebel

Århus

Helsingborg

Panevėžys

LITHUANIA

Esbjerg

DENMARK

København (Copenhagen)

Lund

Karlskrona

Klaipėda

Šiauliai

Utena

Polatsk

Odense

Nyborg

Korsør

Malmö

Simrishamn

Anykščiai

Didžiasalis

Westerland

Tønder

Ystad

BALTIC SEA

Pagėgiai

Kaunas

Vilnius

BELARUS

Flensburg

Nakskov

Nykøbing

Bornholm

Łeba

Kaliningrad

Neman

Chernyakhovsk

Barysaw

Husum

Kiel

Rødby

Sassnitz

Ustka

Gdynia

Hel

Baltiysk

RUSSIA

Alytus

Minsk

GERMANY

Slupsk

POLAND

Gulf of Bothnia

Lofoten

Vesterålen

Vestfjorden

The introduction of Pendolino tilting trains has reduced journey times between the main cities in southern Finland, while Danish internal services received a boost with the opening of the bridge/tunnel across the Storebælt in 1997, which slashed journey times between Copenhagen and places on Funen and Jutland. However, the most important development of recent decades was the construction of the Øresund Link between Denmark and Sweden, which consists of the world's longest single bridge carrying road and rail traffic, and road and rail tunnels – it is familiar to many through the Scandinavian TV thriller series *The Bridge*. Its opening on 1 July 2000 allowed for frequent trains between Copenhagen and Malmö, and a Copenhagen–Stockholm service with journey times cut to five hours on the X2000 trains.

Routes in the wide open spaces of northern Scandinavia pass through unspoilt wilderness. Lines run along the tamer, but still attractive, west coast of Jutland (Denmark), while the lakes and forests of eastern Finland have an appeal all their own – the line from Lappeenranta to Joensuu is particularly attractive.

BERGEN–OSLO

The Bergen line is Norway's best-known railway, renowned for its fabulous scenery as well as being celebrated as an outstanding civil engineering achievement. Although the first passenger service left Bergen for Voss in 1883, it was a narrow-gauge train, which meant this section had to be reconstructed when work started on the extension to Oslo in 1896. The difficulties of building the railway through precipitous and often frozen mountain terrain were so great that it was not opened through to Oslo until 1907, and it was another year before completion of the snow sheds allowed a winter service.

The builders faced numerous problems: the average snowline in Norway is at about 900 metres (3,000ft), compared with 2,100 metres (7,000ft) in Switzerland. A total of 112km (70 miles) of line was above this height, so extensive work was needed to protect the tracks against snow and ice. Another difficulty was the exceptional hardness of the rock, which is mostly gneiss, granite and crystalline schists. The severe weather conditions, coupled with the absence of even rudimentary roads through the wilder parts of the route, meant that work in the open could proceed for only about three months of the year. Even though tunnelling could continue year-round, the excavated rock could not be removed from the workings in winter because of huge drifts – the men even had to crawl in and out of small tunnels through the snow.

Today the line is 489km (304 miles) in length, but originally it was considerably longer; successively built cut-offs, often in tunnel, have both shortened the route and made it less

Oslo–Bergen train in the mountains.

susceptible to the winter storms that threaten to block the track and interrupt services.

BERGEN TO MYRDAL

The temptation to catch the first Oslo train from **Bergen**'s imposing 1913 station should be resisted for at least a couple of days in order to do justice to the city, which is on Unesco's World Heritage list. Although very few medieval buildings survived the fires that periodically ravaged the port, there is plenty to see in this attractive city and good walking in the hills that surround its harbour. To gain an overview of Bergen and to reach walks through wooded hills, take the Fløibanen funicular railway to Fløyen or the cable car to Ulriken.

Almost as soon as the train for Oslo has left Bergen behind, it dives into the 7.6-km (4.75-mile) Ulriken Tunnel, to reach the station at Arna. For much of the first 86km (54 miles), as far as Voss, the railway is seldom out of sight of fjords, much of the line being built on a shelf blasted out of rock faces rising from the water. Numerous tunnels punctuate the line, mostly hewn out of such solid rock that no lining is necessary. The sheer slopes above the fjord prove no impediment to tenacious conifers, which find a purchase in the most inhospitable of crags as far up as the crown of treeless rock at the summit of the surrounding mountains. The

infrequent parcels of land along the foreshore are often occupied by tiny birch-sheltered wood cabins painted in the distinctive damask that can be seen all over Norway. Boat houses, as common here as suburban garages, reach into the clear water.

Shortly after **Dale** is the longest tunnel on the line – the Trollkona, which is 8.7km (5.5 miles) long. From the tunnel the line drops steeply to follow the River Vossa, its banks periodically linked by tiny, pedestrian suspension bridges, to a large lake before the skiing centre of **Voss**. After the line begins another long climb through upland farming country, it follows the north bank of the River Raundal into a spectacular canyon, a sheer drop opening up beneath the railway to the south. Near Mjølfjell the first snow shed indicates how high the line has climbed since leaving the coast; once made of timber, most of the snow sheds have been rebuilt in concrete.

At the end of the climb, at gradients of up to 1 in 46 into a barren, almost treeless bowl, the railway enters a long tunnel to reach **Myrdal**, at an altitude of 866 metres (2,841ft), one of those lonely places that would not exist but for the railway. Sandwiched between two tunnels, the station is best known as the junction for the vertiginous branch to Flåm (see panel below).

HE LONG HAUL TO FINSE

eaving Myrdal on the main line, there
s a fine view down over the Flåm line
o the north before the train enters a
uccession of snow sheds, one of which
ontains Hallingskeid station. From
ere to Finse is the longest stretch of
igh mountain railway in Europe. The
ighest point on the line is at Tauge-
ann 1,303 metres (4,267ft) above sea
evel. In winter, sleds drawn by teams
f huskies may be spotted on the climb
o **Finse**, the highest station on the
oute at 1,222 metres (4,009ft), where
here is a museum commemorating
he navvies who built this extraordi-
ary railway. It is winter for most of
he year at sub-arctic Finse, making
 popular with cross-country skiers; it
s also an access point for two major
rail networks – the Jotunheim to the
orth and the Hardangervidda to the
outh. There are no roads at Finse – it
s totally remote, yet accessible (even
he fastest trains stop here). Because
f this, it was chosen for the filming
f the initial sequences of *The Empire
trikes Back*, depicting battle scenes
on the Ice Planet Hoth. The Blåisen
glacier, running down from the Har-
dangerjøkulen ice cap, is only 5km (3
miles) along a marked path, and visible from the station. Mountain bikes
can be rented from the hotel.

The railway hereabouts is built on
a surprisingly straight course across
the plateau, enabling the train to
bowl along at speed, on grey winter
days whipping up the snow into eddy-
ing wraiths that mask the view of the
monochromatic landscape, broken only
by boulders and birch.

The handsome, wooden station
building at **Haugastøl** serves another
skiing resort which is also popular
in summer as a hiking centre. A few
kilometres before **Ustaoset** the line
crosses the main Oslo–Bergen road
(to which it stays close for most of
the remainder of the journey) and
then follows the north shore of Lake
Ustevatn, with good views of the Hal-
lingskarvet mountain ridge. Holiday
cabins dot the rolling hills as the train
approaches the major winter sports
centre of **Geilo**.

Bergen.

⊘ THE FLÅM BRANCH LINE

This extraordinary 20-km (12.5-mile) line has 20 tunnels and took 17 years to
build, opening for five years of steam traction in 1940 before being electrified.
Trains depart up to 10 times a day for the 50-minute trip. Thoughtfully, the
carriages have opening windows and tip-up seats so that passengers can
move from side-to-side and take photographs. It is one of the steepest non-
rack railways in the world with 16km (10 miles) at a gradient of 1 in 18, requiring the locomotives to have no fewer than five separate braking systems.

The descent of 863.5 metres (2,833ft) in such a short journey is accomplished by a spiral tunnel soon after leaving Myrdal. Near Reinunga is a
lake of the same name, from which a colossal waterfall drops over a series
of walls and slopes into the River Flåm. When the snows melt, the volume
of water makes it worth breaking the journey at Kjosfossen to wonder at
the noise and power of the cataract waterfall. The small village of Flåm is
situated on Aurlandsfjord, a branch of the world's longest fjord, Sognefjord.
However, there is little to detain visitors, apart from a small museum to the
east side of the station, about the history of the railway.

The railway forms part of what is known as 'Norway in a Nutshell', a
hugely popular and widely marketed day circular independent tour, also
using a ferry along Sognefjord, the Myrdal–Voss section of the Bergen railway and a bus from Gudvangen and Voss.

⊘ Essentials

European Rail Timetable nos. 785, 787

Distance: 1,282km (797 miles)

Duration of journey: 6hrs 40 mins (Oslo–Trondheim), 9 hrs 54 mins (Trondheim–Bodø)

Frequency of trains: 3 per day Oslo–Trondheim (+1 night train); 1 per day Trondheim–Bodø (+1 night train)

Oslo Opera House.

ALONG THE HALLINGDAL VALLEY

The train continues its descent through the lovely Hallingdal Valley and its dark coniferous forests, the muffled sound suddenly rising to a metallic roar as the train crosses a river. By **Ål** the line has reached a town large enough to have a few factories, and some passengers reach for a book at this point, although the landscapes rolling past the window remain pleasant enough.

Between Austvoll and **Flå** there is a dramatic stretch where the railway runs along a ledge above the Hallingdalselva River, with great views along the valley, before joining Lake Krøderen and climbing steadily above the water. The line then turns east through sparsely populated hills to burrow through the Haversting Tunnel into a different valley system. This takes the railway down to the junction and sawmill town of **Hønefoss** and through the outlying commuter stations of Oslo. East of **Drammen**, the railway crosses a long bridge over the river mouth, affording views over the branch of the Dramsfjord to the south.

Oslo Sentral station has been skilfully modernised following construction of a tunnel under the city to link previously separate termini; it incorporates the oldest part, which was built in 1877–82.

OSLO–BODØ

Few railways anywhere in the world can have been as long in the building as the line between Oslo and Bodø. The first section to Eidsvoll was opened in 1854 in the presence of Robert Stephenson, who acted as engineer-in-chief. It was another 108 years before the final section formally opened, right at the end of the steam era in Norway. Equally, it is one of the few railways to penetrate the Arctic Circle, offering passengers a safe route through landscapes that even today can be treacherous for motorists. It is a journey offering seascapes, mountain panoramas and some of the loveliest valleys in Norway, and one would be unlucky not to have at least one sighting of reindeer, elk or musk ox. Travel by 'Komfort' classis

the most civilised way to reach the old capital of Trondheim.

The section as far as Trondheim is known as the Dovre Railway, after the range of mountains that it crosses at a height of 1,006 metres (3,300ft). The railway is electrified as far as Trondheim, where diesel traction takes over for the route known as the Nordlandsbanen. It is best to plan the journey with at least one overnight break in Trondheim in each direction: the trip takes just over 6.5 hours between Oslo and Trondheim, and just under 10 hours to reach Bodø. For both sections, the best views are to be had on the left-hand side of the train going north.

NORTH FROM OSLO

Leaving Oslo, trains enter a long tunnel and take the new, high-speed line through an undulating landscape of conifers and birch to **Gardermoen Airport**. The high-speed line continues as far as **Eidsvoll**, where it joins the original tracks to follow the River Vorma to Norway's largest lake, Mjøsa, an important trade route before the railway arrived in the 1880s. As the train skirts the southeastern shore, you may catch a first sight of the lake's *pièce de résistance*, the paddle-steamer *Skibladner*, which has the distinction of being the world's oldest working paddler, built in 1856. Its route and the length of cruises vary from day to day.

From **Tangen**, the line climbs away from the water to give panoramic views to east and west before dropping down to the important railway town of **Hamar**, half way up the eastern side of the lake. Besides the Norwegian Railway Museum and a museum honouring the life of operatic soprano Kirsten Flagstad, the Hedmarksmuseet has 50 or so reconstructed local buildings on a site that incorporates the remains of the cathedral, thought to have been built by the English pope, Nicholas Breakspear, who spent two years in

Norway before becoming Pope Adrian IV in 1154.

LILLEHAMMER TO DOVRE

The town at the northern end of the lake, **Lillehammer**, became famous when it hosted the 1994 Winter Olympics, and to a lesser extent as the setting of the TV series of the same name (2012–2014). It is a popular resort in summer, too, for cycling, walking, canoeing and fishing. Its main cultural attraction is one of the largest open-air folk museums in northern Europe, the Maihaugen, which has nearly 200 buildings brought in from all over the region. The two stocked farms are complemented by displays of rural crafts, and the chance to try your hand at some of them.

The railway follows the much narrower Gudbrandsdal, lined with the usual conifer and birch and punctuated by traditional red-painted farms and side valleys. Leaving **Vinstra**, another station providing access to good skiing country, the train forges along the now broad valley to the forestry centre

Wild musk-ox in Norway's Dovrefjell National Park.

Ski resort near Lillehammer.

of **Otta**. Traditional wooden houses are more in evidence as the railway climbs again, along the eastern flank of the valley through a particularly lovely stretch, with views down into an impressive gorge near the town of **Dovre**.

THE RAUMA RAILWAY

The next station – **Dombås** – is the junction for the 114-km (71-mile) **Rauma Railway** to Åndalsnes, which opened in 1924. After Bjorli, this line follows the plunging descent of the river, but despite dropping at gradients of 1 in 50 it is left perched on a shelf of rock on the mountainside. This is the Trollveggen, one of Europe's tallest cliffs. What appears to be another railway comes into view 137 metres (450ft) below, reached by a giant S-bend. The semi-circle of Stavem Tunnel reverses the train's direction so that it can cross the River Rauma by the 44.5-metre/yd masonry span of Kylling Bridge, where the rails are 59 metres (194ft) above the water. Åndalsnes, the terminus of this line, is of little interest in itself, but

sits on another fjord and is surrounded by high mountains.

Back on the main Trondheim line, the track turns east and describes a horseshoe curve to find a passage over the mountains, allowing passengers to look down on Dombås. Having climbed onto a plateau of wilder country, the line takes a straight course, allowing the train to race across a desolate landscape surrounded by mountains before reaching the lonely, attractive station at **Hjerkinn**, a popular stopping-off place for cross-country skiers. The next station, **Kongsvoll**, is an access point for the walks and climbs of the Dovrefjell National Park, which is served by a timber-built inn of 18th-century origin within 10 minutes' walk of the station.

At the end of this bleak stretch, with the 2,286-metre (7,500-ft) summit of Snøhetta, the tallest mountain in the area, to the west, the line descends through a narrow, steep-sided gorge, lined in winter with frozen waterfalls. Past **Oppdal** and its famous slate quarries, forests enfold the line, and one has to be alert to catch a glimpse of the chasm before **Ulsberg** as the train crosses a viaduct over the River Orkla.

TRONDHEIM AND THE NORDLANDSBANEN

Trondheim is Norway's third city and former capital, but it has the feel of a small, provincial market town and is easily navigated on foot. The station lies on the northern edge of a triangular peninsula on which much of the old part of the city was built, bordered on its southern side by the River Nidelva. You will find the cluster of principal attractions at the southern point of the peninsula: the cathedral (Nidaros Domkirke), the 12th-century remnant of the Archbishop's Palace and the Trondheim Art Museum.

The railway on to Bodø was built as the North Norway Railway

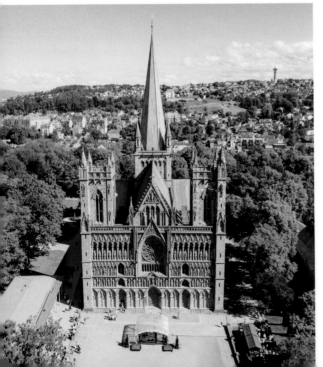
Trondheim cathedral.

Norlandsbanen) and was not finally opened until as recently as 1962, although it was originally intended to go as far as Narvik (which can be reached on the railway from Kiruna in northern Sweden). A major effort was made by the occupying Germans to finish the line during World War II, to convey iron ore from the mines around Narvik. Over 36,000 Yugoslav, Serb, Soviet, Polish and Norwegian prisoners of war were used as labour, often working in appalling conditions.

The line skirts the Trodheimsfjord for some miles from Trondheim, only the rocky foreshore, decaying boats and copses of hardy birch separating the railway from the water's edge. The line climbs along a shelf in the rock, affording more expansive views over the fjord before dropping down to the junction of **Hell**, the name of which has made it one of the most photographed stations in Scandinavia, served by local trains from Trondheim to Storlien in Sweden.

From the chalet-style station at Stjørdal, the railway veers away from the coast through farming country, offering only distant views of the sea until Verdal is reached, where it skirts a shipyard before entering the station. Another stretch of line right beside the water takes the train to Røra, passing small wooden cabins nestling among trees near the shoreline. Steinkjer marks the end of the fjord, but a large lake to the north of the line appears soon after the closed station of Sunnan. Trees gradually cover more and more of the rolling hills through which the railway weaves its course, interrupted by occasional clearings with tidy farms and a few fields.

FOREST RAILWAY

After the end of the lake at **Snåsa**, the line is in forest for much of the way to **Grong**, where several buses meet the train. Two long viaducts take the track into the pretty valley of the River Namsen, which it follows for many miles through deep rock cuttings and short tunnels and across many bridges. The population density is so low that

Hell station.

The Rauma Railway passing Troll Wall.

one wonders how many people are served by stops at some of the more remote stations, like **Lassemoen** and **Namsskogan**. Some stand alone in clearings in the trees, reached by a straight, empty road cut through the forest, in winter resembling a scene from *Dr Zhivago*.

North from **Majavatn**, the station buildings become noticeably more utilitarian and austere. If possible, move to the right-hand side of the coach for the next 20 minutes or so, to appreciate the gorges through which the river flows along Svenningdal. At **Mosjøen**, the line returns briefly to the sea, negotiating headlands by cuttings or tunnels, before a stretch of rolling farmland and a long, delightful section beside the water, with some picture-postcard views.

INTO THE ARCTIC

The River Rana keeps company with the railway through steep-sided Dunderlandsdal. Mid-way between the remote station of **Bolna** and the closed station at Semska, amid a series of snow sheds is the point at which the line crosses the Arctic Circle, marked by a pair of cairns. Visibility in winter can be almost nil, with snow whipped up by the train and the wind creating a white-out. The slopes are barren but for stunted trees and some coarse grass. From **Lønsdal** the train descends steeply through majestic, open country to follow the River Saltelv north to the Saltfjord at **Rognan**. The track now follows the arm of the fjord, though not always within sight of it, all the way to Bodø, pausing at **Fauske**, the last station before journey's end, from where buses run to Narvik for the railway line to Sweden.

It was at a farm near **Bodø** that Louis Philippe (later king of France) was given shelter in 1795 while escaping the Revolution. He was certainly well out of the way: Bodø is so far north it has almost six weeks of midnight sun, from 30 May to 12 July, and a corresponding number of days of mid-winter darkness. At latitude 67° 16', it lies further north than

The Bodø–Trondheim train (Nordlandsbanen), passing the Saltfjellet between Lønsdal and Bolna.

most of Canada, Alaska and Siberia. Much of the 19th-century town was obliterated by German bombing in May 1940, when it was used as a base by British forces.

SWEDEN'S INLANDSBANAN

The Inland Railway (Inlandsbanan) – the 'trans-Siberian' railway of Sweden – runs from Gällivare, a junction on the main electrified line from Kiruna, to Östersund and Kristinehamn, with connections on to Stockholm. The journey offers an unrivalled experience through some of the most remote and beautiful parts of Sweden. It is possible to make stopovers along the route and stay for a night or two in local towns and villages to do some walking in the mountains, or just to enjoy the magnificent wilderness landscapes. Various packages are available combining rail travel with hotel accommodation or trekking.

THE HISTORY OF THE LINE

Plans to lay a line that would open up the endless backwoods of northern Sweden were formulated in the late 1890s, but because of the enormous distances involved, the inaccessibility of the terrain and the difficulty in raising finance, construction did not begin until 1907. One gang started at Östersund, pushing northwards in stages, while another contract undertook the work south from Gällivare – the impetus provided by the need to transport materials to a large hydro-electric power station being constructed near Porjus.

Progress was very slow: the final link between Jokkmokk and Sorsele was not completed until 1937. Meanwhile, south of Östersund, around Sveg, privately-constructed lines were acquired. Link lines were built from the inland track to the main, electrified, parallel route to the east, thus enabling timber to be moved out of the region more quickly.

In such a sparsely populated area, passenger services were maintained by railcars linking the local towns. Through journeys over the whole line took several days, due to lack of connections and infrequency of service. With the improvement of the local roads and the provision of alternative car and bus transport, passenger services were progressively withdrawn from the mid-1960s and the line seemed doomed, apart from sections maintained for the remaining freight traffic.

However, with the privatisation of much of the Swedish State Railways, a separate company was formed in 1993 to exploit the line's tourist potential and for the last few years it has again been possible to travel over the whole length of the line during the short summer holiday period – early June to the end of August – a great way to experience what is termed 'Europe's last wilderness'. Snacks and drinks are served on board, but more substantial meals can be collected from stations along the way,

Inlandsbanan in the Swedish countryside.

European Rail Timetable no. 766

Distance: 1363km (847 miles)

Duration of journey: 13hrs 40 mins (Gällivare–Östersund); 11 hrs 56 mins (Östersund–Kristinehamn)

Frequency of trains: 1 per day (Gällivare–Östersund; summer only)

Inlandsbanan passengers stop to take in the Arctic Circle.

with advance orders taken on the train – an excellent way of sampling local specialities.

GÄLLIVARE TO ARVIDSJAUR

The modern town of **Gällivare**, with its fine wooden station building, is the starting point for the journey. A brightly painted, modern diesel railcar is provided for the service and you are welcomed aboard by your hosts, who give a commentary on local places of interest and look after passengers' needs and answer their enquiries. Many of the passengers are members of groups who are only travelling on a section of the line, as part of a coach excursion by road. The independent traveller is very much the exception, but everyone is made to feel welcome.

On leaving Gällivare, the line runs beside the main line to Kiruna and Narvik before turning southwards and heading off into what will become familiar views for almost the whole of the journey – mile upon mile of forest punctuated by lakes and rivers and the occasional isolated farm. The

economical way in which the line was constructed is immediately apparent, with the original, lightly laid track still in use. Heavy engineering works, apart from the bridges across the many rivers, were avoided and the line generally follows the contours, with gradients undulating, although there are also a few short, steep sections.

After about 90 minutes, the train slows for the first refreshment break of the day at **Vajkijaur**, where a small restaurant is conveniently located adjacent to the road and railway.

The next station is **Jokkmokk**, where the train pauses briefly. At the north end of the station is a granite pillar that commemorates the official opening of the completed Inlandsbanan by the then Crown Prince of Sweden, Gustaf Adolf, on 6 August 1937. Twenty minutes later the train host announces that you are about to cross the **Arctic Circle**; the train stops to let passengers descend to the small platform at Polcirkeln (Polar Circle) to photograph the signs and the line of white stones that marks the location.

By mid-morning the train has reached the closed station of **Varjisträsk**. The building is now used by local hunters and the old waiting room houses some hunting trophies, including a stuffed eagle with outstretched wings. Near Iggejaur, your host announces the approach of one of the major engineering features of the line – a combined road and rail bridge over the River Pite. Passengers are invited to walk across the bridge and rejoin the train on the other side, and most people take advantage of this to stretch their legs and view the rushing waters of the wide river below.

A 30-minute refreshment break at **Moskosel** enables passengers to visit the railway museum that has been set up in the station building, dedicated to the workers who built the line. One of the exhibits is a pedal-driven inspection trolley. Here passengers can pick up food orders before carrying on through to the next station, Arvidsjaur, the first town of any size since leaving Gällivare, 274km (171 miles) to the north. Arvidsjaur is one of the main tourist centres of Lapland and has a beautiful wooden church dating from 1902. It is worth spending a day or two here, as on Friday and Saturday in July and early August one of Sweden's many preserved steam locomotives comes to life to operate evening tours (departing at 5.45pm) to Slagnäs, 53km (33 miles) away. The set of original 1930s coaches includes a small restaurant section serving local specialities. It is a very leisurely trip and the train stops on the way for passengers to take photographs and enjoy the cool evening air. No advance booking is necessary.

The Inlandsbanan stops in Lapland, Dorotea.

SOUTH FROM ARVIDSJAUR

After a lunch of a dish such as reindeer meat eaten on the station platform, the half-hour stop is soon over and a blast on the train's horn quickly gets everyone back on board. Southbound trains reverse here, and head west for over 80km (50 miles), passing the southern end of the vast Lake Storavan. The line takes on a different character here, for not only has the

Arvidsjaur church on a winter evening.

track been relaid, but it is on proper ballast enabling a faster speed and a less bumpy ride.

Sorsele marks the halfway point on the northern section of the Inlandsbanan to Östersund, and also the point where the daily northbound service passes the southbound train. The stationmaster completes his main job of the day in 15 minutes, supervising the arrival and despatch of his two passenger trains. Sadly, there is only 20 minutes to do justice to the excellent railway museum in the old station building.

After Sorsele, the track turns south once again and the scenery becomes more desolate and strewn with large rocks. It is here that herds of reindeer are most likely to be seen and, indeed, the driver has to keep a sharp lookout for them as they are very slow to move out of the way, despite constant sounding of the train's horn. **Storuman** is another tourist centre as well as a railway junction for the freight line to Hällnäs. It is also a centre for the timber industry and train-loads of

logs are despatched from here. It is worth spending a day in the area as there is much to see, including the old Railway Hotel, now the town's library, famous for its beautiful paintings and wrought-iron chandeliers. Sweden's largest wooden church is at the nearby village of **Stensele**; built in 1886, it contains a copy of the world's smallest bible, a quarter of the size of a postage stamp.

Soon after leaving Storuman, the line crosses the River Ume on a long girder bridge and begins a steady climb through desolate rocky country to a summit of 450 metres (1,476ft) near the closed station of Fiandberg, before gradually descending into **Vilhelmina Norra** where there is a 40-minute stop for refreshments.

The area south of here is mainly heathland with scattered clumps of trees and has become a popular area for campers, with stops being made at special halts near the small towns of Dorotea and Hoting to set down passengers who had travelled north on the morning train.

Driving the Inlandsbanan.

To the south of Hoting the line crosses various river tributaries on three impressive bridges, one of which is made of reinforced concrete – the first of its type in Sweden when it was built. There are views of a series of lakes before the train pulls into the station at **Ulriksfors**. This station serves the thriving tourist town of Strömsund, 4km (2.5 miles) to the northwest. The line then climbs steadily through more thickly forested hills to reach a summit close to the station of Munkflohögen, before descending to the Indalsalven Valley where signs of market gardening and several prosperous farms indicate we have left the wilderness behind and are approaching Östersund.

The train now runs parallel to the electrified line from Stockholm to Storlien, on the Norwegian frontier, for the final stretch before terminating at Östersund Central station. Östersund is the largest town in the central Jämtland region, located on the shores of the huge Storsjön lake, Sweden's fifth-largest and the reputed home of the Scandinavian version of the Loch Ness monster.

THE RAILCAR TO MORA

The southern section of the Inlandsbanan is operated separately on an ´out and back' basis from **Mora**, 321km (200 miles) to the south, where the locomotive and coaches now used for the summer tourist service are based. The daily departure is in mid-afternoon and the train leaves the imposing and well-maintained station and follows the main electrified line to Stockholm for 15km (9 miles) as far as Brunflo. Here the Inlandsbanan proper diverges and the line heads south, past the ends of two long narrow lakes before reaching **Hackås**. The village is on the southern shore of Lake Storsjön and is famous for its medieval church with wall paintings from the Middle Ages. For the next stretch there are magnificent views across the water to the mountains before the train arrives at **Åsarna**, and a 15-minute stop.

The scenery changes to open moorland interspersed with pine forests against a backdrop of desolate hills. Negotiating this lonely district the line has some quite steep switchback gradients. The line now takes a westerly course and descends to the fertile valley of the River Ljusnan, passing **Älvros** where the landscape opens up and small farms are again in evidence on the approach to **Sveg**, the former junction for the long-closed line to Hede. After a short stop, the line turns south again and climbs to Gratback, at 524 metres (1,700ft) the highest point on the line. The forests in this area are the home of the brown bear and in a clearing in the forest, the train stops for about thirty minutes whilst the guide escorts passengers to visit one

> **⊙ Tip**
> An excellent way to enjoy Storsjön lake is to take a trip on the oldest steam boat still in service in Sweden, the SS Thomée. Built in 1875, it is now powered by a diesel engine and operates daily excursions from Östersund's small harbour.

High-speed electric train on the St Petersburg–Helsinki line.

Helsinki Central station (HEC).

of the well-established dens of these elusive animals.

Just before arriving at **Orsa** the train stops on the impressive arched steel bridge above the Helvetes waterfall to enable passengers to take pictures of this scenic location. Soon the train arrives at **Mora**, the terminus for InterCity passenger trains from Stockholm, some 4 hours away. Mora is famous for its handicrafts, in particular the gaily-painted red wooden Dala horses.

The line south to Kristinehamn was reopened following closure in the mid-1960s and is operated by Tågab. It makes a delightful final stage, taking 3 hours 44 minutes to travel 296km (184 miles). The line heads through Borlänge, Ludvika, the former iron ore mining town of Grängesberg and Nykroppa before reaching Kristinehamn. The final destination boasts the largest Picasso sculpture (15m/49ft tall) in Europe and stands by the shore of the huge Lake Vänern, with plenty of boat trips, swimming, birdwatching and wild camping.

HELSINKI–ST PETERSBURG

The best travelling experiences give an acute sense of departure and arrival; and the train journey from Helsinki to St Petersburg does exactly that. From leaving the civic-minded, organised capital of Finland it takes just under three and a half hours to reach Finlyandsky *vokzal* (Finland Station) and the anarchic streets of St Petersburg's grand but dilapidated candy-coloured world.

Not that Helsinki isn't an impressive city: take your departure point, the **central station** (Rautatieasema), positioned, as all good stations should be, in the centre of the city. Designed by Eliel Saarinen in 1905 (although not completed until 1919), this superb building combines Helsinki's defining National Romantic (art nouveau) architectural style. Travellers can't fail to glance upwards at the granite building's green clock tower, or miss Emil Wikström's brace of impressive, square-jawed statues holding translucent lanterns on either side of the main doors. The interior of the station is also

a treat. Clean and well signposted, it is easy to find the ticketing hall, change some money into roubles (Helsinki is one of the few places outside Russia where you can do this) and relax in the Eliel restaurant, its stunning murals overlooked by a large painting by Eero Järnefelt.

The high-speed Allegro service, introduced in 2010 and using tilting Pendolino trains, cut the journey time by over two hours to roughly three hours; although what has gone is the character of the old Russian carriages of the old Repin service. The route retraces the 1917 journey made by Lenin, who was greeted at Finland station in St Petersburg (later re-named Leningrad) by a crowd of workers and soldiers who lifted him onto the roof of an armoured car, where he ended his first revolutionary speech in Russia with the words, 'Long live the socialist revolution!'. Six months later the battleship Aurora fired the empty shell that heralded the start of the Russian Revolution. Lenin's journey is commemorated by a statue outside the Finland station.

FIELDS AND FORESTS

The train heads northwest out of Helsinki, stopping at the suburban stations of Pasila and Tikkurila before joining the direct line to Lahti which opened in 2006. Slowly, but surely, the view from the window switches from suburbs to fields, then to the forests of pine, spruce and birch that are the backbone of Finland's paper products industry, the second largest in the world. Some quick ways to identify the different tree species whizzing past your window: pines are the tallest, and tend to have little undergrowth around them; the sun-loving birch has bright, white bark; while spruces can be recognised by their droopy branches and dense, dark-green growth.

The train continues to the winter sports centre of **Lahti**. Although you can't see Lahti's dauntingly huge Salpausselkä ski jump from the train, passengers can get a glimpse of part

Essentials

European Rail Timetable no. 1910

Distance: 416km (258 miles)

Duration of journey: 3hrs 27 mins

Frequency of trains: 5 per day

En route to Lahti.

of the deep-blue lake of Päijänne before the line heads east towards the capital of Kymi province, **Kouvola**, a busy junction where freight trains and cargo trucks jostle for position on the tracks next to the station. From Kouvola it is about three-quarters of an hour to **Vainikkala** and the Russian border. On a sunny day the lakeland countryside is breathtaking, the views providing a welcome break from the continuous forests of pine and spruce.

A SMOOTHER BORDER CROSSING

The Russian railways were built during the reign of Tsar Nicholas I and, as Finland uses the same wide-gauge tracks (a legacy of the days when it was ruled from St Petersburg), travel between the two countries is possible without the time-consuming bogie changing necessary when arriving from countries further south, such as Poland. Remember to adjust your watch in winter, as Russia is an hour ahead of Finland, though in winter both countries are three hours ahead of Greenwich Mean Time. The train picks up speed as it continues toward St Petersburg.

INTO ST PETERSBURG

St Petersburg's Finland Station is an unremarkable building lined with dusty huts selling magazines and food. Go through the station's main doors and you will find a few white taxis waiting to pick up passengers – the station is located north of the River Neva and some way from the main tourist sights and hotels. Taxis are unmetered, and heavy bargaining is essential. Before you start your white-knuckle ride (taxis rule the road in St Petersburg) or take the Metro from Ploshchad Lenina into town, have a look at the huge statue of Lenin in front of the station. Unveiled in 1926, it celebrates his triumphant return from Finland, and is one of the few remaining statues of Vladimir Ilyich Ulyanov left in St Petersburg – neatly setting the tone for your journey into one of Europe's most compelling cities.

Statue of Lenin at Finland Station, St Petersburg.

The numbers here relate to the map on page 280.

MUSEUMS

Danish Railway Museum ❶
Dannebrogsgade 24, DK-5000
Odense
Café, shop
Open: daily 10am–4pm
Features: fascinating displays
Nearest station: Odense
Tel: 66 13 66 30
www.jernbanemuseum.dk

Finnish Railway Museum ❷
Hyvinkäänkatu 9, SF 05800
Hyvinkää
Café, shop
Open: Sept–May Tue–Sat noon–3pm, Sun
noon–5pm; June–Aug daily 10am–5pm
Features: national collection of rail
transport, housed in former station
Nearest station: Hyvinkää
Tel: 040 862 5241
www.rautatiemuseo.fi

Norwegian Railway Museum ❸
Strandveien 161, 2316 Hamar
Restaurant, shop
Open: June–mid-Aug daily
10.30am–5pm; rest of year
11am–3pm, Sun until 4pm
Features: museum dating from
1896, narrow-gauge railway
Nearest station: Hamar
Tel: 40 44 88 80
www.jernbanemuseet.no

Swedish Railway Museum ❹
Rälsgatan 1, 80108 Gävle
Café, bookshop
Open: June–Aug daily 10am–5pm;
Sept–May Tue–Sun 10am–4pm
Features: locos and carriages (closed
for renovations until 2020)
Nearest station: Gävle Central
Tel: 026 455 1450
www.jarnvagsmuseet.se

HERITAGE LINES

Gamle Vossebanen ❺ (Norway)
(Garnes–Midttun)
N 5807 Bergen
Features: steam, museum
Nearest station: Arna
Length: 18km (11 miles)
Gauge: 1,435mm (4ft 8½in)
Tel: 5591 7780
www.njk.no

Krøderbanen ❻ (Norway)
(Vikersund–Krøderen)
3535 Krøderen
Café, shop, historic station, museum
Open: steam late June–Aug Sun
Features: Norway's longest
museum line, historic station
Nearest station: Vikersund (local
trains from Oslo)
Length: 26km (16 miles)
Gauge: 1,435mm (4ft 8½ in)
Tel: 32 14 76 03
www.kroderbanen.museum.no

Rjukanbanen ❼ (Norway)
(Rjukan–Mæl)
Features: historic electrified
lakeside railway built for
transporting chemicals; trips on
rail ferry lake steamer
Nearest station: Notodden
Length: 16km (10 miles)
Gauge: 1,435mm (4ft 8½in)
Tel: 35 09 90 00
www.nia.no/rjukanbanen

Setesdalsbanen ❽ (Norway)
(Grovane–Røyknes)
Grovane, N 4700 Vennesla
Open: mid-June–end Aug Sun; also
Tue–Fri in July
Features: only remaining 1067mm
(3ft 6 inch)-gauge line
Length: 12km (7.5 miles)
Gauge: 1067mm (3ft 6in)
Nearest station: Vennesla
Tel: 38 15 64 82
www.setesdalsbanen.no

Urskog-Hølandsbanen ❾ (Norway)
(Sørumsand–Fossum)
Features: reconstructed station
buildings and workshop along
railway opened 1896
Open: Sun late June–end Aug, Wed
in July
Nearest station: Sørumsand
Length: 4km (2.5 miles)
Gauge: 750mm (2ft 5½in)
Tel: 99 12 82 88
www.u-hb.no

Östra Södermanlands Järnväg ❿ (Sweden)
(Läggesta Nedra–Mariefred/Taxinge
Näsby)
PO Box 53, 64722 Mariefried
Café, shop
Open: certain days, May–Sept
Features: connects with 1903
steamship to Stockholm
Nearest station: Läggesta
Length: 3.2/7km (2/4.4 miles)
Gauge: 600mm (1ft 11⅝ in)
Tel: 0159 21000
www.oslj.nu

Skara-Lundsbrunns Järnvägar ⓫ (Sweden)
PO Box 191, S-5323 Skara
Open: late June–Aug Sun, Tue and
Thu afternoons
Features: roundhouse at Skara
Length: 11.2km (7 miles)
Gauge: 891mm (2ft 11 in)
Tel: 0511 13636
www.sklj.se

Jokoinen Museum Railway ⓬ (Finland)
(Jokioinen–Minkiö–Humppila)
Kiipuntie 49, FI 31360 Minkiö
Open: June–Aug Sun
Features: narrow-gauge museum
at Minkiö
Nearest station: Humppila
Length: 14km (9 miles)
Gauge: 750mm (2ft 5½in)
Tel: 03 433 3235
www.jokioistenmuseorautatie.fi

The Children's Railway in Budapest.

Steam locomotive, Prague.

OTHER EUROPEAN ROUTES

With a dense network of lines snaking through unspoiled countryside to the remotest corners of little-known lands, rail travel in the East of Europe can be a rewarding adventure

Railway journeys in Eastern Europe are not always as straightforward as those in the West but things are changing fast. On the plus side for the railway enthusiast – with plenty of time – most of the countries of the former Soviet bloc (particularly the Czech Republic, Hungary, Romania and Bulgaria) have a few narrow-gauge branch lines winding their way into remote rural backwaters. For convenience, Greece has been included in this section of the book, which also reaches as far as the European part of Turkey, including the city of Istanbul.

Much of the Eastern European railway network developed later than in the West; lines connecting Vienna and Budapest with their domains in the Austro-Hungarian Empire arrived in the 1870s, spreading gradually east and south towards Istanbul. The first Orient Express to complete the journey from Paris entirely by rail did so in 1889. Railway construction was hindered by the mountainous topography of much of south-eastern Europe, as well as the chronic political instability caused by the decline of the Ottoman Empire. In Russia, however, the Moscow to St Petersburg line was completed by 1851.

A COMMITMENT TO RAILWAYS

Eastern Europe's railways took a battering in World War II, after which the Communists set about a large-scale rebuilding operation with gusto; the Soviet authorities always gave railways a high priority, as a symbol of development and progress alongside industrialisation and electrification. Many of the branch lines across a broad swathe of the Hungarian *puszta* date from this period. Previously, many Hungarian towns on the grasslands were isolated and the peasants lived off the land. This was anathema to the Soviet idea of modernisation; throughout the 1950s and 1960s new

Main attractions

Venice: Doge's Palace, St Mark's Square
Berlin: Reichstag, Brandenburg Gate,
Prague: Castle, Charles Bridge, Old Town Square,
Budapest: Vár (Castle), Parliament building,
Istanbul: Blue Mosque, Hagia Sophia
Athens: Acropolis, Temple of Olympian Zeus.

Maps on pages 302, 304, 307, 313

Slovenian railway engineer, near Bohinj.

North Central Europe

0 — 100 km
0 — 100 miles

N

BALTIC SEA

industrial plants were built in rural areas, linked by the extensive rail system that remains today.

The density of the region's railway network is in part due to the fact that Western Europe's long-standing tradition of closing down uneconomic branch lines never caught on. The Soviets were committed to railways, and this mentality has endured, as has a certain pride in the railway system. The fact that car ownership remains lower than in Western Europe, and the motorway network is non-existent in many areas, has also discouraged any cost-cutting measures. EU membership for the Baltic States, Poland, the Czech Republic, Slovakia, Hungary, Romania, Bulgaria and Slovenia, and increasing prosperity generally in Eastern Europe, mean that the old ways are being rapidly replaced with the trappings of modernity.

VENICE–ZAGREB

This is a journey that takes travellers from one of Europe's most slickly packaged tourist cities right into the heart of a region that has recovered from the turmoil of the early 1990s to re-emerge, albeit slowly, as one of Europe's most attractive and unspoiled destinations. It follows a route that takes in swathes of spectacular scenery as it skirts the fringes of the Adriatic Sea, climbs to the southeastern edge of the Alps and furrows its way through rugged mountain gorges.

Like all great journeys it begins in a flush of romance, on the very edge of the **Grand Canal**, crowded with gondolas, tourist-clogged *vaporettos*, water taxis and the sirens of whizzing police boats. Above the aquatic mayhem lie the façades of the grand palaces and the sweeping spires of Canaletto's Venice. In the midst of it all is the functionalism of Venice Santa Lucia railway station where the journey into the Balkans begins.

VENICE TO MONFALCONE

Pulling away from La Serenissima the train eases over the causeway that links the slowly sinking city with the urban sprawl of **Mestre**. The waters stretch away on either side of the track, which appears to be floating over the Venetian Lagoon. Mestre is the adjunct of Venice, where the 'real' people live, an unlovely town, but a major railway junction with lines continuing west on to Padua, Verona and Milan. To the north the track is divided between the line to Treviso and on to the Dolomites, and the second fork that runs eastwards into the Balkans.

One daytime train, the 'Casanova', operates along the 4-hour route to Ljubljana. A connection allows a late evening arrival in Zagreb, the capital of Croatia, but a stay in the Slovenian capital is more pleasant.

Trains between Venice and Budapest continued to run even through the dark days when Slovenia and, to a much greater extent, Croatia were in the grip of a war of independence with the former Yugoslavia. Even when

Essentials

European Rail Timetable no. 89

Distance: 444km (276 miles)

Duration of journey: 7hrs 50 mins

Frequency of trains: 1 per day, change in Ljubljana

1 overnight direct train

Gondola trip in Venice.

civilians were killed by Serb missiles in Zagreb, and Yugoslav war planes were bombing the late President Tudjman's palace, the Venezia Express continued to ferry in passengers, although they were often UN staff and military personnel, rather than the civilians and the occasional tourists who come today.

Striking north from Mestre the line runs along the flat plains that are bordered by the waters of the Adriatic on one flank and the looming peaks of the Dolomites on the other. Even in summer, the sweeping views of Italy's Alpine spine that open up before you on a clear day show that it is still tipped with a sprinkling of snow. The line studiously avoids tackling both the coast and the mountains and the only natural obstacles are the Livenza, Piave and Tagliamento rivers, which are all easily straddled.

Monfalcone is the large port that heralds the line's arrival on the shores of the Adriatic Sea. As the train rolls into town, the uglier face of the Adriatic appears. The cranes and clatter of the port precede the billowing sails and idyllic coves that accompany the short run from here to Trieste. After decades of decay this much ignored corner of Italy is starting to re-emerge; trade with the new Balkan states is a key part of the growth. Thankfully, the train soon leaves behind both Monfalcone and the bustle of the port.

A QUIET RIVIERA

The line now hugs tighter to the Adriatic on the approach to **Trieste**. The wide Gulf of Trieste comes into view and remains there all the way into the city. This is the little visited northernmost corner of the Mediterranean, but despite its relative obscurity, it is every bit as spectacular as the French Riviera, albeit without the glamour and the bustling crowds. Cliffs and wooded slopes hug the northern side of the track, while the waters to the south are full of marinas and yachts, with the shadows of larger freighters in the distance out in the gulf.

The direct train is now routed via Villa Opicina and longer stops in Trieste but the city can be reached by local connections from Venice. You might consider spending a day or two in Trieste, which is both an intriguing modern port town and a delightful backwater. With its unique collage of Austrian, Slavic and – very loosely – Italian influences, the ambience is of a raffish 'Vienna on Sea' with grand façades and boulevards that date back to Trieste's proud days as the main port of the Austrian Habsburg Empire. It was the headquarters of the Italian high command in World War I, and after a turbulent World War II it did not come under Italian administration until 1954.

Trieste's generous waterfront is centred on the 19th-century Piazza

dell'Unità d'Italia (Italy's largest sea-facing piazza), surrounded by a series of handsome buildings. The city is also home to what the locals claim is Italy's finest coffee; you can enjoy testing this claim in the *belle époque* cafés that grace the city-centre streets.

INTO SLOVENIA

Once back on the main line east the train quickly crosses the narrow coastal strip of Italian territory to reach the **Villa Opicina** border station, before the **Sezana** stop signals entry into the Republic of Slovenia, one of Europe's smallest nation states. Slovenia only came into being in 1991, after a relatively painless divorce from Yugoslavia. The two borders on this line are a world away from the clichéd images of gruff Eastern European border guards roughing up unsuspecting travellers and charging dubious spot-fines. Both Slovenia and Croatia – with the former now a member of the European Union, and the latter hoping to join – are keen to stress their modern European credentials and here it shows in polite, efficient passport and customs checks.

The charms of Slovenia are soon apparent as the track starts to climb through the wooded slopes of the Julian Alps. As the scenery becomes more and more rugged, tiny mountain villages and church spires pepper the landscape in scenes reminiscent of Switzerland or Austria. National divisions so often blur in this part of Europe, as is the case here, with the Alpine ranges of Austria, Italy and Slovenia all merging into a continuous whole.

After the effort of negotiating the Julian Alps, the train descends to **Ljubljana**, Slovenia's compact and enjoyable capital. The history of this city of 300,000 inhabitants is apparent in the collage of Italian and Austro-Habsburg architectural styles set out on the banks of the sleepy Ljubljanica River. Italian café culture fills the cobbled streets by the water during the warmer months, while the warmth of beer cellars dominates in winter as the icy temperatures take hold. An eminently

Arriving in Trieste.

walkable city, Ljubljana is easy to explore and its tourist board is happy to point visitors towards the museums, the leafy parks, and the castle that hangs omnipresent over the city.

Ljubljana is also a good base for exploring the rest of the country. To the north is some tremendous Alpine scenery, particularly around Lake Bled, with its picture-perfect church standing serene on an island in the middle of the lake, and Lake Bohinj, a less touristy mountain resort. There is plenty of opportunity for hiking, climbing or just lazing around admiring the mountain views.

From Ljubljana, the railway follows the roaring waters of the Sava, an important waterway that connects the Slovenian capital with its erstwhile compatriots, Zagreb and Belgrade. This is the most spectacular part of the journey as the carriages swing around the tight curves, skip through numerous tunnels, and rumble through the deep rock cuttings necessary to steer the track through this difficult terrain. For much of the journey towards

En route to Dresden, alongside the Elbe.

Zagreb the express hugs the fast-flowing river, with towering mountains on each side. Occasionally a waterside village looms into view before the train swings away into another tunnel or cutting, to emerge in view of another hamlet with a ramble of houses clustered around a picturesque old church.

DOBOVA TO ZAGREB

The border is reached at **Dobova**, where the voltage is switched to the Croatian standard. Border formalities are relatively straightforward these days. For all its ambition to be regarded as a progressive part of modern Europe, much of Croatia is still heavily reliant on small-scale agricultural production, and in the short stretch from the border to Zagreb you will see horse-drawn carts driven by cloth-capped old men, while head-scarfed labourers work the fields; this corner of Europe is still a world away from the modern, mechanised farming further west.

The approach into **Zagreb** passes the usual sprawl of uninspiring apartment blocks and decaying industrial

buildings. Yet this city of almost one million inhabitants has come a long way since being bombarded by Serb rockets in 1991, and has wholeheartedly embraced capitalism. The city has a scenic location, with an old town reminiscent of Prague or Riga and an elegant central business district. On a warm evening when the cafés are full to bursting point with style-conscious young Croatians, it is an invigorating place to be. This is a symbolic end to a journey that takes today's rail travellers across the tracks of the new map of Europe.

BERLIN–BUDAPEST

This journey from the North European Plain to the heart of central Europe includes some stunning river scenery, notably along the Elbe and the Danube, and beautiful rolling landscapes. The Hungaria train is operated by the Hungarian State Railway (MAV). It has comfortable carriages, and the restaurant car is the real thing – proper sit-down service with a waiter, a menu and a wine list. The line passes through four countries, taking in the superb cities of Dresden and Prague en route to one of Europe's most enjoyable destinations.

BERLIN TO THE CZECH BORDER

Having arrived from Hamburg, our train leaves the lower level of the shiny new Hauptbahnhof – a central station built on land freed by the clearing of the Berlin wall, and conveniently close to the Reichstag and Brandenburg Gate. From here the tracks head south across the pancake-flat plain, where there are large tracts of forest and fields stretching into the distance. Settlements are few and far between; this is the middle of the old East Germany, and the few towns and villages are perceptibly poorer than those further west.

About 1 hour and 30 minutes out of Berlin the land begins to rise, and soon changes character completely. Vines appear on south-facing hillsides, cows and horses graze lush pastures. Soon the train is nearing **Dresden**, 'the Florence of the Elbe', with excellent views over the city, none more so than when crossing the river. South of Dresden the track follows the river's course (try to get a seat on the train's left side). This is a beautiful stretch, the river running between craggy, forested hills, with an occasional picturesque town strung along the riverside; Schöna is particularly striking, with a long line of market stalls leading to two tall rock pillars positioned either side of a tributary. Königstein Fortress can be seen on the right, perched 360 metres (1,160ft) above the river. The border station of Bad Schandau is a centre for hiking trails into Sächsische Schweiz National Park – the area is known as the 'Switzerland of Saxony'.

BOHEMIA AND MORAVIA

As the train continues southwards into the Czech Republic, the Elbe (known as the Labe on this side of the border) becomes less visible,

⊙ Essentials

European Rail Timetable no. 60

Distance: 996km (619 miles)

Duration of journey: 11hrs

Frequency of trains: 1 per day (direct)

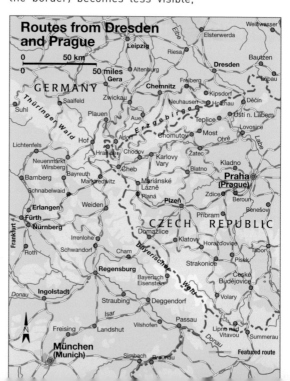

Routes from Dresden and Prague

although the scenery is no less ravishing, with broad, grassy slopes leading up to extensive stands of forest. Passengers are treated to a fine view over the first town in the Czech Republic, **Děčín**, with a handsome *zámek* (castle). As the train heads into central Bohemia the landscape opens up. Just 30km (18 miles) before arrival in Prague, the train passes through the tiny village of Nelahozeves, birthplace of Dvorak, a life-long train enthusiast.

A return to river and hills heralds the approach of **Prague**, where most passengers get off; the train stops at the modern Holesovice station in the northern suburbs before cutting through tunnels to the east – views of the old city are limited. From here the route heads east into the heart of Bohemia, the flattest part of the Czech Republic, where the line passes through forests and fields of maize and sunflowers. Many towns are rendered invisible by solid fences running beside the track – which benefits residents suffering noise

On the Children's Railway, Budapest.

pollution, but is bad news for passengers interested in their surroundings. The big-sky country is interrupted by wooded hills after Chocen and again around **Brezova**, a tranquil-looking hill town. We are now in Moravia, the other, less-visited half of the Czech Republic.

In the hills north of **Brno** we pass peaceful little waterways flanked by pretty gardens. Brno itself is a large city, its historic centre surrounded by belching chimneys and, in common with all the other large towns along the way, overlooked by a gigantic TV tower. South from here to **Breclav** the train picks up speed (most of the previous five hours have been slow going). There are huge, empty fields, A-frame huts, gaggles of geese, and grassy hills in the middle distance. The land begins to assume a fertile, southern flavour – summers are warmer here than elsewhere in the country, and vines appear along the sides of the track. The lake of Chko Palava can be seen on the right, close to the Austrian border.

⊘ EXCURSIONS TO THE WEST OF PRAGUE

The rolling countryside of Western Bohemia is criss-crossed by a maze of branch lines, many of which make rewarding day trips from Prague.

The main line to Plzen and Germany emerges abruptly from the grimy Prague suburbs into delightful countryside, following the River Berounka as it winds its way up into the craggy hills of the Cesky Kras. Karlstejn Castle can be glimpsed briefly on the right, a short distance before its station. After the town of Beroun the terrain flattens out, with sweeping vistas across cornfields to distant manor houses and castles perched on rocky outcrops. West of Plzen the land becomes hilly, wooded and sparsely populated – this part of the Czech Republic was depopulated after World War II, when ethnic Germans were expelled, and remains conspicuously empty today. There are tremendous views into the river gorge on the right before, just over an hour from Plzen, the train pulls into Mariánské Lázné (Marienbad), one of the three famous spa towns of the region that have preserved their 18th- and 19th-century glory. Take the branch line north to Karlovy Vary (Carlsbad), the largest and best-known of the spas. Trains are outstandingly slow (53km/33 miles in 1hr 40 mins), but the route passes through pristine (and protected) forested hills teeming with wildlife.

SLOVAKIA AND THE DANUBE

The Slovak border is crossed north of Kúty, and the train continues south to Bratislava, with good views down to the Danube on the right. Formerly known as Pressburg, the city has, at various times in the past, been under German, Habsburg and Hungarian ownership. Despite its status as a national capital (since 1993), Bratislava is a small city and still feels provincial – the railway station certainly lacks the grandeur of its big-city counterparts.

After passing the steep slopes of the Little Carpathians on the left, the stretch from Bratislava to the Hungarian border is flat and empty. At the border the Danube is regained, and the final stretch from here to Budapest features wonderful scenery as the river, and the track, are squeezed between the Börzsöny and Pilis hills. We pass **Esztergom**, where the giant basilica's 100-metre (330ft) green dome can be seen for miles; and **Visegrad**, with its citadel perched high on a hill. Finally, just under 12 hours after leaving Berlin, the train pulls into **Budapest's Nyugati terminus**.

HUNGARY: ROUTES FROM BUDAPEST

Budapest makes an excellent base for some enjoyable railway excursions. Hungarians are proud of their railways, and within the extensive network there are several preserved lines and other routes of special interest.

THE CHILDREN'S RAILWAY

High in the hills above Budapest is the Gyermekvasút (Children's Railway), a narrow-gauge line that trundles through the woods between Széchenyi-Hegy (accessed by funicular railway from near Moskva Tér in Buda) and Hüvösvölgy. The railway was set up in the late 1940s to encourage children to develop an interest in railways, and is still run by 10- to14-year-olds, with smart uniforms and serious attitudes. Happily, the trains themselves are driven by adults, and cover the distance of 11km (7 miles) in about 40 minutes.

From mid-March until mid-October trains run on a daily basis (departures every 45 minutes); in the winter months there are fewer departures and the railway is closed on Monday. From the halt at János-Hegy a path leads to the hill of the same name, at 529 metres (1,735ft) the highest point around Budapest, with tremendous views over the city. From here you can take a chair lift back down to the city, or after seeing the museum at the Huvösvölgy terminus, catch a bus for the short ride back downhill. For information see www.gyermekvasut.hu.

THE SZALAJKA FOREST RAILWAY

From the attractive town of **Eger** (two hours northeast of Budapest by train), you can head north into the Bükk Hills, taking an hour to reach the town of Szilvásvárad, jumping-off point for the **Szalajka Forest Railway** (be sure to alight at Szilvásvárad Szalajka-v-ölgy, which precedes the main station). From here, follow the road about 600 metres/yds down the hill, past the Peter Kovacs stud farm, where the white Lippizaner horses for which the region is famous are bred; when the main road swings left, a right turn takes you to the Forest Railway. A tiny steam locomotive strains uphill into the dense beech and alder forest, passing trout pools and the *szikla-forrás* spring before arriving at the lovely, grassy glade at Fatyolvizesés. Most people walk the short distance back to Szilvasvarad. The steam train service is somewhat sporadic.

SOUTH OF BUDAPEST

A unique railway line runs through the middle of the riverine forest of **Gemenc**, a protected area on the

⊙ Essentials

European Rail timetable no. 1170 (Zvolen–Banská Bystrica) and 1188 (Banská Bystrica–Kosice); 1190 for the variant route via Jesenké.

Distance: 235km (146 miles)

Duration of journey: 4 hours 25 mins

Frequency of trains: 3 trains per day from Banská Bystrica to Kosice via Brexno; 6 per day direct via Jesenké

Passenger train in the High Tatra Mountains, Slovakia.

Danube, famous for its red deer. The starting point for the line is the small town of Pörböly, a few kilometres west of Baja. There are also boat trips through the park.

Another interesting line runs from the town of **Kecskemét** (depart from the 'KK' station) through Bugac to **Kiskunmajsa**. Trains are infrequent and slow, but this backwater journey gives an opportunity to see an unspoilt part of the *puszta*, the Great Hungarian Plain.

SLOVAKIA: ZVOLEN–KOŠICE VIA BREZNO

This quiet branch line through the hills and forests of Slovakia to the pleasant city of Košice is one of the most enjoyable rail journeys in Eastern Europe. The route can be completed in a little over four hours. Alternatively, you may choose to break your journey in places like Brezno or Dedinky and take time to explore the Low Tatras, or the Slovenský Raj.

There is another line between Zvolen and Košice, which runs on a more southerly track via Jesenské. In common with almost all the railways in Slovakia, this line has its fair share of attractive mountain scenery.

THE SLOVAK HEARTLAND

Zvolen grew rich on profits from the nearby silver mines during the middle ages, although prosperity is far less evident today. The main sight here is the impressive castle, at the base of which stands a replica of the armoured train used in the 1944 Slovak National Uprising. From Zvolen the track follows the wide Hron Valley for an uneventful half hour to **Banská Bystrica**, the administrative capital of central Slovakia and famous as the centre of the 1944 uprising. Get off at the Mesto station, which is reached a couple of minutes before the main station, to have a look around the large, sloping main square. As in the majority of Slovak towns, this roomy, open space is edged with old merchants' houses – mostly dating from the 17th or 18th century – painted in a rainbow of pastel shades.

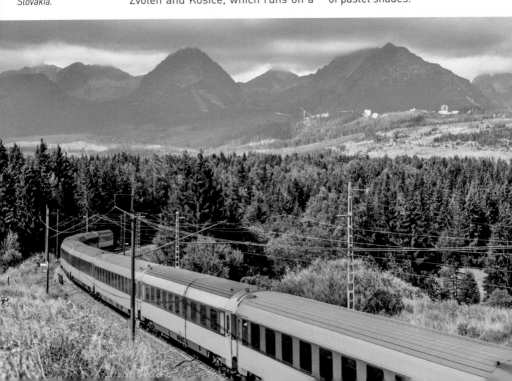

From Banská Bystrica board the Košice train to follow the Hron River as it turns to the east, flanking the long ridge of the Low Tatras to the north. These hills are far more extensive than their loftier namesakes to the north, but less well known and a good deal wilder; this is where Slovakia's remaining populations of bears and wolves can be found.

The train continues past lush meadows, one-horse towns with small wooden stations (all of which are manned) and the occasional concentration of heavy industry, usually in a state of dramatic rusting decline. Brezno is a typically attractive little Slovak town, with a typically remote station – a brisk 20 minutes' walk from the centre. The town makes a good base for hiking in the Low Tatras, with the highest peaks, Chopok (2,024 metres/6,640ft and Dumbier (2,043 metres/6,702ft), accessible from the nearby trailheads at Bystrá or, higher up the valley, the hotel at Srdiecko (where a chair lift operates to the top of Chopok).

THE HRONEC FOREST RAILWAY

The village of **Čierny Balog**, in the green hills 8km (5 miles) south of Brezno, is the terminus of the Hronec Forest Railway, Slovakia's leading preserved narrow-gauge line and the result of a momentous effort by *Strom Života* (Tree of Life), a local environmentalist group which campaigned against the scrapping of the line in the 1980s. In common with many heritage lines in this corner of Europe, this Lilliputian railway was created for forestry purposes, one of around 40 such lines in Slovakia.

There is a museum and a café at the station here. Most trains are steam-hauled and run the 10km (6 miles) up to Hronec, close to the station at Chvatimech on the Zvolen–Brezno line, from the beginning of May until mid-September.

The railway from Brezno south to Tisovec and Jesenské was built to transport iron ore and timber. The section between Pohronská Polhora and Tisovec was so steep that it required a rack section; now that it is no longer

Čierny Hron Railway, an open-air museum in Slovakia.

STEAM IN POLAND

Poland is a wonderful place for railway enthusiasts: in addition to more than a dozen narrow-gauge lines threading their way through its wide open spaces, the western Wielkopolska region is home to Europe's last-surviving regular steam-hauled service. This unlikely throwback to days of yore is based at the small town of Wolsztyn, where an open-air museum showcases steam engines that are still very much in everyday use.

Steam fanatics can indulge their passion with the ultimate experience: driving a steam locomotive, as part of the engine-driving courses that are held regularly in Wolsztyn. In nearby Poznan, meanwhile,

Train departing from Wolsztyn.

there are also opportunities to learn to drive the old city trams.

At the time of going to press there were two daily return steam-hauled departures between Poznan and Wolsztyn. There is also one daily steam train between Wolsztyn and Leszno. (See the European Timetable No. 1099 for schedules.)

The massive steam locomotive, puffing and hissing steam, looks oddly out of place in the utilitarian surroundings of Poznan's main station in the morning rush hour. Among the commuters hurrying along the platform there are usually a few steam enthusiasts gathered around the majestic engine, taking photographs.

Steam train passengers can usually expect to travel in attractive bespoke carriages, but such luxury is definitely not available on this working railway. The drab, dark-green PKP rolling stock is basic in the extreme, consisting of split-level carriages that are in need of a good clean.

A blast of steam from the engine heralds departure on this unique journey, the train heading slowly westwards through the suburbs, whistle sounding. Before long, open fields have replaced the grey blocks of flats and the train picks up speed. Not too much speed, though – it takes a sedate 75 minutes to reach Wolsztyn, 80km (50 miles) to the southwest. The line runs across the northern edge of Wielkopolska National Park, with lakes and forests of birch and pine, before emerging into an open, gently undulating landscape with a scattering of villages. The scenery is not particularly diverting.

Apart from its interest for railway fans, Wolsztyn is also popular with water sports enthusiasts, particularly canoeists, as the surrounding area contains numerous lakes that are linked either by the river or by small canals. The choice of accommodation includes an irresistible opportunity to live like a prince for a fraction of the price, in a tourist hostel, the Dom Turysty, in a neoclassical building that was once a palace. Another hostel, by the Wolsztyn engine shed, represents good-value, basic accommodation.

The line between Wolsztyn and Leszno crosses a region of lakes and woods south of Wolsztyn. From Leszno there are frequent fast trains to Poznan and south to Wroclaw.

put to heavy industrial use, the rack section is closed.

As the main line heads east from Brezno the industry peters out and after Heľpa there are good views of the mountains to the left. If you are tempted to stick your head out of the window, be careful, as the trees and bushes along the tracks are often very close to the train! The temperature starts to drop as the line climbs through pine and spruce forests on the approach to **Červená Skala**, another good base for walking in the hills.

After Telgárt the railway exercises a 360° loop to reach the highest point on the line, at 999 metres (3,277ft), after which the train enters a new kind of landscape as the Low Tatras give way to the limestone pinnacles and gullies of the Slovenský Raj. Passing the famous ice cave of Dobšiná, with its 20-metre (65ft) thick frozen lake, the train arrives at the hill resort and hiking centre of **Dedinky**, photogenically edging the waters of the artificial Palcmanská lake.

EAST TO MARGECANY AND KOŠICE

Soon the Slovenský Raj is left behind and the landscape turns drier as the train heads towards Košice, remaining hilly but with beech trees replacing the dense stands of conifers. The highest peaks here are several hundred metres lower than those further west. The Hnilec and Hornad rivers meet to create Ruzin Lake just before **Margecany**, the junction with the line to Poprad and Žilina. The lake is a popular holiday area and is surrounded by wooden A-frame *chata* (chalets). From here it is a speedy half-hour run to Košice (see following page).

SLOVAKIA: KOŠICE–ŽILINA

The scenic railway line running across northern Slovakia was completed in 1872, when the line from

the town of Bohumín, now on the Czech border with Poland, met the track running north from Košice to Prešov, which had opened a couple of years earlier. The line provides tremendous views of the High Tatras and other mountain ranges, and the frequent departures and relative speed of the trains make it particularly accessible. Most services continue on from Žilina to Bratislava, which is reached in a further 2 hours 40 minutes.

KOŠICE TO THE HIGH TATRA

The centre of Košice, Slovakia's second city, has been beautifully restored, and the exceptionally long, main square is reached from the station by a 10-minute stroll through a leafy park. Perched on the northeastern edge of the Hungarian Plain, Košice was Magyar for most of its history, and has retained its separateness from Bratislava and the Slovak heartland.

Heading north, the train passes the site of the steelworks, which, in common with much of Eastern Europe's

⊘ Essentials

European Rail Timetable no. 1180

Distance: 242km (150 miles)

Duration of journey: fast train 2 hrs 50 mins, slow train 3 hrs 15 mins

Frequency of trains: almost hourly at peak times

Southeast Europe

heavy industry, closed in the 1990s. Almost immediately the hills begin to close in, and before long the junction of Margecany is reached, where the line to Brezno and Banská Bystrica branches off to the west.

Soon after Margecany the railway enters the Spiš region – an area settled by Germans from Saxony in medieval times, after which it was granted trading privileges and became wealthy. The Spiš area is full of wide open spaces, enormous fields and grand sweeping vistas across to the mountains – the Low Tatras to the south, and the spectacular High Tatras to the north; glimpsed from afar, the jagged peaks seem to float surreally above the plain. The range may be high but it is not extensive – only about 30km (18 miles) from east to west. This compactness means that hiking paths are often crowded, in contrast to those of the Low Tatras.

SCENIC BRANCH LINES

Starý Smokovec station, Slovakia.

Before reaching Poprad, the main jumping-off point for the mountains, there are a couple of branch lines leading north through the verdant Spiš countryside to noteworthy attractions; the wonderful castle ruins at Spisske Podhradie, and the handsome town of Levoïa. Trains, however, are few and far between.

From the upper level of **Poprad's** extraordinary station, small electric railcars wind up into the hills. There are regular services to **Stary Smoko-vec**, the main resort, which is full of half-timbered lodges – notably the aptly-named Hotel Grand – as well as several 1970s monstrosities, and on to Strbske Pleso from where a steep rack railway rejoins the main line at **Strba**. The railcars are of the Swiss type (used on all Europe's highland railways), the new ones equipped with extra-large windows to allow passengers to admire the view. Unfortunately, this doesn't amount to much as all the lines run through thick forest with only fleeting glimpses down to the plain and up to the rocky heights. A funicular line runs up to Hrebienok from Stary Smokovec.

STRBA TO ŽILINA

West of Strba, Spiš is left behind as the train crosses a line of wooded hills to descend into the Liptov area. The less-visited western end of the High Tatras still looms large to the north, and the highest peaks of the Low Tatras (including Dumbier, at 2,043 metres/6,702ft) are clearly visible to the south. Just past Liptovsky Mikuláš, the large artificial lake of Liptovská Mara (Liptov Sea) comes into view, with alpine panoramas across to the mountains. The line then passes heavy industry at **Ružomberok**; many Slovak valleys are filled with such industry – often rusting away – and during cold, still, winter weather pollution levels can be extremely high. The grim surroundings of Ružomberok are relieved by its unusual station, complete with carved wooden eaves and a small tower painted in a fetching shade of blue.

Soon the River Váh widens out quite suddenly as a dam is approached. The line passes the Velka Fatra Mountains to the south;

at Kralovany a branch line runs through precipitous mountains to Trstená, close to the Polish border. The Žilina line passes right through the middle of the Mala Fatra range, a popular region for hiking. At the western edge of the mountains, just as the train is passing into the valley around Žilina, there is a great view to the left of the 14th-century castle ruins at **Strečno**. You can also get a glimpse of another ruined castle off to the right – the Stary Hrad.

Žilina itself is an important railway town, where the Košice line meets the line running between Bratislava and Poland.

KRAKÓW–ZAKOPANE

This railway links Poland's undisputed cultural capital with its premier mountain resort, passing through timeless rolling scenery on its ascent to the rugged peaks of the High Tatra. Trains can be crowded in the peak summer season; the best one to catch is the Warsaw–Zakopane which departs Kraków at 11.23.

⊙ Essentials

European Rail timetable no. 1066

Distance: 147km (91 miles)

Duration of journey: 3hrs 6 mins / 4 hrs 6 mins

Frequency of daytime trains: 4 per day (direct)

There are a further 3 trains departing Kraków between 1am and 5am

Hiking in the Tatra Mountains, near Zakopane.

The line south from **Kraków** heads across the plain of the Vistula River, past the attractive church at Skawina before climbing into the first outliers of the Beskid hills, part of the lengthy Carpathian chain. It is not long before the large Benardine monastery of **Kalwaria Zebrzydowska** appears on a hilltop to the right, just past the town itself. The site became a pilgrimage centre in the 17th century after locals experienced visions of crucifixes on the hill, with a type of Via Dolorosa leading to the summit. Pilgrims throng to the complex at Easter and during the Festival of the Assumption in mid-August. From here to Sucha Beskidzka there are expansive views of the Beskid Makowski range stretching to the south and east.

There is a good view of the open-air steam museum on the way out from **Chabówka** station, with numerous steam locomotives in varying states of repair. A branch line heads east to the attractive town of Rabka before crossing the Gorce region and the Beskid Wyspowy range to reach Nowy Sącz.

Train at Larissa station, between Thessaloníki and Athens.

TOWARDS THE MOUNTAINS

The Zakopane line turns south to head directly towards the mountains. On the 30-minute journey to **Nowy Targ** the train passes through timeless scenery – lush, rolling meadows grazed by contended-looking cows, set against a backdrop of dark forests and distant mountains. Nowy Targ marks the start of the Podhale region, home to the Górals, a small ethnic group of highland people. Traditionally farmers and shepherds, they speak their own dialect, and maintain their traditional customs and regional costumes – regardless of living among Poles or, for that matter, the dominant influence of tourism. A distinctive feature of Góral folk culture is the local architecture: ornately carved wooden houses and churches, many of which can be admired in the Tatra villages.

Heading south from Nowy Targ the railway slowly ascends towards the mountains, with increasingly impressive views of the jagged peaks to whet the appetite. Practically the entire southern flank of Poland is

mountainous, but none of the summits are a match for the Tatras (known in Poland as *Tatry*). The highest peaks are over the border in Slovakia, and the range is of modest length, but this has not prevented the Poles from making the most of their Alpine backyard.

Zakopane and its immediate surroundings are decidedly over-developed, the town now sprawling for miles along the valley in a scruffy mélange of half-finished hotels, billboards and tourist schlock. Yet it is not difficult to escape into the mountains, either on the funicular railway up to Gubalówka hill, or simply on foot.

THESSALONÍKI–ATHENS

Travelling by train between Greece's two major cities, Thessaloníki and Athens, is still a great way of discovering parts of mainland Greece even if many of the best views have been sacrificed to speed through route straightening and tunnel-building. This is the line you will come down if you travel to Greece by train from anywhere else in Europe since Thessaloníki is

the connection point for the country's international services. If you are coming from Bucharest or Sofia see European Rail Timetable 61, if you are coming Belgrade (Beograd) see table 62. It's worth noting that the transliteration of Greek names produces some confusing variations in English.

Thessaloníki (sometimes called Salonica), itself, is not to be overlooked. Greece's second city has remains from the time it was under Roman rule and a museum of Byzantine culture.

Just after leaving the northern Greek metropolis of **Thessaloníki**, trains cross a wide, flat, marshy plain that is the river delta for the Axios and Aliakmon rivers. Platy station, the rail junction to Western Macedonia, is the first important stop on this line. Further south, the significant Macedonian archaeological site of **Pella**, with its tombs, is 16km (10 miles) from Adendron station.

Continuing south, the line skirts the Thermaic Gulf. Passengers who can take their eyes off the sea will get inspiring views of snow-capped **Mount**

⊘ Essentials

European Rail timetable no.1400

Distance: 502km (312 miles)

Duration of journey: 5hrs 20 mins average

Frequency of trains: 5 per day and 1 night train

Greece's Volos station was designed by Evaristo de Chirico, father of the famous painter, Giorgio de Chirico.

⊘ A SAD ENDING

Sadly, on January 1 2011, services on the Piraeus, Athens and Peloponnese Railways were suspended indefinitely, as a result of Greece's ongoing economic crises. At the time of writing, there is no suggestion services will be resumed.

A train ride around the Peloponnese – a large peninsula connected to mainland Greece by a land bridge only – was one of the highlights of riding Greece's railways.

There is one remaining railway line on the Peloponnese though: a modern connection running from the port of Katakolo via Pyrgos to Olympia, site of the first Olympic Games in 776BC where there are ancient ruins to visit. See page 318.

Olympus on the other side. If the blue waters are enticing enough, you could get off at Platamon station, which is also a good place to organise treks up Olympus.

TRAVELLING THROUGH CLASSICAL LANDSCAPES

Once out of the canyon, trains immediately pick up speed as they descend onto the fertile Thessaly plain. Though the large city of Larissa is of little interest, the junction station offers rail transfers to Vólos and the Pelion Peninsula. In addition to being a major port with frequent sailings to the Sporades Islands of Skiathos and Skopelos, Volos has a twee, 600-mm gauge steam railway line (The Pelion railway – see page 321) that winds its picturesque way high above the waters of the Pagasitic Gulf from Ano Lechonia through spectacular mountain country to the stone village of Milies.

South from Larissa, trains race along the country's fastest track to the isolated station of Paleofarsalo. Connections can be made here for Trikala and Kalambaka at the base of the Meteora pinnacles, where Greek Orthodox monasteries defy gravity and cling, seemingly by faith alone, to sheer rock outcrop.

Lianokladi station offers rail transfers for Lamia and the small port of Stylis as well as being the jumping-off point for treks to the Agrafa and Brallos natural reserves. Near Lianokladi is the **Gorgopotomos River** where, in November 1942, British commandos and Greek partisans destroyed a crucial railway viaduct in a dramatic raid that disrupted Nazi supply lines.

From the next main station, **Levadia**, you can get to Delphi. After that comes Thiva, the ancient Thebes that once rivalled Athens in importance. There is not much to see today except Mycenaean ruins and an archaeological museum. The town also has associations with the Oedipus legend of Greek mythology.

South of Thebes, trains whisk across Northern European-style fast tracks through Oinoi (the junction with the Eubia rail line), and on to Athens.

Arriving at **Athens** is almost anticlimatic after the dramatic ride from

⊙ EXCURSION TO OLYMPIA

One branch that stills runs in the Peloponnese is the Katakolon line. Board the train at **Pirgos** for a delightful 27-minute ride through wooded countryside to **Olympia**, on a small train that has been lovingly restored after a lengthy absence.

The most salient monuments at the Olympia site (daily summer 8am–8pm) are the **Palaestra training centre**, whose courtyard colonnade has been fully restored; the **workshop of Pheidias**, the celebrated sculptor (identified by a cup found with his name inscribed on it); the **Leonidaion guesthouse**, with its lobular central pool; the Archaic **Hera temple** with its dissimilar columns; the enormous **Zeus temple**, which is now reduced to column sections; and the **stadium** with its 192-metre (630-ft) running course and surviving vaulted entrance.

Nearby is the newer **Olympia Museum** (same hours as site, throughout summer and winter), which is among the best half-dozen of its kind in Greece. In the museum, pride of place goes to the pediment reliefs recovered from the Zeus temple debris, which are now on display in the central hall. The reliefs themselves depict the battle between the Lapiths and the Centaurs, with the god Apollo at the centre of the composition.

Other items well-worth seeking out at the museum include the Hermes and baby Dionysos of Praxiteles, which is showcased in Room 8 at the right rear, together with the Geometric and Archaic bronze gallery, located in Room 2, featuring a gorgon shield ornament, a hammered relief of a mother griffon, various helmets and griffon heads as cauldron ornaments. Also worth seeing is the painted terracotta of Zeus with Ganymede in Room 4, near the heavily damaged Nike of Paionios.

If time permits, the **old museum** nearby (Mon–Fri 9am–4pm) is home to a fine late-Roman mosaic, a statue of Hadrian's lover Antinoös, a stele of Herakles wrestling with the Nemean lion and a bronze miniature of two human wrestlers.

Thessaloníki. For those continuing by rail, there are frequent transfers to the Peloponnese and to the major seaport of Pireaus. For those visiting the capital, the metro has a convenient station not far from the railway station.

KALAVRITA RACK RAILWAY

Diakofto, on the coast of the Gulf of Corinth, is the start of a memorable trip by rack railway to the mountain-top village of Kalavrita. There is no train to Diakofto but there is a bus service from the nearest mainline station at Kiáto, which is connected to Athens. The line at Diakofto was built in 1895 and was an ambitious project for the time. The gauge is just 750mm (2ft 5½in), which facilitates the use of smaller and more flexible rolling stock. The train's top speed is 30-40kmh (18–24mph) on normal track and 6–15kmh (4–9mph) on the toothed sections, which climb gradients of up to 1 in 10.

The highlight of the line comes early on as the train moves 550 metres (1,800ft) up the deep Vouraikos Gorge with its pools and waterfalls, through delightful groves of trees and past enormous boulders gnawed and shaped by time.

The train stops at several small stations: Niamata, Triklia (where the rack mechanism is operated) and Kata Zahlorou, from where it is possible to visit the monastery of Mega Spilaion. This one of the oldest monasteries in Greece (founded in 362 AD) and is named after a cave in which an icon of the Virgin Mary was found. It stands at an altitude of 940m (3,084ft), is eight storeys tall and is built in the shade of a rock on the side of Mt Helmos

After Kerpini you reach the terminus, Kalavitra whose name means 'Good Water'. The main sight for visitors is the Aghia Lavra monastery, founded by a hermit in 961 but destroyed and rebuilt six times in its history. It was here that the Greek revolution of 1821 began. A chapel recalls a massacre of local people by Nazi troops in 1943. Near Kalavitra there is now a large ski resort and it is theoretically possible to swim in the sea and ski in the mountains on the same day.

⊘ Essentials

European Rail Timetable 1455 and see www. trainose.gr

Distance: 22km (13.5 miles)

Duration of journey: 1hr 5mins

Frequency of trains: 3–5 daily

The Kalavrita Rack Railway, near Diakofto.

MUSEUMS AND HERITAGE LINES

Heritage railway lines and museums are few and far between in the eastern parts of Europe – partly because many of the considerable number of forestry and mining lines are still in use as regular passenger services. The numbers relate to the maps on pages 302 and 313.

MUSEUMS

Camlik Outdoor Museum ❶
Camlik Buharli Lokomotif Muzesi, Camlik Köyu, Selçuk, Izmir, Turkey
Open: daily 8am–8pm
Features: a collection of 33 steam locomotives on the premises of the former Camlik station, near the ancient site of Ephesus. Visitors are allowed to clamber on board the engines and get a feeling for the running of them from the inside.
Nearest station: Camlik
Tel: 232 894 8116
www.trainsofturkey.com

OSE Railway Museum ❷
4 Siokou Street, Sepolia, Athens, Greece
Open: Tue–Fri 9am–1pm.
Features: small but delightful museum giving the history of railways in Greece with beautifully preserved engines and carriages. Royal carriages, antique Athenian tramways, instruments, tickets, uniforms and mechanics' tools of the 19th century.
Nearest station (metro): Agios Nikolaos.
Tel: 210 5241323
www.ose.gr

Railway Museum of the Municipality of Kalamata ❸
DEPAK, Kalamata, Greece
Open: daily 8.30am–3pm.
Features: exhibits include an entire station and its area, with a small double-storeyed building for the stationmaster, four platforms and an entrance pavilion with fixed benches for waiting passengers. Seven steam engines and one diesel engine, a manually operated crane (1890), three first class passenger carriages and five first and second class carriages (1885) and eight freight cars of various types (1885–1947).
Nearest station: Kalamata
Tel: 24210 23644
www.ose.gr

Russian Railway Museum ❹
Bibliotechny per, 4, korp. 2, building 1 St Petersburg. (Metro: Baltiyskaya)
Open: Mon, Tue, Wed, Sun 10am–6pm
Features: One of Europe's largest railway museums. It is housed in two buildings, one a former locomotive shed, connected by a suspension bridge. A collection of rare and legendary steam trains, locomotives, electric locomotives, railcars and other rolling stock. Nearby is Varshavsky former railway station.
Tel 812 457-23-16
http://rzd-museum.ru

Steam Locomotive Museum, Sibiu ❺
Str Dorobantilor, nr 22, Sibiu, Romania (opposite the main railway station).
Open: Mon–Fri 9am–3pm
Features: 23 standard-gauge locomotives and 10 narrow-gauge, snow ploughs and steam cranes. Seven of the locomotives are active and used in special train rides for tourists. There are also collections of active and preserved locomotives at several depots. Part of the depot area is still used so care should always be taken. A narrow-gauge steam locomotive based at the depot of the narrow-gauge Sibiu-Agnita railway (follow the narrow-gauge lines east from the station)
Tel: 269-431685
www.turismo.sibiu.ro

Urban Public Transport Museum ❻
Szentendre, Hungary
2000 Szentendre, Dózsa Gy út, suburban railway station (in front of Volán bus station)
Open: Apr–Oct Tue–Sun 10am–5pm
Features: housed in a railway depot, with five exhibition rooms and two display halls to explain the history of public transport in Budapest and other Hungarian cities.
www.bkv.hu

Želeniški Musej (Slovenian Railways Museum) ❼
Parmova 35, SI-1000 Ljubljana, Slovenia
Open: Tue–Fri 10am–6pm
Features: a former boiler room in which are displayed over 60 locomotives and more than 50 other railway vehicles, plus rail-related artefacts.
Tel: 01 291 2641
www.slo-zelenice.si

HERITAGE LINES

Horonec Forest Railway Čierny Balog ❽
Clt 2, 976 52 Čierny Balog, Brezno, Slovakia (see page 311)
Open: May–mid-Sept daily
Features: narrow-gauge steam railway with museum
Gauge: 760mm (2ft 57⁄8 in)
Length: 10km (6 miles)
Tel: 421 48 619 1500
www.chz.sk

Rahmi M. Koç Museum ❾
Hasköy cadessi, Hasköy 80320, Istanbul, Turkey

Open: Tue–Sun 10am–6pm
Features: Industrial museum on
the northern shore of the Golden
Horn. It has a small but unique
collection of rolling stock including
a 1930s railcar and a carriage from
Istanbul's Tunel underground train
that opened in 1875. Other exhibits
include the carriage used by Sultan
Abdülaziz. There is a narrow-
gauge line alone the seashore that
operates at the weekend.
Tel: 212 256 71 73
www.trainsofturkey.com

The Pelion Railway ⑩

(Ano Lehonia–Milies) Greece
Open: Mon & Wed 8am–4pm;
Tue, Thu & Fri 8am–8.30pm, Sat
8.30am–3pm.
Features: the only regularly
operating steam railway in Greece,
with locomotives and rolling stock
dating back to 1903; wonderful
views down over the Pagasitic Gulf.
Nearest station: Volos
Length: 28km (18 miles)
Gauge: 600mm (1ft 11⅝ in)
Tel: 24210 39723
www.trainose.gr

Sargan Mountain Railway – Mokra Gora ⑪

Omladinska b.b. 31000 Uzice,
Serbia
Open: various weekends
8am–6.35pm.
Features: this remarkable railway
is surrounded by rough terrain
that forced engineers to construct

an eccentric figure-of-eight loop
through the hills. The railway is at
the heart of a tourist development
scheme that also includes a 600mm
(1ft 11⅝ in) gauge line into the
forest. There is a museum at Mokra
Gora station.
Length: 15.4km (9.5 miles)
Gauge: 760mm (2ft 57⁄8in)
Nearest station: Uzice
Tel: 381 31 510 288
www.serbianrailways.com

Szilvásvárad–Szalajka Forest Railway ⑫

(see page 309)
Szalajka ut. 6, Szilvásvárad 3348,
Hungary
Open: Apr–Oct daily
Features: narrow-gauge steam line
in the pretty Bükk hills of northern
Hungary; forest walks
Length: 4.5km (3 miles)
Gauge: 760mm (2ft 57⁄8in)
Tel: 06 36 355 197
www.kisvasut.hu

Targu Mures Railway ⑬

Romania
Operates three routes: Targu
Mures–Sovata; Targu Mures–
Mihesu de Campie; and Targu
Mures–Lechinta
Features: steam locomotives haul
refurbished carriages through
beautiful scenery; the lines to the
north are especially interesting
as they climb up into the Band
hills. Several enthusiast trains
have run as far as Band and there

is still an option to repair and
reopen the line as far as Mihesu
de Campie if demand increases.
The Chrzanow Px48 'Duna' type
locomotive 764.053 is the main
steam loco used for hauling
preserved trains. Other Romanian
heritage railways include the
line from Sibiu to Agnita, and
the scenic Aries valley line from
Turda to Abrud.

Wolsztyn Steam Railway ⑭

Poland (see page 312)
Features: unique in Europe, the
steam trains running between
Poznan and Wolsztyn, as well as
Zbasnyek and Leszno, operate a
regular scheduled service. It is
possible to arrange driving courses.
Tel: 08142 860436 (UK number)
www.thewolsztynexperience.org

Znin Railway (ZKP) ⑮

Poland
Open: Apr–Aug
Features: tourist passenger trains
returned to the Znin–Wenecja–
Biskupin–Gasawa line in 1976. The
Wenejca railway museum opened
four years earlier, and contains a
collection of 17 steam locomotives
and a variety of rolling stock and
other items. The museum area (all
outdoors) is being extended. The
railway passes the archaeological
museum at Biskupin
Gauge: 600mm (1ft 11⅝ in)
Tel: 052 30 20 492
www.cleeve.com/znin

Approaching Munich station.

EUROPEAN RAIL TRAVEL

TRAVEL TIPS

EUROPEAN RAIL TRAVEL

The following booking agents sell rail passes, such as the Interrail Pass, for European rail travel. Some agents also sell individual tickets for main-line train journeys in most of Europe (but not for journeys wholly within Eastern Europe). Agencies are increasingly internet-based.

UK

Eurostar
Tel: 0343 218 6186
www.eurostar.com
Tickets can be booked online. In the UK, you can book by telephone or at London St Pancras, Ebbsfleet International or Ashford International stations.
International Rail
PO Box 153 Alresford SO24 4AQ
www.internationalrail.com
Tel: 0871 231 0790
Loco2
Unit K.03, The Biscuit Factory, Drummond Road, Southwark, London, SE16 4DG.

☉ Telephone Numbers

All telephone numbers have the area code included in brackets where applicable. We have not bracketed area codes in those countries, such as Italy and Norway, where the code must always be dialled. For numbers which do not include an area code, such as toll-free '0800' numbers in the UK and the US, brackets are not included.

The initial '0' of the area code is omitted if you are dialling that number from another country. This does not apply to Italian numbers.

No telephone number but they promise to respond quickly to an email hello@loco2.com.
www.Loco2.com
Oui.SNCF
Tel: 09 77 43 10 92
https://en.oui.sncf/en
TrainsEurope
4 Station Approach, March, Cambridgeshire PE15 8SJ
Tel: 0871 700 7722
www.trainseurope.co.uk
Trainline
Tel: 0333 202 2222
www.thetrainline.com

US

Rail Europe
Westchester Avenue
White Plains, NY 10604
Tel: 1-800 622-8600
www.raileurope.com

If possible, always buy your ticket before boarding the train – not doing so can result in a fine. The same is true of reservations; where a train is marked with an 'R' in a square on the timetable, a reservation is required (for more details on reservations see the individual country listings starting on page 329). Travelling on the faster or busier trains may incur a supplement on top of the standard fare; the reservation fee payable on these trains is normally included in this supplement. As a general rule, children under 4 travel free, and those under 12 travel half price.

There is a bewildering array of passes available for rail travel in Europe, valid either for a single country, a group of countries, or the entire continent. Most passes only cover the cost of ordinary services, with supplements required for high-speed trains and overnight services.

Interrail Pass

InterRail passes can only be bought by European nationals or anyone who has lived in one of the countries covered for at least six months. You can buy an Interrail pass a maximum of three months before its start date. Several formats are available: the **Interrail Global Pass** version allows travel in almost all European countries, plus Turkey. Exceptions are Russia and other ex-Soviet states, plus Albania; travel within the country where you bought the ticket is excluded, as is travel on certain privately-run railways – notably in Switzerland and Italy. The Interrail Global Pass is available for 5, 7 or 10 days within a 15-day period, or 15 days, 22 days or one month continuous.

The **Interrail One Country Pass** version is valid for one country for 3, 4, 6 or 8 days in a month. You cannot use this Pass for travel in your own

Buying a ticket in Norway.

⊘ EU Customs Regulations

People entering EU countries from non-member states are allowed to bring in (or take out) 200 cigarettes or 50 cigars or 100 cigarillos or 250g tobacco, 2 litres of alcohol of max. 22 percent proof, or 1 litre of more than 22 percent proof, and 2 litres of

wine. People travelling between EU countries are theoretically permitted to take much larger quantities of tobacco and alcohol with them but they may be required to prove that they are for personal use not for resale.

country of residence. Substantial discounts on many European ferries are included. 1st class and 2nd class passes are available. Prices are about 30 percent lower for those under 26 in second class.

For more information see www.interrail.eu.

Eurail Pass

Eurail Passes are available to people living outside Europe. They can be bought up to 6 months in advance outside Europe, or after arrival in Europe, though the latter costs more. The basic pass has no age limit and covers many of the supplements needed for travel on express or deluxe trains. Passes are valid for periods ranging from 15 days to 3 months, offering unlimited 1st-class travel on the national railways of Austria, Switzerland, Hungary, Germany, France, Belgium, Luxembourg, the Netherlands, Denmark, Finland, Norway, Sweden, Portugal, Spain, Italy, Greece, and the Republic of Ireland. Many private railways and ferries are included in the price. Those aged under 27

⊘ Money

Altogether, 19 European Union states use the euro including most of the countries in this book. Bulgaria, Croatia, the Czech Republic, Denmark, Hungary, Poland, Romania, Russia, Sweden, and the United Kingdom have their own currencies.

Credit cards are widely accepted but it is always useful to have a little cash to hand for use in out-of-the-way places and for small purchases.

Foreign currency and travellers' cheques can be exchanged at banks and currency exchange outlets.

qualify for cheaper pass valid for 2nd-class travel.

The **Eurail Select Pass** is restricted to a specified number of adjoining countries (this means linked by a direct train). Supplements are available to include more countries. Like the other passes, there is a cheaper youth version for those under 27, which covers only second-class travel. Family and group rates are available if you are travelling as a party of 3 or more people. See www.eurail.com for more information.

Regional Passes

The **Balkan Flexipass** provides unlimited 1st- or 2nd-class travel in Romania, Bulgaria, Turkey, Greece, Macedonia, Serbia, Montenegro and other Balkan countries for 3 days within two months.

The **Benelux Pass** allows unlimited travel (except on Thalys trains) throughout Belgium, Luxembourg and the Netherlands for any three days in a month. Under-27 rate available.

The **European East Pass** is available to non-European residents, and offers unlimited rail travel throughout Austria, Czech Republic, Hungary, Poland and Slovakia for any 5 days within a month.

On the platform at Dresden.

Individual countries also offer their own passes for domestic use – see country listings for details.

VISAS AND PASSPORTS

Citizens of European Union Countries only need an identification card or passport for travel between member states. Canadian, US, Australian, New Zealand and UK citizens require a valid passport.

Any non-EU citizens planning to stay over three months in Europe should consult their embassy first..

The situation for UK citizens after the country leaves the European Union in March 2019 is currently unclear. For the latest information, see www.gov.uk.

WHAT TO BRING

For long rail journeys, bring a lightweight towel, earplugs, and an inflatable cushion.

Theft can be a problem, particularly on night trains. Make sure your compartment door is locked if possible, and remember to always padlock belongings.

FINDING YOUR TRAIN

The majority of stations have electronic departures and arrivals timetables prominently displayed in the main station concourse, with the words 'departures' and 'arrivals' clearly marked in English. Otherwise, departures timetables are usually yellow, and arrivals white. Timetables will indicate from which platform the train

☉ Telephones and Internet

Mobile phone coverage and internet access is generally high across Europe; in busier places you will find a choice of Wi-fi hotspots, however there are still a few locations with no network access.

All European countries use the same mobile communications technology and a UK-bought mobile will automatically be transferred to a local network in whichever country you are visiting. Within the EU, mobile operators do not apply international charges under the "roam like at home" rules but there may be a data download limit.

If you come from North America, which uses a different GSM standard, your best option is to buy a European pay-as-you-go SIM card and top it up as and when you need.

Alternatively, there are still fixed public phone booths (usually requiring you to buy a phone card from a newsagent) in many streets, squares and stations; and privately operated call centres where you will be able to talk more quietly. Avoid making international calls from a hotel room where you will pay a surcharge.

Throughout Europe a standardised set of letters is used to denote the type of train. These feature on all timetables and departures/arrivals notice boards: Any train marked with an 'R' in a box requires a seat reservation, to be made in advance. Trains requiring reservations and fare supplements include:

AVE – Spanish high speed train

CIS – Cisalpino tilting trains (Italy and Switzerland)

CNL – CityNightLine

EC – Eurocity international express train

EN – Euronight

Eurostar – high speed train from London to Paris and Brussels

Frecce – high speed trains in Italy

IC – Intercity; standard express train, usually on domestic routes only

ICE – German Intercity Express

InOui the new brand name for French TGV trains

Talgo – Spanish express train

TGV – French Train à Grande Vitesse, to be rebranded inOui

Thalys – High-speed train between France, Belgium and Germany

Trenhotel – Spanish luxury night train

See individual country listings for more details on the types of trains used in each country.

---

departs. Larger stations will also have printed timetables with all train departure and arrival times arranged by destination.

Station platforms are clearly marked and numbered, but things can get complicated when letters are used to sub-divide a particular platform. For example, '13A' may indicate the far end of (the very long) platform 13. If you get on the first train you see (undoubtedly the 13B train) you may find yourself whisked off in the wrong direction.

Finding your seat/berth

Make sure you are in the correct carriage – some carriages at the front or rear of the train may be for a different destination, and split off from the rest of the train at some point down the line. This shouldn't be a

Eurostar.

problem as a guard will normally check your ticket soon after departure, but it pays to be safe. To make things easier, European stations carry train composition boards on the platforms; all you have to do is to find the carriage number on your ticket and then consult the boards to find out if your carriage is in the front, rear or middle of the train. In most countries signs on the platform will help you to find the approximate place at which your carriage will arrive – particularly important when the train is only making a very brief stop.

A board on the side of each carriage indicates the destination of the train as well as its principal stops. A further sign near the doors indicates the carriage number. Seat/berth numbers are clearly marked by the compartment door or, with open-plan seating, next to the seats themselves.

Night trains

The basic form of berth on overnight trains is the **couchette**, simple bunk beds – usually six per compartment in two tiers of three. Sheets and pillows are provided, with toilets and wash basins in each carriage.

Standard sleeping cars cost quite a lot more than couchettes, and have two, three or four berths plus

☉ Cruise Train Operators

Royal Scotsman
Part of Orient Express group www.belmond.com.

El Transcantábrico
Plaza del Emperador Carlos V. 28045 Madrid.
Tel: 91 255 59 12
www.renfe.com

Venice Simplon-Orient-Express
Shackleton House, 4 Battle Bridge Lane, London SE1 2HP
Tel: 0800 913 079

www.belmond.com

Trans-Siberian Express
Russia Experience, 1d The Court, Lanwades Business Park, Kennett CB8 9PW
Tel: 0345 521 2910
www.trans-siberian.co.uk.

Inlandsbanan
Inlandsbanan AB, Box 561, 831 27 Östersund
Tel: (46) 771 53 53 53
www.inlandsbanan.se.

basic washing facilities. Full bedding is provided. First-class sleeping accommodation means one or two berths and usually includes breakfast.

The most luxurious options are the so-called **Hotel Trains** (principally the ÖBB Nightjet services in Germany, Austria and Switzerland, and the Trenhotel services in Spain). These have fewer berths per compartment, armchairs, and private toilets plus showers in first class. Breakfast is included.

LUGGAGE SERVICES

It is possible to arrange to have your luggage sent by train and to pick it up from a particular station. For information, contact the relevant railway company (details in the Railways Across Europe section starting on page 329). Practically all large stations, and many smaller ones, have left luggage facilities – either in the form of lockers or a staffed baggage room.

ACCESSIBLE TRAVEL

The majority of large stations in Western Europe have wheelchair facilities, with staff available to provide assistance. Most fast trains have spaces for wheelchairs.

Information is available from:

Mobility International USA
Offers a travel information service, tours and exchange programmes for people with disabilities.
132 E Broadway Suite 343, Eugene OR 97401
Tel: (541) 343 1284
www.miusa.org

SATH (Society for the Advancement of Travel for the Handicapped)
347 5th Avenue Suite 610, New York, NY 10016
Tel: (212) 447 7284
www.sath.org
A number of organisations in the UK offer advice for disabled travellers including
Can Be Done
Tel 020 8907 2400
www.canbedone.co.uk

A useful source of information is **Disabled Travel Advice** www.disabledtraveladvice.co.uk Tourist offices across Europe can also provide information for **disabled** travellers.

RECIPROCAL HEALTH COVERAGE IN THE EU

Citizens from EU countries are entitled to medical treatment in other EU countries under a reciprocal arrangement. Visitors from EU states should obtain the **European Health Insurance Card** (EHIC) before they leave home. This entitles the holder to free treatment by a doctor and free medicines on prescription. Only treatment under the state scheme is covered. The situation for UK citizens after Brexit is currently unclear. Any traveller from outside the EU is advised to take out private travel insurance: emergency hospitalisation, for instance, and repatriation can be very expensive.

TOUR OPERATORS

Some tour operators run sumptuous five-star trains along famous routes, such as the Trans-Siberian railway line, often using old steam trains.

⊘ Taking Bicycles

Most European trains allow bicycles on board, but advance notice and an extra payment is often required. Bicycles are not allowed on many high-speed trains, however, and in some countries such as Sweden they are not allowed on any long-distance route; for details see individual country listings. A guard will tell you where to store your bike on the train.

Bike hire is often available at stations and some even allow you to return the bike at another station.

If cycling is going to be a large part of your trip, consider joining the Cyclists' Touring Club in the UK, which has fact sheets full of information on all aspects of cycling throughout Europe. Contact CyclingUK at Parklands, Railton Road, Guildford, Surrey GU2 9JX, tel: (01483) 238 301, www.cyclinguk.org.

These 'Cruise Trains' cost about the same as a cruise on a ship, and offer a similar level of opulence.

There are many tour operators around Europe who arrange a wide variety of railway tours.
Abercrombie and Kent
St Georges House
Ambrose Street
Cheltenham GL50 3LG
Tel: 01242 386 500
www.abercrombiekent.co.uk
In the US:
Tel: 888 611 4711
www.abercrombiekent.com
This worldwide tour organisation offers luxury train tours to Russia,

Suite on the Venice Simplon-Orient-Express.

⊘ Hotel Price Categories

A list of selected hotels (convenient for access to railway stations) appears under each country's A–Z section. Prices are for a double room in high season:
€ under 100 Euros (£90 and under)
€€ 100–150 Euros (£90–130)
€€€ 150–200 Euros (£130–180)
€€€€ 200–250 Euros (£180–230)
€€€€€ over 250 Euros (over £230)

⊙ Luxury Trains

Al Andalus
Route: Madrid to Seville via Extramadura. Round trip of Andalusia, taking in Seville Córdoba Granada, Baeza Ubeda Ronda Jerez and Cádiz.
Tel: 912 555 912
www.renfe.com/trenesturisticos

Transcantábrico
Route: San Sebastian to El Ferrol, with side excursions. It also follows La Robla line to Leon. There are two versions: the classic Transcantábrico and the deluxe.
Tel: 912 555 912
www.renfe.com/trenesturisticos

Venice Simplon-Orient-Express
Route: London to Venice. The train follow various other itineraries throughout the year visiting, amongst others, Verona, Vienna and Budapest.
Tel: 0800 913 079
www.belmond.com

Belmond British Pullman
Routes: days out in England on board a classic period train.
Tel: 0800 913 079
www.belmond.com

Belmond Grand Hibernian
Routes: This recreated period train with elegant carriages does various tours of Ireland from Dublin Heuston station.
Tel: 0800 913 079
www.belmond.com

Royal Scotsman
Routes: Tours of the Highlands, lochs, whisky distilleries and other sights of Scotland departing from Edinburgh Waverley.
Tel: 0800 913 079
www.belmond.com

Golden Eagle Luxury Trains
Routes: itineraries visit Italy, the Balkans, Austria and the Alps. Also runs along the Trans-Siberian railway
Tel: 0161 928 9410

the Swiss Alps, Italy, Austria, Great Britain, France, Eastern Europe.

Ffestiniog Travel
First Floor, Unit 6, Former St Mary's Church, Tremadog, Porthmadog, Gwynedd, LL49 9RA
Tel: (01766) 512 400
www.festtravel.co.uk
In addition to booking rail journeys in Europe and North America, Ffestiniog also offers escorted rail journeys throughout the world.

Cocktails are served on the Royal Scotsman.

Great Rail Journeys Ltd
Saviour House, 9 Saviourgate, York YO1 8NL
Tel: (01904) 521936
www.greatrail.com
Great Rail offers exciting trips to nearly all European countries, including an Arctic Circle explorer.

Railtours Ireland
Railtours House, 16 Amiens Street, Dublin 1
Tel: (01) 856 0045

www.railtoursireland.com
Railtours provides a comprehensive variety of rail options in Ireland.

Enthusiast Holidays
146 Forest Hill Road, London SE23 3QR
Tel: (020) 8699 3654
www.enthusiasthols.com
Enthusiast Holidays offers worldwide escorted journeys for the dedicated steam railway traveller.

Voyages Jules Verne
96 Great Suffolk Street, London SE1 0BE
Tel: 020 3131 1339
www.vjv.co.uk
Well-established upmarket travel company.

EUROPEAN RAIL TIMETABLE

The *European Rail Timetable* (formerly known as the Thomas Cook Timetable) is published four times a year and is an essential for any European rail odyssey. For more information, or to buy a print or digital copy, see www.europeanrailtimetable.eu. The *European Railway Atlas* is also a useful complement to the timetable. t

USEFUL WEBSITES

National rail companies' websites are listed under 'Information' in the country-by-country listings. These sites provide timetables, most of which work reasonably well. Ticket agents sites' appear on page 324.
'The Man in Seat Sixty-One' is a well-organised site, tremendously useful for planning a European rail journey with links to all national rail companies: www.seat61.com
Scenic Rail Britain is a valuable online resource, with details and maps of the most picturesque and historic rail routes in Britain: www.scenicrailbritain.com
The European Railway Server provides links to thousands of railway websites across Europe: www.railfaneurope.net
UK heritage railways are well catalogued at www.heritage-railways.com
There is a similar site for French heritage railway at www.facs-patrimoine-ferroviaire.fr
For a reliable, comprehensive European timetable, visit Deutsche Bahn's site at www.bahn.com

COUNTRY BY COUNTRY A-Z

AUSTRIA

The Place

Area: 83,883 sq km (32,371 sq miles)
Capital: Vienna
Population: 8.8 million
Language: German
Time zone: CEST, GMT +1
Currency: Euro (EUR)
Telepone dialling codes:
International code: 43. Area codes:
Vienna 1 (from abroad; when dialling
from elsewhere in Austria use 0222);
Salzburg 662; Innsbruck 512

Visas and Passports

See page 325

Customs

See page 325

Public Holidays

1 January – New Year's Day; 6
January – Epiphany; March/April –
Good Friday, Easter; 1 May – Labour
Day; 12 May – Whit Monday; May –
Ascension Day; May/June – Corpus
Christi; 15 August – Assumption;
26 October – National Holiday;
1 November – All Saints' Day; 8
December – Immaculate Conception;
25 December – Christmas Day; 26
December – Boxing Day.

Tourist Offices

In Vienna

Albertinaplatz/Maysedergasse ,1010
Vienna
Tel: (1) 588 660
Fax: (1) 588 6640
https://www.wien.info/en

In the UK

54 Hatton Gardens, London EC1N
8HN

Tel: (020) 3409 6616
www.austria.info/uk

In the USA

61 Broadway
New York, NY 10006
Tel: (212) 944 7723
www.austria.info

Embassies and Consulates

UK

Jaurèsgasse 12, 1030 Vienna
Tel: (1) 716 130
http://ukinaustria.fco.gov.uk/en/

US

Boltzmanngasse 16, 1090 Vienna
Tel: (1) 313 390
https://at.usembassy.gov/

Money

Credit cards are accepted by major
hotels and many shops in cities.
ATMs accept all major European
debit cards; it is wise to carry a little cash when visiting remote, rural
areas.

Post offices (indicated by a
golden horn symbol) charge little
or no commission, but often give
bad exchange rates. Banks (usually
open Monday–Friday 8am–12.30pm
and 1.30–to 5.30pm) and exchange
offices will change foreign currency
at a better rate.

Health and Emergencies

Austria is a very safe place to travel;
nevertheless, it's always wise to buy
health and travel insurance with

⊘ Useful Numbers

All emergency services: 112
Ambulance and Fire Brigade: 144
Mountain rescue: 140
Police: 133

---

medical cover prior to your trip.
EU citizens need to have their EHIC
(see page 327). It doesn't cover private treatment, but does entitle you
to reduced cost, sometimes free,
emergency medical treatment. The
German for hospital is *krankenhaus*;
emergency room is *notaufnahme*

Austria's standard of medical care
is very good. Visit the local pharmacy
(*apotheke*) for minor problems; most
stay open to 6pm weekdays and noon
on Saturday and usually post a list of
24-hour pharmacies nearby for night
and Sunday duty.

Safety and Crime

Austria is generally very safe, except
for a few areas in Vienna, and the
chief threat here is the pickpocket.
Be vigilant in crowded areas such as
the Westbahnhof, Naschmarkt, the
Prater and especially Karlsplatz.
Keep valuables in your hotel safe.

Business Hours

In general, shops and businesses
open Monday–Friday 9am–6pm (grocery stores from 8am) and Saturday
9am–1pm or 5pm. Small family businesses in rural areas often have lunch
breaks up to 2 hours long. Some
supermarkets and basic provisions
stores in larger stations offer late
night opening, until 10pm. Banks
open Monday–Friday 8am–12.30pm
and 1.30–3pm. Museums are generally open from 9 or 10am–5 or 6pm,
with many closed on Monday.

Train System

Austria's rail network is run by
Österreichische Bundesbahnen
(ÖBB; https://www.oebb.at/en/). The
usual European services are in
operation across the country: EC
(EuroCity international express),
IC (InterCity internal express), EN

(EuroNight) international express services, as well as ÖEC (ÖBB-operated EuroCity), ÖIC (ÖBB-run InterCity), CNL (City Night Line) international overnight train, and ICE German high-speed services. Trains marked 'D' are ordinary express trains (Schnellzug), those marked 'E' (Eilzug) or 'SPR' (Sprinter) are semi-fast regional trains. The usual fare supplements apply for fast trains.

Ticket Details

All trains except most 'E' and all 'R' trains have first and second class. Passengers are required to pay a surcharge on certain InterCity trains; the price of reserved seating is within this additional charge. 'EN' and 'CNL' trains require supplements for couchettes and sleeping cars. ÖBB and most private railways accept Interrail and Eurail passes.

Discount Passes

Interrail and **Eurail** passes are all valid in Austria. The ÖBB Vorteilscard annual card entitles the user to a 50 percent discount on most regular train fares. The classic version is available to everyone but there are cheaper cards available for families, senior citizens, and those under 26. Children under 15, in the company of at least one parent or grandparent travel free with the family card.

Reservations

No supplements or compulsory seat reservations are required for any train category within Austria except CNL. An extra fee is collected for seat reservations, except in first class. If you travel from Austria to neighbouring countries which impose supplements for EC trains, these supplements include the fee for seat reservation inside Austria. Seat, couchette and sleeping car reservations can be made at any ÖBB ticket office. Ticket offices at major railway stations accept credit cards.

Stations in Vienna

Vienna has three main stations: Westbahnhof, Wien Hauptbahnhof and Wien Mitte. Westbahnhof serves much of Austria, Germany, Switzerland, France and Belgium; Wien Hauptbahnhof serves southern Austria, Italy, the Balkans, Greece,

the Czech Republic, Slovakia and Hungary, and some trains to Germany; and Wien Mitte, which serves Vienna International Airport and many InterCity routes. A fourth station, Franz-Josefs-Bahnhof serves domestic routes to the north and west of Vienna.

Train Talk

See Germany section on page 342.

Taking Bicycles

Austria is very bicycle-friendly country. With over 500km (311 miles) of cycle paths in the Vienna area, the tourist office makes a special effort to let travellers know about bike-friendly accommodation, with bicycle hire available from most stations.

On regional trains you can take your bicycle if there is a place on the train. However, not all trains transport bicycles. Check the ÖBB website for more details: https://www.oebb.at/en/.

Where to Stay

For price categories see page 327.

Innsbruck
Grand Hotel Europa
Südtiroler Platz 2, A-6020 Innsbruck
Tel: (05) 125 931
www.grandhoteleuropa.at
19th-century hotel opposite the railway station, in the heart of the city. Bombed in World War II, this historic hotel has hosted Queen Elizabeth II, General Patton, and the crew of Apollo 14. €€€€€

Salzburg
Austria Trend Hotel Europa
Rainerstrassee 31, A-5020 Salzburg

Railjet train in Austria.

Tel: (06) 62 889 930
www.austria-trend.at
Centrally located just 50 metres from Salzburg Hauptbahnhof. Most rooms have good views. €€€
Hotel Der Salzburger Hof
Kaiserschützenstrasse 1,
A-5020 Salzburg
Tel: (06) 62 46970
https://www.dersalzburgerhof.at/en/
Traditional family hotel in the centre of Salzburg, only 200 metres from the Hauptbahnhof. €€€€

Vienna
Hotel Fürstenhof
Neubaugürtel 4, A-1070 Wien
Tel: (1) 523 3267
http://shs-hotels.com/hotel-fuerstenhof/en/
Reasonable and comfortable hotel, with some en-suite rooms. Close to the Westbahnhof. €€€
Hotel Prinz Eugen
Wiedner Gürtel 14, A-1040 Vienna
Tel: (1) 505 1741
https://prinz-eugen-vienna.hotel-rv.com/
Opposite the Belvedere Palace and within 200 metres/yds of the Südbahnhof. €€
Hotel Westbahn
Pelzgasse 1, A-1150 Wien
Tel: (1) 982 1480
https://ana-hotels.com/westbahn
An establishment with friendly service, close to the Westbahnhof, with an old Viennese inner yard and fountain. Historic atmosphere. €€€€

BELGIUM

The Place

Area: 30,528 sq km (11,787 sq miles)
Capital: Brussels
Population: 11.4 million

Languages: Flemish, French and German
Time Zone: GMT +1; EST +6.
Currency: Euro
Telephone Dialling Codes: International code: 32. Area codes: Brussels 2; Bruges 50

Visas and passports

See page 325.

Customs

See page 325.

Public Holidays

1 January – New Year's Day; March/April – Easter Sunday and Easter Monday; 1 May – Labour Day; Ascension Day; Whit Sunday; Whit Monday; 21 July – Independence Day; 15 August – Assumption; 1 November – All Saints' Day; 11 November – Armistice Day; 25 December – Christmas Day.

Tourist Offices

Because of the federalised structure of Belgium, the country's four sections – Brussels, Flanders, French-speaking Wallonia and German-speaking east Belgium – each now have separate tourist information services.

Brussels

Visit Brussels, main information centres, Rue Royale 2, in the City Hall, Grand Place, and at Brussels-Midi railway station, tel: 02-513 8940; www.visitbrussels.be.

Flanders (north of Brussels)

Toerisme Vlaanderen (Flanders Tourist Board), Rue du Marché aux Herbes 61, 1000 Brussels, tel: 02-504 0390; www.visitflanders.com.
In the UK: tel: 020-7307 7738
In the US: tel: 212-584 2336, www.visitflanders.us
German cantons of East Belgium Hauptstrasse 54 Sankt Vith, tel: 080 22 76 64; www.eastbelgium.com

Antwerp Central.

Wallonia (south of Brussels)

OPT (Brussels and Wallonia Tourist Board), Rue du Marché aux Herbes 25 Brussels, tel: 02 899 04 78 or 81 84 41 00; www.opt.be and www.visitbelgium.com
In the UK tel: 020-7537 1132; www.belgiumtheplaceto.be;

Embassies and Consulates

UK

Avenue de Auderghem 10, 1040 Brussels
Tel: (02) 287 6211
www.gov.uk/world/organisations/british-embassy-brussels

USA

Regentlaan 25 (Boulevard du Régent)
B-1000 Brussels
Tel: (02) 811 4000
www.belgium.usembassy.gov

Money

All banks in Belgium exchange foreign money. Most are open Monday–Friday 9am–4pm, with some closing for an hour during lunch. As a rule, exchange offices in larger railway stations maintain longer hours than banks. Many open on Sundays too. Most international credit cards are widely accepted, and there are ATMs all over the country.

Health and Emergencies

All visitors are strongly advised to take out private medical insurance. You may be expected to pay after admittance in case of emergency. It is only possible to claim back 75 percent of the cost with the EHIC; this applies to hospital treatment, doctor and dentist appointments and prescriptions. After regular hours and during holidays you will find the name and address of the nearest chemist on night duty posted on the door of pharmacies.

Safety and Crime

Bag snatching and pickpocketing are the main threats for travellers in Belgium.

Opening Hours

Most shops open Monday–Saturday 10am–6pm, with grocery stores frequently remaining open until 9pm. Some shops close for a lunch break from noon–2pm. Antique and flea markets are generally open Saturday and Sunday.

Train System

Belgian railways are operated by the Société Nationale des Chemins de fer Belges (SNCB), known in Flemish as the Nationale Maatschappij der Belgische Spoorwegen (NMBS). For information see www.belgianrail.be. Trains include the standard European designations of **EC** (international InterCity), and **EN** night trains, as well as high-speed **Thalys** and **Eurostar** services.

Ticket Details

Considerable price reductions apply to children's fares and some deals include discount entry into tourist attractions. The usual supplements are payable on fast trains. Various discounts are available on weekend return journeys.

⊘ Useful Numbers

All emergency services: 112
Ambulance and Fire Brigade: 100
Police: 101

Discount Passes

Interrail and **Eurail** passes are both accepted. The **Benelux Pass** offers unlimited travel on up to 8 days within a one-month period using the railway network in Belgium, Luxembourg and the Netherlands. **Rail Pass** (26+) and **Go-Pass** (under 26 years) allow 10 single journeys, 2nd class (made at any time of day); they are valid for one year and may be shared.

Reservations

Reservations are not available for any journeys wholly within Belgium. They are available for EC and night trains operating international routes and are compulsory for Thalys and ICE services, and can be arranged at main stations and travel agents.

Stations in Brussels

Brussels has three main railway stations, usually marked in both French and Flemish: **Nord/Noord**; **Central/Centraal**; and **Midi/Zuid**.

Midi/Zuid station is the largest of the three, and the departure/arrival point for Eurostar services to/from London. All three stations are connected by the metro system.

Train Talk

See the France section on page 339. In the Dutch- and German-speaking areas of Belgium, you will find that most people speak good English.

Taking Bicycles

Cycling in Brussels is not for the faint-hearted: although cycle lanes do exist, the city is not particularly cycle-friendly. In rural Belgium, by contrast, cycling has long been one of the best ways of getting around. Tourist offices can supply details and maps of local cycle routes. You can rent bicycles from several railway stations around the country (not in Brussels), open 7am–8pm, but you must return them to the same station.

It is also possible to take your own bike on the train by buying a ticket for a one-way trip or for the whole day (giving you unlimited travel within Belgium). There are various restrictions on the use of these services. Folding bikes go free.

Bear in mind if travelling with your bike through Brussels that you cannot load or unload it at Central Station; Midi/Zuid or Nord/Noord stations are recommended instead.

Where to Stay

For price categories see page 327.

Brussels

NH Grand Place Arenberg
15 Rue d'Assaut
Tel: (02) 501 1616
www.nhhotels.com
Close to Central/Centraal station; a comfortable four-star hotel. **€€**

Welcome Hotel
23 Quai au Bois à Brûler
Tel: (02) 219 9546
www.hotelwelcome.com
Small, friendly hotel in city centre; each room is decorated in the style of a different part of the world. **€€–€€€**

Ustel Hotel
6–8 Square de l'Aviation, Brussels
Tel: (02) 520 6053
www.florishotelustelmidi.be
Attractive family-run hotel five minutes' walk from Midi/Zuid station. **€€€**

Praha Hlavni Nadrazi, Prague's main station.

The Place

Bulgaria

Area: 110,910 sq km (42,822 sq miles)
Capital: Sofia
Population: 7.1 million
Language: Bulgarian
Time Zone: EET: GMT +2; EST +7
Currency: Lev (BGN)
Telephone Dialling Codes: International code: 359. Area codes: Sofia 2; Veliko Tarnovo 62; Plovdiv 32

Croatia

Area: 56,542 sq km (21,830 sq miles)
Capital: Zagreb
Population: 4.3 million
Language: Croatian
Time Zone: CET GMT +1; EST +6
Currency: Kuna (KN)
Telephone Dialling Codes: International code 385. Area codes: Zagreb 1; Rijeka 51; Split 21; Dubrovnik 20

Czech Republic

Area: 78,886 sq km (30,458 sq miles);
Capital: Prague
Population: Czech Republic 10.2 million
Language: Czech
Time Zone: CET GMT +1; EST +6
Currency: Koruna (CZK)
Telephone Dialling codes: International code: 420, Area codes: Prague 2; Brno 5; Karlovy Vary 17

Hungary

Area: 93,030 sq km (35,919 sq miles)
Capital: Budapest
Population: 10.1 million
Language: Hungarian (Magyar)
Time Zone: CET GMT +1; EST +6
Currency: Forint (HUF)
Telephone Dialling Codes: International code: 36. Area codes: Budapest 1; Eger 36; Miskolc 46

Poland

Area: 312,685 sq km (120,728 sq miles)
Capital: Warsaw
Population: 38.6 million
Language: Polish
Time Zone: CET GMT +1; EST +6
Currency: Zloty (PLN)
Telephone Dialling Codes: International code: 48. Area codes

Warsaw (6 digits) 22, (7 digits) 2;
Kraków 12; Poznan 61; Zakopane 18

Romania

Area: 237,500 sq km (91,700 sq miles)
Capital: Bucharest
Population: 20 million
Language: Romanian; minorities speak Hungarian and German
Time Zone: EET GMT +2; EST +7
Currency: Leu (RON)
Telephone Dialling Codes: International code: 40. Area codes: Bucharest 1; Brasov 68

Slovakia

Area 49,035 sq km (18,932 sq miles)
Capital Bratislava
Population 5.4 million
Language Slovak
Time zone CET GMT+1. EST +6
Currency: Euro (EUR)
Telephone Dialling codes: International code 421. Area codes: Bratislava 7; Kosice 55 Poprad 52; Banská Bystrica 48

Slovenia

Area: 20,253 sq km (7,819 sq miles)
Capital: Ljubljana
Population: 1.9 million
Language: Slovene
Time Zone: GMT +1; EST +6
Currency: Euro (EUR)
Telephone Dialling Codes: International code: 386. Area codes Ljubljana 01; Maribor 02

Visas, Passports and Customs

The countries covered in the routes in this book are all currently members of the **European Union**, with the UK set to leave in 2019. Citizens of other EU countries can visit EU countries with a valid passport or ID card for up to 6 months or longer. US, Canadian, Australian, New Zealand and South African nationals can stay for up to 90 days without a visa. All EU countries share the same customs arrangements and, broadly speaking, you can take alcohol, tobacco and other goods across internal EU frontiers duty free as long as they are for your personal consumption.

Tourist Offices

Bulgaria

www.bulgariatravel.org
Sofia: St Kliment Ohridski
Tel: 959 2 491 83 44
www.visitsofia.bg

Croatia

www.croatia.hr
Zagreb: Trg bana J Jelacica 11
Tel: 4814051
www.infozagreb.hr

Czech Republic

www.czechtourism.com
Prague: Staroměstské náměstí 5
Prague 1
Tel: (02) 224 861 476

Hungary

http://hellohungary.com
Budapest: Süto utca 2 (off Deák tér)
Tel: (01) 317 9800
www.spiceofeurope.com

Poland

www.poland.travel
Warsaw: pl Defilad 1, (entrance from Emilii Plater Street)
Tel: (022) 53 17 247
www.warsawtour.pl

Romania

www.romaniatourism.com
Bucharest: Piata Universitat underpass
Tel: (01) 021 305 00
www.seebucharest.ro

Slovakia

www.slovkaia.travel
Bratislava: Klobucnicka 2
Tel: (07) 21 61 86
www.visitbratislava.com

Slovenia

www.slovenia.info
Ljubljana: Adamič – Lundrovo nabrežje 2
Tel: 386 1 306 12 15
www.visitljubljana.com

Embassies and Consulates

Bulgaria

UK
9 Moskovska Street, Sofia 1000
Tel: (02) 933 9222
www.gov.uk/world/organisations/british-embassy-sofia

US
16 Kozyak Street, Sofia
Tel: (02) 937 5100
www.bg.usembassy.gov

Croatia

UK
Ivana Lučića 4
10000 Zagreb

Bulgarian BDZ train.

Tel: 385 (1) 6009 100
www.gov.uk/world/organisations/british-embassy-zagreb

US
Ulica Thomasa Jeffersona 2
Tel: 385 1 661 2200
www.hr.usembassy.gov

Czech Republic

UK
Thunovska 14, Prague
Tel: (02) 5740 2111
www.gov.uk/world/organisations/british-embassy-prague

US
Tziste 15, Prague
Tel: (02) 257 022 000
http://cz.usembassy.gov

Hungary

UK
Füge utca 5–7 Budapest
Tel: (01) 266 2888
www.gov.uk/world/organisations/british-embassy-budapest

US
V Szabadság tér 12, Budapest
Tel: (01) 267 4400
http://hu.usembassy.gov

Poland

UK
ul. Kawalerii, Warsaw
Tel: (22) 311 00 00
www.gov.uk/world/organisations/british-embassy-warsaw

Waiting in Sighişoara, Romania.

US
Al Ujazdowskie 29/31, Warsaw
Tel: (22) 504 20 00
www.pl.usembassy.gov

Romania

UK
24 Jules Michelet, Sector 1,
Bucharest
Tel: (01) 201 72 00
www.gov.uk/world/organisations/
british-embassy-bucharest

US
4–6 Dr Liviu Librescu Blvd, Bucharest
Tel: (01) 200 33 00
www.ro.usembassy.gov

Slovakia

UK
Panská 16, Bratislava
Tel: 421 2 5998 20 00
www.gov.uk/world/organisations/
british-embassy-bratislava

US
Hviezdoslavovo nám 4, Bratislava
Tel: (07) 5443 3338
www.sk.usembassy.gov

Slovenia

UK
Trg republike 3, Ljubljana
Tel: (01) 200 3910
www.gov.uk/world/organisations/
british-embassy-ljubljana

US
Prezernova cesta 31, Ljubljana
Tel: (01) 200 5500
www.si.usembassy.gov

Health and Emergencies

Private medical travel insurance is essential when travelling in Eastern Europe. Doctors and hospitals often expect immediate cash payment. Most standard drugs are available in pharmacies but if you need special medication it is best to bring it with you.

It is best to avoid drinking tap water if you can and it is recommended that you wash fruit and vegetables before you eat them, but not in tap water. Bottled mineral water is available everywhere.

Dentistry is a Hungarian speciality, with many visiting the country to benefit from lower prices.

Safety and Crime

The main risk when travelling in Eastern Europe is becoming disoriented. Plan your movements beforehand, keep your wits about you and take the usual sensible precautions. Don't carry all your cash in one place, and avoid displaying large sums of money. Keep to busy places as much as possible. Be alert to scams in which someone will distract your attention so that an accomplice can make off with your bag. Be sure to lock your door securely if on an overnight sleeper train.

Deposit any valuables in the hotel safe, and if you are the victim of a theft, report it immediately to the reception desk at your hotel.

Travelling by train in Eastern Europe

If possible, buy your tickets in advance, online – all railway companies have a reduced version of their website in English. See page 324. If you need to buy a ticket at a station, it can help to write your destination down on a piece of paper.

Interrail and Eurail passes are valid in Eastern Europe but check whether you need to reserve a seat or pay a supplement to use a particular train. Trains that require a reservation are generally marked with a boxed 'r' on timetables.

If for any reason you get on the train without a ticket, go and find the conductor before he finds you.

Train Systems

Bulgaria

Bulgarian railways are operated by Bâlgarski Dârzhavni Zheleznitsi (BDZ; www.bdz.bg). There is an office for international rail travel at Sofia central station.

Bulgarian trains are classed as express (*ekspres*) – marked Ex on timetables; fast (*burz*); and regular (*puticheski*). Reservations are required for the express trains, and a fare supplement payable. Some

☉ Useful Numbers

Every EU state operates the same general emergency number 112.
Bulgaria
General emergencies: 112
Ambulance: 150
Fire: 160
Police: 166
Croatia
General emergencies: 112
Police: 192
Fire: 193
Ambulance: 194
International Directory Enquiries: 902
Local Directory Enquiries: 988
International Operator: 115
Czech Republic
General emergencies: 112
Ambulance: 155
Fire: 150
Police: 158
Hungary
General emergencies: 112

Ambulance: 104
Fire: 105
Police: 107
Poland
General emergencies: 112
Ambulance: 999
Fire: 998
Police: 997
Romania
General emergencies: 112
Ambulance: 961
Fire: 981
Police: 955
Slovakia
General emergencies: 112
Ambulance: 155
Fire: 150
Police: 158
Slovenia
General emergencies, including ambulance and fire: 112
Police: 113

other trains also require reservations – these are marked with a boxed 'r' in timetables.

The Cyrillic alphabet is used in Bulgaria and while names of larger stations may also appear in Latin script, be prepared to decipher timetables with the aid of a dictionary.

Croatia

Croatian railways are run by Hrvatske Željeznice (HŽ; www.hzpp.hr).

Tickets are inexpensive and can be bought in advance. Trains are not usually crowded. IC and icn trains are the fastest, some requiring reservations and a supplementary fare. Reservations are not possible on local trains; a boxed 'r' on timetables indicates that a particular train requires seat reservations.

Czech Republic

The Czech Republic maintains a well-developed railway network. Travelling either first or second class is quite comfortable as well as relatively inexpensive.

The Czech Republic's extensive railways are run by Cёské Dráhy (CD; www.cd.cz). There are also two private train companies serving Slovakia: Regiojet (www.regiojet.sk) and Leo Express (www.leoexpress.com).

The fastest trains are the SC, IC and EC expresses, followed by the Ex trains (supplement payable and reservations required). Semi-fast trains are called spesn´y, slow trains are osobny. Fast trains are marked in red on timetables.

In Prague, most express trains use the main station (Hlavní nádraží), not far from Wenceslas Square. Trains from Berlin arrive at Holesovice station in the north of the city. Other stations are for local services only.

Hungary

Hungarian passenger trains are operated by MÁV (www.mav.hu). Services to Austria are run by another company, GySev (www.gysev.hu)

Departures are displayed on yellow timetables, arrivals on white. The fastest trains are EC (EuroCity), IC (InterCity) and IP (InterPici), all of which require fare supplements and seat reservations. These trains are marked in red on timetables. Standard express trains (gyorsvornat) are significantly slower. The slowest trains are the local személyvonat services.

Tickets can be purchased on the day of departure at the station, although it is advisable to buy them at least 36 hours prior to departure for international services and for all trains in the summer months, when demand is heavy. You may buy your ticket on board for certain services, but this carries an additional modest fee.

For trains to and from Germany, the Czech Republic and Slovakia, and the Danube Bend, generally use Nyugati station in Budapest; for trains to and from Austria, Italy, Slovenia, Croatia, former Yugoslavia, Romania, Bulgaria, Greece and Turkey operate from Keleti station, as well as limited services to Germany, the Czech Republic and Slovakia. The third station, Déli, located west of the Danube in Buda, serves routes to/from western parts of Hungary including Lake Balaton.

Poland

The national rail operator is Polskie Koleje Panstwowe (PKP). For express and premium services see www.intercity.pol; for slower regional trains see www.polregio.pl.

The fastest trains are marked in red on timetables and designated as IC (InterCity; domestic routes) or EC (EuroCity; international routes). Other fast trains (but slower than the IC/EC trains) are marked Ex (ekspresowy); IR fare supplements apply and reservations are required for all these trains. Semi-fast trains (pospieszne) do not require reservations or supplements. Local stopping trains (osobowe or normalne) are very slow. Night trains offer first- and second-class sleeping cars as well as couchettes.

Fast trains are listed in red, slow trains in black. An 'ex' on the timetable denotes an express service; IC

Commuter train in Slovenia.

is for intercity trains. Departures are listed on a yellow board and arrivals on a white board. Main stations are called glowny (abbreviated to Gl).

It is well worth booking a seat, particularly on express services and paying 50 percent extra for a first-class ticket, as prices are inexpensive and second class may be very cramped.

Romania

The Romanian rail network is relatively dense, linking all cities and major towns. Most services are operated by CFR Calatori (www.cfr-calatori.ro) but a few are operated by Regio Calatori (www.regiocalatori.ro) and Softrans (www.softrans.ro)

Most trains are electrified and fairly punctual but branch line services are slow. Fares are cheap by Western standards and first-class travel is inexpensive – although don't expect luxury.

There are three classes of train in Romania: the fastest are the IC (InterCity; domestic) and EC (EuroCity; international) trains, on which a sizeable supplement is payable. Overnight trains generally carry first- and second-class sleepers as well as couchettes; reservations are required. Standard express trains are known as rapid; slower are the semi-fast trains; the slow, frequently stopping, persoane trains are only suitable for shorter journeys. Reservations are obligatory for most services, and it is best to book first-class tickets to avoid overcrowding. Bucharest's main station is the Gara du Nord.

Slovakia

Slovakia maintains a well-developed railway network. Travelling either

Zagreb Central railway station.

first- or second-class is quite comfortable and inexpensive. Železničná Spoločnosť Slovensko is the national operator (ZSSK; www.slovakarail. sk). See also details for the Czech Republic.

IC and EC trains are faster and require a supplement and seat reservation. *Rychlik* are semi-fast trains; *osobny* are slow local trains. Departures are on the usual European departure posters in yellow and arrivals on white. Fast trains are marked in red on timetables. Tickets can be bought in advance or on the day of departure.

Slovenia
Slovenia's national rail operator is Slovenske Železnice (SZ; www.slo-zeleznice.si). Travel on the express ICS trains requires reserved seats and carries a fare supplement. IC trains have a lower fare supplement and reservations are not compulsory for journeys within Slovenia. Tickets may be bought in advance or on the day of travel at stations, or on board the train, although often for an additional charge.

Train Talk

Bulgaria
arrivals *preesteeganye pristigane*
departures *zameenavanye zaminavane*
first class *p'rvoklasen prvoklasen*
platform *peron peron*
railway station *stantsiya stancià*
reservation *rezervatsiya rezervacià*
return *beelyet za oteevanye ee vr'shchane bilet za otivane i vrwane*
second class *vtoreeklasen vtoriklasen*
single *ednopocochen ednopocoçen*
sleeping car *spalen vagon spalen vagon*
ticket *beelyet bilet*

train *vlak vlak*
when...? *koga...koga...?*

Croatia
arrivals *dolazak*
departures *odlazak*
first class *prvu klasu*
platform *platforma*
railway station *stanica*
reservation *reserviranje*
return *povratnu kartu*
second class *drugu klasu*
single *kartu u jednom pravcu*
sleeping car *spavaca kola*
ticket *kartu*
train *vlak*
what time does the train leave? *kada vlak dolazi?*

Czech Republic
arrivals *prijezd*
departures *odjezd/odchod*
first class *první trída*
platform *nastupiste*
railway station *nádrazí*
reservation *místenku*
return *zpáteca jízdenka*
second class *druhé triídy*
single *jízdenka tam*
sleeping car *spací vuz*
ticket *jízdenka*
train *rodeni*
when is the next train to...? *kdy jede dalsí vlak do...?*

Hungary
arrivals *érkezés*
departures *indulás*
first class *else osztály*
platform *vágány*
reservation *helyjegy*
return ticket to *egy retur jegyet... ra/ re*
second class *másodrendi/kettes érdemjegy, másodosztályú*
single ticket please *egy jegyet kérek...-ra/re csak oda*
sleeping car *hálókocsi*

ticket *jegyet*
train *vonat*
railway station *vasútállomás*
when? *mikor?*

Poland
arrivals *przyjazd*
departures *odjazd*
first class *bilet pierwszej klasy*
platform *peron*
railway station *dworzec, samochód, stacja*
reservation *miejscówka*
return *bilet powrotny*
second class *drugiej klasy*
single *w jedna strona*
sleeping car *wagon sypialny*
ticket *bilet*
train *pociag*
when does the train leave for...? *kiedy odjezdza pociag do...?*

Romania
arrivals *sosire*
departures *plecare*
first class *clasa intii*
platform *peron*
railway station *gara*
reservation *resevatie*
return *a returna*
second class *de clasa a dova*
single *bilet simplu*
sleeping car *vagon de dormit*
ticket *bilet*
train *trenul*
what time does the train leave? *la ce ora trenul pleaca?*

Slovakia
arrivals *príchod*
departures *odchod*
first class *prvotriedny*
platform *nastupiste*
railway station *zeleznicná stanica*
reservation *místenku*
return *spiatocny gestovny listok*
second class *sekunda*
single *jednosmerny listok*
sleeping car *lehátkovy vozen*
railway station *zeleznicná stanica*
ticket *lístok*
train *vlak*
when..? *kedy..?*

Slovenia
arrivals *prihod*
departures *odhod*
first class *prvorazreden*
platform *platforma*
railway station *kolodvor*
return *povratna (vozovnica)*
second class *drugorezreden*
single *enosmerna (vozovnica)*
sleeping car *spalnik*
ticket *vstopnica/karta*

train *vlak*
what time does the train leave? *o kateri uri vlak odpelje?*

Where to Stay

Bulgaria

Sofia
Ramada Sofia City Center
131 Maria Louisa Boulevard
Tel: (02) 933 8888
www.wyndhamhotels.com
The closest hotel to the railway station and considered one of the best in Sofia. €€€€

Croatia

Zagreb
Hotel Central
Branimirova 3
Tel: (01) 484 1122
www.hotel-central.hr/eng
Large hotel located opposite the railway station. Doubles are en-suite and include breakfast. €€
Esplanade
Mihanoviceva
Tel: (01) 435 666
www.esplanade.hr
The only 5-star hotel in Zagreb and located just outside the railway station. Also has a casino. €€€€

Czech Republic

Prague
Esplanade
Washingtonova 19, 110 00 Praha 1
Tel: (02) 2450 1111
www.esplanade.cz
Just off Wenceslas Square, in the heart of the old historic centre of town and close to the State Opera and Hlavní station. €€€€
Hotel Ametyst
Jana Masaryka 11, 120 00 Praha 2
Tel: (02) 2292 1921
www.hotelametyst.cz
In the Vinohrady quarter above Wenceslas Square; within easy walking distance of the centre of town. Less than 2km (1 mile) from Hlavní station. €€
Palace
Panská 12, 110 00 Praha 1
Tel: (02) 2409 3111
www.palacehotel.cz
Just off Wenceslas Square, the Art Nouveau Palace dates from 1906. Years of renovation have restored it to its original splendour. €€€

Hungary

Budapest
K+K Hotel Opera
Révay utca 24
Tel: (01) 269 0222
www.kkhotels.com
Next to the Opera House. Less than 1km (0.5 mile) from Nyugati railway station. €€€
Nemzeti Hotel Mercure
Jószef körut 4
Tel: (01) 477 4500
www.hotel-nemzeti-budapest.hu/en
Small elegant rooms in an Art Nouveau building. 500 metres/yds from Keleti station. €€
Radisson Blu Béke
VI, Teréz körut 43
Tel: (01) 889 3900
www.radissonblu.com
The 247 rooms are nicely furnished. Nyugati station is less than 1km (.5 mile) away. Don't miss the cakes in the first-floor Zsolnay Café. €€€€

Poland

Warsaw
Metropol Hotel
Ul Marszalkowska 99a
Tel: (022) 32 53 100
www.hotelmetropol.com.pl
Situated near the central railway station and the Palace of Culture and Science. €€€

Romania

Bucharest
Elizeu
11–13 Elizeu, District Sector 1
Tel +40 722 550 139
www.hotelelzeu.com
Right next to the railway station, with modern en-suite rooms €
Hello
Calea Grivitei nr 143, cod 010708
Tel +40 372 121 800
https://hello-hotels-bucuresti.continental-hotels.ro/en/
Comfortable modern hotel near the station. €

Slovakia

Bratislava
Crowne Plaza
Hodzovo námestie 2
Tel: 0800 980 002
www.lhg.com
A business hotel, but this still bridges the distance between the railway station and the old town

Vintage railway conductor, Podbrdo.

nicely. The former is a kilometre away, the old town less than half that. €€€
Perugia
Zelená 5
Tel: 902 411 111
www.aplendcity.com
Over 2km (1 mile) from the railway station, but superbly situated in the centre. €€€

Slovenia

Ljubljana
Grand Hotel Union
Miklosiceva cesta 1
Tel: (01) 308 1270
www.gh-union.si
Pleasant hotel in the city centre, not far from the railway station. €€€
Hotel Emonec
Wolfova 12
Tel: (01) 200 1520
www.hotel-emonec.com
Just 10 minutes from the station. Simply furnished, with self-service breakfast. €

FRANCE

The Place

Area: 543,965 sq km (210,026 sq miles)
Capital: Paris
Population: 67 million
Language: French
Time Zone: GMT +1; EST +6.
Currency: Euro (EUR)
Telephone Dialling Codes: International code: 33

Area codes: Paris 1; northwest 2; northeast 3; southeast and Corsica 4; southwest 5

Visas and passports

See page 325.

Customs

See page 325.

Public Holidays

1 January – New Year's Day; March/April – Easter Monday; 1 May – Labour Day; 8 May – commemorates the end of World War II; Whit Monday; Ascension Day (always a Thursday); 14 July – Bastille Day; 15 August – Assumption Day; 1 November – All Saints' Day; 11 November – Armistice Day; 25 December – Christmas Day.

Tourist Offices

www.franceguide.com

In Paris

25 Rue des Pyramides (Metro: Pyramides)
Tel: 06 12 34 56 78
www.parisinfo.com

Embassies and Consulates

UK

35 rue du Faubourg St Honoré, 75008 Paris
Tel: (01) 44 51 31 00
http://ukinfrance.fco.gov.uk.

US

2 avenue Gabriel, 008 Paris
Tel: (01) 43 12 22 22
www.fr.usembassy.gov

Money

Banks open Monday–Friday 10am–5pm in Paris. In the rest of France banks open Tuesday–Saturday 10am–1pm and 3–5pm, often closing earlier the day before a public holiday. Only banks displaying a change sign will exchange foreign currency. They charge the best rates. French cash machines accept most international credit and debit cards. Travellers' cheques are widely accepted. Hotels and bureaux de change also exchange currencies, but at a higher commission rate.

TGV trains in Paris.

Health

Health insurance is highly recommended. In emergencies you will be admitted and then charged. For minor ailments it may be worth consulting a pharmacy (recognisable by its green cross sign), which has wider prescribing powers than its UK or US counterparts. They are also helpful in cases of snake or insect bites and can recommend doctors.

Safety and Crime

Sensible precautions with personal possessions are all that should really be necessary when visiting France. Theft and other crime exists in France as elsewhere in Europe. Tourists are frequently targeted on the rail link to and from Charles de Gaulle airport and should never lose sight of their bags.

Opening Hours

Shops: 9am–6pm or later, Tuesday–Saturday. The majority of shops are shut on Monday, and Sunday opening is uncommon. Long lunch hours (from noon or 12.30 for two hours) are still traditional in banks, shops and other public offices; shops in larger towns and cities open continuously.

Post offices: in cities, generally open continuously 8am–6pm weekdays and 8am–noon Saturday – the

⏰ Useful Numbers

Ambulance: 15
Police: 17
Fire: 18

main post office in Paris, at 52 rue du Louvre, 75001 Paris, is open 24 hours every day; in the provinces post offices are open Monday–Friday 9am–noon and 2–5pm and from 9am–noon on Saturday.

Train System

Trains are operated by the Société Nationale des Chemins de Fer Français, universally known as SNCF. For more information see www.en.oui.sncf.

SNCF's services are divided into a number of brands.

High-speed Trains

The majority of long-distance trains, particularly those to and from Paris, are TGVs (Trains à Grande Vitesse, now officially rebranded as TGV inOui) and operate at up to 320km/h (200mph). On most inter-city routes TGVs are faster than air services.

TGVS are comfortable, air-conditioned and have a buffet and bar car. On certain services, passengers can reserve a full meal in advance of travel. However, in a country renowned for its gastronomy, some trains (over relatively long distances) have no catering facilities at all, so it is important to check this before undertaking a long journey.

Fast and comfortable Thalys trains operate between Paris, Brussels, Amsterdam and Cologne and TGV Lyria runs between Paris and Switzerland. Reservations are compulsory on all high-speed prestige services.

Other Trains

Trains in the Ile-de-France (around Paris) form part of SNCF's Transilien network, which connects with the

Metro and RER networks. All other regional trains are classed as TER or Intercité. Standards and punctuality are generally high. If possible avoid travelling on Friday afternoons, Saturday mornings, Sunday evenings and just before and after public holidays.

Intercité trains are generally fast and comfortable long-distance trains that operate in areas that still have no TGV service, and stop more frequently. Some are overnight sleeper services, including some motorail services in which you can put your car on the train, as on the Calais–Avignon route.

Information on local TER trains can be found at www.ter-sncf.com (in French only). From the map of France there are links to the TER pages for each region, with detailed maps of all lines and available stations. It is not usual or necessary to book TER tickets much in advance

Ticket Details

Ticket purchases can be made at the usual ticket windows but also on touch-screen terminals in major stations. These are easy to use and accept major credit cards. Most people, however, purchase online.

Before boarding the train, tickets must be validated by stamping them in a *composteur* – yellow machines at the entrance to station platforms. A return ticket must be stamped before each journey. This is not necessary for hand-written tickets or passes and does not apply to tickets bought outside France. The ticket must be used on the day and in the train indicated but an exchange can be made if there is a change of plan. If you miss your reserved train, it is usually possible to take the next service. If you forget to validate your ticket or boards the wrong train, it is advisable to immediately seek the on-board *contrôleur*.

Fares are divided into three categories: peak (red), standard (white) and off-peak (blue). You can obtain a calendar of these times from SNCF.

Discount Passes

Eurailpass and **Interrail** are valid in France. It should be noted that these tickets do not exempt you from paying for some seat reservations, supplements and overnight accommodation on the train. Reservations must be made before travel on TGVSD,

otherwise you will be charged on the train, with an additional fine added on TGVS. The **France Railpass** (available anyone resident outside France) is valid for 3–8 days within 1 month. A variety of save cards are available including the **Carte Jeune** (for people 12–26 years old), **Carte Sénior** (over 60), a weekend travel card and a card for frequent rail travellers.

Reservations

Most reservations are only possible up to 3 months before departure. A special procedure exists for reservations up to 6 months in advance. Reservations for TGV inOui and Thalys are made automatically when the ticket is purchased, and are included in the ticket price. The passenger can specify the position of the seat and even the direction of travel on certain trains.

Reservations on other trains, including overnight services, may be necessary during peak travel times and on international routes. If you hold a domestic pass, the reservation fee should be waived. However, pass-holder seats are often limited, so be sure to book early. Reservations can be made directly with SNCF, or at any station. The SNCF website (www.en.oui.sncf) has a facility to deliver a ticket free to almost any country in the world if booked a week or more in advance.

Stations in Paris

Paris has several stations: St Lazare for Normandy; Gare du

Tracks into Paris-Montparnasse.

Nord for Calais, Belgium, Cologne, the Netherlands and the UK; Gare de l'Est for northeast France, Luxembourg, Germany and Switzerland; Gare de Lyon for east and southeast France, the Rhône-Alpes, Provence, the Côte d'Azur, Switzerland and Italy; Austerlitz for south and southwest France, Spain and Portugal; Montparnasse for Tours, Bordeaux, Chartres, the Loire Valley and Nantes. Trains for the Loire Valley and points southwest to Bordeaux can depart from either Austerlitz or Montparnasse station.

Train Talk

approximately *environ*
arrival, arrives *arrivée, arrive*
calls at *s'arrête à*
change at *changer à*
connection *correspondance, relation*
daily *tous les jours*
delay *retard*
departure, departs *départ, part*
fast(er) *(plus) rapide*
first class *première classe*
hourly *toutes les heures*
journey *voyage, trajet*
journey time *temps de parcours*
platform *quai*
reservation *réservation*
return ticket *aller-retour*
second class *deuxième classe*
single ticket *aller simple*
station *gare*
ticket *billet*
through train *train direct*
timings *horaires*
train *train*
when does the next train depart for...? *à quelle heure part le prochain train pour...?*

Taking Bicycles

Bicycles can be carried on the majority of SNCF trains including TGVS. Depending on the train, they can be carried free in the baggage compartment, or as packaged luggage on payment of a fee; free of charge on local, regional and non-TGV express trains (except during Mon–Fri peak hours on Paris commuter routes). On most TGVS trains you can put your bike in the luggage van if you reserve space in advance and pay a small fee – this is the same for most overnight trains.

Where to Stay

For price categories see page 327.

Le Negresco hotel, in Nice.

Clermont Ferrand

Hôtel Litteraire Alexandre Vialatte
16 place Delille, 63000
Tel: (04) 73 91 92 06
www.hotelvialatte.com
At the heart of Clermont-Ferrand, close to the railway station. €€

Kyriad Prestige
25 avenue de la Libération, 63000
Tel: (04) 73 93 22 22
www.kyriad-prestige-clermont-ferrand.fr
In the centre of Clermont-Ferrand. A terrace on the roof offers an unrestricted view of the Puy de Dome. €€

Marseille

La Résidence du Vieux Port
18 Quai du Port, 13002
Tel: (04) 91 91 91 22
www.hotel-residence-marseille.com
A first-class, classic-style hotel located in the old port area of Marseille. All rooms have outstanding views of the port and Notre-Dame de la Garde. The railway station is less than 1km (0.5 mile) away. €€€

Sofitel Marseille Vieux Port
36 Boulevard Ch.-Livon, 13007
Tel: (04) 91 15 59 00
www.sofitel-marseille-vieuxport.com
This modern, comfortable hotel is convenient for sightseeing around the old port district. Just over a kilometre from the railway station. €€€€

Nice

Plaza
12 avenue de Verdun, 06004
Tel: (04) 93 16 75 71
www.hotelplazanice.com
Overlooking the Baie des Anges and shaded by magnificent palms, less than 5km (3 miles) from Nice Côte d'Azur Airport; the railway station is only 3 minutes away by car. €€€€€

Négresco
37 promenade des Anglais, 06000
Tel: (04) 93 16 64 00
www.hotel-negresco-nice.com
Nice's most glorious hotel with its great pink dome dominating the promenade des Anglais. It offers every luxury, and impeccable service. €€€€€

Vendôme
26 rue Pastorelli, 06000
Tel: (04) 93 62 00 77
www.hotel-vendome-nice.com
A first class hotel in the heart of Nice, close to the beach and the Acropolis Congress Centre; the railway station is 1km (0.5 mile) away. €€

Nîmes

Best Western L'Orangerie Hotel Nîmes
755 rue de la Tour Evêque, 30900
Tel: (04) 66 84 50 57
www.hotel-orangerie-nimes.fr
Friendly hotel just outside the centre with pretty garden, small pool and good restaurant. €

Paris

Marignan-Champs Elysées
12 rue Marignan, 75008
Tel: (01) 40 76 34 56
www.hotelmarignanelyseesparis.com
A luxury hotel between the Champs Elysées and the fashionable avenue Montaigne, with an Art-Deco facade and modern interior focused round La Verrière, the glass-roofed reception and bar. The restaurant, La Table du Marché, is a favourite with personalities from the worlds of fashion, film and media. All stations easily accessed by Metro. €€€€€

Le Méridien Étoile
81 Boulevard Gouvion St Cyr, BP 75848
Tel: (01) 40 68 34 34
www.lemeridienetoile.com
Situated on the Right Bank between La Défense and the Champs Elysées, this renovated hotel is a 10-minute walk to the Arc de Triomphe. All stations are easily accessed by Metro. €€€€€

Waldorf Madeleine
12 boulevard Malesherbes, 75008
Tel: (01) 42 65 72 06
www.hwparis.com
The fabulous Waldorf Madeleine is within walking distance of the Madeleine Metro station, which offers easy access to all parts of Paris. €€€€

GERMANY

The Place

Area: 357,168 sq km (137,903 s. miles)
Capital: Berlin
Population: 83 million
Language: German
Time Zone: CEST; GMT +1 (+2 from late March until late October)
Currency: Euro (EUR)
Telephone Dialling Codes: International code: 49. Area codes: Munich 89; Frankfurt 69; Cologne 221; Berlin 30; Dresden 351; Nürnberg 911

Visas and Passports

See page 325.

Customs

See page 325.

Public Holidays

1 January – New Year's Day; March/April – Good Friday, Easter Monday; 1 May – Labour Day; May (Thursday) – Ascension Day; May – Whit Monday; 3 October – Day of German Unity; 11 November Armistice Day; 25 December – Christmas Day; 26 December – St Stephen's Day.

Tourist Offices

In Berlin
Europa-Center
Budapester Strasse 45
Tel: (030) 25 00 22
www.berlin-tourist-information.de

In the UK
PO Box 2695, London W1A 3TN
Tel: (020) 7317 0900
www.germany-tourism.de

In the USA

122 East 42nd Street, 52nd Floor, New York, NY 10168
Tel: (212) 661 7200
http://www.germany.travel/en

Embassies and Consulates

UK

Wilhelmstrasse 70/71
Berlin 10117
Tel: (030) 204 570
https://www.gov.uk/world/organisations/british-embassy-berlin

US

Pariser Platz 2
10117 Berlin
Tel: (030) 083 050
https://de.usembassy.gov/

Money

Banks, post offices and bureaux de change (*wechselstuben*) change money. Airports and major railway stations have electronic currency changing machines, used to exchange foreign currency for euros. Banks in major railway stations tend to open every day until 10–11pm. Major credit cards are accepted almost everywhere in the major cities; it's always a good idea to carry a little cash with you though. There are ATMs everywhere in cities and towns. You cannot use travellers' cheques as payment, as they have to be cashed at a bank beforehand.

Health and Emergencies

All non-EU foreign nationals should ensure that they have adequate health insurance before they leave their home country; without insurance medical fees can be very expensive in Germany. For EU citizens, the EHIC covers public health care, which is of excellent quality in Germany. For more information on EHIC see page 327.

If you need a doctor, contact the nearest consulate for a list of English-speaking doctors. In emergencies, either go straight to the nearest hospital's casualty unit or phone for an ambulance. For less major ailments, GPs (*arzt für allgemeinmedizin*) work 9am–noon and 3–6pm weekdays; some are closed on Wednesday.

Pharmacies (*apotheken*) normally open 8am–6.30pm, with some open until noon on Saturdays. They all carry a list on the door of

neighbouring pharmacies that are open at night and over the weekend.

Safety and Crime

Crime exists in Germany as it does all over the world, but it is only in the larger cities that visitors need to be especially cautious. Pickpockets seek their opportunities in crowds so be vigilant. Do not leave luggage unaccompanied at stations or near hotels.

Opening Hours

Shop opening hours are strictly regulated across Germany, although since 2006, the different states (*Lander*) have been allowed to introduce their own rules on shopping hours and this has created some variety. From Monday to Saturday, most shops open from about 9.30am–6pm, and some small local shops open earlier, and close for lunch. In Bavaria, there is a near-complete ban on Sunday opening.

Banks usually open Monday–Friday 8.30am–12.30pm and 1.30–4pm, often with longer hours on Thursday evenings..

Restaurants and pubs close at midnight or 1am. Nightclubs and some bars have licences for extended hours. Only in Berlin are there no late-night restrictions.

Train System

Germany's efficient railway network is run by Deutsche Bahn (DB; https://

ICE train, Frankfurt.

www.deutschebahn.com/en). The usual European **EC** (EuroCity international express), IC (InterCity internal express), and **CNL** (CityNightLine) and **EN** (EuroNight international express) services are in operation across the country. The fastest services are operated by the impressive **ICE** high-speed trains, with superbly designed and appointed interiors. German night trains operating on domestic routes are designated **NZ** (NachtZug); Talgo-designed trains operate on the Hamburg–München and Berlin–München routes. **Thalys** high-speed trains operate between Cologne, Brussels and Paris.

Other services include **IRE** regional express trains, **RE** semi-fast trains, **D** standard express trains, **RB** stopping trains and **S-Bahn** suburban trains.

Fare supplements apply on ICE, Thalys, CNL and NZ services. Lower supplements are charged on EC and IC trains. Reservations are not compulsory except on night trains, Thalys and trains marked 'R' in the timetable, but they are advisable at busy times on inter-city trains.

Ticket Details

Children under 4 years of age travel free of charge, those aged 4 to 11 pay half fare. There are many reduced-fare schemes and passes in Germany, including the **BahnCard 25** and **BahnCard 50**, which offer 25 and 50 percent discounts respectively, for rail travel on most routes. There are reduced versions for children, young people, married couples, families and senior citizens. Advance purchase **Savers** are available for return journeys

with varying discounts according to the day(s) of travel. **Länder-Tickets** are available for unlimited travel between 9am and 3am the following day within a state of your choice, by second class only, for up to 5 people. The **Schönes-Wochenende Ticket** (Happy Weekend Ticket) is valid on Saturday or Sunday from midnight until 3am the following day on all local trains, second class only. Up to 5 people may travel together at no extra charge.

Reservations

It is advisable to make a seat reservation for trains, which costs a little extra. The DB website (www.bahn.com) has all the information you'll need.

Stations in Berlin

As you might expect, there are several busy stations in Berlin: Zoologischer Garten (usually abbreviated to Zoo), formerly the main terminus in West Berlin, and Ostbahnhof, its former East Berlin counterpart are the busiest. Almost all trains stop at both these stations. Trains bound for Russia and Ukraine depart from Berlin Hauptbahnhof. Night trains from all over Germany terminate at Lichtenberg Station. Some other main line trains also stop at the smaller Berlin stations of Friedrichstrasse and Alexanderplatz. The spectacular Berlin Hauptbanhof, which opened in 2006, handles north–south traffic.

Train Talk

arrival, arrives Ankunft, kommt an
change at umsteigen in
connection Anschlusse, Verbindung
daily täglich
delay Verspätung
departure, departs Abfahrt, fährt
entrance Eingang, Einfahrt
every xx minutes alle xx Minuten
except aussen
excuse me entschuldigen Sie, bitte
exit Ausgang, Ausfahrt
fast(er) schnell(er)
first class erste Klasse
from (a town) von xx
hourly stündlich
how far is the station? Wie weit ist es zum Bahnhof?
how much is it? Wieviel kostet das?
journey Reise
journey time Reisezeit

Boarding the train in Munich.

later später
left links
platform Gleis
right rechts
reservation die Platzreservierung
return (ticket) die Rückfahrkarte
second class zweiter Klasse
single (ticket) einfache Fahrkarte
station Bahnhof
stopping trains Nahverkehrszüge
stop hält
straight on geradus
supplement zuschlagpflichtig
through train durchgehender Zug
ticket Fahrkarte
to (a town) nach xx
train der Zug
valid gültig
when is the next train to ...? Wann geht der nächste Zug nach ...?
where do I get a ticket? Wo kann ich eine Fahrkarte kaufen?
where is platform one? Wo ist Gleis eins?

Taking Bicycles

It is possible to take your own bicycle on all local and many IC/EC trains for a small additional fee, but because of limited space it is advisable to check online first at www.bahn.de.

The alternative to taking your bicycle is the Call a Bike scheme (operated by DB), whereby bicycles can be hired at Munich, Berlin, Frankfurt-am-Main, Cologne, Stuttgart, Karlsruhe and many other stations. First up, you'll need to register at www.callabike-interaktiv.de/de or on the app. After registration, you'll be able to book a bike easily online or on the app. Once you've done this, you'll receive a code. Key

in the number on the input display underneath the cover on the bike to release the lock, then remove the bolt.

Where to Stay

For price categories see page 327.

Berlin

Hotel Palace
Europa Centre, Tauentzienstrasse, Charlottenburg
Tel: (030) 25020
www.palace.de
This 1960s-built hotel is right in the centre of the city, and next door to Zoo Garten station. The first floor restaurant is excellent. €€€€

Kempinski Hotel Bristol
Kurfurstendamm, 27 Charlottenburg
Tel: (030) 884 340
www.kempinski-berlin.de
Famous luxury hotel, very convenient for Zoo Station. €€€€€

Pension am Park
Sophie-Charlotten Strasse, 57–58 Charlottenburg
Tel: (030) 321 3485
https://pension-ampark.de/en/
Attractive pension, conveniently located for Zoo station. €€€

Cologne

Brandenburger Hof
Brandenburgerstrasse 2–4, Köln 50668
Tel: (0221) 122 889
www.brandenburgerhof.de
Family-style budget hotel with shared bathrooms on each floor. Full cooked breakfast served in the garden in summer. Close to the river and within walking distance of the cathedral and the Hauptbahnhof. €

Dresden

Hotel Burgk
Burgstrasse 15, Dresden (löbtau)
Tel: (0351) 432510
www.hotel-burgk.de
Just to the west of the main station, only 5 minutes by car from the old town. Small, friendly hotel; impressive breakfast buffet. €€

Kempinski Hotel Taschenbergpalais
Am Taschenberg, Dresden 01067
Tel: (0351) 49120
www.kempinski-dresden.de
Originally an early 18th-century royal castle, which was all but destroyed in World War II, the Kempinski was transformed into Dresden's finest hotel in the 1990s.

Rooms are the most opulent in town. Today, a tiny portion of the bombed ruin has been artfully retained. Less than 1km (0.5 mile) from the main station. €€€€€

Frankfurt

Carlton
Karlstrasse 11
Tel: (069) 241 8280
www.carlton-frankfurt.de
Convenient hotel located in the heart of Frankfurt's business metropolis, with easy access to the railway station and the city's shopping area. €€€€

Munich

Hotel Am Markt
6 Heiliggeiststrasse
Tel: (089) 225014
www.hotel-am-markt.eu
Bavarian, cosy, very quiet, directly on the Viktualienmarkt just 700 metres/yds from the Hauptbahnhof. €€
Hotel Bayerischer Hof
2–6 Promenadeplatz
Tel: (089) 21200
www.bayerischerhof.de
Exclusive family-run grand hotel, famous for its nightclub and Trader Vic's. 500 metres from the Hauptbahnhof. €€€€€
Königshof
Karlsplatz (Stachus)
Tel: (089) 551360
https://www.koenigshof-hotel.de/
Elegant luxury hotel in the centre, 2 minutes from the Hauptbahnhof. €€€€€

Nürnberg

Carlton Hotel Nürnberg
Eilgutstrasse 13-15, Nürnberg 90443
Tel: (0911) 20030
www.carlton-nuernberg.de
A block away from the railway station, the Carlton is one of the best value hotels in Nürnberg, with service and facilities to match more expensive competitors. Popular restaurant, the Zirbelstube, plus lunch on the stone terrace. €€
Dürer-Hotel
Neutormauer 32, Nürnberg 90403
Tel: (0911) 214 665
www.duerer-hotel.de
Situated right under the eponymous castle, and near all the major sightseeing attractions. Modern amenities don't rob the hotel of character. Bistro bar, fitness centre, laundry. Only 1.5km (1 mile) from the main railway station. €€€

GREECE

The Place

Area: 131,950 sq km (50,946 sq miles)
Capital: Athens
Population: 11 million
Language: Greek
Time Zone: GMT + 2; EST +7.
Currency: Euro (EUR)
Telephone Dialling Codes: International code: 30. Area codes: Athens 1; Patras 61, Kalamata 721, Thessaloniki 31

Visas and passports

See page 325.

Customs

See page 325.

Tourist Offices

For all information see www.visitgreece.gr

In Athens

D. Arepagitou 18–20
Tel: 210-33 10 392
www.thisisathens.org

Embassies and Consulates

UK

1 Ploutarchov Street, 10675 Athens
Tel: (01) 0727 2600
www.ukingreece.fco.gov.uk

US

91 Vassilissis Sophias Avenue, 10160 Athens
Tel: (01) 0721 2951
www.gr.usembassy.gov

Train driver's cab, in an ICE train.

Money

All banks and most hotels are authorised to buy foreign currency at the official rate of exchange as set by the Bank of Greece. It is worth carrying a limited sum in US dollars or pounds sterling. Travel agencies give poor rates but charge less commission. Post offices charge a low commission to change cash but don't change travellers' cheques; hotels and agents charge a higher commission than banks. Most banks have ATMs.

Larger hotels, restaurants and shops accept major credit cards. The average *pension* or *taverna* may not. You will find that most brands of card are accepted by the numerous ATMs (different cards in different banks).

Public Holidays

6 January – Epiphany; 25 March – Independence Day; 1 May – May Day; 15 August – Assumption Day; 28 October – "Ohi" Day; 25–26 December.

Health and Emergencies

Citizens of the USA, Canada and the UK do not need any immunisations to enter Greece.

EU residents are entitled to free medical treatment as long as they carry an EHIC (see page 327). Provision may not be of the highest quality, however, plus you will be admitted to one of the lowest-grade state hospitals and have to pay for your own medicine, so it is advisable to take out private medical insurance. Keep receipts for any bills or medicines in order to make a claim.

⊘ Useful Numbers

Ambulance: 161
Police: 100
Tourist police: 171
Operator: 151

There are often long waits for treatment in public hospitals.

On the islands, baby pit vipers and scorpions are a problem in spring and summer. Do not put your hands or feet in places that you haven't checked first. If you swim in the sea, beware of jellyfish. The drinking water is safe, though brackish on certain islands.

Hotel staff will give you details of the nearest hospital or English-speaking doctor. Or contact the Tourist Police, who are always extremely helpful. For minor ailments there's usually an English-speaking pharmacist *(farmakío)* in larger towns and resorts. If you need medication bring the prescription and generic name of the drug.

Safety and Crime

Greece is one of the safest countries in Europe. Crime is rare and but petty theft does sometime occur, and is more likely to have been committed by tourists than by locals.

Opening Hours

All banks open Monday–Thursday 8am–2pm, closing at 1.30pm on Friday. In tourist areas you may find banks open later in the afternoon and on Saturday mornings.

Businesses open at 8.30am and close on Monday, Wednesday and Saturday at 2.30pm. On Tuesday, Thursday and Friday most businesses close at 1.30pm and reopen in the afternoon from 5–8.30pm. Schedules are very flexible in Greece.

Train System

Greek railways are run by Organimós Sidiródromon Éllados (OSE; www.trainose.gr). Many travel agents in Greece can book tickets.

The fastest express trains are the IC (InterCity) expresses, which are air-conditioned and require a fare supplement – reservations are required on certain trains; normal express trains *(taxeia)* are less

reliable; local trains *(topiko)* are very slow. Endorse your ticket at the station before departure if you wish to break your journey.

Ticket Details

Ticket offices close 5 minutes before the departure of the train; if the office is closed, get your ticket on board – find the conductor, don't wait for them to find you. A **Multiple Journey Card** offers unlimited second-class rail travel for 10, 20 or 30 days, but does not include supplements on IC trains. **Interrail**, **Eurailpass** and the **Balkan Flexipass** are all valid.

Reservations

Reservations are recommended, but not essential, on many inter-city trains, although you could have a fight on your hands if someone takes your seat because reserved seats aren't marked. They can be made at any OSE office.

Stations in Athens

Larissa Station (Laríssis) serves trains to Thessaloniki, northern Greece and Bulgaria as well as to Korinthos.

Train Talk

arrivals *afixis*
departures *anahorisis*
first class *próti thési*
platform *platforma*
railway station *strathmós*
reservation *kratisi*
return *i sitírio me epistrofí*
second class *défteri thési*
single *aplo isitírio*
sleeping car *kabines*
ticket *isitírioone énna*
train *tréno*
when is the next train? *póte févyi to tréno?*

Where to Stay

For price categories see page 327.

Athens

Candia
Diligianni Street, 40, Athens 10438
Tel: (021) 0524 6112
www.candia-hotel.gr
A short walk from the railway station, with a roof-top swimming pool and bedroom balconies, some with views of the Acropolis. **€€**

Titania
Panepistimiou Avenue, 52, Athens 10678
Tel: (021) 0332 6000
www.titania.gr
Large hotel near the railway station. Roof garden. **€**

IRELAND

The Place

Area: 70,182 sq km (27,097 sq miles)
Capital: Dublin
Population: 4.7 million
Language: English and Irish (Gaelic)
Time Zone: GMT; EST +5.
Currency: Euro (EUR)
Telephone Dialling Codes:
International code: 353. Area codes: Dublin 1; Cork 21; Tralee 66

Visas and Passports

See page 325.

Customs

See page 325.

Public Holidays

1 January – New Year's Day; 17 March – St Patrick's Day; March/April – Good Friday, Easter Monday;

Dublin Pearse station, Ireland.

1 May – May Day; June first Monday; August first Monday; October last Monday; 25 December – Christmas Day; 26 December – St Stephen's Day.

Tourist Offices

In Dublin
14 Upper O'Connell Street
Tel: 1890 324 583
www.discoverireland.ie

Embassies and Consulates

UK
29 Merrion Road, Ballsbridge, Dublin 4
Tel: (01) 205 3700
www.gov.uk/world/organisations/british-embassy-dublin

US
42 Elgin Road, Ballsbridge, Dublin 4
Tel: 3531 668 8777
www.ie.usembassy.gov

Money

Banks open 9.30am–4.30pm, Monday–Friday. Branches in small towns may close from 12.30–1.30pm. Most Dublin banks open until 5pm on Thursday. Travellers' cheques are accepted at all banks, money-change kiosks and many hotels. Banks generally offer the best rates for cash but bureaux de change open later. ATMs are plentiful.

Health

UK and other EU visitors who go to a doctor (or, in an emergency, a hospital) must present some proof of identity (eg driving licence) and request treatment under the EU health agreement. EU travellers will need their EHIC card for this (see page 327). Medical insurance is highly advisable for all other visitors. Local health boards arrange consultations with doctors. Pharmacies only dispense limited medicines without prescription. They open during normal shopping hours, though some stay open until 10pm in larger towns.

⏲ Useful Numbers

Emergencies: 999 (North), 112 (Republic)

Safety and Crime

Pickpocketing is a problem on crowded shopping streets, and it's not advisable to wander around late at night north of the River Liffey in Dublin. If you get into trouble, contact the Gardaí or Guards (police).

Opening Hours

Banks: 10am–4pm Monday–Friday. Branches in small towns may close from 12.30pm–1.30pm. Most Dublin banks are open until 5pm on Thursday.
Shops: generally 9am–5 or 6pm, 9pm on Thursdays; many smaller newsagents will stay open later and in Dublin mini-supermarkets are open until late in the evening.
Post offices: 9am–5.30pm Monday–Friday; 9am–1pm Saturday.

Train System

Trains in the Irish Republic are operated by Iarnród Éireann (IR; www.irishrail.ie); and by Northern Irish Railways in Northern Ireland (NIR; www.translink.co.uk). Cross-border services are jointly operated. Services are limited on public holidays, especially at Christmas, New Year and Easter.

Ticket Details

Tickets can be purchased from any bus or railway station in the Republic, online, or through a travel agent abroad. Second-class tickets are standard with first-class sometimes also available. Tickets vary according to the amount of flexibility they offer: whether they can be cancelled or not; or whether you use a train other than the one you

On the line near Killiney.

have booked. Reservation is advised on any Intercity train and on any other popular route. Be in your seat at least 5 minutes before departure.

Discount Passes

Interrail and **Eurail** passes are valid for travel in the Republic, excluding city services. Discounts are available from ferry operators Irish Ferries and Stena Line.

Various rail and bus passes are available. If you want to travel freely you may want to consider buying a Trekker ticket, which gives you four consecutive days of travel, or an Explorer, which can be used on any five days out of a specified two-week period. If you are going to be in and around Dublin, you may be best with a Leap Visitor Card.

Stations in Dublin

Connolly Station caters for trains to the north, although some start at Pearse Station and go through Connolly. Heuston Station is for trains to the west and south. Bus No. 90 is an express service between Connolly and Heuston. Connolly and Pearse are connected by DART suburban rail. Heuston Station has cafés and other refreshments, while Pearse and Connolly are less well equipped.

Taking Bicycles

Bicycles are not allowed on the DART or other suburban trains unless folded and suitably covered. On Intercity trains, unfolded bicycles can be stored in the guard's van (caboose) or the cycle racks where provided. You need to buy a separate ticket for your bike, which is very cheap. Alternatively, bikes can be

hired in all the major tourist towns you are likely to visit.

Where to Stay

For price categories see page 327.

Dublin

Jurys Christchurch Inn
Christchurch Place, Dublin 8
Tel: (01) 454 0000
www.jurysinn.com
New, less expensive addition to a long-established chain of hotels. Well located for the old city and Temple Bar. €€€€
Othello Guesthouse
Lower Gardiner Street, Dublin 1
Tel: (01) 855 4271
www.athelloguesthouse.com
Handy, inner north-city location near Connolly Station. Well equipped for the price. €€
The Parliament Hotel
Lord Edward Street, Dublin 2
Tel: (01) 670 8777
http://parliament.indublinhotels.com/en/
Opposite Dublin Castle and adjacent to the lively Temple Bar district, the Parliament's Edwardian façade veils a contemporary interior. Facilities include a bar and international restaurant. €€€
Shelbourne Hotel
St. Stephen's Green, Dublin 2
Tel: (01) 663 4500
www.marriott.com
Long established as Dublin's most prestigious hotel, with plenty of old-world atmosphere. The lounge is a great place for afternoon tea, or enjoy a pint of Guinness in the Horseshoe Bar. €€€€€

Killarney

Great Southern Hotel
East Avenue, Killarney, Co.Kerry

Tel: (064) 663 8000
www.greatsouthernkilarney.com
Monumental Victorian railway hotel adjacent to town centre. Swimming, tennis, sauna and Irish entertainment nightly from May to September. €€€€

ITALY

The Place

Area: 301,338 sq km (116,346 sq miles)
Capital: Rome
Population: 60 million
Language: Italian
Time Zone: GMT +1; EST +6.
Currency: Euro (EUR)
Telephone Dialling Codes: International code: 39. Area codes: Palermo 091; Florence 055; Pisa 050; Genoa 010; Rome 06; Milan 02; Naples 081; Venice 041. Area codes are included in all calls, including those made from within the same area. The initial 0 is never omitted.

Visas and passports

See page 325.

Customs

See page 325.

Public Holidays

1 January – New Year's Day; 6 January – Epiphany; March/April – Easter Sunday, Easter Monday; 25 April – National Day of Liberation; 1 May – Labour Day; Whit Sunday; 15 August – Assumption; 1 November – All Saints' Day; 8 December

– Immaculate Conception; 25 December – Christmas Day; 26 December – St Stephen's Day.

Tourist Offices

In Rome
Via de San Basilio 51 (Piazza Barborini)
Tel: 06 06 08
www.italia.it; www.turismoroma.it

Embassies and Consulates

UK
Via XX Settembre 80a (Porta Pia), 00187 Roma RM
Tel: 06 4220 0001
www.ukinitaly.fco.gov.uk.

USA
Via Vittorio Veneto 119/A, 00187 Roma
Tel: 06 46741
www.it.usembassy.gov

Money

Banks are generally open 8.30am–1.30pm, and for an hour in the afternoon (usually 3–4pm), from Monday to Friday. Given the long queues for money changing in Italy, it is simplest to get cash from ATMs. Be aware when using credit cards that many banks charge large fees for cash advances. Travellers' cheques are easily exchanged at banks, which offer the best rates. Hotels and bureaux de change also exchange currencies.

In cities, most of the restaurants, hotels, shops and stores will take major credit cards, but in some rural areas especially, you may be able to pay only in cash.

Health and Emergencies

Health insurance is recommended. Most hospitals have a 24-hour emergency department called *Pronto Soccorso*. For more minor complaints, seek out a *farmacia*, identified by a sign displaying a red cross within a white circle. Normal opening hours are 8.30am–12.30pm

High-speed Alstom AGV train, Milan.

and 3–7.30/8pm Monday–Saturday. Outside these hours the address of the nearest *farmacia* on night duty is posted in the window.

Safety and Crime

Tourist-targeted crime consists mainly of pickpocketing and bag snatching. Be extra cautious in Rome and Naples; do not leave bags unattended on any train. Always ask for ID before surrendering a ticket or paying any so-called fine.

Opening Hours

Shops open 9am–1pm and 3.30 or 4–7.30 or 8pm although department stores and shops in cities tend to open 9.30am–7.30pm. Almost everything closes on Sunday. Shops often also close on Monday (sometimes in the morning only) and some shut on Saturday.

Train System

Most Italian trains are operated by the Ferrovie dello Stato (FS; www.trenitalia.com), under the brand name Trenitalia. Some private companies compete on the most profitable lines with Trenatalia or run certain lines exclusively. These other operators include Ferrovie Emilia Romagna (FER, www.fer-online.it) around Bologna; Ferrovie Nord Milano (www.ferrovienord.it) from Milan; SAD (www.sad.it) in the Dolomites; and Trenord www.trenord.it) in Lombardia. Train information is available from staff at *uffici informazioni* at most major stations.

Types of Train
The figureheads of the network are the Frecciarossa luxury high-speed trains between major cities; next down are the only slightly slower Frecciargento trains, and then the Frecciablanca and *InterCity* trains, which stop rather more frequently. All are air-conditioned and very comfortable. Supplements (supplementi) are charged for these trains, and it is obligatory to reserve a seat, although this can be done up to a few minutes before the train departs. On long-distance routes, overnight sleeper trains are also available.

More local trains may be called Regionale, Diretto, Interregionale (cross-country) or, rather

Verona Porta Nuova railway station, Italy.

inappropriately, *Espresso*. They are much slower, since they generally stop at many stations. No reservations are necessary for regional trains.

Ticket Details

Trenitalia tickets for first and second class come as base (fully flexible), economy and super economy (non-refundable and non-transferable to another train). Queues at stations can be long so it's best to buy tickets at travel agents, or online at www.ferroviedellostato.it. Fares are calculated per kilometre. Passengers must stamp local tickets in the station before boarding and if, for some reason, that is not possible, try to find the conductor before they find you. Reservations can be made at most travel agencies as well as at stations.

Discount Passes
Interrail and **Eurail Pass** are valid for travel in Italy. If you haven't got a pass, you can economise by buying a 10-journey travel ticket but this must be used in conjunction with a travel card.

City Stations

Rome: Termini station handles most main national and international traffic. Ostiense and Tiburtina serve long-distance north–south trains.
Milan: Most long-distance trains terminate at Centrale. Some trains terminate at Porta Garibaldi station.
Naples: Most long-distance trains terminate at Napoli Centrale, which is connected to the new high-speed interchange, Stazione Napoli-Afragola. Mergellina and Campi Flegrei stations are further west and

handle mainly local trains. Trains to Pompeii and Sorrento depart from Stazione Circumvesuviana.

Train Talk

arrival, arrives *arrivo, arriva*
calls at *ferma a*
change at *cambiare a*
departure, departs *partenza, parte*
every xx minutes *ogni xx minuti*
first class *la prima classe*
how much is it? *quanto costa?*
journey *viaggio, percorso*
platform *binario*
railway station *stazione (ferroviaria)*
return *un biglietto di andata e ritorno*
second class *seconda classe*
single *un biglietto di andata sola*
sleeping car *vagone letto*
ticket *biglietto*
train *treno*
when does the train depart for...? *quando parte il treno per...?*
where? *dove?*

Taking Bicycles

It is possible to carry bicycles in the luggage cars on R *(Regionale)*, IR *(Interregionale)* and D *(Diretto)* trains, for a small fee. They are not generally permitted on fast IC, EC or EuroNight trains. You can board all regional, inter-regional, direct and suburban trains bearing a bicycle symbol but you will need a ticket. Transport is free for bikes when they are in a bike bag.

Where to Stay

For price categories see page 327.

Cagliari
Sardegna Hotel Cagliari
Via Lunigiana 50, Cagliari I-09122
Tel: 080 70 286245

www.sardegnahotelcagliari.it
A good three-star hotel situated only 2km (1 mile) from the railway station. €€€

Milan

Mennini
Via Napo Torriani 14
Tel: 02 669 0951
www.hotelmennini.com
A first-class hotel, located only 150 metres from central railway station, and close to the Castello Sforzesco, La Scala Opera Theatre, Via Montenapoleone and Piazzo dell Scala. €€€€

Excelsior Gallia
Piazza Duca d'Aosta 9, 20124 Milano
Tel: 02 6785 787
www.starwoodhotels.com
Located beside Stazione Centrale, with many superb rooms that feature original Art Deco marble bathrooms. The staff are friendly and professional. The hotel also has an excellent restaurant. €€€€

Michelangelo
Piazza Luigi di Savoia 6
Tel: 02 67551
www.michelangelomilan.com
Set close to the Stazione Centrale, the Michelangelo is one of the best-run hotels in Milan, and, despite its anonymous setting in a tower, it has not lost the personal touch. Sound facilities and efficient service. €€€€

Naples

Grand Hotel Vesuvio
Via Partenope 45
Tel: 081 76 40 044
www.vesuvio.it
Situated in a sunny waterfront position overlooking the Bay of Naples and dominating the Santa Lucia harbour. Most rooms have a balcony or terrace with an excellent view of the Mediterranean and Vesuvius. Just over 500 metres/yds from the railway station. €€€€€

NH Napoli Ambassador
Via Medina 70
Tel: 081 410 5111
www.nh-hotels.com
Italy's tallest hotel gives panoramic views of Naples. Situated in the heart of the city close to the Piazza del Municipio, and less than 500 metres/yds from the railway station. €€€€

Palermo

Villa Igiea
Salita Belmonte 43
Tel: 091 631 2111
www.villa-igiea.com
Overlooking the Bay of Palermo and set in splendid terraced gardens of jasmine with a swimming pool, the Villa Igiea is one of Sicily's best hotels. €€€€€

NH Palermo
Via Foro Italico 22b
Tel: 091 616 5090
www.nh-hotels.com
A first-class hotel with a magnificent swimming pool in luxuriant gardens. The hotel is on the seafront and just a few steps from the gardens of Villa Giulia. The harbour and the railway station are just 500 metres/yds away. €€€

Rome

Hotel Doria
Via Merulana 4, 00185 Roma
Tel: 06 446 5888
www.doriahotel.it
A simple hotel just five minutes' walk from Stazione Termini. Small and clean, it has a TV and mini-bar in some rooms. €€€€

St Regis
Via Orlando Vittorio Emanuele 3, 00185 Roma
Tel: 06 47091
www.stregisrome.com
Between the railway station and the Via Veneto area, this exclusive, dignified hotel is very well run and stylish. It is set in a patrician palace and graced with Chinese and Japanese rugs, chandeliers and antiques. €€€€€

Select
Via V Bachelet 6
Tel: 06 445 6383
www.hotelselectgarden.com
Close to the station, this small friendly hotel has the feel of a secluded villa. Good value. €€

Rome's St Regis hotel.

Venice

Abbazia
Priuli dei Cavaletti, 66–8 Cannaregio
Tel: 041 717 333
www.abbaziahotel.com
Converted monastery with 39 rooms and the hotel is framed by a garden. Within easy reach of the railway station (150 metres/yds) and Piazzale Roma. €€€€

Hotel Carlton and Grand Canal
Santa Croce, 578
Tel: 041 862 0480
www.carlton.hotelinvenice.com
Well-equipped hotel on the Grand Canal, convenient for the station. €€€€

PORTUGAL

The Place

Area: 92,345 sq km (35,655 sq miles), including Madeira and the Azores
Capital: Lisbon
Population: 10.6 million
Language: Portuguese
Time Zone: GMT (summer time GMT + 1); EST +6;
Currency: Euro (EUR)
Telephone Dialling Codes: International code: 351
All domestic calls are 9-digit numbers, with no area codes.

Visas and Passports

See page 325.

Customs

See page 325.

⏱ Useful Numbers

All emergencies (Police, Fire, Ambulance): 112

Public Holidays

1 January – New Year's Day; mid to late February – Carnival (preceding Lent); March/April – Good Friday, Easter; 25 April – Anniversary of the Revolution (1974); 1 May – Labour Day; 10 June – Portugal and Camões Day; early June – Corpus Christi; 15 August – Day of the Assumption; 5 October – Republic Day; 1 November – All Saints' Day; 1 December – Restoration of Independence; 8 December – Day of the Immaculate Conception; 25 December – Christmas Day.

Tourist Offices

www.visitportugal.com
Lisboa Welcome Centre, is in Praça do Comercio (tel: 910-517 886
www.visitlisboa.com

Embassies and Consulates

UK

Rua São Bernardo 33, Lisbon
Tel: (21) 392 4000
www.ukinportugal.fco.gov.uk

USA

Av. das Forças Armadas, Lisbon
Tel: (21) 727 3300
www.pt.embassy.gov

Money

There are banks in all but the smallest towns. Changing cash at a bank or ATM is far cheaper than paying the higher rate of commission on travellers' cheques. Visa, AmEx, Maestro and MasterCard are widely accepted. ATMs, usually called *multibanco*, take all major cards. Travellers' cheques are accepted in banks.

Health

Private treatment must be paid for, so it is best to take out health insurance. For minor complaints, consult a pharmacy – a list of those open late is in the window of each and also in newspapers. As part of the EU, emergency medical treatment is free or reduced-cost provided you have an EHIC (see page 327) and your passport or ID card. Beware of sunburn. Use sunscreen and wear a hat. Tap water is generally drinkable, but it is best to use bottled water (*água mineral*).

Safety and Crime

Portugal has a well-deserved reputation for non-violence, though petty theft is becoming a problem in some areas of Lisbon and Porto. Report theft to the police within 24 hours in order to claim insurance.

Opening Hours

Shops: 9am–1pm and 3–7pm Monday–Friday, 9am–1pm Saturday. Large supermarkets remain open all day Saturday and half-day Sunday and holidays.
Banks: main branches open 8.30am–3pm Monday–Friday; closed Saturday, Sunday and holidays. Some in Lisbon open until 6pm.
Post Offices: 9am–6pm Monday–Friday. Some central offices have extended opening hours.

Train System

Caminhos de Ferro Portugueses (CP; www.cp.pt.) is Portugal's national operator.
The main categories of train in Portugal are Alfa Pendular (AP) a high-speed tilting train (*rápido*) between Lisbon and the Algarve, and in the North, Oporto and Braga. Intercidades (Intercity trains), also known as *directos*; and interregional (IR), semi-fast trains known as *semidirectos*. *Regionais* and *Suburbano* services are local stopping trains. Sud-Express trains are international train services to Vigo, Madrid and Paris.

Ticket Details

Tickets cost very little, with a choice of first- or second-class, smoking or non-smoking. Because everyone who takes the Douro line on a regular basis knows the 'glamour view' (the Douro River) is on the right-hand side (going to Pocinho, on the left side coming back) seats in these coveted positions fill up early. Latecomers are advised to go for one of the relatively empty and still-inexpensive 1st-class compartments. Look for the sign that

Local train in the Duoro Valley.

says *bilheteiras* (tickets). There are fines for boarding the train without a ticket or pass.

Discount Passes

The **Interrail** and **Eurail Pass** are valid in Portugal. The Portugal Rail Pass (for visitors to the country only) gives unlimited travel in the country for three or seven days within a month. First- and second-class versions are available. The Tourist Travel Card gives unlimited travel in and around Lisbon and Porto and in the Algarve.

Reservations

Seats must be reserved in advance on AP and IC trains, plus international services. Fare supplements are also payable. Bookings can be made at any CP office or through selected ticket agents.

Stations in Porto/Lisbon

Porto: Fast trains to Lisbon depart from Campanhã station, just outside the city centre; most other trains depart from the central São Bento station, calling in at Campanhã as they exit the city.
Lisbon: There are four railway stations in Lisbon plus Barreiro on the south side of the River Tagus. Trains for the north of Portugal, Spain, France and beyond depart from Santa Apolónia and the ultra-modern Oriente station. Those heading for Sintra and Figueira da Foz on the coast north of Lisbon depart from Rossio station, while local trains to Cascais and Estoril depart from Cais do Sodré station. Trains to the Algarve depart from Barreiro, on the

Rossio station, Lisbon.

other side of the Tagus and reached by ferry from Lisbon; buy inclusive ferry/train tickets at Sul e Sueste station.

Train Talk

arrivals *chegadas*
daily *cadadia*
departures *partida*
exit *a saída*
first class *primeira classe*
how much is it? *Quanto custa?*
platform *plataforma*
railway station *estação*
reservation *reserva*
return *retorn-bilhete/bilhete de ida e volta*
second class *segunda classe*
single *bilhete de ida*
sleeping car *uma couchette*
ticket *bilhete*
train *comboio*
when does the train depart for...? *a que hora parta el comboio para...?*
where is the...? *Onde é...?*

Taking Bicycles

Bicycles may be carried on many Portuguese trains, depending on available space. It is best to find out the specific requirements for your journey before you travel. Coimbra Urban, Inter-regional and Regional services charge a fee to carry bicycles at weekends, on public holidays and off-peak times – ask the ticket inspector for a bicycle ticket. Bikes can only be taken on the fast AP trains if they are disassembled first.

Where to Stay

For price categories see page 327.

Lisbon

Alfama Terrace
Travessa dos Remedios 15
Tel: 965 258 461
www.alfamaterrace.com
A short walk from Santa Apolónia station. Air-conditioned apartments with private terraces. €€

Porto

Hotel Infante de Sagres
Praça D. Filipa de Lencastre, 62
Tel: 351 223 398 500
www.hotelinfantesagres.pt
Splendid old hotel right in the centre of Porto, with rooms that are full of character. Less than 500 metres/yds from São Bento station. €€€€€
Mercure Porto Centro
Praça de Batalha, 116
Tel: 22 204 3300
www.accorhotels.com
Overlooking the old centre of Porto, and just 250 metres/yds from São Bento station; 140 air-conditioned rooms. €€€

RUSSIA

The Place

Area: 17.1 million sq km (6.59 million sq miles)
Capital: Moscow
Population: 145.4 million
Language: Russian
Time Zone: Russia has 11 time zones. Moscow and St Petersburg are GMT +3; EST +8
Currency: Ruble (RUB)
Telephone Dialling Codes: International code: 7. Area codes: Moscow 495 or 499; St Petersburg 812

Visas passports and customs

To obtain a tourist visa from a Russian embassy or consulate, you will need a valid passport, an official application form and three passport photographs. If you apply personally, rather than through a travel agency, allow ample time, as it can take up to a month.

Carry your passport and visa at all times in Russia: the police have the right to check your identity at will.

It is best to check with the Russian consulate or embassy in your home country about what you can and can't take into or bring out of Russia. It is prohibited to export antiquities and art or cultural objects except for those imported and declared on entry. As a general rule, anything of value, including personal jewellery and electronics, should be declared upon entry to avoid a hassle when leaving. Computers, electronic notebooks and related hardware must be presented for scanning at the airport at least two hours prior to departure.

Public Holidays

2 January – 2nd day of New Year; 7 January – Russian Orthodox Christmas; 23 February – Defenders of the Motherland Day; 8 March – International Women's Day; Good Friday; 1 May – Labour Day; 9 May – Victory Day; 12 June – Independence Day; 7 November – Day of Accord and Reconciliation; 12 December – Constitution Day.

Tourist Information

www.russiatourism.ru
8/10 Neglinnaya Street, Building 1, Suites 13 & 14, Moscow, Russia 107031
Tel +7 495 623 797
www.mos.ru

Embassies and Consulates

UK

Smolenskaya Naberezhnaya 10 Moscow

⊘ Useful Numbers

Fire: 101
Police: 102
Ambulance: 103

Tel: +7 495 956 7200
www.gov.uk/world/organisations/
british-embassy-moscow

US

Bolshoy Devyatinskiy Pereulok No. 8, Moscow
Tel: +7 (095) 728 5000
www.ru.usembassy.gov

Health and Emergencies

You must take out health insurance up to a minimum of RUB 100,000 before entering Russia. Check with your doctor or the Russian embassy about recommended vaccinations to have.

It is recommended that you wash fruit and vegetables before you eat them. You should not drink tap water even in small quantities. Bottled mineral water is available everywhere.

Money

The currency in Russia is the ruble (abbreviated to RUB), and divided into 100 kopeks. US dollars and euros are not legal tender in Russia: they must be changed at a bank and never with a street trader. Major credit cards are accepted, but in some places you will only be able to pay with cash.

Safety and Crime

The usual precautions apply in Russia. Remain vigilant and don't allow yourself to be distracted in crowds. When travelling alone on a train, do not fall asleep. A useful website for emergency information is www.en.mchs.ru

Opening hours

Business hours in Russia are unpredictable, but as a general rule you can expect businesses to operate from 8 or 9am until 5 or 6pm, and to shut for anything between 1 and 3 hours for lunch in the afternoon.

Train System

The national train operator is Rossiskiye Zheleznye Dorogi (RZhD), known in English as Russian Railways. Russian Railways website is www.eng.rzd.ru. Other excellent sources of advice in English are www.realrussia.co.uk, (which even includes

a visual guide to a Russian railway ticket) and www.seat61.com. Russian Railways oversees a vast network of 83,000km (50,000 miles) of track. Russia has direct international rail connections with Beijing, Berlin, Budapest, Helsinki, Nice, Paris, Prague, Sofia, Tallinn Vienna and Warsaw. The top Russian train is the Sapsan, which came into service at the end of 2013. It can reach speeds of 250km/h (155mph). For the Trans-Siberian Railway, see page 92.

Tickets and Reservations

Tickets can be bought at railway stations, from travel agents, over the phone or online at www.eng.rzd.ru/. For all but local trains reservation is necessary and passports and visas must be presented. Interrail and Eurail passes are not recognised in Russia.

Most trains operate over long distances and seats convert to berths. There are three categories: Spalny (CB) first-class two-berth; Kupeiny (K) second-class four-berth; and Platskartny (Pl) open-plan dormitory cars. There are also cheap 'hard seat' carriages known as Obshchi (O), best avoided for anything other than short journeys.

For a detailed explanation of Russian railway tickets (including a visual guide), see www.poezda.net/en.

Stations in Moscow and St Petersburg

There are nine major stations in Moscow. Belorusskaya serves Belarus, Poland, the Czech Republic,

Grand Europe Hotel, St Petersburg.

Slovakia, Austria and Germany; Oktyabrskaya (also known by its former name, Leningradskaya) serves routes north to Helsinki and St Petersburg; Kiyevskaya serves routes running south and southwest to the Ukraine, Moldova, Hungary, former Yugoslavia, Croatia, Romania and Bulgaria. The Trans-Siberian Express operates from Yaroslavskaya.

St Petersburg has five principal stations Finlyandski (famous for its associations with the returning exile, Lenin) serves Finland; Glavny (also known as Moskovsky), serves Moscow and Murmansk; Vitebski serves the Baltic States, Ukraine, Belarus, Poland, the Czech Republic, Hungary and Germany.

Train Talk

arrivals *priyezd priezd*
departures *otyezd otezd*
first class *pervoklassnee pervoklassnyj*
platform *plataforma platforma*
railway station *vokzal vokzal*
reservation *zakaz zakaz*
return *obratnee bilyet obratnyj bilet*
second class *vtoroy klass vtoroj klass*
single *bilyet v odeen konyets bilet v odin konec*
ticket *bilyet bilet*
train *poyezd poezd*
when does the train depart for...? *kogda otkhodeet poyezd v kogda otxodit poezd v...?*

Where to stay

Moscow

Arbat
Plotnikov per, 12
Tel: (499) 271 28 01
www.arbat-photel.ru/en
Three-star hotel in the heart of the city, 5–10 minutes' drive from the Kremlin, and just 150 metres/yds from the pedestrianised Arbat. The nearest metro station is Smolenskaya, a 3-minute walk. €€€€
Baltschug Kempinski
Ul. Balchug, 1
Tel: (495) 287 2000
www.kempinski-moscow.com
Luxury hotel on the river bank, 5 minutes' walk from the Kremlin. The nearest metros are Novokuznetskaya and Tretyakovskaya. €€€€
Marriott Grand
Tverskaya Street, 26/1
Tel: (495) 937 0000

www.marriott.com
Comfortable Art Nouveau five-star hotel in the heart of the city centre, surrounded by traditional 18th-century buildings. Facilities include sauna and pool. The nearest metro is Mayakovskaya – about 5 minutes' walk. €€€€

Radisson Slavyanskaya
Berezhkovskaya Nab, 2
Tel: (495) 941 8020
www.radissonblu.com
Luxury hotel in the west of the city with several fine restaurants and a good view of the river. Next door to Kievsky railway terminal and metro. €€€€

St Petersburg

Corinthia
Nevskij Prospekt, 57
Tel: 812 380 2001
www.corinthia.com
Comfortable five-star hotel in the centre of town, which has preserved its original historical style facade. The nearest metro is Ploschad Vosstanya/Mayakovskaya. €€€€

Grand Hotel Europe
Ulitsa Mihailovskaya, 1/7
Tel: (812) 329 6000
www.belmond.com
A five-star hotel dating to the beginning of 19th century and in the heart of the city. Tchaikovsky spent his honeymoon here, and George Bernard Shaw dined with Maxim Gorky. The nearest metro is Gostiny Dvor. €€€€

St Petersburg
Pirogovskaya Nab, 5/2
Tel (812) 380 1919
www.hotel-spb.com

Ticket inspector in Norway.

Overlooking the River Neva, close to Finlyandsky station. €€€€

SCANDINAVIA

The Place

Finland

Area: 338,145 sq km (130,559 sq miles)
Capital: Helsinki
Population: 5.5 million
Language: Finnish, Swedish in some places
Time Zone: GMT +2; EST + 7. Clocks advance 1 hour late March until late October
Currency: Euro (EUR)
Telephone Dialling Codes: International code: 358. Area codes: Helsinki 09; Tempere 03; Turku 02

Norway

Area: 323,759 sq km (125,004 sq miles)
Capital: Oslo
Population: 5.3 million
Language: Norwegian
Time Zone: GMT + 1; EST +7. Clocks advance 1 hour from late March until late October
Currency: Krone (NOK)
Telephone Dialling Codes: International code: 47. All numbers are 8-digit – no area codes required

Sweden

Area: 449,964 sq km (173,732 sq miles)
Capital: Stockholm
Population: 9.1 million

Languages: Swedish, Finnish, Sami
Time Zone: GMT + 1; EST +7. Clocks advance 1 hour from late March until late October
Currency: Krona (SEK)
Telephone Dialling Codes: International code: 46. Area codes: Stockholm 8; Göteborg 31; Malmö 40; Ostersund 63

Visas and Passports

Scandinavian citizens may freely move between their countries without a passport, but still need some form of ID. Citizens of most other countries require a passport for stays of less than three months.

Customs

Finland

As with other EU countries – see page 325.

Norway

Customs allowances are very similar to those of the EU countries. On top of the tax-free quota you may bring in 4 litres wine or liquor against payment of duty.

Sweden

As with other EU countries – see page 325.

Tourist Offices

Finnish

In the UK
Lyric House, 149 Hammersmith Road, London W14 0QL
Tel: (020) 7838 6200
https://www.visitfinland.com/

In the US
655 3rd Avenue, New York, NY 10017
Tel: (212) 885 9700
https://www.visitfinland.com/

Norwegian

In the UK
Charles House, 5th Floor, 5 Lower Regent Street, London SW1Y 4LR
Tel: (020) 7839 8820
www.visitnorway.co.uk

In the US
655 Third Avenue, Suite 1810, New York, NY 10017
Tel: (212) 885 9700
www.norway.org

Train in Finland.

Swedish

In the UK
Travel and Tourism Council, Swedish Embassy, 11 Montagu Place, London W1H 2AL
Tel: (020) 7724 5868
www.visitsweden.com

In the US
Tourism Council: PO Box 4649, Grand Central Station, New York, NY 100163-4649
Tel: (212) 885 9700
www.visitsweden.com

Embassies and Consulates

UK

Finland
Itäinen Puistotie 17, 00140 Helsinki
Tel: (09) 2286 5100
https://www.gov.uk/world/organisations/british-embassy-helsinki

Norway
Thomas Heftyesgate 8, 0244 Oslo
Tel: 23 13 27 00
https://www.gov.uk/world/organisations/british-embassy-oslo

Sweden
Skarpögatan 6–8, Box 27819, 11593 Stockholm
Tel: (08) 671 3000
https://www.gov.uk/world/organisations/british-embassy-stockholm

US

Finland
Itäinen Puistotie 14B, FIN-00140 Helsinki
Tel: (09) 616 250
https://fi.usembassy.gov/

Norway
Morgedalsvegen 36, 0378 Oslo
Tel: 21 30 85 40
https://no.usembassy.gov/

Sweden
Dag Hammarskjölds Väg 31, SE-115 89, Stockholm
Tel: (08) 783 53 00
https://se.usembassy.gov/

Money

Finland is the only Scandinavian country to adopt the Euro. Credit and debit cards are accepted almost everywhere, with Visa, American Express, Mastercard and Diner's Club the most common. ATMs are ubiquitous.

Health and Emergencies

The standard of health provision is very high in Scandinavia, and even in remote areas you should have no problem getting medical help. In Norway and Finland, if you are ill ask your hotel, tourist office or a pharmacy for the address of an English-speaking GP. There is no GP system in Sweden, so the place to go for any type of treatment is the nearest hospital. Casualty *(akutmottagning)* deals with serious problems, but out-patients clinics *(vårdcentral or husläkarmottagning)* are a better option since you will normally be seen within an hour. Take your passport with you and your EHIC, if applicable. Note that you will still need to pay part of the cost, which is non-refundable. Make sure you keep receipts if you have medical insurance.

☉ Useful Numbers

All emergency services (ambulance, fire and police) 112

For minor problems, head for a pharmacy. Most larger cities have all-night pharmacies; if closed a list will usually be posted on the door of each informing you of nearby all-night pharmacies. Mosquitos in the far north in high summer can be vicious.

Safety and Crime

Scandinavia is generally a law-abiding region. Crime figures are low, and the streets of the cities are by and large safe. Petty theft is the most likely danger so keep an eye on your passport and cash.

Opening Times

Finland
Shops generally open from 9am–8pm; in Helsinki many open until 9pm weekdays and 6pm on Saturdays. Supermarkets open from 9am–8pm weekdays, and until 4pm on Saturday. Banks are open Monday–Friday 9am–4.15pm. Some exchange bureaux open later, particularly at airports and main railway stations, and at international ferry terminals.

Norway
Shops are open Monday–Friday 9am–5pm, until 7pm on Thursday, and on Saturday from 9am–3pm. Shopping centres tend to stay open until 8pm on weekdays and 6pm on Saturday. Banks are open on weekdays from 8.30am–3.15pm (until 4.30 or 5pm Thursday).

Sweden
Shops open Monday–Friday 9.30am–6pm, and on Saturdays until 3 or 4pm. In larger cities many open on Sunday, usually noon–4pm. Banks are open Monday–Friday 10am–3pm (4pm Thursday, 6pm in some larger cities), and closed on Saturdays.

Train Systems

Finland
Finland's railways are run by VR Ltd (www.vr.fi). There are five main types of train. The **Pendolino** (S) is a high-speed tilting train. A fare supplement is payable and there are first- and second-class compartments. The new double-decker **InterCity** (IC) expresses have first- and second-class, provide service for wheelchair users, have a play space for children, luggage lockers,

Onboard the Inlandsbanan.

bicycle and ski locks and designated compartments for families, passengers with pets and allergy sufferers. **Express** *(pikajunat)* and **regional** *(taajamajunat)* trains have second-class compartments only. **Sleeper trains** operate between Helsinki, Tampere, Oulu and Rovaniemi.

Norway

Norwegian railways are operated by the Norges Statsbaner (NSB; www.nsb.no). Express trains are either tilting **Signatur** services or the standard **Ekspresstog (Et)**; other tilting trains include **Agenda**. Other trains generally only have second-class seating. Signatur and some other express trains have 'family' carriages with a play area for children. Night trains with couchettes and sleepers (first/second-class) operate on the Oslo–Stavanger, Oslo–Bergen, Oslo–Trondheim and Trondheim–Bodø routes. Supplement fares are payable on Signatur and Et trains.

Sweden

Swedish trains are run by Swedish State Railways (Statens Järnvägar; SJ; www.sj.se/en); several local lines are run by smaller companies – rail passes are not always valid on these lines; check with a tourist office. 95 percent of Swedish trains are electric. High-speed **X2000** trains are the most prestigious, operating on most long-distance routes in the country. Other fast trains are called **InterCity**, on which a smaller fare supplement is payable. X2000 and selected InterCity trains have family coaches, with play areas for children. Overnight trains with first- and second-class sleepers and couchettes operate on the Stockholm–Malmo–Copenhagen route, and between Stockholm and northern Sweden.

Ticket Details

Finland

Tickets are sold at railway stations, travel agencies and online at www.sj.se/en. Several train passes are valid for travelling in Finland: the **Finnrailpass** is good for unlimited travel on all trains in Finland for 3, 5 or 10 days within one month; the **Eurail Scandinavia Pass** offers you unlimited travel in Denmark, Finland, Norway and Sweden for 4–10 days travel (second-class) within a two-month period; and the **Interrail Pass** is also valid.

Norway

The **Eurail Norway Pass** offers 3–8 days of second-class travel within one month. For non-Europeans it also qualifies you for additional discounts on several ferries. **Interrail, Eurail Scandinavia Pass** and **Eurailpass** are valid in Norway.

Sweden

An adult passenger (not using a rail pass) can be accompanied by two children (under 16) at no extra charge on X2000 and InterCity trains. Under 26s pay 70 percent of the full fare. The **Eurail Sweden Pass** offers unlimited first- or second-class rail travel within Sweden. Choose between 3–8 travel days within one month. A **Tågplus** ticket enables you to use rail, bus and ferry networks. **Eurail Scandinavia Pass** and **Interrail Pass** are all valid.

Reservations

Finland
Advance tickets on S220 (Pendolino), InterCity (IC) and Express (P) trains indicate a seat reservation. Seats may be booked for allergic or disabled passengers, and in Express

trains a seat in the children's playroom car or video car. It is not possible to book a seat in advance on a regional train
Norway
Seat reservations are compulsory on Signatur and Et trains, and on other trains marked with a boxed 'R' on timetables. An additional fee has to be paid for reservation of seats, couchettes and sleepers.

You can buy tickets from www.nsb.no and collect them on the train, or have them sent to an address in Norway. Seat reservations can be made up to 90 days before travel.
Sweden
Seat reservations are recommended on most services: they are necessary on X2000 and overnight trains, but not on InterCity services. Reservations can be made on most long-distance journeys; reserved seats must be claimed no later than 15 minutes after departure. See www.sj.se/en/ for more details. X2000 and some InterCity trains have a special carriage with a wheelchair lift and a bookable space for a wheelchair.

Train Talk

Finland

arrivals *saapuvat*
change here for *matkustavat vaihtavat junaa*
daily *päivittäin*
departures *lähtevä*
first class *primaarinen kurssi*
how much is it? *paljonko tämä maksaa?*
platform *ulkoportaat*
railway station *rautatieasema/asema*
reservation *reservaatti*
return *korko*
second class *sekunti kurssi*
sleeping car *makuuvaunu*
thank you *kiitos*
ticket *lippu*
train *juna*
when? *j?*
where is...? *missä on...?*

Norway

arrival *ankomst*
daily *daglig*
departure *avgang, a€€ik, avreise*
first class *første klasse*
how much is it? *hvaor mye koster det*
platform *perrong*
railway station *stasjon*
reservation *reservasjon*
return *tur-retur*
second class *andre klasse*

single *en vei*
sleeping car *sovevogn*
ticket *billet*
train *tog*
where is...? *hvor er...?*

Sweden

arrival hall *ankomsthall*
change here *byter om tåg*
daily *daglig*
departure hall *avgångshall*
first class *förstklassig*
how much is it? *vad kostar det?*
platform *kateder/läktare*
please *tack/var så god*
railway station *station*
reservation *reservera*
return journey *återfärd/tur och retur*
second class *andraklassbiljett*
single *enda/enkel/ogift*
sleeping car *so€€agn*
ticket *biljett*
train *tåg*
when? *när?*
where is ...? *var är ...?*

Bicycles

Finland

To transport a bicycle on Pendolino and IC trains you need to book in advance. One bicycle per passenger is admitted for transportation in the guard's van, for a fee. Bicycles cannot be taken on Helsinki region commuter trains during rush hour Monday–Friday (7–9am and 3–6pm).

Norway

Bicycles can be taken free on most trains (on fast trains look for the bicycle symbol on timetables) but a charge is made for carrying bikes on the Bergen and Flåm railways. Reservations for transporting bikes

Grand Hotel in Oslo.

can only be made in Norway and should be made well in advance for long-distance and intercity trains (www.nsb.no); on most local trains, you can't reserve: if there is space, you can take your bike.

Sweden

Bicycles are only permitted on the Øresund line serving Gothenburg–Copenhagen and Kalmar–Alvesta–Copenhagen routes, and for half the price of a standard ticket. Microcycles and children's cycles may be taken aboard as hand luggage without charge. You can also take your bicycle on a train in Skåne as the local transport provider (Skånetrafiken) reserves space on the Pågatågen trains

Where to Stay

Finland Hotels

For price categories see page 327.

Helsinki
€€
Radisson Blu Royal
Runeberginkatu 2, 00100
Tel: 358 (0) 20 1234 701
https://www.radissonblu.com/en/royalhotel-helsink
Sunny, open dining and bar areas and the usual good service. About a 10-minute walk from the centre. €€€€

Norway Hotels

For price categories see page 327.

Bergen
Grand Hotel Terminus
Zander Kaaes Gate 6
Tel: 55 21 25 00

www.ght.no
In a great location opposite the station, this elegant hotel has been a popular stopover for wealthy tourists since 1928. The comfortable rooms are beautifully decorated and the restaurant serves fine Norwegian cuisine with many dishes unique to Bergen. Closed at Easter.
€€€

Oslo
Bristol
Kristian IV's Gate 7
Tel: 22 82 60 00
www.bristol.no
Famous hotel, with ornate lobby and antiques in the bedrooms. Less than 500 metres/yds from the station.
€€€
Grand Hotel
Karl Johans Gate 31
Tel: 23 21 20 00
www.grand.no
On Oslo's main thoroughfare since 1874, this exclusive hotel has been the site for many Nobel Prize celebrations and where visiting heads of state tend to stay. Less than 500 metres/yds from Sentral station.
€€€€
Clarion Royal Christiania Hotel
Biskop Gunnerus' gate 3, N-0106
Tel: 23 10 80 00
www.royalchristiania.no
Magnificent atrium, spacious rooms, wonderful service and breakfasts; convenient location less than 100 metres/yds from Oslo Sentral station. €€€€

Trondheim
Clarion Grand Olav Hotel
Kjøpmannsgata 48, 7010 Trondheim
Tel: 73 80 80 80
https://bit.ly/2scET25/
Top-class hotel in the heart of Trondheim. Close to shops, bars and restaurants. Less than 1km (0.5 mile) from the railway station. €€€

Sweden Hotels

For price categories see page 327.

Östersund
Scandic Hotel South
Krondikesvagen 97, Östersund, 83146
Tel: (063) 127 560
www.scandichotels.com/hotels/sweden/ostersund
First-class hotel with satellite TV, gymnasium, sauna and solarium.
€€€

Stockholm
Radisson SAS Royal Viking Hotel Stockholm
Klarabergsgatan and Vsagatan
Tel: (08) 5065 4000
www.radissonblu.com/en/royalvikinghotel-stockholm
Modern and tastefully designed rooms in the very heart of Stockholm; convenient for the station. €€€€

Scandic Continental Hotel
Vasagatan S-101, 22 Stockholm
Tel: (08) 5173 4200
www.scandichotels.com/hotels/sweden/stockholm/scandic-continental
A first-class hotel located in the city centre. Facilities include a sauna and relaxation room. €€€€

SPAIN

The Place

Area: 505,988 sq km (195,363 sq miles)
Capital: Madrid
Population: 47 million
Language: Spanish (Castilian), plus Catalan, Basque and Galician
Time Zone: GMT +1; EST +6.
Currency: Euro (EUR)
Telephone Dialling Codes: International code: 34
All numbers should be dialled with their area code, for local, long-distance and international calls. Madrid 910-918; Barcelona 930-938; Seville 854; Alicante 865; Palma de Mallorca 971; San Sebastián 943; Bilbao 94

Visas and passports

See page 325.

Customs

See page 325.

Public Holidays

1 January – New Year's Day; 6 January – Epiphany; March/April – Good Friday, Easter; 1

⊙ Useful Numbers

All emergency services: 112
Police: 091
Municipal Police: 092
Emergency Medical Care: 061
Fire Department: 080

May – Labour Day; 15 August – Feast of the Assumption; 12 October – Columbus Day or Día de la Hispanidad; 1 November – All Saints' Day; 6 December – Constitution; 8 December – Immaculate Conception; 25 December – Christmas Day. These are all national holidays – numerous other regional ones occur.

Tourist Offices

www.spain.info

In Madrid

Plaza Mayor
Tel: (91) 5787 810
www.esmadrid.com

In Barcelona

Plaça de Catalunya
Tel: 932 853 834
www.barcelonaturisme.com

Embassies and Consulates

UK

Torre Espacio, Paseo de la Castellana 25, Madrid.
Tel: (91) 7146 300
http://ukinspain.fco.gov.uk.

USA

Serrano 75, Madrid
Tel: (91) 587 2200
https://es.usembassy.gov/.

Money

Banks give the best rates for travellers' cheques and foreign currency, but you can also use the numerous currency exchange shops (casas de cambio), which stay open later. Shop around. Airport bureaux, travel agencies and hotels also change money, at bad rates – although commission is low. Banks give cash against your credit card.

ATMs are plentiful. Credit cards are accepted in most shops and businesses and for long-distance train tickets. You will need to produce your passport or ID card on these transactions.

Health and Emergencies

Spain has countless pharmacies (farmacias), each with a white sign with a flashing green cross. They tend to open 9.30am–1.30pm and 4.30–8pm Monday–Friday; 9am–1.30pm Saturday. In most towns a

system operates whereby there is one pharmacy open round-the-clock in each area. A sign in front of each should indicate which are open on which nights.

If you have a serious problem, get the number of an English-speaking doctor from your consulate, the police, tourist office or closest pharmacy. The EHIC card only covers emergency public, not private health care. You are advised to take out insurance before travelling.

Safety and Crime

Bag-snatching and pickpocketing are probably the worst problems – and tourists are a major target, so take care in crowds and busy tourist areas, especially the big cities. Avoid flashing money around. Keep valuables in the hotel safe and don't carry large sums of money or your passport (take a photocopy instead). If robbed, contact the local police station – the Policía Municipal or Policía Local are the most sympathetic. Most insurance companies require an official statement (denuncia) before they will accept a claim.

Opening Hours

Banks: hours vary. Most open 9am–2pm Monday–Friday, and some on Saturday until 1pm, though not usually between June–Sept or on Thursday afternoons. All close on Sunday and holidays. Several branches in the business districts open until 6pm or later.
Shops: open 9.30 or 10am–1.30 or 2pm and then reopen in the afternoon from 4.30 or 5 until around 8pm Monday–Saturday. Many close on Saturday afternoons in summer and all day Sunday. Large stores tend to open 10am–9pm Monday–Saturday and on a fixed number of Sundays.
District post offices: 9am–2.30pm Monday–Friday; all close on Sunday.
Principal post offices: open daily 9am–2pm and 4–7pm.

Train System

Most Spanish railways are run by the Renfe Operadora (www.renfe.com). FEVE, a subsidiary of Renfe, operates services on the Transcantábrian route (see page 165). Other operators are FGV (http://fgv.es) around Valencia; FGC (http://fgc.cat) in

AVE train in Madrid.

Catalonia; Euskotren (www.euskotren.eus) in the Basque Country and SFM (www.trensfm.com) on the island of Mallorca.

Renfe services are divided into three categories. Suburban and commuter networks extend out from the main cities and serve areas of dense population. The most useful trains for visitors are the medium- to long-distance services, which are marketed under a series of brand names, including Alaris, Altaria, Aliva, Arco, Talgo and Euromed.

The third division of Renfe is the high-speed AVE (Alta Velocidad Española) network that connects Madrid with Barcelona and Seville. The AVE line from Barcelona continues north over the French border to join with the SNCF rail system. AVE trains are extremely comfortable and, like all Spanish trains, generally punctual.

Ticket Details

Most trains offer first-class *(preferente)* and second-class *(turista)* tickets; a super first-class *(club)* is available on AVE trains. Ticket price depends not on distance, but on category of ticket and time of travel – costing more at peak times.

Discount Passes

Interrail and Eurail are valid in Spain. Renfe issues its own pass for visitors, which allows unlimited travel for one or six months; for more details see www.renfe.com.

Reservations

Except for local trains, you will need to reserve a seat or face paying a higher reservation fee paid to the conductor on board.

City Stations

Madrid has two main railway stations. Trains for the north, northeast and northwest of Spain operate from Chamartín, in the north of the city. The station also handles the slower trains for southern and eastern Spain. Fast trains for the east, west and south, including AVE trains, operate from Atocha, nearer to the city centre. Trains for the southwest and Portugal mostly use Atocha.

Barcelona's main station is Sants although some trains operate out of França.

Several other cities have more than one station. Some have a station on the high speed AVE line as well as a normal station for all other services

Train Talk

arrival, arrives *llegada, llega*
change at *cambiar en*
confirmation *confirmación*
connection *correspondencia, enlace*
daily *diario*
delay *retraso*
departure, departs *salida, sale*
excuse me *perdón*
exit *salida*
first class *primera clase*
how much is this? *cuánto es?*
platform *andén*
railway station *estación de tren*
reservation *plaza reservada*
return *ida y vuelta*
single *ida solo*
second class *segunda clase*
sleeping car *coche/carro cama*
straight on *todo recto*
this way to... *por aquí a...*
ticket *billete*
to the left *a la izquierda*
to the right *a la derecha*
train *tren*
when does the train depart for...? *¿a qué hora sale el tren para...?*
where is the...? *¿dónde está el ...?*

Taking Bicycles

To take a bicycle on an AVE train you will need to fold it or dismantle it so that it fits into a carrying case. On local trains, there is usually no problem taking your bike for free except during rush hour. For all other trains you will need to pay a small fee but there is a limit to the number of bikes that can be carried on any one train.

Where to Stay

For price categories see page 327.

Bilbao

Carlton
Plaza Federico Moyúa, 2
Tel: (94) 416 2200
www.aranzazu-hoteles.com
Orson Welles and Ernest Hemingway have both stayed here, so it's fair to say that this place breathes history. Less than 1km (0.5 mile) from Abando station **€€€€**

Ercilla
Ercilla, 37–39
Tel: (94) 470 5700
www.hotelercilla.es
A highly popular hotel with a fine restaurant, the Bermeo. Easy walking distance from Abando station. **€€€**

Nervión
Paseo Campo Volantín, 11
Tel: (94) 445 4700
www.barcelo.com
Located beside the estuary, this monolithic operation offers up-to-date comforts and is 5 minutes from the Guggenheim Museum. Also close to Abando station. **€€**

Villa de Bilbao
Gran Vía, 87
Tel: (94) 441 6000
www.nh-hotels.com
Centrally located with excellent service, this business hotel offers a fine breakfast and La Pergola, a gourmet dining choice. Less than 500 metres/yds from Abando station. **€€€€**

Madrid

Weare Chamartín
Agustín de Foxá, s/n
Tel: (91) 334 4900
www.weare-chamartin.com
Comfortable hotel close to Chamartín station in the northern suburbs. **€€€€**

Eurobuilding
Padre Damián, 23
Tel: (91) 353 7300
www.hotelnheurobuilding.com
In the heart of the business district of northern Madrid, handy for Chamartín station. Has many facilities including shops, restaurants and a swimming pool. **€€€€**

Prado
Prado, 11
Tel: (91) 369 0234
www.pradohotel.com
Recently remodelled and centrally located hotel, about 1km (0.5 mile) from Atocha station. €€€
Wellington
Velázquez, 8
Tel: (91) 575 4400
www.hotel-wellington.com
An old-fashioned, stylish hotel. Close to good shops, and across the Parque del Retiro from Atocha station. €€€€

San Sebastián

Londres y de Inglaterra
Zubieta, 2
Tel: (94) 344 0770
www.hlondres.com
Lovely hotel by the beach, just across from the old part of town. €€€
María Cristina
Paseo República Argentina, 4
Tel: (94) 343 7600
www.hotel-mariacristina.com
Originally opened in 1912, it has been entirely remodelled and is the top hotel in the city. Close to Donostia Station. €€€€
Monte Igueldo
Paseo del Faro 134
Tel: (94) 321 0211
www.monteigueldo.com
A romantic retreat, with beautiful sea views. €€
Niza
Zubieta, 56
Tel: (94) 342 6663
www.hotelniza.com
One block in from La Concha, San Sebastián's wonderful beach, this is a handy spot at a reasonable price. €€

Seville

Alfonso XIII
San Fernando, 2
Tel: (95) 491 7000
www.hotel-alfonsoxiiisevilla.com
Old-style elegance in this classic hotel, built in neo-Mudéjar style in the 1920s. Handy for the station. €€€€€
Simón
García de Vinuesa, 19
Tel: (95) 422 6660
www.hotelsimonsevilla.com
One of the best-value choices in the centre of the city, offering pleasant but no-frills lodgings in an 18th-century house around an Andalucían patio. Within 1km (0.5 mile) of the railway station. €€

SWITZERLAND

The Place

Area: 41,284 sq km (15,940 sq miles)
Capital: Bern
Population: 8.4 million
Languages: Swiss-German, French, Italian, Romansch
Time Zone: GMT +1; EST +6. Clocks advance 1 hour from late March until late October
Currency: Swiss franc (CHF)
Telephone Dialling Codes: International code: 41. Area codes: Zürich 43; St Moritz 81; Lucerne 41; Geneva 22

Visas and passports

No visa is required for citizens of EU countries, the US, Australia, New Zealand, Canada or Japan for stays of up to 3 months.

Customs

Customs allowances are very similar to those of the EU countries (see page 325).

Public Holidays

1 January – New Year's Day; 2 January – St Berchtold's Day; March/April – Good Friday and Easter Monday; 1 May – Labour Day; Ascension Day; 12 May – Whit Monday; 1 August – National Day; 25 December – Christmas Day; 26 December – St Stephen's Day.

Tourist Offices

In Zürich
Tödistrasse 7, CH-8027 Zürich
Tel: (01) 288 1111
www.myswitzerland.com/en

In the UK
30 Bedford St, London WC2E 9ED
Tel: (020) 7420 4900
www.myswitzerland.com/en

In the USA
608 Fifth Avenue, New York, NY 10020
Tel: (212) 757 5944
www.myswitzerland.com/en

Embassies and Consulates

UK
Thunstrasse 50, 3005 Bern

Tel: (031) 359 7700
https://www.gov.uk/world/organisations/british-embassy-berne

US
Sulgeneckstrasse 19, 3007 Bern
Tel: (031) 357 7011
https://ch.usembassy.gov

Money

Travellers' cheques and currency (only bank notes) can be changed at banks, bureaux de change, airports, travel agents, main railway stations – which stay open late and at weekends and charge no commission – and major hotels, which often offer the worst rates. You can settle bills in larger hotels, shops and restaurants with foreign money, more often than not at a bad rate of exchange, although change is likely to be in Swiss francs. ATMs are easy to find.

Health and Emergencies

The quality of medical treatment in Switzerland is very high, but also very expensive; so make sure you take out some health insurance. Although Switzerland is not an EU member, under the EHIC scheme (see page 327), nationals of EU countries are entitled to emergency medical treatment. In case of emergency, go to the nearest doctor or to

The Rhaetian Railway.

the emergency station in the nearest hospital. You will have to pay up front for treatment and claim it back later. Larger towns have an emergency doctor's number printed in the local press, or dial 111, which can also give you contact details of 24-hour pharmacies.

Safety and Crime

Switzerland has very little crime. Nevertheless, it is better not to walk alone at night in some parts of bigger cities. Be vigilant for pickpockets in crowded places.

Business Hours

Shops tend to open daily from 8 or 9am–6.30pm, and until 4pm on Saturday. Once a week (Thursday or Friday) shops open until 9pm. Outside city centres businesses close for 1–2 hours for lunch. In tourist areas shops have longer hours and often open on Sunday. Expect these hours to deviate in rural areas. Banks **are open from** 8am–5pm Monday–Friday, once a week they extend their hours; elsewhere 8.30am–noon and 1.30–4.30 or 5.30pm Monday–Friday.

Train System

The vast majority of Swiss services are run by **SBB** (www.sbb.ch), and as you may expect, they are extremely punctual, so make sure you arrive on the platform on time. Trains you may encounter in Switzerland include **ICE** (German high-speed trains), **CIS** (Cisalpino high-speed tilting trains operating routes into Italy), **EC** (EuroCity international express), **IC** (InterCity domestic express), **EN** (EuroNight express night train), **CNL** (CityNightLine luxury night train), **IR** (InterRegio fast regional train), **RE** (RegioExpress semi-fast regional train) and **R** (trains that stop at all stations).

Ticket Details

Inter-city trains have first- and second-class compartments and leave every hour. The larger lakes are serviced by boats; tickets are usually covered by a rail pass.

Discount Passes

Interail and Eurail passes are valid for many services in Switzerland;

The Golden Pass Panoramic train, near Lake Geneva, Switzerland.

see www.interrail.eu for more details. Also worth considering is the **Swiss Pass**, a personal network ticket issued for 4, 8, 15 or 22 days, 1 month, or for 3, 4, 5 or 6 days within a month (referred to as a Flexipass), which enables its bearer unlimited mileage on SBB and many private railways, post buses and boats (and in 38 cities and towns on buses and trams too). The **Swiss Card** is also good for a round trip ticket from one of the Swiss borders or airports to a holiday resort area in Switzerland. Valid for a month, it also gives 50 percent reduction on all other journeys you make (some mountain railways might not be included). The **Swiss Transfer Ticket** is a return ticket from the border or airport to your holiday resort, valid for one month. You have to buy it outside Switzerland, ideally at the tourist office in your own country.

Reservations

Switzerland is unusual in that reservations and fare supplements are not generally required, except on international routes and night trains. Reserve tickets for trains and boats at railway stations or at tourist offices; you can buy tickets on post buses and Intercity trains, but it's more expensive to do it this way.

Stations in Geneva

In Geneva, Cornavin is the main station; Gare Geneve Eaux-Vives in the east services trains to Annecy and St Gervais. Other main Swiss cities each have one principal station.

Train Talk

See France, Italy, and Germany sections on pages 339, 347 and 342.

Taking Bicycles

It is possible to carry bicycles on most Swiss trains but check the timetable – if nothing is written in the comments section you can take a bike on the train. You only have to make a reservation for a bike if taking ICN trains. Generally on international trains (ICE and Cisalpino) you are not allowed to take bikes as trains are narrow, so there is no space.

Where to Stay

For price categories see page 327.

Geneva

Balzac
Rue de l'ancien Port 14
Tel: (022) 731 0160
www.hotel-balzac.ch
Large, comfortable rooms, near the lake and a five-minute drive from the station. €€€€

Kipling
Rue de la Navigation 27
Tel: (022) 544 4040
www.hotelkiplinggeneva.com/en
Colonial-style decoration in a quiet street five minutes' walk from the station. €€

Strasbourg
Rue Pradier 10
Tel: (022) 906 5800
www.hotelstrasbourg.ch
Pleasant hotel with a good location on a quiet street close to the station, just a two-minute walk. €€€

Luzern

Hotel Monopol
Pilatusstrasse 1
Tel: (041) 226 4343
https://www.monopolluzern.ch/en/
This elaborate 19th-century grand hotel is convenient for the railway station (less than 1km/0.5 mile)

or the lake. Rooms are individually furnished – some modern and some period. Room service, laundry, babysitting. €€€€

Wilden Mann Hotel
Bahnhofstrasse 30
Tel: (041) 210 1666
www.wilden-mann.ch
Seven antique houses (the oldest dating from the 16th century) make up this cosy, higgledy-piggledy hotel right on the Bahnhofstrasse. The beauty of the original houses is combined with modern amenities. Less than 100 metres/yds from the station. €€€€

St Moritz

Carlton Hotel
Via J. Badrutt 11
Tel: (081) 836 7000
www.carlton-stmoritz.ch
Just 1km (0.5 mile) from the railway station, this elaborate ochre-coloured château has a view of the lake and the mountains and is one of the loveliest hotels in St Moritz. €€€€€

Waldhaus am See
Via Dim Lej 6
Tel: (081) 833 6000
www.waldhaus-am-see.ch
Overlooking the lake, this large three-star hotel offers reasonably-priced rooms, but prices rise in the high season. Only 200 metres/yds from the station. €€€€€

Zürich

Hotel Montana
Konradstrasse 39
Tel: (043) 366 6000
www.hotelmontana.ch
Close to the station and old town. Includes a highly-rated French restaurant. €€€

Leoneck
Leonhardstrasse 1
Tel: (044) 254 2222
www.leoneck.ch
Near the main shopping area and just 200 metres/yds from station. Restaurant serves Swiss food. €€

TURKEY

The Place

Area: 779,452 sq km (300,948 sq miles). Turkey straddles Europe and Asia. Only the European part, including the city of Istanbul, is included in this book.
Capital: Ankara

Population: 80 million
Language: Turkish and others
Time Zone: Apr–Sept GMT +2; EST +7. Oct–Mar GMT+3; EST +8.
Currency: Turkish lira (TRY)
Telephone Dialling Codes: International code: 90. Area codes: Istanbul European (Throce) side 0212; Istanbul Asian (Anatdia) side 0216

Visas and Passports

Citizens of most countries will require an electronic visa to enter Turkey. Go to www.evisa.gov.tr where you will be asked to fill in a form and pay the required fee.

Customs

You are allowed to bring into the country up to 200 cigarettes, 50 cigars, 200g pipe tobacco, 5 litres wine or spirits. Possession of narcotics is treated as an extremely serious offence; penalties are harsh.

It is strictly forbidden to take antiques, including rugs and carpets, out of the country. Should you buy anything old or old-looking, be sure to have it validated by the seller, who should get a clearance certificate from the Department of Antiquities. Respectable carpet dealers should be familiar with the procedure.

Tourist Offices

www.goturkeytourism.com

In Istanbul

Sultanahmet Square
Tel: (0212) 518 1802
Karaköy Harbour
Tel: (0212) 249 5776

Embassies and Consulates

UK

Sehit Ersan caddesi 461A, Cankaya Ankara
Tel: (0312) 455 3344
www.gov.uk/world/organisations/british-embassy-ankara

US

110 Ataturk Boulevard, Ankara
Tel: (0312) 455 5555
www.tr.usembassy.gov

Money

Banks open Monday–Friday 8.30am–noon and 1.30–5pm. Some stay open at lunchtime and some are

open daily in transit areas. Almost all banks have 24-hour ATMs. Travellers' cheques are accepted, for a charge, at the majority of banks as well as at private exchange offices.

Major credit cards are widely accepted by shops, restaurants, hotels and petrol stations.

Public Holidays

1 January – New Year's Day; 23 April – National Sovereignty and Children's Day; 19 May – Atatürk's Commemoration and Youth and Sports Festival; 30 August – Victory Day; 29 October – Republic Day.

Health and Emergencies

If you fall ill, the standard of healthcare in Turkey is not high, so it is essential to have medical insurance. Most drugs are available without prescription from pharmacies (eczane). Traveller's diarrhoea is the main risk. Drink only bottled water, wash and/or peel all fruit and vegetables, and ensure cooked food is piping hot. It's safest to eat freshly prepared local produce.

Safety and Crime

Turkey has an enviably low crime record but unfortunate incidents do

Sirkeci railway station.

happen. Tourists are regarded as guests, so are generally very well treated. Tourist areas are regularly patrolled by special Turizm or Foreigners' Police, who should do their best to help you and should speak some English.

Opening Hours

Shops generally open Monday–Saturday 9.30am–7pm; some only shut for the night at midnight. Shops are usually closed on Sunday, but increasing numbers of large shops stay open all week.

Train System

Türkiye Cumhuryeti Devlet Demiryollari (TCDD; www.tcdd.gov.tr) is Turkey's national operator.

This book only covers Turkish railways in Europe – effectively the line from Bulgaria to Istanbul. For journeys beyond Istanbul consult the TCDD website.

Ticket Details

Tickets are sold at TCDD stations and by appointed agents. Purchase tickets and reserve seats or sleepers in advance. It's best to reserve seats when you can.

Stations in Istanbul

Istanbul has two magnificent, historical stations: Sirkeci station in Eminönü, in the heart of old Constantinople, and Haydarpafla across the Bosphorus on the Asian side of Istanbul. At the time of writing, both stations are currently closed for long-term refurbishments see www.goturkeytourism.com for up-to-date details. Trains from Europe use Halkali station in the city's western suburbs; trains to the rest of Turkey and further into Asia, depart and arrive at Pendik suburban station.

Train Talk

arrivals *varis*
departures *birakmak*
first class *birinci sinif*
platform *peron*
railway station *gar/istasyon*
reservation *salkama*
return *gidis-dönüs*
second class *ikiuci sinif*
single *biletinde*

ticket *bilet*
train *tren*
what time does it leave? *kaçta kalkiyor?*

Where to Stay

For price categories see page 327.

Istanbul

Hotel Romance
Hüdavendigar Cd. 5, Sirkeci
34410 Sultanahmet
Tel: (0212) 512 8676
www.romancehotel.com
Very close to Istanbul's main attractions, and less than 500 metres/yds from Sirkeci station. €€

Hotel Saba
Sehit Mehmet Pasa Yokusu, 8
34400 Sultanahmet
Tel: (0212) 458 0262
www.saba.com.tr
Comfortable hotel in the historic centre of Istanbul and less than 1km (0.5 mile) from Sirkeci station. €€

UNITED KINGDOM

The Place

Area: 242,514 sq km (93,638 sq miles)
Capital: London
Population: 65 million
Language: English
Time Zone: GMT; EST+5.
Currency: Pound sterling (GBP)
Telephone Dialling Codes: International code: 44. Area codes: London 020; Edinburgh 0131; York 01904; Glasgow 0141.

Visas and passports

See page 325.

Customs

See page 325.

Public Holidays

1 January – New Year's Day; March/April – Good Friday, Easter

Useful Numbers

Emergencies: 999 (you will be directed to the police, fire brigade or ambulance service according to your needs)

Monday; first Monday in May; last Monday in May; last Monday in August; 25/26 December – Christmas/Boxing Day.

Embassies and Consulates

US Embassy
33 Nine Elms Lane, SW8 5DB
Tel: 0207 499 9000
https://uk.usembassy.gov/

Money

Banks open 9.30am–4.30pm Monday–Friday, and often Saturday morning in shopping areas. Most have ATMs where international credit or cashpoint cards can be used. There is no commission on sterling travellers' cheques, but a charge for changing cash into British currency.

Travel agents operate bureaux de change at comparable rates. Privately run bureaux de change (many open 24 hours) often have low exchange rates but high commissions. Post offices and Marks & Spencers bureaux de change do not charge commission when purchasing foreign currency. International credit cards are accepted in most shops, hotels and restaurants.

Health and Emergencies

Most visitors have to pay for medical and dental treatment and should have health insurance. In the case of minor accidents, your hotel will know the location of the

UK Tourist Offices

www.visitbritain.com
Edinburgh
3 Princes Street
Tel: (0131) 473 3868
www.visitscotland.com
Inverness (Scottish Highlands)
36 High Street
Tel: (01463) 234 353
www.visithighlands.com
London
Britain and London Visitor Centre
Piccadilly Circus,
Tel: (020) 8846 9000
www.visitlondon.com
York
1 Museum Street
Tel: (01904) 550 099
www.visityork.org

Southern Rail and Thameslink trains, London.

nearest hospital with a casualty department.

You can buy over-the-counter and prescription medicines at Boots, the UK's largest chain of pharmacies.

Safety and Crime

UK cities are no more dangerous than any others; unfortunately, many of the rougher spots are around railway stations. If arriving on a late train when there is no public transport available, use only an official taxi from a marked taxi rank. Keep a vigilant eye on your bags in the station and beware of pickpockets.

Opening Hours

Most shops are open Monday–Saturday 9am–5.30pm (but larger shops stay open later), and Sunday 10am–4pm. Post offices are also open Monday–Friday 9am–5.30pm, and on Saturday, from 9am–12.30pm. Pubs are generally open Monday–Saturday 11am–11pm (later in Scotland), and noon–10.30pm on Sunday.

Train System

The railway system in the UK has several idiosyncrasies to distinguish it from the rest of Europe. A major difference is that the British system was privatised in the 1990s and is run by many different operating companies. This has proved a mixed blessing. While some people claim competition has raised standards and improved services, others believe it is worse off than when it was under national ownership. Another peculiarity is the extent

to which timetables vary between weekdays and weekends. Unlike the rest of Europe, Britain's trains are not labelled on timetables by number – but rather by their final destination.

Ticket Details

There are three basic tickets, in ascending order of cost: **Advance** are single fares for a specific train booked in advance; **Off-Peak** and **Super Off-Peak** fares can be purchased at any time but cannot be used during the busiest times of the day; and **Anytime** tickets, which can be used on any train. The further in advance the ticket is booked, the cheaper it will be. It is best to buy tickets from a station ticket office or the train operator itself, either by telephone or online. The best place to start is the National Rail enquiries website www.nationalrail.co.uk. Other useful websites for information and booking are www.trainline.com and www.raileasy.co.uk.

London Bridge station.

Eurostar

Eurostar (www.eurostar.com) operates services connecting the UK with mainland Europe, arriving at and departing from London St Pancras. Most Eurostar tickets can be purchased up to 120 days before the date of travel.

Discount Passes

There is a wide variety of **BritRail** (www.britrail.net) passes for use in the UK and Ireland, covering different areas and days of travel. They are only for the use of visitors to Britain. **Interrail** passes are valid in the UK – although for a few trains you will need to have a Global Pass. **Eurail** passes are not valid in England, Scotland and Wales but are valid in Northern Ireland.

Reservations

Reservations are not necessary on most trains, but are advisable for long-distance services, especially Friday to Sunday. Reservations can be made online, in person or over the phone with a credit card.

Stations

There are 10 major termini in London: London Bridge for Kent; Charing Cross for East Sussex and Kent; Waterloo for Surrey, Hampshire and Dorset; Victoria for Gatwick and West Sussex; Paddington for Oxford, Bristol, the West Country and south Wales; Marylebone for Stratford and Birmingham; Euston for the West Midlands, Manchester, Liverpool and Glasgow; St Pancras for the East Midlands, Sheffield and Eurostar services; King's Cross for Cambridge, Peterborough, Leeds,

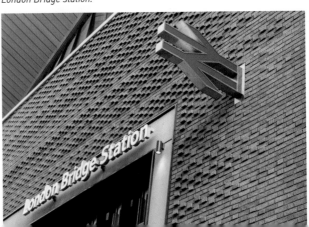

York, Newcastle and Edinburgh; Liverpool Street for East Anglia and Cambridge.

In Glasgow, there are two main stations: Queen Street (Edinburgh and northern Scotland) and Glasgow Central (London, Glasgow and southern services).

Taking Bicycles

Most lines allow bicycles, but many limit it to non-peak times. Check your timetable for more detailed information. Bicycles are often prohibited on trains running through city centres.

Indoor pool at the Waldorf Hilton.

Where to Stay

For price categories see page 327.

Edinburgh

Holyrood Aparthotel
1 Nether Bakehouse, EH8 8PE
Tel: (0131) 524 3200
www.holyroodaparthotel.com
A deluxe hotel located in the heart of Edinburgh. The hotel is near the Palace of Holyrood and the Scottish Parliament Building. €€€€

Salisbury Hotel
45 Salisbury Road, EH16 5AA
Tel: (0131) 667 1264
www.the-salisbury.co.uk
Upmarket B&B in listed Georgian house. 1.5km (1 mile) from Waverley Station. €€€

Glasgow

Euro Hostel
318 Clyde Street, G1 4NR
Tel: 08455 399 956
www.eurohostels.co.uk
Reasonably priced, en-suite hostel, with a range of rooms suitable for families as well as backpackers. Close to Central Station. €

Malmaison
278 West George Street, G2 4LL
Tel: (0141) 378 0384
www.malmaison.com
Smart hotel, with decor inspired by the Paris Malmaison and an excellent brasserie. five minutes' walk from Central Station. €€€€

Inverness

St Ann's House
37 Harrowden Road, IV3 5QN
Tel: (01463) 236157
www.stannshouse.com
Well maintained family-run guesthouse, 10 minutes' walk from the city centre, rail and bus stations. €€

Westbourne Guest House
50 Huntly Street, IV3 5HS
Tel: (01463) 220700
www.westbourne.org.uk
Situated on the west bank of the River Ness, five minutes' walk from the centre and rail and bus stations. €€€

London

Crescent Hotel
49–50 Cartwright Gardens, Bloomsbury, WC1H 9EL
Tel: (020) 7387 1515
www.crescenthoteloflondon.com
Attractive family-run hotel with 27 rooms, handily situated for Euston and King's Cross/St Pancras stations. €€€

Elizabeth Hotel
4 Lancaster Terrace W2 3PF
Tel: (020) 7402 66 41
www.londonelizabethhotel.com
Friendly hotel in an elegant period square, just south of Paddington station. There are 49 standard, superior and suite rooms. €€€€

The Mad Hatter Hotel
3–7 Stamford Street, SE1 9NY
Tel: (020) 7401 9222
www.fullershotels.com
Good value small hotel south of the River Thames, conveniently situated for Waterloo Station. €€€

Strand Palace
372 The Strand, WC2R 0JJ
Tel: 020 7379 4737
www.strandpalacehotel.co.uk
In the heart of London's theatre district, with easy access to Waterloo, Euston, King's Cross/St Pancras International and Victoria stations. €€€€€

The Waldorf Hilton
Aldwych, WC2B 4DD
Tel: (020) 7836 2400
www.hilton.co.uk/waldorf
Recently restored and steeped in history, the Waldorf is situated in the heart of Theatreland in sophisticated surroundings. Convenient for all the main stations. €€€€€

York

Dean Court
Duncombe Place, YO1 7EF
Tel: (01904) 625 082
www.deancourt-york.co.uk
Comfortable 40-room traditional hotel close to the Minster and in its own traffic-free zone. Less than 1.5km (0.5 mile) from the station. €€€

FURTHER READING

Bradshaw, George *Bradshaw's Continental Railway Guide 1913.* Nostalgic reprint of classic guide to travel in more sedate times.

Bryson, Bill *Neither Here Nor There: Travels in Europe.* A journey around the continent partly using trains.

Chesshyre, Tom *Ticket to Ride: Around the world in 49 unusual train journeys.* A collection of fascinating routes including in Britain and continental Europe.

Christie, Agatha *Murder on the Orient Express.* The much-filmed whodunit that will forever be as famous as the train itself.

Dow, Andrew *Dow's Dictionary of Railway Quotations.* An A-Z of bon mots, as well as a discussion about railway jargon and clichés.

Greene, Graham *Stamboul train.* A novel set on a journey of the Orient Express from Ostend to Istanbul, later filmed.

Harrison, Rebecca *From Steam to Screen Cinema, the Railways and Modernity.* An exploration of our fascination with two technologies: rail transport and the media.

Kennedy, Ludovic *A Book of Railway Journeys.* Anthology of prose and poems on rail travel in Britain Europe and the rest of the world.

Marchant, Ian *Parallel Lines.* Contrasts between the real railways of Britain and "the railway of our dreams".

Nesbit, Edith *The Railway Children.* A classic novel for children made into a film about children living near a railway line.

Portillo, Michael *Great Continental Railway Journeys.* Book of a successful TV documentary by the politician turned presenter.

Merridale, Catherine *Lenin on the Train.* An account of the revolutionary's famous journey across half of Europe from Zürich to Petrograd.

Smith, Mark *The Man in Seat 61: A Guide to Taking the Train through Europe.* By the creator of the highly informative rail website, seat61.com.

Various *Cycle Escapes London.* A handy collection of picturesque cycle rides in and around London, making use of local trains, with handy details of which services allow bicycles on board.

Zola, Emile *La bête humaine* (*The beast in Man*). A classic thriller set on the Paris to Le Havre line.

⊙ Send us your thoughts

We do our best to ensure the information in our books is as accurate and up-to-date as possible. The books are updated on a regular basis using local contacts, who painstakingly add, amend and correct as required. However, some details (such as telephone numbers and opening times) are liable to change, and we are ultimately reliant on our readers to put us in the picture.

We welcome your feedback, especially your experience of using the book "on the road". Maybe you came across a great bar or new attraction we missed. We will acknowledge all contributions, and we'll offer an Insight Guide to the best letters received.

Please write to us at:
Insight Guides
PO Box 7910
London SE1 1WE

Or email us at:
hello@insightguides.com

CREDITS

PHOTO CREDITS

Alamy 6M, 6BL, 7BR, 8/9, 12/13, 22, 40, 55, 72/73, 80, 95B, 104, 107, 112B, 159, 180B, 317, 319
Andreas Gerth/swiss-image.ch 195
Andy Mettler/swiss-image.ch 208
AWL Images 44, 70/71, 130
Belmond 6BR, 16B, 78, 82B, 82T, 83, 84, 85B, 85T, 102, 106, 327, 328, 351
Ben Zurbriggen Fotografie/ Freilichtmuseum Ballenberg 203B
Christophe Merlet 134T
Christian Houge/Visitnorway.com 285
Colin Barker 114B
David Gubler 288
Deutsche Bahn AG 4, 15B, 17, 56, 60, 61, 67, 91B, 250/251, 252, 253, 258/259, 261, 265, 266, 269, 270, 271, 273B, 273T, 274, 306, 322, 324T, 325, 338, 341, 342, 343
Gasteinertal Tourismus GmbH, Marktl 246
Getty Images 1, 14, 18/19, 24, 25, 26, 27, 28, 29, 30, 31, 32, 33, 34, 35, 36, 38, 39, 42, 43, 52, 53, 54, 57, 58, 62, 65, 74, 94, 115, 144, 149, 150, 152/153B, 168, 210/211, 212, 220, 290B
Gjertrud Coutinho 279
Harald Eisenberger/Austrian National Tourist Office 230/231
Harald Eisenberger/ÖBB 240T
Hilton Hotels 363
Håkan Wike/Inlandsbanan AB 68/69,

278, 289, 290T, 292, 354
iStock 7BL, 15T, 45, 49, 59, 79, 88T, 89, 91T, 95T, 96/97, 109, 112T, 120, 122T, 124, 131, 134, 135, 138, 147, 148B, 151, 156, 163, 172, 173, 177, 215, 224, 227B, 241, 244, 257, 263, 264, 267B, 283, 286, 303, 305, 313, 320, 331, 332, 336, 339, 340, 344, 346, 349, 350, 357, 364
Jan Geerk/swiss-image.ch 192, 194, 206T
Jungfrau Region 185
Karl-Heinz Hug/swiss-image.ch 198
Leif Johnny Olestad/visitnorway.com 287B
Marcus Gyger/swiss-image.ch 188/189B, 207
Ming Tang-Evans/Apa Publications 308
Nederlandse Spoorwegen 326
Nikada 267T
Northern Ireland Tourist Board 98
NSB 324B, 352
OBB 330
PPR/Verkehrshaus der Schweiz/ Roger Hofstetter 66
Public domain 20, 21, 37, 41, 51, 228
Renfe 167B
Rhaetische Bahn 7TR, 75, 184, 193, 196, 197, 199, 358
Roger Hofstetter/Verkehrshaus der Schweiz 203T

Roland Gerth/swiss-image.ch 191
Shutterstock 7TL, 46, 48, 50, 63, 64, 86, 88B, 90, 92, 99, 101, 105, 108, 110, 111B, 111T, 113, 119, 121, 123B, 139, 141, 142, 143, 145, 146, 148T, 153T, 155, 157, 158, 165, 166, 167T, 171, 174, 180T, 181, 188T, 213, 216, 217, 218, 219, 221T, 221B, 222, 226, 227T, 229, 232, 234/235, 237, 239, 240B, 242T, 242B, 243, 245, 248, 258, 260, 262, 268, 272, 281, 284B, 284T, 287T, 291, 294, 295T, 296, 298/299, 300, 301, 310, 311, 312, 314, 315, 316, 333, 334, 335, 337, 347, 355, 360, 362B, 362T
Sipa USA/REX/Shutterstock 170
Starwood Hotels & Resorts 348
Stephen Miles 117
Stuart Petch 114T
SuperStock 47, 128/129, 160/161, 162, 169
Swedish Railway Museum 297
Swiss Travel System 10/11, 16T, 23, 182/183, 187, 190, 200, 201, 202, 204/205, 206B, 328/329
swiss-image.ch 359
Tourism Ireland 122, 345
Tourismus Salzburg 247B, 247T
Vastavalo/Juhana Konttinen/Visit Finland 295B
VR 353
zettel/Foap/Visitnorway.com 276/277
ÖBB/Robert Deopito 233

COVER CREDITS

Front cover: The Bernina Express, Switzerland *iStock*
Back cover: Glenfinnan Viaduct, Scotland *iStock*
Front flap: (from top) Oriente Station,

Lisbon *iStock*; Grand Suite on the Venice Simplon Orient Express *Belmond*; The Matterhorn Gotthard Bahn, Switzerland *Swiss Travel System*; Steam train in the Yorkshire

Dales *iStock*
Back flap: Track in Germany *Deutsche Bahn AG*

INSIGHT GUIDE CREDITS

Distribution
UK, Ireland and Europe
Apa Publications (UK) Ltd;
sales@insightguides.com
United States and Canada
Ingram Publisher Services;
ips@ingramcontent.com
Australia and New Zealand
Woodslane; info@woodslane.com.au
Southeast Asia
Apa Publications (SN) Pte;
singaporeoffice@insightguides.com
Worldwide
Apa Publications (UK) Ltd;
sales@insightguides.com
Special Sales, Content Licensing and CoPublishing
Insight Guides can be purchased in bulk quantities at discounted prices. We can create special editions, personalised jackets and corporate imprints tailored to your needs. sales@insightguides.com
www.insightguides.biz

Printed in China by CTPS

All Rights Reserved
© 2019 Apa Digital (CH) AG and Apa Publications (UK) Ltd

First edition **2002**
Second edition **2019**

www.insightguides.com

Editor: Tom Fleming
Authors: Nick Inman and Tim Locke
Head of DTP and Pre-Press: Rebeka Davies
Update Production: Apa Digital
Picture Editor: Tom Smyth
Cartography: original cartography Original Cartography, updated by Carte

CONTRIBUTORS

This fully-updated edition was commissioned by **Rachel Lawrence** and edited by **Tom Fleming** at Insight Guides' London office. **Penny Phenix** proofread and indexed this guide.

Nick Inman and **Tim Locke** have comprehensively updated this edition, which builds on the original work of authors and updaters, including **Tom Le Bas**, **Anthony Lambert**, **David Lawrence**, **David Haydock**, **Gary Buchanan**, **Robin McKelvie**, **Marcus Brooke**, **Sylvia Suddes**, **Claire Griffiths**, **Martha Ellen Zenfell**, **Peter Lemney**, **Nick Inman**, **Roland Beier**, **Donald Wilson**, **Zane Katsikis**, **John Wilcock**, **Jason Mitchell** and **Christina Park**.

ABOUT INSIGHT GUIDES

Insight Guides have more than 45 years' experience of publishing high-quality, visual travel guides. We produce 400 full-colour titles, in both print and digital form, covering more than 200 destinations across the globe, in a variety of formats to meet your different needs.

Insight Guides are written by local authors, whose expertise is evident in the extensive historical and cultural background features. Each destination is carefully researched by regional experts to ensure our guides provide the very latest information. All the reviews in **Insight Guides** are independent; we strive to maintain an impartial view. Our reviews are carefully selected to guide you to the best places to eat, go out and shop, so you can be confident that when we say a place is special, we really mean it.

Legend

City maps

	Freeway/Highway/Motorway
	Divided Highway
	Main Roads
	Minor Roads
	Pedestrian Roads
	Steps
	Footpath
	Railway
	Funicular Railway
	Cable Car
	Tunnel
	City Wall
	Important Building
	Built Up Area
	Other Land
	Transport Hub
	Park
	Pedestrian Area
	Bus Station
	Tourist Information
	Main Post Office
	Cathedral/Church
	Mosque
	Synagogue
	Statue/Monument
	Beach
	Airport

Regional maps

	Freeway/Highway/Motorway (with junction)
	Freeway/Highway/Motorway (under construction)
	Divided Highway
	Main Road
	Secondary Road
	Minor Road
	Track
	Footpath
	International Boundary
	State/Province Boundary
	National Park/Reserve
	Marine Park
	Ferry Route
	Marshland/Swamp
	Glacier Salt Lake
	Airport/Airfield
	Ancient Site
	Border Control
	Cable Car
	Castle/Castle Ruins
	Cave
	Chateau/Stately Home
	Church/Church Ruins
	Crater
	Lighthouse
	Mountain Peak
	Place of Interest
	Viewpoint

INDEX

COUNTRY ABBREVIATION LIST

Austria (AT)

Belarus (BY)

Britain (GB)

Bulgaria (BG)

Croatia (HR)

Czech Republic (CZ)

Denmark (DK)

Finland (FI)

France (FR)

Germany (DE)

Greece (GR)

Hungary (HU)

Ireland (IE)

Italy (IT)

Norway (NO)

Poland (PL)

Portugal (PT)

Romania (RO)

Russia (RU)

Serbia (RS)

Slovakia (SK)

Slovenia (SI)

Spain (ES)

Sweden (SE)

Switzerland (CH)

Turkey (TR)

European Railway Atlas

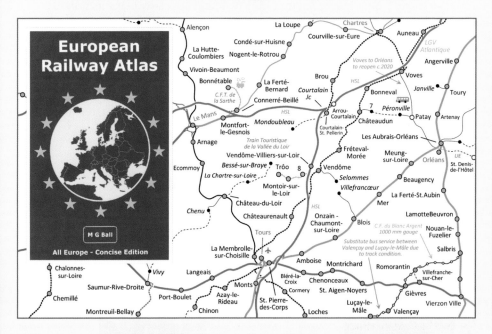

All Europe Concise Edition (Detail as illustrated) - £19.95 + p&p

Or for more detail there's the Regional Series of fourteen books showing <u>all</u> stations - £5.95 to £13.95 + p&p

All come with a FREE PDF version to download to your device and take on your travels when you buy direct from:

www.europeanrailwayatlas.com

INSIGHT ⊙ GUIDES

OFF THE SHELF

Since 1970, INSIGHT GUIDES has provided a unique perspective on the world's best travel destinations by using specially commissioned photography and illuminating text written by local authors.

Whether you're planning a city break, a walking tour or the journey of a lifetime, our superb range of guidebooks and phrasebooks will inspire you to discover more about your chosen destination.

INSIGHT GUIDES

offer a unique combination of stunning photos, absorbing narrative and detailed maps, providing all the inspiration and information you need.

PHRASEBOOKS & DICTIONARIES

help users to feel at home, when away. Pocket-sized with a free app to download, they go where you do.

CITY GUIDES

pack hundreds of great photos into a smaller format with detailed practical information, so you can navigate the world's top cities with confidence.

EXPLORE GUIDES

feature easy-to-follow walks and itineraries in the world's most exciting destinations, with our choice of the best places to eat and drink along the way.

POCKET GUIDES

combine concise information on where to go and what to do in a handy compact format, ideal on the ground. Includes a full-colour, fold-out map.

EXPERIENCE GUIDES

feature offbeat perspectives and secret gems for experienced travellers, with a collection of over 100 ideas for a memorable stay in a city.

www.insightguides.com

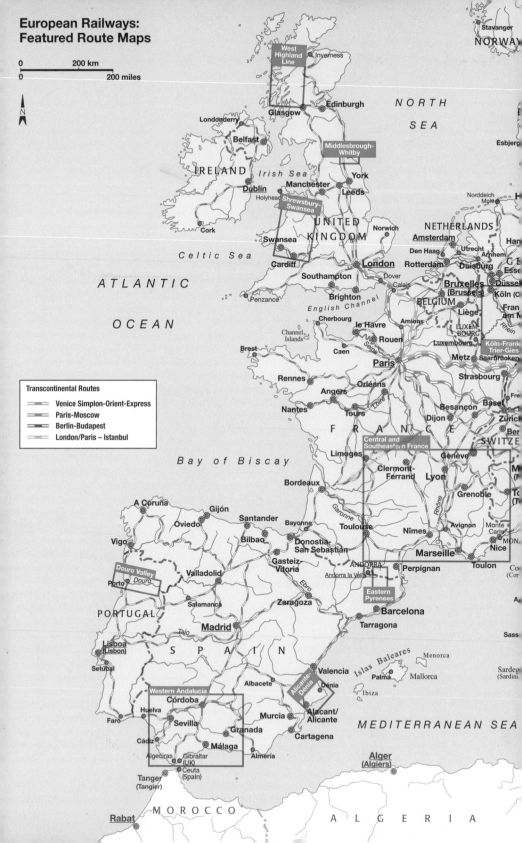

European Railways:
Featured Route Maps

0   200 km

0   200 miles

N

Transcontinental Routes

— Venice Simplon-Orient-Express
— Paris-Moscow
— Berlin-Budapest
— London/Paris – Istanbul

West Highland Line

Middlesbrough-Whitby

Shrewsbury-Swansea

Central and Southeastern France

Douro Valley

Eastern Pyrenees

Western Andalucía

Alicante-Dénia

NORWAY
Stavanger

NORTH SEA

Inverness
Glasgow
Edinburgh

Londonderry
Belfast

IRELAND
Irish Sea

Dublin
Holyhead

Cork

Celtic Sea

Manchester
York
Leeds

Swansea

Cardiff

UNITED KINGDOM

Norwich

Southampton
London
Brighton
Penzance
Dover
Calais

English Channel

Cherbourg
le Havre
Rouen

Brest
Channel Islands
Caen

ATLANTIC OCEAN

Rennes
Orléans

Angers
Tours

Nantes

FRANCE

Limoges

Bay of Biscay

Bordeaux

A Coruña
Gijón
Santander
Oviedo
Bayonne
Vigo
Bilbao
Donostia-
San Sebastián
Gasteiz-
Vitoria
Valladolid

Salamanca
Zaragoza

PORTUGAL

Porto
Douro

MADRID

Tajo

Lisboa
(Lisbon)

SPAIN

Setúbal

Albacete

Huelva
Córdoba

Faro
Sevilla
Granada
Murcia

Cádiz
Málaga
Almería

Algeciras
Gibraltar
(UK)
Ceuta
(Spain)

Tanger
(Tangier)

Rabat

MOROCCO

ALGERIA

NETHERLANDS
Amsterdam
Den Haag
Utrecht
Arnhem
Rotterdam
Duisburg

Norddeich
Mole

Esbjerg

**Bruxelles
(Brussels)**

BELGIUM

Liège

Köln (C

Düssel

**LUXEM-
BOURG**
Luxembourg

Metz

Fran
am M

Rhein

Köln-Frank
Trier-Gies
Saarbrücken

Amiens

Paris

Strasbourg

Besançon
Dijon

Basel

Zürich

Ber

SWITZE

Clermont-
Ferrand
Lyon

Genève

Grenoble

Toulouse
Nîmes
Avignon
Monte
Carlo
MON.

Marseille
Nice

Perpignan
Toulon

ANDORRA
Andorra la Vella

Barcelona
Tarragona

Valencia

Ebro

Dénia

Alacant/
Alicante
Cartagena

Islas Baleares
Menorca
Palma
Mallorca
Ibiza

Sardeg
(Sardini

Sass

MEDITERRANEAN SEA

**Alger
(Algiers)**

Garonne

Rhône

Seine

Loire